CHANGING PARADIGMS IN HISTORICAL AND SYSTEMATIC THEOLOGY

General Editors
Sarah Coakley   Richard Cross

This series sets out to reconsider the modern distinction between 'historical' and 'systematic' theology. The scholarship represented in the series is marked by attention to the way in which historiographic and theological presumptions ('paradigms') necessarily inform the work of historians of Christian thought, and thus affect their application to contemporary concerns. At certain key junctures such paradigms are recast, causing a reconsideration of the methods, hermeneutics, geographical boundaries, or chronological caesuras that have previously guided the theological narrative. The beginning of the twenty-first century marks a period of such notable reassessment of the Christian doctrinal heritage, and involves a questioning of the paradigms that have sustained the classic 'history-of-ideas' textbook accounts of the modern era. Each of the volumes in this series brings such contemporary methodological and historiographical concerns to conscious consideration. Each tackles a period or key figure whose significance is ripe for reconsideration, and each analyses the implicit historiography that has sustained existing scholarship on the topic. A variety of fresh methodological concerns are considered, without reducing the theological to other categories. The emphasis is on an awareness of the history of 'reception': the possibilities for contemporary theology are bound up with a careful rewriting of the historical narrative. In this sense, 'historical' and 'systematic' theology are necessarily conjoined, yet also closely connected to a discerning interdisciplinary engagement.

This monograph series accompanies the project of *The Oxford Handbook of the Reception of Christian Theology* (OUP, in progress), also edited by Sarah Coakley and Richard Cross.

CHANGING PARADIGMS IN HISTORICAL AND SYSTEMATIC THEOLOGY

General Editors: Sarah Coakley (Norris-Hulse Professor of Divinity, University of Cambridge) and Richard Cross (John A. O'Brien Professor of Philosophy, University of Notre Dame)

RECENT SERIES TITLES

Kant and the Creation of Freedom

A Theological Problem

CHRISTOPHER J. INSOLE

OXFORD

UNIVERSITY PRESS

OXFORD
UNIVERSITY PRESS

Great Clarendon Street, Oxford, OX2 6DP,
United Kingdom

Oxford University Press is a department of the University of Oxford.
It furthers the University's objective of excellence in research, scholarship,
and education by publishing worldwide. Oxford is a registered trade mark of
Oxford University Press in the UK and in certain other countries

First Edition published in 2013

Impression: 1

British Library Cataloguing in Publication Data
Data available

ISBN 978-0-19-967760-3

Printed in Great Britain by
the MPG Printgroup, UK

Acknowledgements

I am grateful to the Department of Theology and Religion at the University of Durham, for periods of research leave in 2008 and 2011. The research benefited greatly from conversations at seminars at the Universities of Aberdeen, Cambridge, Durham, Nottingham, and Oxford. For their support and encouragement of the project, I thank Tom Perridge and Sarah Coakley. For feedback, encouragement, and assistance on diverse aspects of the project, I am indebted to Lewis Ayers, John Barclay, Nigel Biggar, Andrew Chignell, James Driscoll, Alex Englander, Claire Feeley, Carol Harrison, Laurence Hemming, Desmond Hogan, Chris Joby, Patrick Kain, Karen Kilby, Rae Langton, Kathy Lehav, Gerard Loughlin, Mark McIntosh, Justin Mihoc, Paul Murray, Oliver O'Donovan, James Orr, Stephen Plant, Jean Porter, Marcus Pound, Robert Song, Hilary Walford, and Francis Watson. I give special thanks to David Dwan and to Phil Shiner for their steadfast confidence in the project, their good humour, support, and care. For her constant friendship and intellectual stimulation, and for letting me talk about Kant (a lot), but not all the time, I thank and celebrate my wife Lisa. The book is dedicated to our son, Rory Hugh Insole.

Contents

Method of Citation

References to Kant, with the exception of the *Critique of Pure Reason*, refer to the Akademie edition, *Kant's gesammelte Schriften*, edited by the Royal Prussian (later German) Academy of Sciences (Berlin: Georg Reimer, later Walter de Gruyter & Co., 1900–). These references are cited by volume: page number, and are prefaced by an abbreviation of the title of the work, as set out below. Citations to the first *Critique* are to the A (first-edition) or B (second-edition) pages, as translated in *The Cambridge Edition of the Works of Immanuel Kant: Critique of Pure Reason* (CPR), ed. and trans. Paul Guyer and Allen Wood (Cambridge: Cambridge University Press, 1998). I occasionally refer to Kant's notes on his copy of the *Critique of Pure Reason*, given in Benno Erdmann, *Nachträge zu Kants Kritik der reinen Vernunft* (Kiel: Lipsius & Ticher, 1881). For these references, I use E. followed by the page reference. Italics in the quotations represent either Kant's original emphases represented in the Akademie edition by bold gothic script, or a Latin passage (or occasionally a Greek word) in a predominantly German text. Unless otherwise stated, and where available, I use the standard translation provided in *The Cambridge Edition of Works of Immanuel Kant* (Cambridge: Cambridge University Press, 1992–). The Cambridge Edition provides marginal Akademie edition volume: page references. In a number of instances I have modified the translation; I indicate in footnotes where this is the case. In other cases, where there is no translation available, I use my own translation. Again, I indicate this in footnotes.

Correspondence	*The Cambridge Edition of the Works of Immanuel Kant: Correspondence*, ed. and trans. Arnulf Zweig (Cambridge: Cambridge University Press, 1999)
Lectures on Ethics	*The Cambridge Edition of the Works of Immanuel Kant: Lectures on Ethics*, ed. Peter Heath and J. B. Schneewind, trans. Peter Heath (Cambridge: Cambridge University Press, 2001)
Lectures on Logic	*The Cambridge Edition of the Works of Immanuel Kant: Lectures on Logic*, ed. and trans. Michael Young (Cambridge: Cambridge University Press, 2004)
Lectures on Metaphysics	*The Cambridge Edition of the Works of Immanuel Kant: Lectures on Metaphysics*, ed. and trans. Karl Ameriks and Steve Naragon (Cambridge: Cambridge University Press, 1997)
Notes and Fragments	*The Cambridge Edition of the Works of Immanuel Kant: Notes and Fragments*, ed. Paul Guyer, trans. Curtis Bowman, Paul Guyer, and Frederick Rauscher (Cambridge: Cambridge University Press, 2005)

Practical Philosophy	*The Cambridge Edition of the Works of Immanuel Kant: Practical Philosophy*, ed. and trans. Mary J. Gregor (Cambridge: Cambridge University Press, 2008)
Rational Theology	*The Cambridge Edition of the Works of Immanuel Kant: Religion and Rational Theology*, ed. and trans. Allen W. Wood and George di Giovanni (Cambridge: Cambridge University Press, 1996)
Theoretical Philosophy 1	*The Cambridge Edition of the Works of Immanuel Kant: Theoretical Philosophy, 1755–1770*, ed. and trans. David Walford and Ralf Meerbote (Cambridge: Cambridge University Press, 1992)
Theoretical Philosophy 2	*The Cambridge Edition of the Works of Immanuel Kant: Theoretical Philosophy after 1781*, ed. Henry Allison and Peter Heath, trans. Gary Hatfield, Michael Friedman, Henry Allison, and Peter Heath (Cambridge: Cambridge University Press, 2002)
APV	*Anthropologie in pragmatischer Hinsicht* (1798), in *The Cambridge Edition of the Works of Immanuel Kant: Anthropology, History and Education*, ed. and trans. Robert B. Louden and Günter Zöller (Cambridge: Cambridge University Press, 2008), 7: 117–333
BL	*Blomberg Logic (1770s)*, in *Lectures on Logic*, 24: 301
CF	*Der Streit der Fakultäten. The Conflict of the Faculties* (1798), in *Rational Theology*, 7: 5–115
CHH	*Mutmaßlicher Anfang der Menschengeschichte* (1786). *Conjectures on the Beginning of Human History*, in *Kant: Political Writings*, ed. H. S. Reiss and trans. H. B. Nisbet (Cambridge: Cambridge University Press, 2005), 8: 107–23
CJ	*Kritik der Urtheilskraft* (1790). *The Cambridge Edition of the Works of Immanuel Kant: Critique of the Power of Judgement*, ed. Paul Guyer, trans. Paul Guyer and Eric Matthews (Cambridge: Cambridge University Press, 2000), 5: 167–484
Coll.	*Moral Philosophy: Collins' Lecture Notes* (1784–5), in *Lectures on Ethics*, 27: 243–471
Corr.	*Correspondence* (1749–1800), in *Correspondence*, 10: 7–12: 370
CPrR.	*Kritik der praktischen Vernunft* (1788). *Critique of Practical Reason*, in *Practical Philosophy* (Cambridge: Cambridge University Press, 2008), 5: 3–309

DFW	*Declaration concerning Fichte's Wissenschaftslehre* (1799), in. *Correspondence*, 12: 370–1
DL	*Dohna-Wundlacken Logic* (early 1790s), in *Lectures on Logic*, 24: 676–784
DR	*Danziger Rationaltheologie* (1784), 28: 1231–1319
DS	*Von dem ersten Grunde des Unterschiedes der Gegenden im Raume* (1768). *Concerning the Ultimate Ground of the Differentiation of Directions in Space*, in *Theoretical Philosophy 1*, 2: 375–83
EaT	*Das Ende aller Dinge* (1794). *The End of all Things*, in *Rational Theology*, 8: 328–339
GW	*Grundlegung zur Metaphysik der Sitten* (1785). *Groundwork of the Metaphysics of Morals*, in *Practical Philosophy*, 4: 385–463
Her.	*Kant's Practical Philosophy: Herder's Lecture Notes* (1762–4), in *Lectures on Ethics*, 27: 3–78
HL	*Heschel Logic* (1780s), in *Lectures on Logic*; page numbers refer to original manuscript
IC	*Untersuchung über die Deutlichkeit der Grundsätze der natürlichen Theologie und der Moral* (1763). *Inquiry Concerning the Distinctness of the Principles of Natural Theology and Morals*, in *Theoretical Philosophy 1*, 2: 273–301
ID	*De mundi sensibilis atque intelligibilis forma et principiis* (1770). *Concerning the Form and Principles of the Sensible and Intelligible World [Inaugural Dissertation]*, in *Theoretical Philosophy 1*, 2: 385–419
JL	*Jäsche Logic*, in *Lectures on Logic*, 9: 3–150
LF	*Gedanken von der wahren Schätzung der lebendigen Kräfte* (1747). *Thoughts on the True Estimation of Living Forces*, my translation, 1: 1–182
LPR	*Philosophische Religionslehre nach Pölitz* (1817). *Lectures on the Philosophical Doctrine of Religion*, in *Rational Theology*, 28: 993–1126
MD	*Metaphysik Dohna* (1792), in *Lectures on Metaphysics*, 28: 656–90
MetM.	*Die Metaphysik der Sitten. The Metaphysics of Morals* (1797), in *Practical Philosophy*, 6: 203–430
MH	*Metaphysik Herder* (1762–4), in *Lectures on Metaphysics*, 28: 39–53
MK₂	*Metaphysik K₂* (early 1790s), 28: 709–816

	the Existence of God, in *Theoretical Philosophy 1*, 2: 63–163
Opt.	*Versuch einiger Betrachtungen über den Optimismus* (1759). *An Attempt at Some Reflections on Optimism*, in *Theoretical Philosophy 1*, 2: 27–35
PJ	*Preface to Reinhold Jachmann's Examination of the Kantian Philosophy of Religion* (1800), in *Rational Theology*, 8: 441
PM	*Metaphysicae cum geometria iunctae usus in philosophia naturali cuius specimen I. continet monadologiam physicam, quam consentiente amplissimo philosophorum ordine* (1756). *The Employment in Natural Philosophy of Metaphysics Combined with Geometry, of Which Sample I Contains the Physical Monadology*, in *Theoretical Philosophy 1*, 1: 473–87
PP	*Zum ewigen Frieden. Ein philosophischer Entwurf* (1795). *Perpetual Peace: A Philosophical Sketch*, in *Practical Philosophy*, 8: 341–86
Pr.	*Prolegomena zu einer jeden künftigen Metaphysik, die als Wissenschaft wird auftreten können* (1783). *Prolegomena to any Future Metaphysics that Will be Able to Come Forward as Science*, in *Theoretical Philosophy 2*, 4: 255–383
R	*Reflexionen* (1753–1804). *Reflections*, 17: 229–19: 654
Rel.	*Die Religion innerhalb der Grenzen der Bloßen Vernunft* (1794). *Religion within the Boundaries of Mere Reason*, in *Rational Theology*, 6: 3–202
TP	*Über den Gemeinspruch: Das mag in der Theorie Richtig sein, stimmt aber nicht für die Praxis. On the Common Saying: That May be Correct in Theory, but it is of no Use in Practice* (1793), in *Practical Philosophy*, 8: 275–312
UNH	*Allgemeine Naturalgeschichte und Theorie des Himmels* (1755). *Universal Natural History and Theory of the Heavens*, ed. Milton K. Munitz and trans. W. Hastie (Michigan: University of Michigan Press, Ann Arbor Paperbacks, 1969), 1: 215–368
Vig.	*Notes on the Lectures of Mr Kant on the Metaphysics of Morals: Vigilantius* (1793), in *Lectures on Ethics*, 27: 479–732
VL	*Vienna Logic* (1780s), in *Lectures on Logic*, 24: 787–940

WRP   *Welches sind die wirklichen Fortschritt, die die Meta-*
       physik seit Leibnitzens und Wolf's Zeiten in Deutschland
       gemacht hat? (1793/1804). *What Real Progress Has*
       Metaphysics Made in Germany since the Time of Leibniz
       and Wolff?, in *Theoretical Philosophy 2*, 20: 259–351

1

Introduction

Kant struggles with a problem that is irreducibly theological: how can it be said that human beings are free, given that they are created by God? This is the central exegetical claim of this book. Kant's claimed solution to this problem is in turn the object of the book's theological and philosophical analysis. The problem is theological, in that it concerns the relationship between divine and human action. The problem is irreducible, in that it arises from a reflection on the unique metaphysical properties of the creator, given certain doctrinal assumptions, rather than from more general philosophical concerns.

Kant's thought is typically divided into a 'pre-critical' and a 'critical' period, with a date around 1770 considered as the vital watershed. Tracking how Kant struggles with this theological problem will offer illumination on two fronts. First of all, on the exegetical front, I show that the theological problem in part generates the shift from his pre-critical to his critical philosophy, and that it explains the particular and sometimes surprising way in which he expresses his critical philosophy. Secondly, I will argue that the way in which Kant addresses this theological problem in the critical period should be significant in determining how contemporary theologians and philosophers of religion receive and use Kant's thought.

According to a 'standard' interpretation,[1] Kant was a fairly conventional rationalist until he came under the influence of Newton and Hume, which

---

[1] Sustained scholarly defences of this narrative are not as common as one might suppose, given its prevalence. One can find something like the narrative—from rationalism to Newtonian science—defended in Michael Friedman, *Kant and the Exact Sciences* (Cambridge, MA: Harvard University Press, 1992), and Martin Schönfeld, *The Philosophy of the Young Kant: The Precritical Project* (New York: Oxford University Press, 2000); but in its more careful scholarly form the narrative loses the blunt creedal power that it can have when it is simply assumed as a framework. In English-speaking scholarship the 'standard interpretation' is the underlying premiss for the 'Oxford school' of Kant interpretation, where at least *that which is of value* in Kant's critical work is thought to be in stark discontinuity with his rationalist background: see Peter Strawson, *The Bounds of Sense: An Essay on Kant's Critique of Pure Reason* (London: Methuen, 1966), and Jonathan Bennett, *Kant's Analytic* (Cambridge: Cambridge University Press, 1966), and *Kant's Dialectic* (Cambridge: Cambridge University Press, 1974). This narrative is also in the background when Kant's thought is used as a resource for doing practical philosophy without substantial ontological commitments: see Katrin Flikshuh, *Kant and Modern*

precipitated his critical turn, at which point Kant realized the inadequacy of metaphysical and theological speculation ungoverned by the data of experience. Kant himself is partly responsible for this standard narrative, writing in 1783 that it was the 'remembrance of David Hume' that woke him from his 'dogmatic slumber' (*Pr.* 4: 260). In its own terms, there is nothing particularly slumbering about Kant's work prior to the critical period, with distinctive contributions to metaphysics, natural philosophy, and theology. Kant's presentation of his intellectual trajectory in these terms might have been more tactical than biographical; Allen Wood suggests that Kant framed his work in these terms in order to provide a 'striking way' to help an audience immersed in Wolffian philosophy to 'find its own path to his critical philosophy through reflection on Hume's sceptical challenges'.[2] In any case, when we read the sentence after this well-rehearsed quotation, Kant explains that he was provoked by Hume's insight into a 'part of' the *problem* of how we have knowledge of causation, while insisting at the same time that he was 'very far from listening to [Hume] with respect to his conclusions' (*Pr.* 4: 260). Kant's undoubted respect for and debt to Hume is consistent with Kant's critical *solution* having continuities with an epistemically disciplined rationalism.

In recent Kant scholarship, there has been a resurgence of interest in Kant's metaphysical and rationalist commitments, which more scholars now recognize continue into the critical period.[3] These commentators tend to stress the

---

Political Philosophy (Cambridge: Cambridge University Press, 2000), and Onora O'Neill, *Constructions of Reason: Explorations of Kant's Practical Philosophy* (Cambridge: Cambridge University Press, 1989). There is a recent literature in German that insists upon the central importance of Hume in Kant's intellectual trajectory: see Hans Gawlick and Lothar Kriemendahl, *Hume in der deutschen Aufklärung: Umrisse der Rezeptionsgeschichte* (Stuttgart: Fromann-Holzboog, 1987). Aspects of the standard interpretation also resonate with strands of late nineteenth- and early twentieth-century Neo-Kantianism; in particular the scientifically oriented 'Marburg school' of interpreters, who emphasized Kant's epistemology at the expense of his metaphysics: see Hermann Cohen, *Kant's Theorie der Erfahrung* (2nd edn; Berlin: Dümmler, 1885), and Paul Natorp, *Die logischen Grundlage der exacten Wissenschaften* (Leipzig and Berlin: Teubner, 1910).

[2] Allen W. Wood, 'Kant's Life and Works', in Graham Bird (ed.), *A Companion to Kant* (Oxford: Wiley-Blackwell, 2010), 10–31 (p. 13).

[3] Karl Ameriks, *Kant's Theory of Mind: An Analysis of the Paralogisms of Pure Reason* (Oxford: Oxford University Press, 2000), and 'The Critique of Metaphysics: Kant and Traditional Ontology', in Ameriks, *Interpreting Kant's Critiques* (Oxford: Oxford University Press, 2003), 112–34; Alison Laywine, *Kant's Early Metaphysics and the Origins of the Critical Philosophy* (Atascadero, CA: Ridgeview Publishing Company, 1993); Robert Adams, 'Things in Themselves', *Philosophy and Phenomenological Research*, 57/4 (1997), 801–25; Houston Smit, 'The Role of Reflection in Kant's *Critique of Pure Reason*', *Pacific Philosophical Quarterly*, 80/2 (1999), 203–23; C. A. Dalbosco, *Ding an sich und Erscheinung: Perspektiven des transzendentalen Idealismum bei Kant* (Würzberg: Königshausen und Neumann, 2002); Rae Langton, *Kantian Humility: Our Ignorance of Things in Themselves* (Oxford: Oxford University Press, 2004); Eric Watkins, *Kant and the Metaphysics of Causality* (Cambridge: Cambridge University Press, 2005); Elena Ficara, *Die Ontologie in der 'Kritik der reinen Vernunft'* (Würzberg: Königshausen und

continuity of Kant's thought with the metaphysics of German thinkers such as Leibniz, Wolff, Baumgarten, Crusius, and Knutzen; in this, recent commentators stand in a line with earlier commentators such as Max Wundt, Erich Adickes, Heinz Heimsoeth, and Lewis White Beck.[4]

As part of this movement, Kant's indebtedness to rational theology, both in the pre-critical and the critical periods, has been given proper acknowledgement.[5] There has also been important work on the extent to which Kant's practical commitment to freedom is an independent and irreducible strand in his justification for transcendental idealism,[6] the claim that space and time are features of how we receive the world, rather than being features of the world in itself. This book attempts to draw out more systematic links between these two dimensions of Kant's thought: theology, and the importance of freedom in the emergence of transcendental idealism. The relationship between these two dimensions of Kant's thought has certainly been noticed and commented

Newmann, 2006); Anja Jauernig, 'Kant's Critique of the Leinizian Philosophy: *Contra* the Leinizians, but *Pro* Leibniz', in Daniel Garber and Bétrice Longuenesse (eds), *Kant and the Early Moderns* (Princeton and Oxford: Princeton University Press, 2008), 41–64; Andrew Chignell, 'Real Repugnance and Belief about Things-in-Themselves: A Problem and Kant's Three Solutions', in James Krueger and Ben Lipscomb (eds), *Kant's Moral Metaphysics: God, Freedom and Immortality* (Berlin: de Gruyter, 2010); and Nicholas Stang, 'Did Kant Conflate the Necessary and the A Priori?', *Noûs*, 45.3 (2011), 443–71.

[4] Max Wundt, *Kant als Metaphysiker; ein Betrag zur Geschichte der deutschen Philosophie im 18ten Jahrhundert* (Stuttgart: F. Enke, 1924); Erich Adickes, *Kant und das Ding an sich* (Berlin: Pan Verlag, 1924); Heinz Heimsoeth, 'Metaphysical Motives in the Development of Critical Idealism', in *Kant: Disputed Questions*, ed. and trans. by Moltke S. Gram (Atascadero, CA: Ridgeview Publishing Company, 1984), 194–235; Lewis White Beck, *Early German Philosophy: Kant and his Predecessors* (Cambridge, MA: Harvard University Press, 1969).

[5] J. Kopper, 'Kants Gotteslehre', *Kant-Studien*, 47 (1955–6), 31–63; H.-G. Redmann, *Gott und Welt: Die Schöpfungstheologie der vorkritischen Periode Kants* (Göttingen: Vandenhoeck and Ruprecht, 1962); Joseph Schmuker, 'Die Gottesbeweise beim vorkritischen Kant', *Kantstudien*, 54/4 (1963), 445–63; Allen W. Wood, *Kant's Moral Religion* (Ithaca, NY, and London: Cornell University Press, 1970); Pierre Laberge, *La Théologie Kantienne précritique* (Ottawa: Éditions de L'Université d'Ottawa, 1973); Allen W. Wood, *Kant's Rational Theology* (Ithaca, NY: Cornell University Press, 1978); Mark Fisher and Eric Watkins, 'Kant on the Material Ground of Possibility: From "The Only Possible Argument" to the "Critique of Pure Reason"', *Review of Metaphysics*, 52/2 (1998), 369–95; Robert Adams, 'God, Possibility and Kant', *Faith and Philosophy*, 17/4 (2000), 425–40; Schönfeld, *The Philosophy of the Young Kant*, 183–208; Frederick Beiser, 'Moral Faith and the Highest Good', in *The Cambridge Companion to Kant and Modern Philosophy*, ed. Paul Guyer (Cambridge: Cambridge University Press, 2006), 588–639; Andrew Chignell, 'Kant, Modality, and the Most Real Being', *Archiv für Geschichte der Philosophie*, 91/2 (2009), 157–92; Nicholas Stang, 'Kant's Possibility Proof', *History of Philosophy Quarterly*, 27/3 (2010), 275–99; Patrick Kain, 'The Development of Kant's Conception of Divine Freedom', in Brandon Look (ed.), *Leibniz and Kant* (Oxford: Oxford University Press, forthcoming).

[6] Desmond Hogan, 'Three Kinds of Rationalism and the Non-Spatiality of Things in Themselves', *Journal of the History of Philosophy*, 47/3 (2009), 355–82; and 'How to Know Unknowable Things in Themselves', *Noüs*, 43/1 (2009), 49–63. See also Ameriks, *Interpreting Kant's Critiques*, ch. 6.

upon,[7] as has the transposition of cognitive and creative tasks from the divine mind to the human mind.[8] What there has not been is a sustained treatment of the movement from Kant's pre-critical position on the status of space, time, and causation, to his critical position, which keeps as its central focus Kant's changing conception of the relationship between divine action and human freedom.

This book fills this gap in Kant scholarship. It also does something distinctive in relation to this material, by engaging theologically with the fundamental premises that drive Kant forward. Throughout the book, as I set out Kant's shifting account of the relationship between divine action and human freedom, I analyse in detail where some theologians might have real difficulties with Kant's account, both of the problem and of the solution. In this respect, I consider the book to be a contribution to another recently burgeoning literature, which engages Kant's philosophical theology and philosophy of religion in its own terms, using Kant as a source of consolation and insight where possible, but also being critical where appropriate.[9]

My aim is both to offer a new interpretation of a strand of Kant's work, and to set out an alternative perspective on the significance of Kant for theology. Kant's philosophy has often been received as presenting a challenge to theology's

---

[7] See Ameriks, *Interpreting Kant's Critiques*, 162–71; Henry Allison, *Kant's Theory of Freedom* (Cambridge: Cambridge University Press, 1995), 61–2; Andrew Chignell, 'Kant, Possibility and the Threat of Spinoza', *Mind* (forthcoming).

[8] Henry Allison, *Kant's Transcendental Idealism: An Interpretation and Defense* (New Haven, CT: Yale University Press, 1983), 19–25, and Laywine, *Kant's Early Metaphysics and the Origins of the Critical Philosophy*, esp. 124–45. Although Allison pursues a more epistemological reading of the critical Kant, he is often acute at noticing the traditional theological lines of thought being traced over.

[9] Wood, *Kant's Moral Religion*; Gordon E. Michalson Jr., *Fallen Freedom: Kant on Radical Evil and Moral Regeneration* (Cambridge: Cambridge University Press, 1990); Phillip J. Rossi and Michael Wreen (eds), *Kant's Philosophy of Religion Reconsidered* (Bloomington and Indianapolis: Indiana University Press, 1991); Adina Davidovich, *Religion as a Province of Meaning* (Minneapolis: Fortress Press,1993); Stephen R. Palmquist, *Kant's System of Perspectives: An Architectonic Interpretation of the Critical Philosophy* (Lanham, MD: University Press of America, 1993); John Hare, *The Moral Gap: Kantian Ethics, Human Limits, and God's Assistance* (Oxford: Clarendon Press, 1996); Jacqueline Mariña, 'Kant on Grace: A Reply to his Critics', *Religious Studies*, 33/4 (1997), 379–400; Gordon E. Michalson Jr., *Kant and the Problem of God* (Oxford: Blackwell, 1999); Stephen R. Palmquist, *Kant's Critical Religion: Volume Two of Kant's System of Perspectives* (Aldershot: Ashgate Publishing, 2000); Chris L. Firestone and Stephen R. Palmquist (eds), *Kant and the New Philosophy of Religion* (Bloomington and Indianapolis: Indiana University Press, 2006); Peter Byrne, *Kant on God* (Aldershot: Ashgate Publishing, 2007); Chris L. Firestone and Nathan Jacobs, *In Defense of Kant's Religion* (Bloomington, IN: Indiana University Press, 2008); Chris L. Firestone, *Kant and Theology at the Boundaries of Reason* (Aldershot: Ashgate Publishing, 2009); Pamela Sue Anderson and Jordan Bell, *Kant and Theology* (London and New York: T&T Clark International, 2010). For a helpful contextualizing of the recent interest in Kant's philosophy of religion, see Andrew Chignell, 'Introduction: On Defending Kant at the AAR', *Faith and Philosophy*, 26/2 (2012), 144–50. This issue of *Faith and Philosophy* is largely given over to a symposium on Kant's philosophy of religion, centred around Firestone and Jacob's *In Defense of Kant's Religion*.

presumption to speak of God.[10] The account set out in this book presents a different possibility: that theology can present some challenges, or at least some illumination, to aspects of Kant's epistemology and metaphysics, by understanding these as motivated and justified, in part, by a problematic conception of the relationship between divine action and human freedom. Kant is not simply the scourge of metaphysics and theology, but has intrinsically theological difficulties of his own that generate aspects of his critical philosophy. Corresponding to these complementary aims, Kant interpretation and theological engagement with Kant, I have in mind two main constituencies of readers: readers interested in Kant, and those concerned with systematic and philosophical theology. Not all readers will be members of both groups, and so might become frustrated by too much Kant, or too much theology. If the book succeeds, the reader interested in either area *will be* interested in the other by the end, if not at the beginning.

The project by its nature compels us to engage with a wide range of Kant texts, from 1749 to the early 1800s. Such coverage has associated risks, in the same way that an exclusive focus on one period or a few texts of Kant's œuvre has its own limitations. Although the path I follow will open up a wide view of the Kantian landscape, I do not attempt to survey Kant's entire corpus. The aim is to track, in a disciplined way, one specific strand running through the entire development of Kant's thought: how, for Kant, can it be said that we are free, given that we are created by God? All the material in the book is selected and oriented to this purpose. Where material is not relevant to our task, it is not treated; where philosophical and textual controversies cross our path, they are treated only to the extent that they bear upon our central question. My judgement on what is excluded or included, and to what extent, will inevitably be controversial, but this is the criterion that I have attempted to apply. I aim to give an accurate and distinctive interpretation of Kant's construal of the relationship between divine action and human freedom, by my own interpretation of primary texts, informed by an extensive secondary literature. It is not my intention, though, to give a philosophical evaluation of the plausibility of Kant's metaphysics or epistemology. There is already an extensive literature dedicated to this. The book draws on this literature, but does not seek to be a contribution on this front.

I draw upon a wide range of Kant's published and unpublished (by Kant) works and correspondence, his *Reflexionen*, and Kant's lectures on metaphysics,

---

[10] See, for example, Nicholas Wolterstorff, 'Is it Possible and Desirable for Theologians to Recover from Kant?', *Modern Theology*, 14/1 (1998), 1–18. This can be the case even where the theologian considers that Kant's challenge can and should be addressed. See, for example, Donald MacKinnon's discussion of Kant in *Themes in Theology: The Three-Fold Cord: Essays in Philosophy, Politics, and Theology* (Edinburgh: T&T Clark, 1987), ch. 2; and more recently Paul Janz, *The Command of Grace: A New Theological Apologetics* (London: T&T Clark, 2009), where the epistemic humility of Kant plays an important role.

ethics, and theology given from the 1760s to the 1790s. The relative weight to be given to these lecture-notes is contested, based as they are upon student transcriptions of Kant's lectures. As well as the question of the reliability of the note-takers, it is not always clear the extent to which Kant is endorsing a position, or simply rehearsing a traditional account for the benefit of his students.[11] Mindful of this, I am careful not to base controversial aspects of my interpretation of Kant on these lectures alone, although evidence from the lectures might be enlisted when clarifying or supporting an interpretation that is more broadly warranted on the basis of other texts. If there is an exception to this cautious practice, it is in my use of the lecture notes to map Kant's struggle with reconciling divine and human freedom in the 1760s and 1770s. This exception is warranted for two reasons. First of all, the clarity, pervasiveness, and repetition of the same themes across different note-takers leave us in no doubt concerning the drift of Kant's thought at this time. Secondly, the concerns we find expressed in these lectures cannot be rehearsals of traditional positions, quite simply because they do not reflect any sort of traditional position. Rather, they disrupt traditional certainties and resolutions, reflecting distinctively Kantian anxieties that arise from a problem that opens up in his thought.

For the most part, I use the terms 'action' and 'freedom' interchangeably, when framing the question of how, for Kant, divine and human freedom/action interact. In general, the terms 'action' and 'freedom' cannot be used interchangeably without further comment. Conceptually speaking, we might insist that there can be unfree actions (if I am determined, or if I am coerced, where these situations are considered to be destructive of freedom); and, more controversially, we might also claim that there can be freedom without action (if I have a potential to do something that I never act upon, where omissions are not counted as actions). The 'further comment' needed to warrant using these terms interchangeably is a grammatical reflection. By a 'grammatical reflection', I mean a consideration of the rules governing the correct use of concepts *within a context*. For Kant, in line with the theological tradition, God acts in creating and sustaining the world. A distinctive claim of the Christian tradition, in contrast to some versions of Neo-Platonism and pantheism, is that God acts *freely* in creating and sustaining the world. As part of the free creation of the world, God creates and sustains human beings, who are also in some sense *free*. A question then arises as to what shape human action must

---

[11] Perhaps the most controversial set of notes are the *Lectures on the Philosophical Doctrine of Religion* (1783–4). These lectures were first published in 1817 by the Kantian Karl Henrich Luwig Pölitz. For a positive assessment of the value of these lecture notes, see Wood, *Kant's Rational Theology*, 149, and 'Translator's Introduction' in Kant, *Lectures on Philosophical Theology* (Ithaca, NY: Cornell University Press, 1978), 9–18. For a largely negative assessment of the value of these lecture notes, see Byrne, *Kant on God*, 4–5. Byrne finds that the *Lectures* violate Kant's critical epistemic discipline, with 'affirmations that are more religiously conservative, less sceptical, than those found in the critiques' (p. 4).

have if it is to be action-that-is-free, both in relation to other created things, and in relation to the creator's action-that-is-free. We can use action and freedom interchangeably, because, when we speak about action, we are concerned, in this book, with 'action-that-is-free', and when we speak about freedom, we are concerned with the ability to perform an 'action-that-is-free'. All the work is yet to be done, of course, in ascertaining what is involved, for God and for us, in performing an action-that-is-free.

An account of how Kant relates divine and human action-that-is-free needs to begin with an outline of what Kant understands divine action-that-is-free to consist in. While Kant's conception of human freedom shifts considerably, his conception of divine freedom remains largely stable across the development of his thought. Chapter 2 sets out this conception. We find that Kant has, in his bones, a positive and teleological conception of freedom, expressed paradigmatically and perfectly in divine freedom, where what matters for freedom is that the will is oriented to the good. There are theological difficulties with such a conception of divine freedom, which are explored in Chapter 3. I will set out how, for Kant, God's creation of a world that conforms to the highest good is necessary, but free, in that such a creation is an expression of God's own 'well-pleasedness in himself' (*LPR* 28: 1061). From some theological perspectives, this conception does not say enough about divine sovereignty, binding the divine will to a divine nature over which God has no control, where the divine nature is itself bound to an external category of reason or goodness. In Chapter 3 I explore some of the fundamental theological issues that will determine how positively or negatively one receives Kant's theological rationalism. Although I do not defend Kant's rationalism about God, I do suggest that it is not obviously 'beyond the pale' from a broadly orthodox perspective, if one accepts that the divine nature is internal to the divine will, and that goodness and rationality are internal to the divine nature. By exploring the 'non-moral dependence' of all possibility upon God, we will see that, for Kant, God is the source of all goodness and rationality; therefore, goodness and rationality can only ever be 'internal' factors shaping the divine nature and the divine will. This helps to explain why, for Kant, it in no way threatens divine freedom that God is unable to do other than the good. Understanding Kant's conception of perfect divine freedom will provide an illuminating interpretative puzzle when we move on, in Chapter 3, to consider how important the capacity to do other than the good becomes for Kant's conception of significant human freedom.

Having set out Kant's conception of divine freedom, and explored some of the deep premises that undergird this conception, I move on in Chapter 4 to set out Kant's account of human freedom in the 1750s. At this stage in his thought, Kant considers that human freedom is compatible with God being the creative and sustaining source of our existence, and of all our actions. To be free, human beings do not need to enjoy an ultimate responsibility for their actions, and they do not need to enjoy the possibility of doing other than they

do. Chapter 4 tracks how Kant's position on human freedom shifts significantly in the 1760s and 1770s, such that he begins to reach out for a notion of
transcendental freedom, whereby human beings enjoy ultimate responsibility
for their actions (as God does), and where human beings (unlike God) have
the possibility of acting other than they do. As this latter ability involves our
being able to do other than the good, we will see that Kant considers it to be a
regrettable feature of our freedom. In the 1760s and 1770s, Kant sometimes
expresses a distinctively theological problem with our having such transcendental freedom, asking how we can be free if our existence is 'derived from
another'.

Part of the intellectual matrix of ideas and problems that gave rise to Kant's
critical philosophy was the question of how to allow a conceptual space for
created freedom, given the existence and role of a creator. I conclude
Chapter 4 by reflecting on the way in which Kant, in the 1760s and 1770s,
begins to consider God to be an 'alien' and 'external' cause on the creature.
This, for many historical and contemporary theologians, would indicate a
problematic model of the way in which divine action and human freedom
relate, as if both are somehow competing for the same conceptual space. This
controversy, of how to conceive the relationship between divine action and
human freedom, is at the heart of our theological engagement with Kant.
I begin this engagement in Chapter 4 with a brief discussion of Aquinas's
account of the uniquely interior quality of divine action, whereby God can
never be a violent or alien cause on the creature.

By the 1780s, Kant understands transcendental idealism to be the guarantor
of human freedom, in relation to the creator. Chapter 5 analyses the shape of
this solution, as understood by Kant, setting out the relationship between
transcendental idealism and the possibility of noumenal first causation;
human transcendental freedom is located in a non-spatial and non-temporal
sphere, where we can regard ourselves as not determined by any antecedent
causes. In this context, I address the issue of whether my interpretation
illegitimately projects a pre-critical notion of 'substance' onto Kant's critical
use of the term. I show that Kant does use the category of noumenal substance,
and explain why such a usage need not be inconsistent with the epistemic
discipline of Kant's critical period, at least on a plausible, and in my view
correct, interpretation of what this epistemic discipline amounts to.

The notion that in some sense our empirical actions derive from a case of
atemporal first causation is found by some commentators to be scarcely more
credible than a flat contradiction. This has led these commentators to deny
that Kant holds this view in any significant sense. In Chapter 6, I defend the
claim that Kant is in fact committed to the notion of atemporal first causation,
explaining why this would not seem an implausible or epistemically undiscip-
lined claim to Kant. Chapter 6 moves onto address a challenge to the fundamental coherence of the notion of noumenal first causation: in particular, with

reference to the inexplicability of our ability to do other than the good. I conclude that Kant has no good answer to this problem, and that he knows this, but that some theologians might like him better for his studied admission of incomprehensibility.

Even if it is permitted that Kant could speak about noumenal substances without violating his own epistemic discipline, there might still be some scepticism about the specific substantial commitments concerning God that I ascribe to Kant. Kant could hardly be said to have a 'theological problem' in his critical period, if he no longer believes in God in a significant sense. In Chapter 7, I defend the position that Kant continues to believe in God in the critical period, albeit that Kant's warrant for this belief arises from practical rather than theoretical reason. I argue against deflationary readings of these commitments, which hold that Kant merely intends us to proceed 'as if' certain claims were true, while bracketing out any fundamental commitment to their being so.

Chapter 8 drills down on an aspect of Kant's transcendental idealism that has not received much attention: specifically, Kant's claim that God is not the creator of appearances (*CPrR.* 5: 102), and that space is 'not a thing as a divine work' (R. 6057, 18: 439). I acknowledge that the specific theological claim, that God is not the creator of appearances, does not seem to follow from the epistemic thesis that space and time are features of our reception of the world. The further theological claim seems, on the surface, to be unnecessarily sensationalist and extravagant. At any rate, Kant makes the claim, and our task is to make some sense of it. This I claim to have done by the end of the book. Part of the answer to the interpretative puzzle comes at the end of Chapter 8. By ensuring that God is not the cause of space, time, and causation, Kant considers that he has solved the problems that arise from our being created by God. In some texts at least, Kant no longer finds it problematic that we are dependent upon God. Furthermore, and of particular interest to theologians, it is specifically our dependence upon *God* that is an unproblematic type of dependence. God creates us in a reciprocal and non-determined community of noumenally free beings, the 'Kingdom of Ends'. If we were dependent upon other *created* causal determining factors, that would indeed threaten freedom; but an implication of transcendental idealism, on Kant's account, is that we are dependent upon God alone, and not upon contingent and created determined series. I suggest that this theological implication of transcendental idealism is further developed by Schleiermacher.

Questions still remain, though, about the precise nature of this relationship between divine and human action, and the scope of our 'unproblematic' dependence upon God. The final two chapters move on to interrogate these issues: to establish Kant's position (Chapter 9), and to reflect on the significance of Kant's position for the theological reception of his thought (Chapter 10). Chapter 9 takes us to the heart of Kant's theological problem, by focusing on the precise 'causal joint' between God's creative action and our free actions. I track this issue in Kant by attending to some debates in late medieval and early modern philosophy. This is the discourse out of which, and in which, Kant's position on the issue is explicitly worked out, although the narrow and technical discussion is itself motivated by, and oriented to, a cosmic and perennial question. In short, the issue is how we can relate the claim that God is the creator *ex nihilo*, such that everything that exists is dependent entirely and utterly upon God, with the claim that the creature has an existence that is distinct from God, and is capable of an action that belongs properly to the creature, and is not just an aspect of divine action.

The mainstream medieval tradition understood that it was not a sufficient account of the scope of divine action to say that God's action on creatures is exhausted by God bringing the substances into existence, and conserving them in their existence. In the eyes of theistic philosophers such as Aquinas, Suarez, and Leibniz, this view, known as 'mere conservationism', fails to describe the total and immediate dependence of the creature upon God in all the creature's modes of being, including in the actions of the creature. When the creature acts, God also acts directly and immediately, so that, as David Burrell puts it, 'God not only causes each thing to be, and thus makes it able to act, but God also acts in its acting by causing it to be the cause that it is'.[12] Divine action is regarded as 'concurring' with human action in a single cause: hence this understanding of divine and human action is known as a 'concurrence' account. By analysing a wide range of texts where Kant explicitly discusses conservation and concurrence, I demonstrate that Kant is a 'mere conservationist', and that, when we understand this, we see precisely why Kant asserts that 'it would be a contradiction to say that God is the creator of appearances' (*CPrR.* 5: 102), in so far as appearances are (in part) the effects of creaturely actions.

In the final chapter, I conclude by considering some of the profound difficulties and antagonisms in the debate around the nature of divine and human action. These difficulties are at work, I suggest, in wildly different estimations of Kant's importance—or wholesomeness even—for Christian theology. I suggest that although there is much in Kant that the theologian might find surprisingly illuminating and consoling, the specific issue of Kant's conception of the relationship between divine and human action will be, for orthodox theologians, a real stumbling block. Kant's views will be a stumbling block in two senses: first of all, there will be a 'problem with Kant', if his account is considered to be at odds with Christian orthodoxy; secondly, Kant takes us to the 'problem of the problem', in that it is unclear whether a fully

---

[12] David Burrell, *Freedom and Creation in Three Traditions* (Notre Dame, IN: University of Notre Dame Press, 1993), 69; Burrell offers this as a commentary on Aquinas, *Summa Theologiae*, Blackfriars Edition, ed. Thomas Gilby OP et al., 60 vols (Cambridge: Cambridge University Press, 2006), 1.105.5.

transparent account could ever in principle be given of the concurrence between divine and human action. The extent to which this troubles us will depend upon some fundamental theological and philosophical premises, as well as our expectations about what we expect philosophy to do in relation to theological doctrines.

When I began researching this book, I was motivated by a sense that Kant was a largely pernicious influence on philosophy and philosophical theology: replacing tasks done (rather successfully, I thought and still think) by God in the thought of a thinker such as Aquinas, with a somewhat inflated and Titanic human subject. In some ways it can help when writing about Kant if one does not self-identify as a Kantian. It means that Kant does not always have to be right, conforming to contemporary intellectual fashions and one's own sense of the plausible. In the course of engaging with Kant's texts, I found that he is also not always wrong. In any case, I am now convinced that there is not much 'Titanism' to Kant's depiction of the human subject. I do think that there is a problem with Kant's account of divine action and human freedom, but also that Kant takes us to the 'problem of the problem', and is good to think with, even where we disagree. Above all, Kant is an honest thinker, who worries at some of the defining problems in modern philosophical theology relentlessly and without subterfuge.

In the final twist, by drawing on strands of Kant's thought covered over the course of the book, alongside a few late enigmatic texts, I sketch a reconstruction of Kant, arguing that a concurrence account of divine action and human freedom might be not only consistent with strands of his wider philosophy, but even positively harmonious with it, in some cases making other areas of his thought work more successfully. Whether this reconstruction is thought to be an improvement, a piece of vandalism—or perhaps just rather pointless— will more likely depend on views brought to the book than those derived from it.

2

The Creation

This book is occupied with the question of how, for Kant, it can be said that human beings are free, given that we are created by God. In order to understand precisely what the question means 'for Kant', we need to understand what the content of the key concepts would be for the philosopher: human freedom, God and divine freedom, and the divine creation of a world with free beings. This chapter is dedicated to providing an exposition of Kant's understanding of the nature of God and divine freedom, and of the divine creation. The next chapter looks at some of the fundamental theological challenges to this conception. We begin the consideration of created human freedom in Chapter 4.

William Rowe distinguishes two fundamental views about divine freedom in Western philosophical thought. According to the first view, 'God is free in creating a world or in acting within the world he has created provided nothing *outside* of God determines him to create the world he creates, or determined him to act in a particular way in the world he has created'.[1] The second view insists that 'God is free in creating or acting within his creation' only if 'it was in his power not to create what he did or not to act within his creation as he did'.[2] On this conception, it is crucial for divine freedom that there are alternative possibilities open to God, or that God is able to do otherwise.

In this chapter we will see that Kant emphatically ascribes to a version of the first view. The conception that emerges incrementally across the chapter is one where the ability to do otherwise does not feature as an important criterion for divine freedom. In the first section of this chapter I draw on recent work by Andrew Chignell, in order to set out a distinction between logical and real possibility that does important work in Kant's account of divine freedom (as well as in other areas of his philosophy). In the second section, I explore how in Kant's early thought the divine will is shaped by the requirement that, if God chooses to create, God must create the best really possible world. There is evidence from his later work that Kant comes to the view that God must

---

[1] William L. Rowe, *Can God Be Free?* (Oxford: Oxford University Press, 2004), 14.
[2] Rowe, *Can God Be Free?* 4.

choose to create (although this is still an act of 'divine free will'), and that God must create a world that achieves the 'highest good'. It is unclear in his later thought whether Kant understands the world that achieves the 'highest good' as the best really possible world, or whether the highest good can be realized in a number of ways.[3] What matters for our purposes is that God's 'inability to do otherwise' is not construed by Kant as a lack or impotence on the part of God. Rather, this 'inability' is an expression of God's perfect goodness and rationality. In the third section, I set out the way in which the divine will as 'holy' is shaped by perfect goodness and the rational moral law.

Over the course of the book, I will show that Kant's conception of human freedom shifts considerably. The same cannot be said when it comes to his conception of divine freedom. Although there are significant epistemic shifts in the status of propositions about God, the content of these propositions ('what the concept *God* means, whether or not we consider that such a God exists') remains remarkably stable. For this reason, and in partial support of this claim for continuity (which is further defended in Chapter 7), I draw in this chapter and the next on a range of texts from the 1750s to the 1790s. As hinted at above, we will see in the second section of this chapter that there are some specific areas where Kant's conception of the relationship between divine freedom and the creation changes; but these shifts are not so much revolutions, as developments or revisions of themes already embedded in his earliest thought, which is itself saturated in the categories of rationalist scholastic theology.

LOGICAL AND REAL POSSIBILITY

In setting out Kant's position on divine freedom, I will be careful to avoid the language of 'constraints', 'limitations', or 'restrictions' on the divine will, as for Kant—and for the rationalist tradition within which he works—these are not constraining factors on the divine will, but rather constitute what is distinctive and praiseworthy about the *divine* will.[4] I will use blander expressions, and talk of factors that 'shape' and 'direct' the divine will; although, equally, this should not be read as an endorsement of Kant's account of divine freedom. I explore difficulties with Kant's conception of divine freedom in the next chapter.

Any position on divine omnipotence and divine freedom will have to define itself in relation to categories of logical possibility and impossibility. More usually, philosophical theologians will carve out a notion of omnipotence that allows God to do anything that is logically possible, so that the only restriction

---

[3] For this point, I am indebted to an anonymous reader for OUP.
[4] For this point of terminological caution, I am indebted to an anonymous reader for OUP.

upon divine power is that God cannot bring about a logically impossible situation, or bring it about that a logically impossible proposition is true.[5] When interpreting the conception of divine power and freedom that the pre-critical Kant ascribes to God, we also need to explore how divine power and freedom are related to Kant's notion of 'real possibility' and 'real repugnance', which is a more restrictive category than logical possibility and impossibility. Having done this, we will then be in a position to understand the nature of divine freedom in relation to the creation of the world.

In *The Only Possible Argument in Support of a Demonstration of the Existence of God* (1763), Kant sets out three conditions that must be met for something to be considered 'possible'. First of all, it must not be self-contradictory, as 'anything which is self-contradictory is internally impossible' (*OPA* 2: 77). Kant calls this the 'formal' or the 'logical element in possibility' (*OPA* 2: 78). Secondly, the possibility must have a thinkable content. There must be a 'material element', which 'is itself something and can be thought' (*OPA* 2: 77). Kant gives as an example a 'triangle which has a right angle' (*OPA* 2: 77). The 'material' elements in this, or the 'data', are the 'triangle and the right angle'. The 'formal element' is the 'agreement' of 'one with the other, in accordance with the law of contradiction' (*OPA* 2: 77).

It is not entirely clear what Kant's criteria are for being a 'material element', or being a 'something which can be thought'. Commentators must resort to reconstructions on the basis of the relatively spare account given by Kant. Chignell offers a plausible construal,[6] drawing upon Kant's *New Elucidation*, where Kant writes that 'in every comparison the things which are to be compared must be available for comparison', and 'where nothing at all is given there is no room for either comparison, or, corresponding to it, for the concept of possibility' (*NE* 1: 395). Chignell suggests that one aspect of satisfying the 'material' conditions of possibility is that 'the thing in question must have some positive predicates whose content determines its existence in one way rather than another'.[7] As Kant puts it, 'if things differ from each other, then they differ in virtue of something which is present in one thing and not in the other' (*Opt.* 2: 31). 'Empty' concepts are predicates that fail to pick out genuine properties. Even if they are logically consistent, they do not give us a content that is 'available for use by thought'. Examples of such predicates, Chignell suggests, would include *being such that 2 + 2 = 4, not being a horse, not being Sherlock Holmes*, and the 'thought-entities' of rationalist metaphysics (A602/B630). Although these are suggestive examples of

[5] For a discussion of recent formulations of omnipotence, see Richard Swinburne, *The Coherence of Theism* (Oxford: Clarendon Press, 1993), 153–66.

[6] Andrew Chignell, 'Kant, Real Possibility, and the Threat of Spinoza', *Mind* (forthcoming); page references to this article refer to an off-print of the article, provided by the author, as it will appear in *Mind*, except for the pagination, which will change according to the location of the article.

[7] Chignell, 'Kant, Real Possibility, and the Threat of Spinoza', pp. 9–10, offprint; see *NE* 1: 395–6.

'empty predicates', Chignell concedes that it is not clear that Kant is able to provide a non-circular account of what it is to be 'available for use by thought' or to 'determine something's existence in one way rather than another'. For our purposes, though, this is as close as we need to get to Kant's 'material criterion' for possibility.

These formal and material conditions on possibility can also be found in Leibniz, for whom the 'giveness' of the conceptual content of possibilities is grounded in 'God's understanding'.[8] Where Kant innovates upon the tradition is in his addition of a third requirement for possibility: that it be 'really possible' in the sense that the 'positive, contentful predicates' must be '*really harmonious* with one another'.[9] The opposite of this, 'real repugnancy', occurs when 'something, as a ground, annihilates by means of a real opposition the consequence of something else' (*OPA* 2: 86). Chignell distinguishes in this context between 'predicate-cancelling' and 'subject-cancelling' real repugnance. We have predicate-cancelling real repugnance where 'two predicates of a thing are opposed to each other, but not through the law of contradiction' (*NM* 2: 171). For example, if the 'motive force of a body in one direction' is met by the 'equal tendency of the same body in the opposite direction', then these forces do not contradict each other 'as predicates', although there is a 'true opposition' (*NM* 2: 171). Kant considers that this distinction between a real and a logical opposition applies across a range of spheres. In psychology the distinction reveals that displeasure is not just a lack of pleasure, but a real and positive state that cancels out pleasure (*NM* 2: 180–2). In moral philosophy, some evils are not just negations of the good, but 'positive grounds which cancel the good' (*NM* 2: 182). In natural science the distinction between real and logical opposition can help us to see that any 'state of matter can only ever be changed by means of an *external* cause' (*NM* 2: 192).

We have subject-cancelling real repugnance when the ascription of predicates to a subject cancels out the possibility of the subject itself, such as would occur, for example, if we ascribed 'to what has an understanding and will' the 'impenetrability of bodies, extension and the like' (*OPA* 2: 85). More contemporary examples would include the non-logical repugnance that some philosophers derive from metaphysical facts about natures, when, for example, we combine the properties *being water* and *being XYZ*, where *XYZ* is distinct from *being H$_2$O*.[10]

Kant construes the scope of real possibility as more narrowly limited than the scope of logical possibility. When asking about the scope of divine

---

[8] See Gottfried Wilhelm Leibniz, *Monadology*, in *Philosophical Texts*, ed. and trans. R. S. Woolhouse and Richard Francks (Oxford: Oxford University Press, 1998), 268–81 (pp. 273–4, §43–4); for this reference, I am indebted to Chignell, 'Kant, Real Possibility and the Threat of Spinoza', p. 11, offprint.

[9] Chignell, 'Kant, Real Possibility and the Threat of Spinoza', p. 11, offprint.

[10] Chignell, 'Kant, Real Possibility and the Threat of Spinoza', pp. 11–12, offprint.

freedom, we will need to answer the questions, not only of whether the divine will is shaped by logical possibility, but also of whether the divine will is shaped by real possibility; and, if so, how Kant avoids compromising the independence and sovereignty of God.

GOD NECESSARILY CREATES THE BEST REALLY POSSIBLE WORLD

It is usual to separate out 'emanation' and 'free-creation' accounts of the relationship between God and the world, where the former conceive of the world unfolding by necessity from (or as an expression of) the divine nature, while the latter conceive of the world coming into being as a result of the divine will. Kant unambiguously wishes to align himself with the latter account, but we need further degrees of nuance, if we are to capture Kant's precise position. As we have seen above, Kant thinks that for something to be 'really possible' its 'positive, contentful predicates' must be '*really harmonious* with one another'.[11] Worlds, which are populated by substances, must also be 'really harmonious' as well as logically possible, and so I talk below about worlds being 'really possible'. A logically possible world might not be a really possible world, as some logically possible worlds might contain predicate- or subject-cancelling real repugnance. Incorporating Kant's distinction between real and logical possibility, there are at least five possible construals of the relationship between God and the world, which will help us to locate Kant's position (further qualifications to the 'Necessary Free Creation' account will be introduced below):

Emanation 1 (Pantheism): God is identical with the world; where one represents things 'as if the world itself were God' (*LPR* 28: 1092).

Emanation 2: God is separate from the world, but where the world necessarily comes into being, and does so in the form that it does, without it being willed by God; where 'God is regarded as the cause of substances by the necessity of his nature' (*LPR* 28: 1092).

Necessary Free Creation: God is separate from the world, but the divine will necessarily chooses to create a world, and, given God's perfect goodness, the divine will necessarily creates the best really possible world. God could not do otherwise than to create a world, and to create this world, from all really possible worlds.

Contingent Free Creation 1: God can choose whether or not to create a world, but, if God does decide to create a world, God must choose the best possible world out of all really possible worlds.

[11] Chignell, 'Kant, Real Possibility and the Threat of Spinoza', p. 11, offprint.

Contingent Free Creation 2: God can choose whether or not to create a world, and can choose any really possible world.

Kant consistently avoids emanationist accounts, emphatically distinguishing God from the created world (*OPA* 2: 90–1; *ID* 2: 414; *LPR* 28: 1091–1199). Kant encountered an emanationist approach in Spinoza's substance monism, where (as Kant understands Spinoza) the world is construed fundamentally as a single divine substance. Kant identifies Spinoza's erroneous conception of substance as responsible for such monism (*MH* 28: 51–2; *LPR* 1041–2, 1052, 1269).[12] 'Contingent Free creation 2' is a model that comes up in recent philosophy of religion as a problem for theodicy (bracketing for the moment the distinction between real and logical possibility). For example, J. L. Mackie observes that, if the only restriction upon divine omnipotence is that God cannot do the logically impossible, then God can create any logically possible world.[13] Mackie finds no logical contradiction in the claim that 'God creates a world where everybody as a matter of fact freely chooses to do the good'. This has an edge, as it would seem to render God morally reprehensible for not creating such a logically possible world where people have freedom, but choose only the good. Kant considers a version of 'Contingent Free Creation 2' in his *Optimism* essay, when he dismisses the view that God 'might choose this of all possible worlds, not because it was better than the other worlds which lay within his power to choose, but quite simply because it so pleased him' (*Opt.* 2: 29–30).

Kant's pre-critical position falls out somewhere between 'Necessary Free Creation' and 'Contingent Free Creation 1'. Kant insists that if God creates a world, God does so freely (through his will); because of God's perfect goodness, God must create the best really possible world. This is ambiguous, as it stands, between the claim that it is necessary that God creates a world, and the claim that *if* God creates a world (where God could do otherwise), then God necessarily creates the best really possible world. If it is necessary that God creates a world, such that, given the divine nature, God could not have willed otherwise, then Kant gravitates towards the 'Necessary Free Creation' view; if it is not necessary that God creates a world, such that

---

[12] For a full discussion of Kant's attitude to Spinoza, see Chignell, 'Kant, Real Possibility, and the Threat of Spinoza'; Beth Lord, *Kant and Spinoza: Transcendental Idealism and Immanence from Jacobi to Deleuze* (Basingstoke: Palgrave Macmillan Press, 2011); Pierfrancesco Basile, 'Kant, Spinoza and the Metaphysics of the Ontological Proof', *Metaphysica: International Journal for Ontology and Metaphysics* 11/1 (2010), 17–37; Henry Allison, 'Kant's Critique of Spinoza', in Richard Kennington (ed.), *The Philosophy of Baruch Spinoza* (Washington: Catholic University of America Press, 1980), and J. C. Morrison, 'Christian Wolff's Criticism of Spinoza', *Journal of the History of Philosophy*, 31/3 (1993), 405–20.

[13] J. L. Mackie, *The Miracle of Theism* (Oxford: Oxford University Press, 1982), 150–76. For an argument that God might not be able to create any logically possible world—for example, where all free creatures in fact choose the good—see Alvin Plantinga, *God, Freedom and Evil* (Grand Rapids, MI: William B. Eerdmans, 1974), 29–55.

God could have willed otherwise, then Kant gravitates towards the 'Contingent Free Creation 1' view.

The textual evidence is itself ambiguous. The implied meaning of texts from 1749 into the 1760s seems to suggest 'Contingent Free Creation 1'. In the *New Elucidation* Kant writes that it is 'entirely a matter of choice for God, and can therefore be admitted or omitted according to His pleasure' whether substances are in 'reciprocal connection', or whether 'substances can exist in accordance with the law which specifies that *they are in no place* and that they stand in no relation at all in respect of the things of our universe' (*NE* 1: 414). If it 'can be admitted or omitted according to His pleasure' whether substances stand in connection with other substances, it would seem to imply—although Kant does not explicitly state here—that whether or not substances exist at all can also 'be admitted or omitted according to His pleasure' (*NE* 1: 414; see also *LF* 1: 21–2). Even if this is not the case, and God is for some reason compelled to create substances, if these substances stand 'in no relation at all' (*NE* 1: 414), this would not yet be the creation of a 'world'. A world, for Kant, involves substances being *connected* (*LF* 1: 21–2; *ML₂* 28: 196; *MD* 28: 657, and *MMr.* 29: 852).[14] If God were to create isolated substances, God would not have yet created a *world*, until he had determined to place these substances in connection with other substances. This placing of substances in connection with each other, we have been told, can be 'be admitted or omitted according to His pleasure' (*NE* 1: 414). Therefore, God's ability to choose whether or not to place substances in connection in fact *entails* that God can choose whether or not to create a *world*. These passages, where Kant invokes the rather peculiar ability of God to create isolated or connected substances, will occupy us later on in the next chapter (pp. 48–52) when considering the scope of divine freedom with respect to created essences.

Further evidence for the 'Contingent Free Creation 1' view in Kant's early thought comes from *The Only Possible Argument*, where he tells us that 'things exist because God willed that they should exist' (*OPA* 2: 100), which is followed by the comment that 'the ground of which has to be sought in a free choice', which 'must, for that very reason, be contingent' (*OPA* 2: 101). The clear implication of this passage would seem to be that it is contingent upon the free choice of the divine will whether anything created exists at all.

In his *Optimism* essay Kant sets out that, by virtue of the divine nature, if God in his freedom decides to create a world (*Opt.* 2: 100), God necessarily creates the best of all possible worlds, and does so from a range of really possible worlds that are available to God but that God does not actualize: 'Since God chose this world and this world alone of all the possible worlds of

---

[14] For the references to the metaphysics lectures, I am indebted to Lucas Thorpe, 'Is Kant's Realm of Ends a *Unum per Se*? Aquinas, Suarez, Leibniz and Kant on Composition', *British Journal for the History of Philosophy*, 18/3 (2010), 461–85 (pp. 478–82).

which He had cognition, He must for that very reason, have regarded it as the best' (*Opt.* 2: 34; also *Opt.* 2: 29–32; *OPA* 2: 109, 53, and *NE* 1: 404). Kant acknowledges that 'not being able to choose other than that which one distinctly and rightly recognises as the best constitutes, perhaps, a constraint which limits the will' (*Opt.* 2. 34), but that this is not a 'necessity which cancels freedom' (*Opt.* 2. 34), as any freedom that would be cancelled out by such a constraint would not be worth having: 'thanks for the freedom which banishes into eternal nothingness the best which it was possible to create' (*Opt.* 2. 34).

In his later thought, Kant is able to give a more positive account of the 'constraints' upon the divine will; I permit myself such a term here as Kant's language itself suggests it (*ein Zwang des Willens*). It is in the course of providing this positive account, as Patrick Kain demonstrates, that Kant moves towards a 'Necessary Free Creation' account.[15] By the 1780s Kant sets out a full and positive account of how the divine will is determined to create, and to create the 'most perfect world' (*LPR* 28: 1061–2), not by something external to God, but by virtue of God's cognition of his self-sufficiency. God necessarily cognizes himself, and, being necessarily the all-sufficient ground of everything possible, God's cognition of his all-sufficiency determines God to bring the world into existence:

God cognizes himself by means of his highest understanding as the all-sufficient ground of everything possible. He is most well-pleased with his unlimited faculty as regards all positive things, and it is just this well-pleasedness with himself which causes him to make these possibilities actual. (*LPR* 28: 1061)

In 'cognizing himself, he cognizes everything possible which is contained in him as its ground', where this 'well-pleasedness of a being with itself as a possible ground for the production of things is what determines its causality' (*LPR* 28: 1061–2), so that the 'product of such a will will be the greatest whole of everything possible, that is the *summum bonum finitum*, the most perfect world' (*LPR* 28: 1061–2).

It is at a point such as this where we might need to be cautious before ascribing a position to Kant on the basis of the *Lectures on the Philosophical Doctrine of Religion* (1783–4).[16] As I acknowledged in the previous chapter, it is not always clear where Kant is endorsing a position, and where he is rehearsing a traditional viewpoint. We do have an earlier endorsement of this notion of divine self-sufficiency, which is compatible with the later account, except that it does not fully draw out the consequences for creation (see *OPA* 2: 151–4). More significantly, when ascribing such a conception to the critical Kant, we find him

---

[15] For my discussion of this development in Kant's thought I am indebted to Kain, 'The Development of Kant's Conception of Divine Freedom', in (ed.) Brandon Lock, *Leibniz and Kant* (Oxford: Oxford University Press, forthcoming), 19–25, manuscript; page references refer to the manuscript of the chapter provided by the author, rather than to the edited book.

[16] For this note of caution, I am indebted to an anonymous reader for OUP.

endorsing a similar viewpoint in his published work *Theory and Practice* (1793), where Kant writes that 'the cause of God's will consists in the fact that despite his highest self-contentment, things external to him shall exist insofar as he is conscious of himself as an all-sufficient being':

> The Deity . . . although subjectively in need of no external thing, still cannot be thought to shut himself up within himself but rather [must be thought] to be determined to produce the highest good beyond himself just by his consciousness of his all-sufficiency; and this necessity in the supreme being (which in the human being is duty) cannot be represented *by us* other than as a moral need. (*TP* 8: 280n)

Given the corroboration from this published work, it is plausible to ascribe to Kant the view that we should conceive of God necessarily creating a world by virtue of God's cognition of his 'all-sufficiency'. This raises a sharp question: in what sense can a 'necessary' act of the will be considered 'free'? This is taken up more fully in the next chapter, where I discuss the relationship between perfect freedom and perfect goodness. At this point, it is important at least to understand why Kant himself thinks that there is a significant difference between 'Necessary Free Creation' and 'Emanation 2'. Kain suggests that the key for Kant is to distinguish between 'what is contained in or follows *immediately* from God's nature' and what follows, 'even if necessarily and fully determinatively, only via God's understanding and will'.[17] So in the mid-1770s Kant writes that the 'the absolute necessity of his nature and his essence does not make his actions absolutely necessary' (*ML₁* 28: 335). As Kain puts it, the 'consequence of God's essence' is 'mediated by his understanding and will', and so 'is part of God's nature and thus internal to God, rather than external to him'.[18] The crucial difference between 'Emanation 2' and 'Necessarily Determined Free Creation' is that, according to the latter, God is the cause of substances *via* his will (albeit a necessarily determined one). As Kain puts it, Kant's distinction here is between 'what is contained in or follows *immediately* from God's nature and what follows, even if necessarily and fully determinately, only via God's understanding and will'.[19]

In this way Kant distinguishes his position from 'Emanation 2', where God is separate from the world, but where the world necessarily comes into being, and does so in the form that it does, where 'God is regarded as the cause of substances by the necessity of his nature' (*LPR* 28: 1092). Kain captures the way in which Kant sets out the distinction, although we might wonder if Kant's formulation itself really leads us to the heart of the matter. After all, the divine will and understanding—invoked by 'Contingent Free Creation 1' accounts—are still 'aspects of the divine nature', and so, in a sense, the world comes about 'by the necessity' of the divine nature, where the divine

---

[17] Kain, 'The Development of Kant's Conception of Divine Freedom', p. 13, manuscript.
[18] Kain, 'The Development of Kant's Conception of Divine Freedom', p. 13, manuscript.
[19] Kain, 'The Development of Kant's Conception of Divine Freedom', p. 13, manuscript.

nature encompasses will and understanding. The crucial difference would not seem to be that on the emanationist account the world arises 'from the divine nature', and on the contingent free creation account it does not; rather the difference lies in what we consider to constitute the divine nature. On an emanation account, there is no divine will as such, but just a structure of necessity, whereas the free creation account ascribes an irreducible role to the divine will as part of the divine nature. This enables Kant to state that 'an all-sufficient being can produce things external to itself only through will and not through the necessity of its nature' (*LPR* 28: 1061), where this should be read as 'not merely through the necessity of its nature-conceived-of-without-a-will'. Similarly, the distinction between the emanation and the free-creation account of creation does not seem to be securely delivered by Kant's conviction that God does not *need* the existence of the world, and the existence of the world does not 'really affect him', as Kain puts it.[20] It is not clear, *prima facie*, what would prevent a Spinozistic emanationist finding a way of saying that substance *S* arises from God by necessity, without God needing *S* or being effected by *S*: for example, before *S* arose, God was still without need or dependence, and, if *S* ceased to exist, God would continue to exist without *S*.

We also need to consider a further possible shift in Kant's later thought, brought to light by Chignell. As we will see, on Chignell's interpretation, this shift indicates a further tightening of the parameters of divine choice, although not, for Kant, any sort of restriction on divine freedom. Chignell draws attention to a passage in the third *Critique*, where Kant writes that the distinction of 'possible from actual things' is 'merely subjectively valid for the human understanding, since we can always have something in our thoughts although it does not exist, or represent something as given even though we do not have any concept of it' (*CJ* 5: 402)[21]. Such a distinction is valid *only* for a limited (human) understanding, and would not apply if our understanding were divine and 'intuitive'. When our reason follows 'the unremitting demand' to assume an 'original ground' (God) existing 'absolutely necessarily', then we postulate a being 'in which possibility and actuality can no longer be distinguished at all, and for which idea our understanding has absolutely no concept, i.e., can find no way in which to represent such a thing and its way of existing'. So we see that, in the case of divine cognition, 'there would be no such distinction (between the possible and the actual)':

For an understanding to which this distinction did not apply, all objects that I cognize would *be* (exist), and the possibility of some that did not exist, i.e. their contingency if they did not exist, as well as the necessity that is to be distinguished from that, would not enter into the representation of such a being at all. (*CJ* 5: 402–3)

---

[20] Kain, 'The Development of Kant's Conception of Divine Freedom', pp. 21–22, manuscript.
[21] Chignell, 'Kant, Real Possibility, and the Threat of Spinoza', pp. 34–38, offprint.

Chignell derives from these passages the conclusion that, for the mature Kant, God's creation of the actual world itself produces real possibilities, such that the actual world is the only really possible world (and so the best). On this account, God does not choose one world from among a range of really possible worlds. There are no really possible worlds other than the one actually instantiated by God. In order to arrive at this interpretation, Chignell needs to construe Kant's reference to the 'actual' (*Wirklich*) to mean something along the lines of 'that which is instantiated as part of the created world', where 'to exist' (*existieren*) would mean 'to be a created substance in relation with other substances that together constitute a world'. If this is how we understand Kant's references to 'actuality' and 'existence', then it does indeed follow that, at a fundamental *ontological* level (from a 'God's-eye point of view'), it would be impossible to draw a distinction between the created world that God brings into existence and the really possible. This follows directly from the claim that for the divine understanding there is no 'distinction between the merely possible and the actual', if the 'actual' means that which is instantiated in the created world. Then it would indeed be entailed that God does not choose from really possible worlds; but that the actual world constitutes what is really possible, even if (and as Chignell acknowledges) this is not Kant's earlier position, as in the 1750s and 1760s Kant talks of God choosing from possible worlds.[22] The distinction between the really possible and the actual will continue to do important epistemological work *for us*, because we do not experience everything that is part of the created world that God makes 'actual'.

I have nothing invested in the accuracy of Chignell's interpretation. There is another plausible way in which we can construe this passage from the third *Critique*. It is possible that Kant is just drawing upon a consideration that we find in his earlier thought: that for God there is no extensional distinction between the actual and the really possible, because everything that is really possible is grounded in the actuality of the divine understanding. As we will see in the next chapter (pp. 37–47), being 'actual' or 'existent' in this context does not mean being part of the created world that God instantiates, but being grounded in the divine understanding. For God, that which is really possible is coextensive with the actual because all possibilities are grounded in the divine understanding. On this reading, that all really possible worlds (of which there are more than one) are grounded in the actuality of the divine understanding would be compatible with asserting that in God 'possibility and actuality can no longer be distinguished at all' (*CJ* 5: 402).

Nonetheless, for the sake of completeness, if Chignell is correct in his interpretation of this passage from the third *Critique*, to capture Kant's mature

---

[22] Chignell, 'Kant, Real Possibility and the Threat of Spinoza', 37, n. 51, offprint.

take on divine creation ('Necessary Free Creation'), we would need to modify the clause pertaining to really possible worlds, along the following lines:

> Necessary Free Creation*: God is separate from the world, but the divine will necessarily chooses to create a world, and given God's perfect goodness, the divine will necessarily creates the only (and best) really possible world. God could not do otherwise than to create a world, and to create this world.

One further qualification should be noted. The notion of the 'best really possible world' does not play a developed and explicit role in Kant's critical philosophy. In his critical philosophy, as we have seen above, Kant is committed to the view that God necessarily creates the 'highest good' by virtue of his cognition of his own self-sufficiency (*TP* 8: 280n). Furthermore, as I will discuss in Chapter 7, Kant bases the requirement that we believe in God and immortality upon a commitment to the 'highest good', where we postulate that in a future state happiness will be distributed in proportion to moral virtue (*CPrR*.5: 110–32). A commitment to the highest good is compatible with the concept of the best really possible world, but is also compatible with the view that there is no single 'best' way in which the highest good might be realized. On this point, it makes a difference what status we ascribe to notes based upon Kant's lectures in the 1780s. In the *Lectures on the Philosophical Doctrine of Religion* (1783–4), Kant is recorded as saying that the product of a divine will 'will be the greatest whole of everything possible, that is the *summum bonum finitum*, the most perfect world' (*LPR* 28: 1061–2). Kant— if we are hearing Kant accurately—might be endorsing the notion of 'the most perfect world', or he might simply be rehearsing a traditional point of view that he once endorsed, but without continuing to commit himself to the notion that there is a 'most perfect world'. Apart from a suggestive reference in the second *Critique* to the 'highest derived good' as 'the best world' (*der bestan Welt*) (*CPrR*, 5: 125), we have no independent corroboration from Kant's published sources on this issue, and so we had better remain agnostic.

In summary, the safest formulation of Kant's mature position is the following:

> Necessary Free Creation**: God is separate from the world, but the divine will necessarily chooses to create a world, and given God's perfect goodness, the divine will necessarily creates a world that achieves the highest good (however that is construed).

This formulation is ambiguous between 'Necessary Free Creation' as set out on p. 16, 'Necessary Free Creation*' as set out directly above, and a view where there is no really best possible world, but a range of worlds that can achieve the highest good.

What is significant for our purposes, though, is that on any plausible interpretation, at all stages in his thought, Kant presents us with a divine will that necessarily acts in a particular way without being able to do otherwise, because of God's perfect goodness. In the 1750s this involves God necessarily creating the best really possible world, if God creates a world at all. In his later thought, this involves God necessarily (but freely) bringing about the highest good, a view that is compatible with a range of positions on whether or not there is a best really possible world, or whether there are really possible worlds that are not actual. Kant insists that a divine will subject to significant shaping factors is nonetheless perfectly free. Such a conception of divine freedom is heavily contested, and we investigate some of the issues raised by this claim in the next chapter. In order to begin to appreciate why Kant finds this an acceptable account of divine freedom, we need to explore Kant's understanding of perfect freedom, and its close relationship to perfect goodness and the moral law.

DIVINE FREEDOM AND THE HOLY WILL

Kant's account of how God necessarily but freely creates a world exemplifies a wider principle: that God, who is perfectly free—without any external coercion, dependence, or needs—necessarily follows rational norms. In this, God provides the paradigm for perfect freedom, which we can only participate in to a degree. In 1755 Kant writes that as '*spontaneity* is action which issues from *an inner principle*', when '*this spontaneity is determined in conformity with the representation of what is best it is called freedom*' (*NE* 1: 402). In the 'most exact sense', Kant writes in 1769–70, 'freedom properly consists only in the possibility of *doing something good*' (*R* 4227; 17: 466). Freedom is 'the capacity to be determined only through reason, and not mediately, but immediately, hence not through the matter, rather through the form of the laws. Thus moral' (*R* 5436; 18: 181). Although 'necessitation by stimuli is wholly repugnant' to freedom, 'necessitation by motives is not opposed to freedom', because: 'The power of free choice, so far as it acts according to motives of the understanding, is freedom, which is good in all regards. This is the absolute freedom, which is moral freedom' (*ML₁*, 28: 255).

If human beings 'were completely intellectual', Kant writes, 'then all of their actions would be actively determined but still free' (*R* 4227; 17: 466): that is to say, determined by the law of reason, but still free, as freedom is the capacity of reason to follow the moral law. In *Reflexion* 4337 Kant provides a pithy statement of the difference between divine and human freedom:

Contingently preferred actions (the freedom of human beings) are those that are not determined through any rules. Necessarily preferred actions (divine freedom) are those that are determined only in accordance with the rule of the good power of choice. (*R* 4337; 17: 510)

As divine freedom involves being determined through the rule of the good power of choice, Kant writes that God's 'freedom allows itself to be grasped most easily, but not the freedom of his creatures' (*R* 4787; 17: 728):

We can very well understand and have insight into divine freedom, but not human freedom. If the human power were merely intellectual, then we could have insight into his power of choice through reason; likewise if he were a brutum. But not as a sensible and rational being, since his action is subsequently a phaenomenon, but antecedently a noumenon under practical laws. (*R* 4788; 17: 728)

This notion of perfect freedom carries onto into Kant's critical work. It is shown in the *Groundwork* (1785), where Kant writes that 'a free will and a will under moral laws are one and the same' (*GW* 4: 447). If 'reason infallibly determines the will', as is indeed the case with God, then 'the will', in such an instance, 'is a capacity to choose *only that* which reason independently of inclination cognizes as... good' (*GW* 4: 412). Therefore, God always acts according to perfect freedom. God's 'volition is of itself necessarily in accord with the law' (*GW* 4: 414), and 'his maxims necessarily harmonize with the laws of autonomy' (*GW* 4: 439). Because divine volition is necessarily in accord with the law, 'no imperatives hold for the *divine* will and in general for a *holy* will', and the '"ought" is out of place here' (*GW* 4: 414). Notions such as an 'imperative', 'duty', and 'ought' have a role only where a will must struggle to do the good (see also *CPrR.* 5: 32, 37, 83; *Vig.* 27: 519, 623; *Mro.* 29: 605, 611; *MetM* 6: 379, 386, 417).[23]

Although Kant talks at points of God *commanding* the moral law, it is not God's command that grounds morality.[24] Rather, God *commands* that which

---

[23] For a full account of the significance of the distinction between the holy will and the human will, see Terence Irwin, *The Development of Ethics: A Historical and Critical Study. Volume III: From Kant to Rawls* (Oxford: Oxford University Press, 2009), 157–63, and Robert Stern, *Understanding Moral Obligation: Kant, Hegel, Kierkegaard* (Cambridge: Cambridge University Press, 2012), 75–88. For these further references to Kant's texts, I am indebted to Stern, *Understanding Moral Obligation*, 85.

[24] Here I disagree with John Hare's account of Kant as a form of divine commands theorist about moral obligation. See Hare, 'Kant's Divine Command Theory and its Reception within Analytical Philosophy', in D. Z. Phillips and Timothy Tessin (eds), *Kant and Kierkegaard on Religion* (New York: Palgrave Macmillan, 2000), 263–77; 'Kant on Recognizing our Duties as God's Commands', *Faith and Philosophy*, 17 (2000), 459–78; *God's Call: Moral Realism, God's Commands, and Human Autonomy* (Grand Rapids: William B. Eerdmans, 2001), 87–119; *God and Morality: A Philosophical History* (Oxford: Wiley-Blackwell, 2009), 122–75. From the Kant texts cited here, and given the wider picture of Kant's philosophical theology that emerges in this chapter and the next, I think it is clear that Kant can speak of God commanding morality, while explicitly distancing himself from the implication that the content or force of morality derives from the divine will. For a fuller critique of Hare's voluntarist reading, to which I am indebted here, see Stern, *Understanding Moral Obligation*, 58–67. Stern does not explore the extent to which morality, for Kant, might still depend upon God, inasmuch as reason as such depends 'non-morally' upon the divine understanding/nature. This strand is stronger, of course, in Kant's pre-critical work, but could still be (tentatively) ascribed to the critical Kant (see pp. 229–33).

is the moral law, precisely because it is the moral law, independently of and prior to any action of the divine will: 'An action must be done, not because God wills it, but because it is righteous or good in itself; it is because of this that God wills it and demands it of us' (*Col.* 27: 262).

Speaking about those who derive 'morality from the divine will', Kant tells us that although 'any moral law' is also a divine command, the moral law does not 'flow from such a command': 'God has commanded it because it is a moral law, and His will coincides with the moral law' (*Coll.* 27: 277; see also *Coll.* 27: 283, 302, 307, 309; *Her.* 27: 10, 15, 18, *Mro.* 29: 627–8). The holiness of the divine will is such that 'the dispositions' of the 'divine' are coincident with 'objective morality', so that, 'if we act in accordance with the latter, we also act in accordance with the divine will' (*Coll.* 27: 263). This is consistent with Kant's position in the first *Critique*, where he writes: 'We will not hold actions to be obligatory because they are God's commands, but will regard them rather as divine commands because we are internally obligated to them' (A818–19/B846–7; see also *LPR* 28: 1002–3; *Rel.* 6: 3–7, 183).

This does not diminish divine freedom, as God's 'freedom increases with the degree of morality' (*Coll.* 27: 268), where the divine will 'intrinsically wills what is good' (*Coll.* 27: 268–9). This is not the same as saying that the moral law is independent of God, for reasons that are set out in the next chapter: as we will see, that which does not depend upon the divine will still depends upon *God*, in that all possibility depends upon the divine understanding/nature.

The position that Kant defends, in both pre-critical and critical philosophy, that God's perfect freedom is compatible with God being unable to do other than the good, is put forward by the medieval theologian Anselm (among others). For Anselm, all that is required for freedom is 'the power to preserve rectitude of will for the sake of that rectitude itself', whether or not the will can do otherwise.[25] This, Anselm affirms, is a complete (*perfecta*) condition for freedom.[26] Not all commentators have agreed with Kant, or Anselm, that 'God's freedom allows itself to be most easily grasped' (*R* 4787; 17: 728), with some suspecting an incoherence in the notion of a free being who necessarily complies with rational norms.[27] Certainly such an account will not be acceptable to those for whom 'the ability to do otherwise' is criterial for freedom. Such an account might also be regarded as problematic in terms of whether we can ascribe ultimate responsibility to God for his actions, with some

---

[25] Anselm, *De libertate arbitrii* 3, in *S. Anselmi Cantuariensis Archiepiscopi Opera Monia*, ed. F. S. Schmitt (Stuttgart-Bad Canstatt: Friedrich Fromann Verlag, 1968), 1: 212. Cited and quoted by Thomas Williams and Sandra Visser, 'Anselm's Account of Freedom', *Canadian Journal of Philosophy*, 31/2 (2001), 221–44 (p. 221).

[26] Anselm, *De libertate arbitrii*, 13. I am indebted for this reference to Williams and Visser, 'Anselm's Account of Freedom', 221.

[27] For this formulation of the problem I am indebted to Kain, 'The Development of Kant's View of Divine Freedom', pp. 6–7, manuscript.

commentators considering that it is no better to be constrained by metaphysical necessity than physical necessity. In neither case, it might be objected, is there a 'participation' in 'the light of reasons',[28] where the actions of the moral agent are an 'expression of her own mental activity' motivated 'by her recognition of the appropriate conceptual connections', and 'not merely the result of the operation of beliefs and desires in her'.[29] It is to this cluster of theological and philosophical anxieties about divine freedom that I turn in the next chapter.

---

[28] Douglas Lavin, 'Practical Reason and the Possibility of Error', *Ethics*, 114 (2004), 424–57.
[29] Christine M. Korsgaard, 'The Normativity of Instrumental Reason', in Garrett Cullity and Berys Gaut (eds), *Ethics and Practical Reason* (Oxford: Clarendon Press, 1997), 221, 336.

3

Is God Free?

We have seen in the previous chapter that the divine will, for Kant, is extensively shaped by rational and moral factors, such that it is lacking in scope for alternative actions when it comes to God's 'free' decision to create a world. In this chapter I ask whether the 'shaping factors' upon divine freedom are incompatible with what the orthodox Christian wants to say about the extent and depth of divine freedom and sovereignty. If Kant's conception is indeed incompatible with Christian orthodoxy, then one of the guiding lines of enquiry in this book has reached a swift dead end: that is, the question of what Kant's legacy should be for Christian theologians reflecting on the relationship between divine and human freedom. The answer might seem to be that Kant is largely irrelevant to this task, as he works so far outside the bounds of Christian orthodoxy on a doctrine as fundamental as the creation.

In this chapter, I will attempt to set out as sympathetic a construal as I can manage of Kant's conception of divine freedom, explaining why it is at least a close relation of strands of traditional theology that are hardly 'beyond the pale'. I suggest that one's theological attitude to Kant will be heavily shaped by two issues: first of all, whether one considers that the divine nature is 'external' to the divine will, and, secondly, whether one considers categories such as 'goodness' and 'rationality' to be external to the divine nature.

In the first section we see that Kant does not think that the divine nature is external to the divine will. In the second section I explain why Kant would not think that goodness or rationality are external factors to the divine nature. This is because of the dependence of all possibilities upon the divine understanding. One way in which this dependence manifests itself is that although the divine will brings substances into existence, the divine will cannot choose the essential properties of substances. The real possibilities that determine these essential properties still depend upon God, but upon the divine understanding rather than the divine will. Kant calls this a 'non-moral' dependence upon God. Whether a substance exists at all depends upon the divine will and is called a 'moral' dependence. Goodness and rationality are in no sense 'external' to the divine nature, because the structure of *all* real possibility depends upon and is grounded in the divine nature, without being dependent upon the divine will. At this point, in the third section, it will be necessary to refute an alternative reading of the pre-critical Kant, presented by Rae Langton, which suggests a much greater degree of arbitrary choice for the divine will with respect to the structure of real possibilities that determine the essences of created substances. I argue that the texts cited by Langton do not challenge my claim that, for Kant, God does not have a choice over the shape of real possibilities (which constitute the essences of created substances), although the shape of real possibilities depends upon the divine nature/understanding (rather than the divine will).

In the final section of the chapter, I ask what implications Kant's conception of divine freedom has for our understanding of the emergence of Kant's critical philosophy. I claim that studying Kant's conception of divine freedom opens up something of an interpretative puzzle. The question that arises will be this: given that the 'ability to do otherwise' is not part of Kant's conception of meaningful divine freedom, and given the reasons why it is not, why does this ability become *such* an important aspect of how Kant conceives what is required for human freedom? The discussion in the next chapter, where I track Kant's shifting conception of human freedom in relation to God, will be framed by this question. Only against the background of Kant's conception of divine freedom do certain aspects of his philosophy of freedom look appropriately strange, and in need of explanation. I will also return to this question in the final chapter, where I ask whether Kant, from within his own resources, could have configured the relationship between divine and human freedom in a more traditional way.[1]

IS THE DIVINE NATURE EXTERNAL OR INTERNAL TO THE DIVINE WILL?

In the previous chapter, we saw that Kant's conception of divine freedom is significantly shaped by God's perfect goodness. In Kant's early thought, this leads Kant to affirm that God creates the best really possible world, if God creates at all; in his later thought, Kant affirms that God necessarily creates a world, and that this world achieves the highest good. A consideration of Kant's fundamental theological premises about divine freedom is in order, because, on some accounts, the factors that shape this freedom would be unacceptable violations of divine omnipotence and independence. In particular, Kant's later position, that God necessarily creates a world, might seem to be obviously and

---

[1] Material from this chapter, especially pp. 37–52, has been published in my 'Intellectualism, Relational Properties and the Divine Mind in Kant's Pre-Critical Philosophy', *Kantian Review*, 16/3 (2011), 399–428.

wildly beyond the pale of Christian orthodoxy. Thomas Flint would speak for many when he claims that the view that 'God's will was necessarily constrained (by his perfect knowledge and goodness, perhaps) to perform a certain creative action' is 'inconsistent' with 'orthodox Christian belief', and goes past boundaries 'beyond which the clearheaded orthodox Christian dare not stray'.[2]

In this section I explore two strategies that Kant might adopt in justifying the claim that God can be free, even if God has no choice: the first is a Leibnizian strategy that distinguishes between types of necessity; the second strategy, a version of which can be found in Aquinas (on some interpretations), claims that God's goodness is somehow 'diffusive of itself', necessarily bringing about the creation, but without compromising divine freedom. I find that Kant presents a variant of the second strategy. I conclude the section by reflecting on the deep theological issues at stake when it comes to accepting or denying such an approach. Everything turns on two fundamental considerations. First of all, whether or not one accepts that for God, and God alone, the divine nature is appropriately 'internal' to the divine will; and, secondly, whether one can accept that properties such as 'goodness' and 'rationality' are in some sense appropriately internal to the divine nature.

In the opening of Chapter 2, I commented that conceptions of divine freedom in Western thought tend to divide into those that consider God to be free just if God is not 'constrained' by anything external to the divine nature, and those that regard God as free only provided that God could have done otherwise. These options parallel 'compatibilist' and 'incompatibilist' conceptions of human freedom. Compatibilism considers an action to be free provided that the agent wants to do the action, and her wanting to do the action arises in some sense from her nature, which includes her beliefs and desires. Incompatibilism, on the other hand, insists that an action is significantly free only provided that the agent could have done otherwise—that is, if there was an 'alternative possibility' (AP), and if in some sense the 'ultimate responsibility' (UR) for the actions rests with the agent.[3] In Kant's case we would have to say that although God is the ultimate source of his actions, when it comes to the creation there is no ability for God 'to have done otherwise'. As such, Kant's analysis of God's freedom has strong 'compatibilist' features.

According to this approach, God could have the 'ultimate responsibility' for his actions that the incompatibilist seeks, sufficient for the ascription of

[2] Thomas Flint, 'Two Accounts of Providence', in Thomas V. Morris (ed.), *Divine and Human Action: Essays in the Metaphysics of Theism* (Ithaca, NY, and London: Cornell University Press, 1988), 147–81 (p. 152).

[3] I am indebted here to Robert Kane, *The Significance of Free Will* (Oxford: Oxford University Press, 1998).

freedom, without the ability of doing otherwise. Such a claim brings about a cluster of objections. There is disagreement about whether the capacity of 'being the originating source of actions without being able to do otherwise' can be described as 'freedom' at all, without, as Wittgenstein puts it, 'language going on holiday'.[4] Rowe takes the view that if God was not free to do otherwise than to create the best possible world, then God 'does not enjoy freedom with respect to creation'.[5] If God is not free to do otherwise, Rowe reflects, then God is '*not responsible* for his possession of the properties that constitute his nature', and so God is not 'responsible, and praiseworthy, for his necessarily doing what he sees to be best'.[6] Rowe's focus is on the claim that God necessarily creates a world, and that this world must be the best possible world; but similar considerations would apply to Kant's suggestion that God necessarily creates a world, and that this world must achieve the highest good.

Other philosophers express different fundamental intuitions here. Bergmann and Cover concede that God is not free to do otherwise, but insist that what matters is that a 'good action flows from God himself—that God agent-caused it, that nothing distinct from God . . . caused him to perform that act, that he is *responsible* for that act'.[7] Where people are inclined to resist this view, Bergmann and Cover insist, it is because they have wrongly conflated 'couldn't do otherwise' with 'forced'.[8] Wierenga points out that it is usual to make 'certain refinements' to our naive understanding of concepts when applying them in the special case of God, and that this is what we need to do when speaking of divine 'freedom'. Few philosophers, for example, insist that divine omnipotence involves God being able to do that which is logically or metaphysically impossible, and, just as 'certain refinements need to be made to the naive concept of omnipotence', so we should expect the same in the case of God's freedom, in the light of God's perfect goodness.[9] In what follows I investigate what might be the theological grounds for such a refinement of the concept of divine freedom, in the light of God's perfect goodness.

Leibniz presents a strategy that can be employed by thinkers who want to defend divine freedom, without ascribing to God the ability of doing otherwise. Leibniz argues that there are alternative logical and metaphysical possibilities for God sufficient for freedom, even though morally God could not have done otherwise. Kant would have been familiar with this strategy from reading Leibniz's work, and Kain discerns an implicit debt to Leibniz on this

---

[4] Ludwig Wittgenstein, *Philosophical Investigations* (Oxford: Blackwell, 1973), §38.
[5] Rowe, *Can God be Free?*, 35.
[6] Rowe, *Can God be Free?*, 141.
[7] Rowe, *Can God be Free?*, 400.
[8] Rowe, *Can God be Free?*, 399.
[9] Edward Wierenga, 'Perfect Goodness and Divine Freedom', *Philosophical Books*, 48/3 (2007), 207–16 (p. 214).

point.[10] Nonetheless, I argue that the textual evidence suggests that Kant was sceptical of Leibniz's distinction between types of necessity.

Leibniz's Distinction between Types of Necessity

Leibniz preserves a sense in which God is 'free to do otherwise', by distinguishing between logical, metaphysical, and moral necessity.[11]

God is bound by a moral necessity to make things in such a manner that there can be nothing better: otherwise . . . he would not be satisfied with his work, he would blame himself for its imperfection; and that conflicts with the supreme felicity of the divine nature.[12]

God chose between different courses all possible: thus metaphysically speaking, he could have chosen or done what was not the best; but he could not morally speaking have done so.[13]

One must confess that there is evil in this world which God has made, and that it would have been possible to make a world without evil or even not to create any world, since its creation depended upon the free will of God.[14]

In 'absolute' terms God had it in his power to create any logically possible world, including one with no evil in it (although this would have been a less good world overall than the one he did create). Hence Leibniz says that, 'metaphysically speaking', God 'could have chosen or done what was not the best';[15] at the same time, morally speaking, because of perfect goodness, God 'cannot fail to act in the most perfect way, and consequently to choose the best'.[16] Not all commentators have been able to understand Leibniz's distinction between metaphysical and moral freedom.[17] If God is perfectly good and omnipotent, the objection runs, then God chooses to create the best of all possible worlds. God, for Leibniz, is indeed perfectly good and omnipotent, therefore God necessarily chooses to create the best of all possible worlds, even if a being who was omnipotent and not perfectly good could have done otherwise. Where 'if p then q' is true as a hypothetical necessity, and where

---

[10] See Kain, 'The Development of Kant's Conception of Divine Freedom', p. 14 ff, manuscript.

[11] In my discussion of Leibniz, I am indebted to Rowe, *Can God Be Free?*, ch. 1.

[12] Gottfried Wilhelm Leibniz, *Theodicy: Essays on the Goodness of God, the Freedom of Man and the Origin of Evil*, ed. Austin M. Farrer and trans. E. M. Huggard (New York: Cosimo, 2009), 253, §201.

[13] Leibniz, *Theodicy*, 271, §234.

[14] Leibniz, 'Summary of the Controversy Reduced to Formal Arguments', in *Theodicy*, 377–88 (p. 378).

[15] Leibniz, *Theodicy*, 271, §234.

[16] Leibniz, *Theodicy*, 252, §201.

[17] For this point, I am indebted to Rowe, *Can God Be Free?*, 15–17.

we assert *p*, then *q* seems to follow with necessity, and without any other possibility.

We do not need to settle this issue here: the important question is whether Kant relies on this Leibnizian distinction. It is true, as Kain shows, that Kant draws on Leibniz's distinction between a brute absolute necessity, which should not be ascribed to the divine will, and a morally determined (because value-cognizing) free will.[18] It is questionable, though, whether Kant approves of using this distinction to claim that in some sense God 'could have done otherwise'. As we will see in the next chapter, in 1755 Kant endorses Crusius' attack on the Leibnizian use of the distinction between absolute and moral necessity. The distinction, Kant complains, 'has no power at all to break the force and effective power of necessity' (*NE* 1: 399), and 'does little to diminish the force of the necessity or the certainty of the determination': 'For just as nothing can be conceived which is *more true* than *true*, and nothing *more certain* than *certain*, so nothing can be conceived which is *more determined* than *determined*' (*NE* 1: 400).

On this point, Kant would seem to be in agreement with Rowe that if God's actions are shaped by necessity, it would not diminish the force of this necessity that the binding constraint is derived from moral rather than logical considerations. This does not seem to be the way in which Kant preserves divine freedom in the face of the necessity of perfect goodness.

God's Goodness as 'Diffusive of Itself'

The strategy that Kant explicitly uses to account for divine freedom involves grounding the determination of the divine will in considerations that are properly 'internal' to the divine nature. As we saw in the previous chapter (pp. 19–20), God is 'determined to produce the highest good beyond himself just by his consciousness of his all-sufficiency' (*TP* 8: 280n), where it is his 'well-pleasedness with himself which causes him to make these possibilities actual' (*LPR* 28: 1061). The 'product of such a will will be the greatest whole of everything possible, that is the *summum bonum finitum*, the most perfect world' (*LPR* 28: 1061–2).[19] Kant aligns himself here with a tradition in Christian theology that understands God's perfect goodness as in some sense 'diffusive of itself', where God creates in order to express the divine goodness. When explaining why God creates, Aquinas writes that 'the

---

[18] See Kain, 'The Development of Kant's Conception of Divine Freedom', p. 14, manuscript. See also *LPR* 28: 806, 1068, 1092, 1276, 1280–1; *R* 3911, *R* 4125, *R* 4128, *R* 4129, *R* 4738, and *R* 4739. I am indebted to Kain for these references.

[19] For a full discussion of this positive account, to which I am indebted, see Kain, 'The Development of Kant's Conception of Divine Freedom', pp. 19–25, manuscript.

communication of being and goodness arises from goodness': 'This is evident from the very nature and definition of the good . . . the good is diffusive of itself and of being. But this diffusion befits God because . . . God is the cause of being for other things.'[20]

It is important to stress that Aquinas, unlike Kant, denies that God's goodness *requires* him to create a world. Furthermore, Aquinas, unlike the early Kant, does not believe that there is such a thing as the best possible world. For Aquinas, perhaps like the later Kant (depending upon our interpretation see p. 23), God has a choice of which world to create, although any world created will necessarily be a diffusion of divine goodness.[21] Nonetheless, self-styled Thomists, such as Norman Kretzmann, have considered that the only consistent theological conclusion from Aquinas's account of goodness as 'diffusive of itself' is that 'God's goodness requires things other than itself as a manifestation of itself', and that it is correct to say that 'God therefore necessarily (though freely) wills the creation'.[22] My suggestion is not that Kant was drawing on Aquinas here. There is no evidence for that. Rather, Kant's own answer to the question of how God can be said necessarily (though freely) to will the creation reaches for some of the same Neoplatonic resources that Aquinas himself drew upon, where these resources are mediated to Kant through German rationalism. Relating this tradition to Aquinas shows that Kant is not working entirely outside of a major strand in Christian thought, even if he is working on the edge of it, or stretching the bounds.

This conception of divine freedom, as well as receiving support from traditional thinkers (Anselm and Aquinas), is defended by some recent philosophers, who endorse the view that the divine will can be determined by the perfect goodness of the divine nature, without violating perfect freedom. Edward Wierenga defends such a conception by drawing upon insights from 'compatibilist' accounts of freedom. Wierenga observes that 'canny compatibilists' will not allow that freedom is compatible with *any* 'antecedent causal conditions', but only with the 'right ones, arising in the right matter'.[23] Much ink has been spilt over what might constitute the 'right causal conditions', but most strategies for identifying the right conditions circle around 'the customary way in which people come to have beliefs and desires, not through drugs or

---

[20] Thomas Aquinas, *Summa Contra Gentiles*, ed. and trans. Vernon J. Bourke (Notre Dame, IN: University of Notre Dame Press, 1975), 1: 37.

[21] Aquinas, *Summa Theologiae*, 1a.25.6.3.

[22] Norman Kretzmann, 'A General Problem of Creation', in Scott MacDonald (ed.), *Being and Goodness: The Concept of the Good in Metaphysics and Philosophical Theology* (Ithaca, NY: Cornell University Press, 1991), 208–49 (p. 229). In my discussion of Aquinas, I am indebted to Kretzmann, and to Rowe, *Can God Be Free?*, ch. 3.

[23] Edward Wierenga, 'The Freedom of God', *Faith and Philosophy*, 19/4, (2002), 425–36 (p. 434); for a defence of a similar view, see also Thomas Talbott, 'On the Divine Nature and the Nature of Divine Freedom', *Faith and Philosophy*, 5 (1988), 3–24.

hypnosis or nefarious neurosurgeons manipulating their brains'.[24] What matters to the 'canny compatibilist' is that 'the beliefs and desires are the agent's *own*, that they are internal to the agent'.[25] Where compatibilism is rejected, it is often because of a conviction that 'the relevant causal conditions are thus not really internal to the agent'; because, 'if determinism is true, an agent's beliefs and desires themselves have antecedent causes stretching back to before the agent even existed', in a way that stretches the claim that the antecedent causes are 'really internal' to the agent.[26] The incompatibilist does not so much challenge the compatibilist insight that freedom is consistent with the right sort of 'internal' antecedent causal conditions, as doubt the claim that causal conditions—without a distinct moment for a will that could do otherwise—could ever be 'internal' in the requisite way. At this point Wierenga sets out his claim that 'the compatibilist's insights' might be *uniquely* applicable 'to the case of God':

Even if in some circumstances C God's knowing that A is the best action, his wanting to do A, and his being able to do A is a logically sufficient condition of his doing A in C, it is nevertheless in virtue of *his own nature* that he knows that A is the best action, wants to do A, and is able to do A. There is no long chain stretching back to things separate from him that give him this constellation of knowledge, desire, and ability; it is due to his *own* knowledge and power and goodness. I see no reason not to say, accordingly, that God is free, even when he does what is best.[27]

In Kant, and Aquinas, we see just such a resort to God's own nature to explain the determination of the divine will: God is not determined to 'produce the highest good' by anything 'external' to his 'all-sufficiency'. Whether such a strategy is accepted or not will turn on whether it is accepted that the divine nature is 'internal' in the right sort of way to the divine will. For those inclined to reject the strategy, the conceptual separation of the divine will and divine understanding (or divine nature) seems in practice to subordinate the divine will to the divine understanding/nature; inasmuch as the divine understanding/nature is synonymous with the structure of reason itself, the divine will is then subordinated to a structure of reason/nature. The structure of the divine nature does indeed seem to 'trump' the freedom of God. Precisely because the divine will is *separated* from the divine understanding (or nature), a theologian might complain, there is a sense in which reason being grounded in the divine nature does not mitigate the impact of the fact that it is *the structure of reason* that does the important work. Throughout this section we have asked whether the divine nature is external or internal to the divine will. We find, though, that

---

[24] Wierenga, 'The Freedom of God', 434.
[25] Wierenga, 'The Freedom of God', 434.
[26] See Peter van Inwagen, *An Essay on Free Will* (Oxford: Clarendon Press, 1983), and Kane, *The Significance of Free Will*.
[27] Wierenga, 'The Freedom of God', 434.

there is a further and deeper question, about whether goodness and rationality are in some sense external to the divine nature, determining the divine nature from 'without'. Even if the divine nature is not 'external' to the divine will, are the properties of the divine nature themselves problematically external to this nature?

Kant does have reasons for considering that the divine nature is not external to the divine will, and that goodness and rationality are in no way external to the divine nature. These reasons derive from the rationalist tradition of conceiving the divine nature, whereby the very structure of all possibilities are grounded upon the divine understanding, depending for their possibility on God, albeit not upon the divine *will*. The next section explores this aspect of Kant's philosophical theology.

There are other theological strategies for resolving this problem, not adopted by Kant, and so not discussed extensively here. An extreme voluntarism simply asserts that the divine will determines the structure of goodness and rationality. Some philosophers of religion have taken this to the point where the divine will chooses and creates the divine nature (a position known as 'theological activism').[28] A more traditional solution is found in the doctrine of divine simplicity, whereby God's nature is understood as identical with God's will, with God's existence, and with all of God's actions.[29] Wes Morriston acknowledges that this 'doctrine does have the advantage' of solving the problem that God is 'stuck' with the divine nature. Like other commentators, Morrison is overwhelmed by the 'known disadvantages of the doctrine':[30] that it is hard to grasp how all of God's properties could be identical with each other, and with God's existence and nature. Similarly, Bergmann and Cover acknowledge that divine simplicity might solve the problem of how God can be perfectly free and perfectly good, but do not further explore this avenue,

---

[28] See Thomas V. Morris, 'Absolute Creation', in *Anselmian Explorations: Essays in Philosophical Theology* (Notre Dame, IN: Notre Dame University Press, 1987), 161–78. For criticisms of 'theological activism', see Wes Morriston, 'Is God Free? Reply to Wierenga', p. 97, and Bergmann and Cover, 'Divine Reponsibility without Freedom', p. 394. The question arises as to whether or not the divine will could have given himself a different nature. If the answer is 'yes', it would seem that God could have created his nature as less than perfectly good, and so less perfect than it could be (and so less than Godlike); if the answer is 'no', then again it seems that God is 'stuck' with his nature (Morriston, p. 97). It is also, as Cover and Bergmann comment, 'difficult to render comfortable to the intellect' the idea 'of God's actively creating those very properties—those very aspects of the divine nature—that are logically necessary for his creative activity' (p. 394). Kant, in any case, would find 'theological activism' extremely uncomfortable, and there is no hint of such a notion in his work.

[29] For sympathetic discussions of divine simplicity, see Alexander Pruss, 'A New Free Will Defence', *Religious Studies*, 39 (2003), 211–33; and Eleonore Stump and Norman Kretzmann, 'Absolute Simplicity', *Faith and Philosophy*, 2/4 (1985), 353–82.

[30] Wes Morrison, 'Is God Free? Reply to Wierenga', *Faith and Philosophy*, 23/1 (2006), 93–8 (p. 93).

explaining that 'we've enough on our plate without adding divine simplicity'.[31] For the medieval tradition, our inability to grasp divine simplicity was regarded as a consideration in its favour. I will have something to say in later chapters about the attitude of philosophers of religion to traditional doctrines that are theoretically 'hard to grasp'. At this point, it is sufficient to comment that, although Kant invokes the 'simplicity' of God (*OPA*, 2: 84–85; *LPR*, 28: 1038), by this he means just the 'indivisibility' of God, that God cannot be split apart or 'fall apart from inside', to use Keith Yandell's felicitous phrase.[32] There is no evidence in Kant of commitment to, or detailed knowledge of, the deeper resonances of the doctrine of simplicity, where every property and action of God is identical with every other property and action, and with God's nature and existence.

ARE GOODNESS AND RATIONALITY EXTERNAL OR INTERNAL TO THE DIVINE NATURE?

All Possibility Depends upon the Divine Nature

Kant's argument in *The Only Possible Argument for the Existence of God* (1763) goes from sheer possibility to the existence of God. Recently, there have been some logically sophisticated reconstructions and evaluations of the success of the proof.[33] We are not here concerned with whether Kant succeeds in proving the existence of God. It is sufficient for our purposes, of interpreting Kant's conception of the dependence of all possibility upon the divine nature, to give an outline of how Kant himself thinks the proof works.

There is a finely grained interpretative issue relating to *The Only Possible Argument* as to whether possibilities are grounded in God by being thought in the divine understanding, or by being exemplified in the divine nature; even to explain what is at stake in this discussion would be a distraction at this point in our discussion, and so I remain neutral on the issue. What matters here is that possibilities are grounded in God, but not by virtue of being chosen by the divine will. I will refer to both the divine understanding and the

---

[31] Michael Bergman and J. A. Cover, 'Divine Responsibility without Freedom', *Faith and Philosophy*, 23/4 (2006), 381–408 (p. 405).

[32] Keith Yandell, 'Divine Necessity and Divine Goodness', in Thomas V. Morris (ed.), *Divine and Human Action* (Ithaca, NY, and London: Cornell University Press, 1988), 313–44 (p. 318); Yandell dismisses the doctrine of simplicity as incompatible with the doctrine of the Incarnation.

[33] See Stang, 'Kant's Possibility Proof', 275–99; Chignell, 'Kant, Modality and the Most Real Being'; Adams, 'God, Possibility and Kant'; Schönfeld, *The Philosophy of the Young Kant*, 183–208; Fisher and Watkins, 'Kant on the Material Ground of Possibility'; Wood, *Kant's Rational Theology*, 64–79. For our purposes here, nothing hangs on the success or otherwise of Kant's proof.

divine nature, depending on the context. Kant uses both terms, and I reflect his usage, depending on which text I am discussing.

The broad outline of the proof is as follows. As we saw in the previous chapter (pp. 13–16), for something to be possible it must avoid self-contradiction (*OPA* 2: 77), and must have a thinkable content (*OPA* 2: 78), which Chignell describes as the requirement that 'the thing in question must have some positive predicates whose content determines its existence in one way rather than another'[34] (the contrast being with properties such as 'being such that 2 + 2 = 4'). As we also saw in the previous chapter (p. 15) Kant innovates upon his rationalist predecessors by stipulating that to be thinkable something must be 'really possible', with predicates that are *really harmonious* with one another'.[35]

At this point, what is sometimes called an 'actualist premiss' does important work. The actualist premiss states that something can exist only if it is grounded upon and caused by a reality that is greater than it. As Robert Adams[36] comments, this belongs to the 'same historical family' as the fourth of Thomas Aquinas's five ways, where a proof for the existence of God is 'based on the gradation observed in things':

Some things are found to be more good, more true, more noble, and so on, and other things less so. But such comparative terms describe varying degrees of approximation to a superlative . . . Something therefore is the truest and best and most noble of things, and hence the most fully in being . . . There is something therefore which causes in all other things their being, their goodness, and whatever other perfection they have. And this we call 'God'.[37]

Kant applies the actualist premiss to conclude that something can only be really possible, if the possibility itself has an ontological reality. Possibilities can have thinkable content only if the possibilities exist. This means that everything that is really possible (and so really harmonious) must already be actual somewhere; and that a similar grounding in actuality must support any harmony that exists between all that is really possible. The ontological reality of the sum total of real possibilities and their harmony is contained, Kant considers, in God, the *ens realissimum*, a most real being possessing all perfections and attributes.[38] Kant claims that 'absolute impossibility' is

---

[34] Chignell, 'Kant, Real Possibility, and the Threat of Spinoza', pp. 9–10, offprint.

[35] Chignell, 'Kant, Real Possibility, and the Threat of Spinoza', p. 11, offprint.

[36] Adams, 'God, Possibility and Kant', 425.

[37] Aquinas, *Summa Theologiae*, 1a.2.3.

[38] There is some controversy among commentators as to whether this condition of possibility should be construed in ontological or epistemic terms: that is, whether the condition of possibility is the actual ontological reality of the sum total of possibilities, or some sort of weaker condition of epistemic thinkability. I agree with Schönfeld's evaluation that the epistemic option might be 'tempting if one proceeds from the transcendental viewpoint of the critical Kant, but seems questionable considering the objectives of the precritical Kant' (*The Philosophy of the*

'synonymous' with the 'cancellation' of all possibility (*OPA* 2: 79), such that the negation of all possibility is impossible. Hence, that which is required to ground all possibility must necessarily exist: 'For if nothing exists, then nothing which could be thought is given either, and we contradict ourselves if we still wish to say that something is possible' (*OPA* 2: 78). In Kant's words:

All possibility presupposes something actual in and through which all that can be thought is given. Accordingly, there is a certain reality, the cancellation of which would itself cancel all internal possibility whatever. But that, the cancellation of which eradicates all possibility, is absolutely necessary. Therefore, something exists absolutely necessarily. (*OPA* 2: 83)

This leads Kant to the divine mind:

There exists something absolutely necessary. It is one in its essence; it is simple in its substance; it is a mind according to its nature; it is eternal in its duration; it is immutable in its constitution; and it is all-sufficient in respect of all that is possible and real . . . I am certain that the being, whose existence we have just proved, is precisely the Divine Being. (*OPA* 2: 89)

All of these properties are generated by a standard scholastic reflection on what must be involved in absolute perfection: that there can be no dependence, which means that there can be no composition of parts, or changeability, or temporality; which generates in turn the claims that God is simple, immutable, and eternal. The movement of Kant's thought here is recognizably similar to Leibniz's account of the pre-existence of all possible essences in the divine being:

Neither those essences nor the so-called eternal truths pertaining to them are fictitious. Rather, they exist in a certain realm of ideas, so to speak, namely in God himself, the very source of every essence and of the existence of the rest. The very existence of the actual series of things shows that we seem not to have spoken without grounds. For the reason for things must be sought in metaphysical necessities or in eternal truths, since (as I showed above) it cannot be found in the actual series of things. But existing things cannot derive from anything but existing things, as I already noted above. So it is necessary that eternal truths have their existence in a certain absolute or metaphysically necessary subject, that is, in God, through whom those things which would otherwise be imaginary are realized.[39]

The structure of possibilities is the structure of possible ways in which the world can be. From the depositary of possibilities, which constitutes the divine understanding, the divine will actualizes some possibilities, and not others.

Young Kant, 296). For alternative readings, see Redmann, *Gott und Welt*, and Laberge, *La Théologie Kantienne précritique*.

[39] Gottfried Wilhelm Leibniz, *The Ultimate Origination of Things* (1697), in *Philosophical Essays*, ed. Roger Ariew and Daniel Garber (Indianapolis and Cambridge: Hackett, 1989), 149–155 (pp. 151–2).

The divine will decides to actualize some possibilities (albeit without being able to do otherwise), but is not able to manipulate or alter the structure of these possibilities. In this, God's will is indeed 'constrained' (or shaped), but not by something external to God: God's will is constrained fundamentally by God's nature, which in turn is the ground of all possibility. Every law of nature is an actualization of a subset of possibilities contained in the divine nature. The same conceptual momentum—from possibility, to thinkability, to the divine nature—can be evidenced at every level: from the smallest aspect of creation to the creation itself. Reflection on the momentum can be provoked by contemplating the most abstract a priori possibility, or a complex, concrete, and embodied actuality. At the most abstract end of the spectrum, the possibility in mind could be an a priori mathematical or geometrical truth. All one needs for the argument is this notion of a priori possibility:

> The argument for the existence of God which we are presenting is based simply on the fact that something is possible. It is, accordingly, a proof which can be conducted entirely *a priori*. It presupposes neither my own existence, nor that of other minds, nor that of the physical world. (*OPA* 2: 91)

Equally, something as fleshed out as the laws of nature concerning the structure and behaviour of air (an example Kant uses) can be analysed in terms of the same conceptual progression from real possibility, to a grounding in the divine being. In this way, as Schönfeld suggests, Kant achieves his 'precritical project',[40] of reconciling rationalistic and Newtonian perspectives. Kant himself seems to indicate satisfaction along these lines in the preface of *The Only Possible Argument*, where he writes:

> It might seem that the periodic occurrence of fairly detailed physical explanations in a work would be damaging to the unity which one must observe in reflecting upon one's subject. However, since my intention in these cases has been especially focused on the method of using natural science to attain cognition of God, I could scarcely have achieved this purpose without deploying such examples. (*OPA* 2: 68)

This progression, from the micro to the macro, is reflected in the overall structure of the work, with part I dedicated to an ontological a priori argument ('In Which Is Furnished the Argument in Support of a Demonstration of the Existence of God' (*OPA* 2: 70)), and part II where Kant builds an a posteriori argument from design, 'in which the existence of God is inferred a posteriori from the unity perceived in the essences of things' (*OPA* 2: 93).

The laws that determine the structure and behaviour of air are a part of the divinely willed instantiation of real possibilities contained in the divine under-standing. This provides a momentum from the a priori argument of part I to the a posteriori argument from the appearance of harmony, order, and design

---

[40] Schönfeld, *The Philosophy of the Young Kant*, 194.

in the world. The a priori and a posteriori approaches are best understood, not as separate arguments, but as two meditations on the same structure of dependence:[41] from real possibility (the ground of structure, order, harmony), to thinkability, to being grounded in the divine being. When we admire the appearance of design in the universe, we are contemplating 'unity, harmony and order', which are sub-strands 'to be found in the possibilities of things':

Our mature judgement of the essential properties of the things known to us through experience enables us, even in the necessary determinations of their internal possibility, to perceive unity in what is manifold and harmoniousness in what is separated. It follows that the *a posteriori* mode of cognition will enable us to argue regressively to a single principle of all possibility. We shall thus finally arrive at the self-same fundamental concept of absolutely necessary existence, from which the *a priori* mode of cognition initially started out. (*OPA* 2: 92)

Part I of *The Only Possible Argument* has been the subject of more intense study, with sophisticated modal reconstructions and critiques. Of more interest to us, when tracking the relationship between the divine will and the divine nature/understanding, is part II of the proof, where Kant addresses the question of the 'essences of things' (*OPA* 2: 93), which he explains are necessary and binding, even upon the will of God. When we encounter order and harmony, it would be 'quite alien to the nature of the things themselves' to say that they 'stand in this harmonious relation' because 'a Creator has ordered them this way' (*OPA* 2: 96). God does not make the 'claws of a cat' retractable 'with a view to protecting them from wear' (*OPA* 2: 96). Kant considers that positing this sort of design invites Voltaire's satirical comment that God has given us noses 'so that we can wear spectacles' (*OPA* 2: 131). Rather, we should say that the 'simple law was the source of further usefulness and harmoniousness, not by art, but rather by necessity', and that there inheres 'in the very essence of things themselves universal relations to unity and cohesiveness', such that 'a universal harmony would extend throughout the realm of possibility itself' (*OPA* 2: 96).

Although God decides—in a sense, perhaps without being able to do otherwise (see pp. 16–24)—upon 'the existence of things' he does not decide their internal possibilities; rather the 'internal possibility of things, namely, furnishes Him . . . with the material' for the creation (*OPA* 2: 100). The 'essences of these materials' contain within themselves 'an extraordinary adaptedness to harmony' (*OPA* 2: 100). Kant is explicit that this 'adaptedness and harmony' should 'not be attributed to a free choice' (*OPA* 2: 101) of God, because the harmony 'is inherent in the very possibility of the things in question', so that 'the element of contingency, presupposed by any [divine] choice, here disappears' (*OPA* 2: 103). The 'union of numerous diverse

---

[41] On this point I am indebted to Schönfeld, *The Philosophy of the Young Kant*, 190–7.

consequences' that we find in the world is 'not a contingent union', and so not a 'product of a free will' (*OPA* 2: 101). Kant even says that it would be 'absurd' to attribute the 'great harmony' of 'beautiful relations' to 'a will' (*OPA* 2: 101). There is no legitimacy in an appeal to the 'divine power of choice', when the 'essences' of things 'contain within themselves an agreement which is extensive and necessary' (*OPA* 2: 131).

Kant illustrates this with concrete examples drawn from the harmony and lawfulness that constitute the earth's atmosphere, 'the possibilities of the pump, respiration, the conversion of liquids . . . into vapours, the winds, and so on' (*OPA* 2: 101). For example, 'the characteristic of air, in virtue of which it offers resistance to the material bodies moving in it', is to be 'regarded as a necessary consequence of its nature' (*OPA* 2: 102). It is 'inherent in the essence of the thing itself' that 'a celestial body in its liquid state should, entirely necessarily . . . strive to assume a spherical form', which 'harmonizes with the other purposes of the universe better than any other possible form' (*OPA* 2: 102).

The *existence* 'of all this harmoniousness along with its consequences' continues to be 'attributed to the power of choice of the first cause' (*OPA* 2: 101), to the 'wise choice of Him who created them on account of that harmony' (*OPA* 2: 103). It would be false to say that the harmonious connection of the essences do not depend upon *God*. Although they do not depend on the divine *will*, they do depend entirely on the divine *nature*. It is not Kant's intention to restrict the extent of the dependence of the creation on the divine mind, as if the essences of things are somehow independent of God. Rather, Kant seeks to differentiate two types of total dependence on God, which Kant names 'moral' and 'non-moral' dependence. We have a 'moral' dependence when 'God is the ground of that thing through his will', and a 'non-moral' dependence in the case of the 'internal possibility of things', of which the God is the 'ultimate ground' (*OPA* 2: 100).

Non-Moral Dependence upon God

It is this distinction between moral and non-moral dependence on God that lies behind Kant's discussion in *The Only Possible Argument* of the distinction between 'existence' and the properties that constitute an essence. This antici- pates Kant's critical refutation of the ontological argument (A592/B620– A602/B630), which revolves around the observation that 'existence' is 'not a real predicate' (A598/B626). Kant opens *The Only Possible Argument* by observing that, when God utters 'His almighty *Let there be* over a possible world' by bringing it into existence, 'he adds no new predicate to it', but 'posits it with all its predicates' (*OPA* 2: 74). This understanding of existence, as not adding any new predicates, is related to Kant's position that 'all determinations and predicates of the real thing are also to be found in the mere possibility of that same thing' (*OPA* 2: 75), independently of the divine will, but not of the divine nature.

The picture that emerges from *The Only Possible Argument* involves the divine will being provided with the really possible essences that are grounded in the divine nature, rather than the divine will shaping and deciding on the structure of really possible essences. Real possibilities, and the harmonious combination of all real possibilities, are grounded in the divine nature, and they are dependent upon God in the sense that all the reality that they have comes from their participation in the self-sufficient All-Reality that is God: but they are dependent upon God in a 'non-moral' and uncreated sense, analogous to the way in which we might say that 'omnipotence' is dependent upon the divine nature, in so far as it is part of the divine nature, although omnipotence is not therefore created by God, as God does not (traditionally) create his own nature.

The non-moral dependence of all possibilities upon God is important to Kant in a number of ways. First of all, it provides Kant with a theological objection to forms of natural theology, or 'physico-theology'. The natural theologian looks for proofs for the existence of an intelligent designer, on the basis of the evidence of order in the universe. Such proofs, Kant considers, presume that the 'admirable adaptation' we see in the world must be 'foreign to nature' left to its own resources, and that nature 'abandoned to its own general laws . . . would bring forth nothing but disorder' (*UNH* 1: 223). Kant is particularly focused here on proofs based upon order in inorganic nature; the case of organic order, as we will see below, is more complex (*UNH* 1: 230). Kant insists that (inorganic) matter is 'bound to certain necessary laws':

Matter, which is the primitive constituent of all things is therefore bound to certain laws, and when it is freely abandoned to these laws it must necessarily bring forth beautiful combinations. It has no freedom to deviate from this perfect plan. (*UNH* 1: 227–8)

It is true that the harmonies that necessarily exist in nature have their source in God, but they are grounded in the divine understanding, rather than in the divine will. For this reason, God does not need to bring about the harmonies in nature through a 'special government' (*UNH* 1: 224; see also *OPA* 2: 123–36). The harmony and lawfulness of nature can be supported only by being grounded in a 'common origin', an 'Infinite Intelligence, an Understanding [*Verstand*]' (*UNH* 1: 225). When nature unfolds according to 'its inherent essential striving', it is this essential striving that itself constitutes 'the most splendid evidence of its dependence on that pre-existing Being who contains in Himself not only the source of these beings themselves but their primary laws of action' (*UNH* 1: 226).

That which seems to be a consideration against the need for God (*qua* divine will), the orderliness of nature without divine intervention, becomes for Kant a consideration in favour of the need for God (*qua* divine understanding), as the source of the general order in nature: 'Reasons which, as used in the hands of opponents, are dreaded as prejudicial, are rather in themselves powerful weapons by which to combat them' (*UNH* 1: 225). Kant's position is a subtle one: in order for nature to be such that it does not require the constant intervention of a divine will, there needs to be a divine understanding, supporting and sustaining the structure of the laws of nature. 'There is a God', Kant tells us, 'just because nature even in chaos cannot proceed otherwise than regularly and according to order' (*UNH* 1: 228).

The non-moral dependence of all real possibilities upon God is also important to Kant for another reason, close to the heart of this chapter. In this chapter we have identified two underlying issues of central importance in determining whether Kant has given a theologically adequate account of divine freedom. First of all, there is the question of whether the divine nature is external to the divine will. Secondly, there is the further question of whether goodness and rationality are external to the divine nature. If goodness and rationality are external to the divine nature, then it looks as if Kant's account of divine freedom would be compromised. This at least is Kant's view: 'To what limitations, emanating from a separate ground, would not the Independent Being be subject, if not even these possibilities were grounded in that Being?' (*OPA* 2: 151)

'All the unity and harmony I observe around me', Kant writes, 'is only possible because a Being exists which contains within it the grounds not only of reality but also of all possibility' (*OPA* 2: 152–3):

This Supreme Being embraces within itself everything which can be thought by man, when he, a creature made of dust, dares to cast a spying eye behind the curtain which veils from mortal eyes the mysteries of the inscrutable. God is all-sufficient. Whatever exists, whether it be possible or actual, is only something in so far as it is given through Him. If it be permitted to translate the communings of the Infinite with Himself into human language, we may imagine God addressing Himself in these terms: *I am from eternity to eternity: apart from me there is nothing, except it be through me.* This thought, of all thoughts the most sublime, is still widely neglected, and mostly not considered at all. That which is to be found in the possibilities of things and which is capable of realizing perfection and beauty in excellent schemes has been regarded as a necessary object of Divine Wisdom but not itself as a consequence of this Incomprehensible Being. The dependency of other things has been limited to their existence alone. As a result of this limitation, a large share in the ground of so much perfection has been taken away from that Supreme Nature, and invested in I know not what absurdity. (*OPA* 2: 151)

It is important to appreciate the full sweep of all those things that are non-morally dependent upon the divine nature/understanding. It includes, Kant tells us, *all possibility*, 'everything which can be thought by man', 'whatever exists, whether it be possible or actual' (*OPA* 2: 151). As we have seen, it includes the abstract possibility of a geometrical proof, and the concrete atmospheric realities of air and water (*OPA* 2: 101–3). It also includes all principles of order, harmony, beauty, rationality, and goodness (*OPA* 2: 91–2, 101–3, 151–4). The divine '*all-sufficiency*' that grounds all possibility is 'expanded to include all that is possible or real', and 'designates everything which can be conceived under the notion of perfection' (*OPA* 2: 154). When discussing the question of freedom (divine and human), I frequently express Kant's position by saying that goodness and rationality are grounded non-morally in the divine nature/understanding, rather than in the divine will. This way of speaking is warranted, by virtue of the totalizing scope of the divine all-sufficiency, which includes 'everything which can be conceived under the notion of perfection' (*OPA* 2: 154), including therefore goodness and rationality.

Although Kant's claim in 1759 that God creates the best of all really possible worlds is associated closely with Leibniz,[42] Kant seeks to distance his account of the creation from Leibniz.[43] One of Kant's objections to Leibniz is that he has indeed neglected the 'most sublime' thought that all possibility, as well as all of reality, depends upon God. Kant complains (almost certainly unfairly) that Leibniz conceives of the divine will as constrained by a notion of possibility that is inappropriately 'independent' from God, a 'necessary object of Divine Wisdom' (*OPA* 2: 151), as if 'all possibility is spread out before God', so that 'God beholds it, considers it, and examines it' (*R* 3705; 17: 237), and then wills into existence the best possible world that God can manage given the restraints of possibility. Kant is perhaps troubled by passages where Leibniz talks of God being '*bound* by a moral necessity' to 'make things in such a manner that there can be nothing better'.[44] Had Kant access to other texts, he might have been reassured by Leibniz's explanation that 'the Dependence of everything upon God extends to all that is possible ... the possibility of things, even to those that have no actual existence, has itself a reality founded in the divine existence',[45] and that 'these possibilities or ideas of things coincide ... with God himself'.[46]

---

[42] Leibniz, *Theodicy*, 206–7, §134.

[43] For the discussion of Kant's treatment of Leibniz, I am indebted to Kain, 'The Development of Kant's Conception of Divine Freedom', pp. 14–15, manuscript.

[44] Leibniz, *Theodicy*, 253, §201.

[45] Gottfried Wilhelm Leibniz, *Causa Dei Asserta per Justitiam Eius*, §§7–8, in *Die Philosophischen Schriften*, ed. C. I. Gerhardt, 7 vols (Berlin: Weidmann, 1875–90), 6: 440–62 (p. 440).

[46] Gottfried Wilhelm Leibniz, 'Letter to Wedderkopf' (May 1671), in *Philosophical Papers and Letters*, ed. and trans. Leroy E. Loemker, 2nd edn (Dordrecht: Kluwer Academic Publishers, 1989), 146–7.

Kant's unfairness to Leibniz aside, we can see that in his dismissal of the view that possibilities are 'external' to God, Kant addresses precisely the question of why the divine will is not impacted upon by something 'outside' the divine nature, when necessarily choosing to create a world, where this world is necessarily populated by particular substances with non-negotiable essences. God is not just a powerful agent alongside other agents, but the very ground of possibility itself. As Kant explains in *The Only Possible Argument*, 'the ground of possibility, that is to say, the essence of God, will be in the highest harmony with his own will':

The reason for this is not that God is the ground of internal possibility in virtue of his own will. The reason is rather this: the same infinite nature is related to all the essences of things as their ground . . . Accordingly, the possibilities of things themselves, which are given through the divine nature, harmonize with his great desire. Goodness and perfection, however, consist in this harmony. And since goodness and perfection harmonise in one single principle, it follows that unity, harmony and order are themselves to be found in the possibilities of things. (*OPA* 2: 91–2)

What is possible for God is grounded, not in the divine will 'choosing' the structure of possibilities, but in the divine nature, the source of all possibility. The divine will is in the 'highest harmony' with the divine nature, which harmony itself grounds the harmoniousness between all real possibilities.

We might, though, still have a sense that there is something inappropriately 'brute' in this explanation. So with respect to essences, for example, we might ask: what makes *these* the essences that are grounded in the divine nature? Following Chignell, I think the answer here is just that 'here is where Kant's spade is turned':[47] these just are the essences that are so grounded. Is this a 'brute' and arbitrary fact? There are two ways in which someone might think that it is, in a way that they find objectionable. First of all, one might find the whole business of 'turning your spade' and finding bedrock—wherever this is done—arbitrary, non-explanatory, and gratuitously foundationalist. Secondly, one might find God in particular to be an unsatisfactory place to do this: because the concept of God is incoherent, or because it itself seems to need to be grounded. One might also combine elements of both reactions.

Both forms of objection are worthy of exploration in their own right, but neither provides grounds for us to worry about the interpretation of Kant, as both anxieties would be incomprehensible to the rationalist mindset. On the first point, the rationalist is driven to find a unified, plenitudinous, and rational resting place that grounds the entire hierarchy of being, without being part of this hierarchy, and that provides a sufficient reason and ground for everything that exists. On the second point, intrinsic to the grammar of the concept of God is that God provides an all-sufficient reason for everything that

---

[47] Chignell, 'Kant, Real Possibility, and the Threat of Spinoza', 37, offprint.

is, in a way that resolves and cuts off a regress of explanation. If one has a purported being 'God', but then needs to seek for the ground of God, then what one has discovered, from the rationalist point of view, is that the purported being cannot be God, a being no greater than which can be conceived, who does not need a ground because God is the ground of all grounds.

GOD, FREEDOM, AND CONTINGENCY: RAE LANGTON'S ALTERNATIVE INTERPRETATION

The account of divine freedom that I have ascribed to Kant construes the divine will as heavily shaped by rational norms. Even the (uncreated) structure of the essences of created substances are not determined by the choice of the divine will, although it is the divine will that 'decides' (subject to perfect goodness) to create these substances. In turn, these essences of created substances determine their causal and relational properties, as is shown in Kant's atmospheric examples. In recent discussions of *The Only Possible Argument*, the focus has been on Kant's claim that an absolutely necessary being is required to ground all possibility as such. The issue of the status of the divine will, in relation to the divine nature/understanding, has received some comment, but has not been the focus of interest or argument.[48] One commentator in particular, though, has taken a firm line on the role of the divine will in Kant's early philosophy. Rae Langton has offered an interpretation of some of Kant's pre-critical texts that suggests that the divine will has unlimited choice in determining the causal properties of substances.

As we have seen in the previous section, Kant considers that the causal properties of substances are determined by the essences of substances, which in turn are a subset of the totality of real possibilities grounded in God (*OPA* 2: 92–6, 100–3, 131, 151–3; *UNH* 1: 225–8). If Langton is right that God can change the causal properties of substances by an act of will, then the divine will can change the structure of real possibilities, a subset of which provides the essences of created substances. If Langton's interpretation is accurate, then I have seriously overestimated the extent and importance of the factors that shape Kant's conception of the divine will. It is important, therefore, that I address the texts cited by Langton, and show why they are consistent with my reading. My treatment is limited to the specific issue of the scope of divine will. I make no comment here on Langton's wider interpretation of Kant. I consider

---

[48] Chignell construes Kant along more intellectualist lines ('Kant, Modality and the Most Real Being', 181), and Stang along more voluntarist lines ('Kant's Possibility Proof', 296–7).

first of all the texts that Langton herself draws upon to support her thesis. I then consider other passages that Langton does not cite, but that might be thought to support Langton's claim about the scope of the divine will.

An Argument from the Possibility of Isolated Substances

Langton cites the following passage from *Living Forces* in support of her thesis about the extensive scope of the divine will.

A substance is either in connection and relation with another substance outside of itself, or it is not. Because any self-standing being contains the complete source of all its determinations in itself, therefore it is not necessary to its being that it stand in connection with another thing. Therefore substances can exist and nonetheless have no external connection at all with other substances, or they can stand in a real connection with other substances. (*LF* 1: 21–2)[49]

In *Living Forces* Kant explains that, for there to be a 'world', we require substances to be in connection with one another. Given that it is possible for things to exist without being in connection, it is therefore possible for substances to exist, but not to belong to a world. Equally, it is possible that substances are connected with each other, but not with this world, such that there exists another world. Kant criticizes the view, propounded in the 'lecture halls', that 'there could not exist more than a single world' (*LF* 1: 22). It is 'really possible' that 'God has created many millions of worlds' (*LF* 1: 22). It remains 'undecided whether they really exist or not', and we commit the mistake of thinking otherwise because we fail to understand that we have a world only when things 'stand in a real connection with other things' (*LF* 1: 22).[50] This is a view that Kant reiterates in the *New Elucidation* (1755):

There could be, if God so willed, a number of such substances, free from any connection with our universe, but, nonetheless, linked with each other by means of a certain connection with their determinations so as to produce place, position, and space: they would constitute a world banished beyond the limits of the world, of which we are parts, that is to say, they would constitute a solitary world. For this reason, the possibility that there might be, had it so pleased God, a number of worlds, even in the metaphysical sense, is not absurd. (*NE* 1: 414)

These texts are peculiar in a number of respects. First of all, it is controversial that a cogent conceptual distinction can be drawn between the creation of substances, and their being placed in interconnection with other substances. Secondly, it is not clear how this insistence relates, if it does at all, to Kant's *Optimism*, where he insists that, if God chooses to create a world, it must be

---

[49] My translation.   [50] My translation.

the best really possible world. What matters for our purposes is not whether or not Kant is correct in holding out for the possibility of isolated substances, but precisely what this implies for the scope of divine freedom. In this connection, Langton draws on the following passages where Kant asserts that relations between substances arise because of the 'arbitrary will' of God, which can be 'omitted or not omitted at his pleasure'.[51]

Newtonian attraction . . . is brought about by the . . . connection of substances . . . it is the most fundamental law of nature governing matter, remaining constantly in force only in virtue of God's immediately sustaining it. (*NE* 1: 415)

But no substance of any kind has the power of determining other substances, distinct from itself, by means of that which belongs to it internally (as we have proved). It follows from this that it only has this power in virtue of the connection, by means of which they are linked together in the idea entertained by the Infinite Being. (*NE* 1: 415)

Since the reciprocal connection of substances requires that there should be, in the effective representation of the divine intellect, a scheme conceived in terms of relations, and since this representation is entirely a matter of choice for God, and can therefore be admitted or omitted according to His pleasure, it follows that substances can exist in accordance with the law which specifies that *they are in no place* and that they stand in no relation at all in respect of the things of our universe. (*NE* 1: 414)

Langton understands this as suggestive of a looseness of fit between the properties the substance has intrinsically (roughly speaking 'independently of the presence of other created substances') and those that it has in relation to other substances ('relational properties'). God could in principle create the very same substance but superadd different relational/causal properties. Langton considers that Kant shares with many recent philosophers a commitment to the contingency of the causal and relational properties of substances and the laws of nature that govern/describe these causal and relational properties.[52] On Langton's interpretation 'Kant's intuition' is that 'things could be just as they are with respect to their intrinsic properties, yet different with respect to their causal powers', because of the 'contingency of the connections—if any— between intrinsic properties and causal powers'.[53] So, for example, 'in a world where the laws of nature were different, things might not have an attractive power, despite having the very same intrinsic properties that attractive things actually have'.[54] Langton calls this the 'Humean intuition', more 'in deference to the contemporary literature than to Hume himself', that 'there could be two universes containing the same objects, with the same intrinsic properties; but the laws of nature are different, so they have different powers'.[55]

---

[51] Langton, *Kantian Humility*, 121.   [52] Langton, *Kantian Humility*, 121.
[53] Langton, *Kantian Humility*, 118.   [54] Langton, *Kantian Humility*, 118.
[55] Rae Langton, 'Kant's Phenomena: Extrinsic or Relational Properties? A Reply to Allais', *Philosophy and Phenomenological Research*, 73/1 (2006), 170–85 (p. 175).

Langton's interest in these passages is primarily in terms of their implications for our knowledge of the intrinsic properties of substances: if the connection between intrinsic properties and causal powers is so deeply contingent, we cannot hope to derive knowledge of the intrinsic properties of substances from studying the causal and relational properties of substances, where our only experience of substances is by definition relational (the substances in relation to our cognitive powers). I make no comment on Langton's wider interpretation. Our interest is in just one strand of the evidence—pertaining to divine freedom—that Langton presents for her interpretation.

The difficulty with Langton's reading is that Kant does not actually say that God is free, as she parses it, 'to add or not to add *any powers he pleases*',[56] or that 'God could make the facts about substances and their intrinsic properties one way, and facts about their causal powers a different way'.[57] What Kant precisely says in the texts cited is that God is free to bring about, or not to bring about, 'the connection of substances' (*NE* 1: 415). As 'substances can exist . . . in no relation at all in respect of the things of our universe' (*NE* 1: 414), the creative act that is 'unconstrained and arbitrary'[58] is the act of placing substances in relation with one another *at all*. That the 'existence of substances' is 'insufficient on its own' to 'establish their reciprocal interaction' means, for Kant, that there must be a 'common cause of all things . . . that is to say, God', who decides to connect substances (*NE* 1: 414). This is compatible with the view that Langton ascribes to Kant, that God can add or not add *any power he pleases*, but it is distinct from it. It would be possible for God to be able to connect or not to connect substances, but for substances necessarily to have certain dispositions and relational properties that constitute this connection, in the event of God deciding to place substances in connection with each other. For clarity, we can set out the two possible interpretations of these texts:

> Interpretation One: the divine will can place substances in connection with each other or not; and the divine will can constitute these connections in any way that God chooses.

> Interpretation Two: the divine will can place substances in connection with each other or not; but having done so, the divine will cannot constitute these connections in any way that God chooses.

In terms of their philosophical cogency, both positions have their own peculiarities, which I do not intend to go into. The point is not which is correct as an

---

[56] Langton, *Kantian Humility*, 119.

[57] Rae Langton, 'Humility and Co-Existence in Kant and Lewis: Two Modal Themes, with Variations', in Barry Loewer and Jonathan Schaffer (eds), *The Blackwell Companion to David Lewis* (Oxford: Blackwell, forthcoming), 15, manuscript; the page references are to the unpublished chapter as supplied by the author, rather than to the edited book.

[58] Langton, *Kantian Humility*, 119.

account of the universe, but which is Kant's position. These texts from *Living Forces* and the *New Elucidation* do not by themselves definitively settle the interpretative issue in either direction, and Langton's construal is a viable reading of these passages taken in isolation. Two considerations, though, lead us to favour 'Interpretation Two'. First of all, 'Interpretation Two' is compatible with the clear parameters of the account that Kant presents in *Universal Natural History* and *The Only Possible Argument*, set out above (see pp. 37–47). In these texts we saw that although the divine will decides to create substances, the essences of these substances are determined by the divine nature/understanding, rather than the divine will. If 'Interpretation One' were correct, we would not expect Kant to say that the 'internal possibility of things... furnishes Him... with the material' for the creation (*OPA* 2: 100), or that the 'adaptedness and harmony' of substances should 'not be attributed to a free choice' (*OPA* 2: 101) of God, because the harmony 'is inherent in the very possibility of the things in question', so that 'the element of contingency, presupposed by any [divine] choice, here disappears' (*OPA* 2: 103). It is hard to square 'Interpretation One', while it is easy to reconcile 'Interpretation Two', with the claim that the 'union of numerous diverse consequences' that we find in the world is 'not a contingent union', and so not a 'product of a free will' (*OPA* 2: 101); that it would be 'absurd' to attribute the 'great harmony' of 'beautiful relations' to 'a will' (*OPA* 2: 101); and that there is no legitimacy in an appeal to the 'divine power of choice', when the 'essences' of things 'contain within themselves an agreement which is extensive and necessary' (*OPA* 2: 131).

Secondly, it is suggestive that in passages that surround the cited quotations, Kant identifies the 'divine understanding [*divino intellectu*]' (*NE* 1: 413), rather than the divine will, as the 'common principle' of the existence and interaction of substances, which 'maintains them in a state of harmony in their reciprocal relations' (*NE* 1: 413). It is 'the scheme of divine understanding [*intellectus divini schema*]' that establishes 'the relations of things to each other', such that 'it is most clearly apparent from this that the universal interaction of all things is to be ascribed to the concept alone of this divine idea [*divinae ideae*]' (*NE* 1: 413). Although the divine will is given a role, in that whether or not there are relations between substances is a matter that can 'be admitted or omitted in accordance with His pleasure', the 'reciprocal connection of substances' once activated is located in the 'divine intellect [*intellectus divini*]' (*NE* 1: 414). Whenever Kant discusses the reciprocal connection of substances in the *New Elucidation*, he refers to the divine understanding, intellect, or 'the idea entertained by the Infinite Being' (*NE* 1: 415). This is more consistent with 'Interpretation Two'. The divine will determines whether or not to place substances in connection with each other; nonetheless, having placed the substances in connection, the divine will cannot constitute these connections in any way that God chooses, as the shape of these connections is grounded in the divine understanding, not the divine will.[59]

An Argument from Organic Order

There is in fact one area where Kant talks about the divine will choosing to order nature in ways that are contingent.[60] For reasons that I set out here, when properly contextualized and understood, this aspect of Kant's thought does not offer support for Langton's thesis about the ability of the divine will to determine arbitrarily the relational properties of substances.

When discussing organic order, Kant writes that there are 'innumerable arrangements in nature which are, from the point of view of the universal laws of nature, contingent': 'As such they have no other foundation than the wise intention of Him who willed that they should be connected thus and not otherwise' (*OPA* 2: 121). When we contemplate the 'structure of an animal', the intricacy of the organism leads us to concede the existence of a designer:

Its organs of sense perception are connected with the organs of voluntary movement and life, and connected in such an ingenious fashion that once one's attention has been drawn to it, one would have to be of an ill-natured disposition (for no one could be so unreasonable) not to recognise the existence of a Wise Author, who had so excellently ordered the matter of which the animal was constituted. (*OPA* 2: 125)

Kant reflects that, when contemplating the 'products of the plant- and animal-kingdoms' (*OPA* 2: 118), 'the unity of all the combined advantages (in which perfection consists) is obviously contingent and ascribable to a wise choice' (*OPA* 2: 119). Although Langton does not refer to these passages, it might seem that they lend support to her claim that, for Kant, the divine will can place substances in connection with each other or not, and can constitute these connections in any way that God chooses. To see that this is not correct, we need to move through three stages. First of all, we need to appreciate the extent to which Kant limits any appeal to contingent design. Secondly, it is important to understand why Kant thinks that the evidence of organic design takes us only to a great architect, rather than to a Supreme Being who is the creator of the world *ex nihilo*. Thirdly, we will see why such 'architectural' work is

---

[59] For a fuller account of Langton's argument, see my 'Intellectualism, Relational Properties and the Divine Mind'. Desmond Hogan makes a similar objection to Langton's theory in 'Kant's Theory of Divine and Secondary Causation', in Brandon Look, *Leibniz and Kant* (Oxford: Oxford University Press, forthcoming), pp. 13–14, manuscript.

[60] I am indebted to James Orr for pointing out to me that I needed to address this aspect of Kant's thought, both in conversation and in his work towards a Ph.D. (Cambridge) work 'Natural Purposiveness as a Theological Problem in Kant's Pre-Critical and Critical Philosophy'. Orr's doctorial research concerns, among other things, the lines of continuity and discontinuity between Kant's pre-critical and critical treatment of physico-theology.

possible, for Kant, if the architect is also the Supreme Being, where real possibilities are grounded in the divine understanding of this being, not the divine will.

First of all, Kant is hesitant about the status of such appeals to a 'Wise Author'. He cautions us that, just because 'a natural connection harmonizes with what accords with a wise choice', it 'does not follow that it is also, from the point of view of the universal laws of causality, contingent, or that it has been especially instituted by an artificial provision' (*OPA* 2: 122). Kant is clear that it would be wrong to extend considerations that apply to organic matter to inorganic order: for example, Kant reiterates that the harmonious arrangement of 'the clouds, rain, winds, the dusk, and so forth' is 'necessary' and not a product of contingent design (*OPA* 2: 118). When setting out his 'rules of the revised method of physico-theology', Kant insists that 'one will presume that the necessary unity to be found in nature is greater than strikes the eye' (*OPA* 2: 126). Significantly, Kant goes on immediately to stress that this 'presumption will be made not only in the case of inorganic nature, but also in the case of organic nature':

For even in the case of the structure of an animal, it can be assumed that there is a single disposition, which has the fruitful adaptedness to produce many different advantageous consequences. Initially, we may have supposed that a variety of special provisions must have been necessary to produce such effects. Careful attention to the necessary unity of nature is both consonant with philosophy and advantageous to the physico-theological method of inference. (*OPA* 2: 126)

Although Kant concedes that 'one would have to be of an ill-natured disposition' (*OPA* 2: 125) not to 'recognise the existence of a Wise Author', his tone throughout discourages the 'lazy self-complacency' that makes an 'overhasty appeal to a divinely ordered and directed instituted provision as if it were an explanation in the philosophical sense of the word' (*OPA* 2: 121). Allowing that a divine will designs the structure of organisms is consistent with Kant's insistence that nature is governed by necessary laws, grounded not in the divine will but in the divine understanding.

In fact, as Kant goes onto show, not only are necessary laws and contingent design consistent, but the grounding of the laws of nature in the divine understanding (not the divine will) is a fundamental condition for the possibility of contingent design. To approach this conclusion, we need to move to our second consideration. After conceding that the ingenious order that we find in organisms leads us to 'recognise the existence of a Wise Author', Kant goes on to make an important qualification:

Nothing more than this can be inferred from our own example. Whether this matter has existed eternally and independently in its own right, or whether it has also been generated by this same Author—these are issues which cannot be decided by reference to our example. (*OPA* 2: 125)

In a passage that anticipates an objection to physico-theology that Kant will repeat in the first *Critique* (A620/B648–A630/B658), Kant writes that contemplating complex organic order serves only 'to prove the existence of an Author of the connections and artificial combinations in the world':

It does not prove the existence of an Author of matter itself, nor does it prove the origin of the constituent parts of the universe. This considerable defect must expose all those who avail themselves of this method alone to the error known as 'refined atheism'. According to this brand of atheism, God is strictly regarded as the Architect of the world, not its Creator: He orders and forms matter, but He does not produce or create it. (*OPA* 2: 122)

Physico-theology does not by itself lead us to *God*, in the sense of a being no greater than which can be conceived, or, in Kant's terms, a being who enjoys 'absolute necessity' and 'all-sufficiency', who is the ground of all possibility. The possibility of physico-theology, as I will argue, in fact depends upon a more fundamental theological level at which nature is ordered. If we can understand why this is the case, we will also see why Kant's concession to contingent divine design still fits within 'Interpretation Two', rather than 'Interpretation One'. This leads us to the third stage of our reflections about the divine will in relation to organic order.

The reason why contingent design depends upon more fundamental necessities is as follows. As we have seen, the evidence of intricate organic order can take us only to a 'Wise Author', not to a 'Wise Being' who is the ground of all that is. When we arrive at the conclusion that a designing 'Wise Author' exists, the evidence that has led us here does not by itself tell us whether or not this 'matter has existed eternally and independently in its own right', or whether it was 'generated by this same Author' (*OPA* 2: 125). At this point, Kant reflects upon what makes possible the work of the 'Wise Author'. What makes such designing work at all possible is that 'not all natural perfection is the work of artifice': 'The rules of great usefulness are also connected together with necessary unity, and . . . this agreement inheres in the very possibilities of things themselves' (*OPA* 2: 125). Precisely because this 'unity is itself, nonetheless, grounded in the possibilities of the things themselves', there 'must be a Wise Being', that is to say, a being who grounds all real possibilities:

In the absence of which none of these natural things would themselves be possible, and in which, as in a great ground, the essences of such a multiplicity of natural things are united into such regular relations. But then it is clear that not only the manner of their connection, but the things themselves, are possible only in virtue of this Being. That is to say, they can only exist as the effects of this Being. It is this argument which first reveals the complete dependency of nature upon God. (*OPA* 2: 125)

Even granting the role of the divine will in designing organic complexity (which Kant does, with some hesitancy), the picture that emerges is not that set out by Langton, where God's will decides by *fiat* the fundamental relational properties that belong to substances. Rather the divine will is presented (as it were) with the essences that are grounded eternally in the divine understanding, and creates organic complexity out of the 'possibilities of the things themselves', where the 'essences of such a multiplicity of natural things' are already 'united' into 'regular relations' (*OPA* 2: 125). Although organic complexity might have a 'moral dependence' upon the divine will (acting freely, although in conformity to divine goodness), the fundamental essences that make possible organic order have a 'non-moral dependence' upon the divine understanding. This might seem to create a conceptual split between God as the 'Wise Author' of organic order, and God as the 'Wise Being' who grounds the possibility of such order. Kant is aware of this, and explains that the (non-moral) ground of the possibilities that constitute all essences 'underlies not only the essence of all things', but also the 'essence of wisdom, goodness and power', which is expressed in any action of God as the 'Wise Author'. From this underlying 'unity' it 'follows that all possibility must of necessity harmonize with' the properties of God as designer (*OPA* 2: 125). Although the creation comes about because of the wise choice of God, at an ultimate level of explanation, the 'widely extended unity' that makes up 'nature's perfection' is not 'inferred from the wise choice as its cause': 'It is rather derived from a ground in the Supreme Being which is such that it must also be a ground of great wisdom in Him' (*OPA* 2: 119). Kant concludes gnomically that 'unity is thus derived from a Wise Being, but not through His wisdom' (*OPA* 2: 119). We can now see that by this Kant means that the 'unity' that underlies the possibility of organic and inorganic order arises because of the divine 'wisdom/wise choice', but that this 'wisdom/wise choice' itself depends ultimately upon the divine understanding, which is itself not a product of divine choice, but the precondition of it.

On the basis of a wide range of texts, 'Interpretation Two' is more plausible as a reading of passages where Kant talks about the divine choice of whether or not to put substances into connection with each other. 'Interpretation Two' is also preferable as a reading of other passages, which Langton does not consider, where the divine will sets fundamental possibilities into contingent patterns of organic order. Our thesis has never been that the divine will plays no role in the creation for Kant. Everything in the divine creation comes through the divine will. It is rather that the divine will is non-negotiably but non-coercively shaped by God's perfect goodness and the structure of real possibilities, which are grounded in the divine understanding, not constituted by the divine will. It seems likely that for Kant 'the role a property plays is not, after all, something contingently worn, not a cloak that can be thrown off (so to speak) when travelling from world to possible world'.[61] Langton has not

---

[61] Langton, 'Humility and Co-Existence in Kant and Lewis', p. 16, manuscript.

provided persuasive grounds to doubt the claim that, for Kant, although the divine will is free, and the world depends upon the divine will, there are significant ways in which the divine will does not have or need freedom of *choice*, in the sense of an ability to do otherwise.

A FRAMING INTERPRETATIVE QUESTION: WHAT IS THE PROBLEM WITH FREEDOM?

In this chapter I have set out some of the fundamental theological presuppositions that will determine how acceptable one finds Kant's conception of divine freedom. I do not in the end offer a defence or critique of Kant's position, except to suggest that it is not wildly and obviously beyond the bounds of a strand of orthodox (albeit contestable) theology. In any case, whatever we think of Kant's conception of divine freedom, we now have a full account of the extent to which divine freedom is shaped by rational and moral factors.

Understanding the contours of Kant's conception of divine freedom can evoke a sense both of enlightenment and of puzzlement in relation to the wider development of his thought. First of all, we have a clear intimation of something that will become very important to Kant: the perfect freedom of autonomy, or, as Langton nicely puts it, 'the radical, but deeply puzzling, idea that a free will and a will under moral laws are "one and the same"'. We see it here first, albeit that it is enjoyed only by the divine mind. In the next chapter we trace the course of Kant's thought about human freedom from 1755 to the 1770s, where we see that Kant moves from compatibilism about human freedom, to a troubled desire to ascribe aspects of (what Kant previously regarded as) divine freedom to the human creature.

It is here that Kant's conception of divine freedom generates a puzzle about the importance that our guiding question—'how can it be said that we are free given that we are created by God?'—will have for Kant in the 1760s and 1770s. Here we address the second objective of the book, of exploring the work done by an irreducible theological problem in the emergence of Kant's critical philosophy. God enjoys perfect freedom. We have seen that Kant consistently insists, into the critical period, that perfect freedom is not threatened but constituted by being necessarily shaped by rationality and perfect goodness. Across the development of his thought, Kant considers that God's enjoyment of perfect freedom is compatible with God's creative act being heavily shaped by necessary factors. God's enjoyment of perfect freedom is constituted by God necessarily willing and conforming to rational norms. Even down to the very substances and laws of nature that God creates, the divine will must follow the shape of real possibilities that are grounded in the divine nature/

understanding, where God does not enjoy a freedom 'to do otherwise' with respect to these essences. All of this is viable for Kant, because he has in his bones a positive and teleological conception of freedom, where what matters for freedom is that an agent wills the good. God is paradigmatically free, in that goodness and rationality can only ever be 'internal' factors shaping the divine will.

Against this framework, the puzzling question is this: why does it become so important for Kant, when thinking about *our* freedom, that we enjoy the ability to do otherwise, and, on the back of this—because it is the only way that we can secure such an ability—that we are ultimately responsible for our actions? In his earlier thought, as we will see in the next chapter, neither the ability to do otherwise nor being ultimately responsible for our actions is required for human freedom; indeed, neither option is coherently ascribable to human beings at all. Kant's sense that it is important that we have an ability to do otherwise, and ultimate responsibility, precedes his capacity to give a feasible account of how this is possible theologically speaking. The first shift in Kant's thought is a conceptual one in terms of what is required for human freedom. The next chapter explores the question of why this shift occurs, given Kant's consistent account of perfect divine freedom and the intimate relationship between freedom and rationality.

Broadly speaking, two interrelated provisional answers emerge. First of all, God seems to shift from being an 'internal' to an 'external' cause for human creatures: in his early thought, our willing (or otherwise) to follow the moral law is determined by God, but is still internal to the human creature in a way that is compatible with freedom. As his thought develops in the 1760s and 1770s, God seems to become a determining cause that is in some respects 'external' to the human creature, so that determination by God is not compatible with human freedom. This, at least, is the way that Kant puts it at points, although in further chapters we will see that the picture becomes more complicated and theologically nuanced in the late 1770s and 1780s. Secondly, derivatively upon the fundamental theological shift in the conception of divine–human interaction, Kant seems to want to distance us from divine action in order to secure meaningful freedom for us; he does this by claiming that we are 'able to do otherwise' than we do, although this ability, central to 'transcendental freedom', always remains a function of a limitation and a lack in human beings. Fundamentally, our 'ability' to do otherwise is not so much a capacity, as a failing, albeit one that Kant is convinced we need in order to secure meaningful human freedom.

4

The Problem

This chapter traces the emergence of a problem for Kant: the problem of how we can be said to be free, given that we are created by God.[1] This problem arises for Kant as a shift occurs in his conception of what is required for human freedom to be possible. The shift in Kant's thought that I track is this: in the 1750s Kant considers that human freedom does not require the agent to be able to do otherwise (the 'alternative-possibility' condition (AP)), nor does Kant require the agent to be ultimately responsible for his or her actions (the 'ultimate-responsibility' condition (UR)). Over the course of the 1760s and 1770s, Kant changes his mind on both points, requiring for significant human freedom both that we can do otherwise than we do, and that we are ultimately responsible for our actions. The freedom that satisfies both conditions is what Kant calls 'transcendental freedom'.

This way of putting the issue means that we can steer our way through a knotty terminological dispute as to whether Kant's mature position is best described as fundamentally 'compatibilist' or 'incompatibilist'. Commentators focus on different strands in Kant's account of divine and human freedom, and decide variously that Kant is more fundamentally compatibilist or incompatibilist, usually acknowledging in each case that Kant fits the description in an unusual and qualified sense.[2] What is clear is that, in his ascription of

---

[1] Material from this chapter, and from subsequent chapters, has appeared in my article 'Kant's Transcendental Idealism, Freedom and the Divine Mind', *Modern Theology*, 27/4 (2011), 608–38.

[2] For recent discussions on different sides of the terminological issue, see Simon Shengjian Xie, 'What is Kant: a Compatibilist or an Incompatibilist? A New Interpretation of Kant's Solution to the Free Will Problem', *Kant-Studien*, 100/1 (2009), 53–76; and Coleen P. Zoller, 'The Pre-Critical Roots of Kant's Compatibilism', *Philosophy and Theology*, 19/1–2 (2007), 197–213. Xie focuses on the ultimate responsibility required by Kant's transcendental freedom, and the fact that we can do otherwise, but neglects that the ability to do otherwise is not essential for freedom as such. Zoller concentrates on Kant's intellectualist notion of perfect freedom, which involves following the moral law, whether or not one can do otherwise. Zoller is correct to perceive this continuity in Kant's conception of perfect freedom across his thought, although she neglects the shift from the pre-critical to the critical Kant, whereby Kant begins to ascribe to us ultimate responsibility for whether or not we follow the moral law. Allen Wood suggests that Kant's critical moral philosophy is a compatibilism between compatibilism (in the phenomenal

transcendental freedom to human beings in the 1770s, Kant moves away from the sort of compatibilism he espoused in 1755. By the 1770s Kant considers that freedom entails our ability to do otherwise (AP), and that we are ultimately responsible (UR) for our actions. In this sense, I think it is not misleading to say that he moves towards an incompatibilist position. Our task is to investigate how and why Kant moves from not requiring AP or UR for human freedom, to admitting the former and requiring the latter: this describes Kant's transition from a compatibilist conception of freedom to a transcendental conception of freedom. I will permit myself to talk of transcendental freedom as an 'incompatibilist' analysis, in the sense that transcendental freedom, like other incompatibilist accounts, insists on AP and UR.

Having, in the first section, set out the compatibilist account of freedom that Kant provides in the 1750s, I track the shift to incompatibilism in Kant's thought by looking at three sets of texts. In the second section I look at some reflections on Rousseau in the early 1760s. In the third section I attend to a passage in the *Only Possible Argument*, which I read alongside some related *Reflexionen* from the mid-1760s. Finally, in the fourth section, I analyse passages from Kant's 'Lectures on Metaphysics' in the 1770s. By the 1770s we find Kant formulating his difficulty in blunt theological terms, asking how we can be free, if we are created by God. Before interrogating the grounds for this shift, I dispatch (in the fifth section) a suggestion that Kant has in fact resolved the issue of the relationship between divine and human action in the 'Metaphysik Herder' lectures.

In the chapter up to this point, I will have furthered one of the two main objectives of the book, of exposing an immanent theological difficulty that in part motivates the emergence of Kant's critical philosophy. The remainder of the chapter turns to the second objective, of engaging theologically with Kant on the question of divine action and human freedom, with a view to evaluating his legacy on this front.

At this point in our discussion, the framing question set in the previous chapter will become relevant. Given Kant's account of the perfect freedom enjoyed paradigmatically by God, which does not require God's ability to do otherwise, why does it become so important for Kant in the 1760s and 1770s that human beings enjoy this ability? In the sixth section I explore a suggestion from Derk Pereboom, which helps us to raise this question in a particularly sharp way. Pereboom questions whether Kant *needs* the ultimate responsibility and ability to do otherwise that characterizes transcendental freedom at

realm) and freedom (in the noumenal): see Allen W. Wood, 'Kant's Compatibilism', in Allen W. Wood (ed.), *Self and Nature in Kant's Philosophy* (Ithaca, NY, and London: Cornell University Press, 1984), 73–101. It is true that, for Kant, the appearance of determinism does not conflict with a more fundamental transcendental freedom, but, as Xie argues, this is not really a compatibilist concept of *freedom*: as 'by separating freedom and determinism into two different worlds', Kant 'must have recognized their incompatibility in the first place' ('What is Kant', 53).

all, in order to sustain the perfect freedom that is involved in following the moral law. If Pereboom is correct, Kant could (and should) have steered away from transcendental freedom (the demand that we are able to do otherwise, and that we are ultimately responsible for our actions) in the 1760s and 1770s, and simply have affirmed perfect freedom as a possibility for (some) human beings. That the responsibility for these human beings achieving perfect freedom rests ultimately in God would not endanger what matters about perfect freedom, which is that we are rationally motivated to follow the moral law. I argue that the scenario put forward by Pereboom—perfect freedom but without transcendental freedom—is ambiguous between two readings. On one reading, human beings always do act according to perfect freedom, albeit that they are determined to. On the other reading, some human beings are some of the time determined to act according to perfect freedom, and some human beings are some of the time determined not to.

I explain why Kant would not accept the first account, where determined human beings always choose the good, and why he has strong grounds for his refusal: we cannot know that this scenario is a real rather than a merely logical possibility; and, in any case, this suggestion does not describe the world that we inhabit, and so the world created by God. The second reading of Pereboom's suggestion is in fact a version of Kant's 1755 position: God determines that some human beings some of the time act according to perfect freedom, and that some human beings do not.

It turns out, therefore, that the live options for Kant are indeed his 1755 position or transcendental freedom. I will suggest that although we have identified a cluster of motivations, aspirations, and anxieties that frame this shift in Kant's thought, we do not really have a clear argument that explains his transition to transcendental freedom. In the seventh section, I examine Patrick Kain's sympathetic account of Kant's differentiated characterization of divine and human freedom. Kain argues that it is coherent for Kant to claim that it is essential for our distinctively creaturely freedom to be able to do otherwise, and to be ultimately responsible for our actions, even if the ability to do otherwise is not a necessary part of perfect divine freedom. Kain suggests that our ability to do other than the good arises because we, unlike God, are impacted upon by 'alien causes', where we can choose to prioritize 'our dignity' and the moral law, or 'our needs and wants'.[3]

Kain's reference to 'alien causes' takes us directly to the heart of the matter. Freedom involves not being determined by 'alien causes'. The crucial question is therefore: what constitutes a cause that is 'alien' to the creature? I find that Kant moves from thinking that God is not an alien cause, to thinking that God is an alien cause, and that this is a sheerly conceptual and

---

[3] Kain, 'The Development of Kant's Conception of Divine Freedom', p. 29, manuscript.

theological move. In relation to this theological move, I set out a mainstream pre-modern theological perspective, according to which this way of seeing the problem is itself the problem, as God can never be an alien cause to the creature. This is just the first stage in our theological conversation with Kant about the relationship between divine and human action, as Kant shows more subtlety as he moves closer, in his own view, to solving the problem of created freedom.

KANT'S PRE-CRITICAL COMPATIBILISM

Kant's earliest writings in the late 1740s and 1750s grapple, among other things, with the problem of causation.[4] The notion of causation between substances (finite created beings) was under pressure in Kant's context because of perceived problems with the scholastic 'way of influence'. Critics of this position characterized it as positing something passing 'from one substance into another',[5] with properties somehow hovering between substances.[6] As Kant understood it, there were three main options for explaining causation, or the appearance of causation (*NE* 1: 415; *ID* 2: 409): occasionalism, pre-established harmony, and intersubstantial causation. Two of these options 'explain' causation by denying that it is fundamentally real, even if the systematic appearance of causation has a 'reality' as a well-founded phenomenon. Malebranche's occasionalism asserts that there are no causal relations between created substances: with each event, God acts directly on the individual substance. Leibniz's pre-established harmony similarly identifies the only intersubstantial causal movement in the universe to be that which runs from the creator to each individual created monad. The representation of the world afforded to each monad unfolds according to an eternally determined plan. There is an appearance of harmony and interconnection between the separate and unconnected monads, only because of the pre-established design in the divine mind. Although these monads are causally isolated, God produces 'the same effect that would be noticed if they communicated through the

---

[4] For an extensive account of Kant's intellectual context, to which I am indebted in this section, see Watkins, *Kant and the Metaphysics of Causality*, pt 1, and Laywine, *Kant's Early Metaphysics and the Origins of the Critical Philosophy*, 37–42.

[5] Gottfried Wilhelm Leibniz, 'Extract from a Letter Written by Monsieur Leibniz about his Philosophical Hypothesis (1696) ("Third Explanation of the New System")', in *Philosophical Texts*, 191–3 (p. 192, §5).

[6] I do not thereby endorse this interpretation of the scholastic account. For a defence of the scholastic account, see Alfred J. Freddoso, who claims that scholastics 'all deny that *transeunt* action involves the literal *transfer* of some entity—i.e. perfection or form—from the agent to the patient', in 'God's General Concurrence with Secondary Causes: Pitfalls and Prospects', *American Catholic Philosophical Quarterly*, 67 (1994), 131–56 (p. 139).

transmission of species or qualities, as the ordinary philosophers imagine they do'.[7] The case for an intersubstantial causal connection between substances was made in Germany by philosophers influenced by Newton, such as Knutzen and Crusius, who maintained—as Kant interpreted them—that substances had real causal relations with other substances, by virtue of their existence alone.

Kant's intervention in this debate is to insist that God is required both to bring substances (finite created beings) into existence, and in a conceptually separate act (as we saw in the previous chapter, pp. 48–52), to place substances in a real reciprocal connection with one another, thus constituting a world. Kant argues in 1755 that substances are genuinely connected (contrary to Leibniz), but not connected by virtue of their existence alone (contrary to Knutzen and Crusius): they are 'linked together' in 'the idea entertained by the Infinite Being' (*NE* 1: 415), such that the 'origin ... of the reciprocal connection of things ... is to be sought outside the principle of substances', in God alone (*NE* 1: 416). This 'interaction between substances by means of truly efficient causes' can be 'ascribed to an internal force of the substance', but nonetheless this internal force rests entirely on 'divine support' (*NE* 1: 416).

There are two principles—'extremely rich in consequences' (*NE* 1: 410)— that govern the interconnection of substances: the principles of succession and coexistence. The 'principle of succession' asserts that no substance has the power to change itself: 'No change can happen to substances except in so far as they are connected with other substances; their reciprocal dependence on each other determines their reciprocal changes of state' (*NE* 1: 410). Without this 'connection of substances', 'succession and time would likewise disappear' (*NE* 1: 416). As Laywine points out, we see here something like the Newtonian principle of inertia applied at a more fundamental level;[8] more fundamental, because Kant is describing a truth not just about matter, but about any substances whatsoever. The Newtonian conception of force 'presupposes place, direction and change', while for the early Kant 'force applies in more spheres than bodies', and includes, for example, 'a change of perception in a soul'.[9] The second of the principles set out in the *New Elucidation*, the 'principle of coexistence', is made up of two claims. First of all, 'finite substances, do not, in virtue of their existence alone, stand in relationship with each other'; and, secondly, the 'divine understanding' as the 'common

---

[7] Gottfried Wilhelm Leibniz, *A New System of the Nature and Communication of Substances, and of the Union of the Soul and Body* (1695), in *Philosophical Essays*, ed. Roger Ariew and Daniel Garber (Indianapolis and Cambridge: Hackett, 1989), 138–45 (p. 144).

[8] Laywine, *Kant's Early Metaphysics and the Origins of the Critical Philosophy*, 36. See also Paul Guyer, *Kant and the Claims of Knowledge* (Cambridge: Cambridge University Press, 1987), 11–12. Guyer makes the suggestion that in the 'principle of succession' we see Kant anticipating the arguments of the 'Refutation of Idealism' (B275–94).

[9] Laywine, *Kant's Early Metaphysics and the Origins of the Critical Philosophy*, 36.

principle of their existence' is required to sustain the substances 'in a state of harmony in their reciprocal relations' (*NE* 1: 413).

Following Leibniz, Kant ascribes to a version of the 'principle of sufficient reason', whereby there are sufficient determining grounds for everything that happens. When discussing his version of the principle of sufficient reason, Kant uses what he stipulates to be a synonymous term, 'the principle of the determining ground' (*NE* 1: 391). The principles of succession and coexistence are, for Kant, how 'the principle of the determining ground' manifests itself in relation to created substances: everything has a determining ground, where for substances, these grounds are the real intersubstantial relations of coexistence and succession, which in turn depend upon the divine mind (*NE* 1: 411). We will return in Chapter 8 to the fate of these two principles in Kant's critical thought; the two principles do not share the same critical end, for reasons that are close to the heart of this book.

It is important to understand that this gesture towards the divine mind, as the source of causation, is more than a rather grudging acknowledgement—halfway to deism—that as God is the creator of everything, he must be the creator of causation as well, although in truth we could ground causation perfectly adequately without reference to God. Kant's claim about causation is that it positively and emphatically requires a divine mind. In 1755 Kant writes that the 'reciprocal interaction' and 'external connection' between substances even makes it possible 'to infer with the greatest certainty that there is a supreme cause of all things, and indeed, only one, that is to say, God' (*NE* 1: 414).

As Friedman helpfully puts it, for Kant:

purely mechanistic explanation is itself the best proof of a divine origin of the universe; for it is God, and God alone, who has established these fundamental laws of interaction (laws which have such harmonious consequences of necessity) as belonging to the very essence of matter.[10]

A 'mechanical connection', for Kant, is a 'connection of bodies through which they act according to laws of motion' (*MH* 28: 49), with the laws of interconnection dependent entirely upon the divine mind. That there is lawful mechanism is a clear indication, for Kant, of the existence and activity of a divine mind. We might say that not only is the existence of causation a proof for the existence of God, but also that the existence of God functions as a guarantor for the existence of intersubstantial causation. Because of God, intersubstantial causation is possible; without God, substances could not be causally related.

Alongside this treatment of causation in the *New Elucidation* we find an extensive treatment of the theme of human freedom. In his 1755 account of intersubstantial causal relations between substances, we have just seen

---

[10] Friedman, *Kant and the Exact Sciences*, 11.

that Kant distinguishes his position from both Leibniz and Crusius: against Leibniz, Kant insists on intersubstantial reciprocal relations between substances. Against Crusius, Kant argues that substances do not enjoy intersubstantial relations by virtue of their existence alone. Similarly, on the question of freedom, Kant argues for a position that is distinct from both Leibniz and Crusius. We can get a good sense of Kant's position by tracking the precise nature of his criticism of both thinkers in turn.[11]

First of all, as mentioned in the previous chapter (pp. 32–33), Kant is critical of Leibniz's attempt to distinguish between types of necessity. Leibniz claims that, although our actions are necessary given our motives, they are not absolutely necessary, as a world in which we do otherwise is not ruled out by the principle of contradiction, even if it is impossible on other grounds. In the *Theodicy* Leibniz attempts to distinguish between hypothetical necessity, whereby actions and events are certainly determined by previous states, and an 'absolute' necessity, which would involve it being logically impossible that the actions or events did not occur:

Nevertheless, objective certainty or determination does not bring about the necessity of the determinate truth. All philosophers acknowledge this, asserting that the truth of contingent futurities is determinate, and that nevertheless they remain contingent. The thing indeed would imply no contradiction in itself if the effect did not follow; and therein lies the contingency. The better to understand this point, we must take into account that there are two great principles of our arguments. The one is the principle of *contradiction*, stating that of two contradictory propositions the one is true, the other false; the other principle is that of the *determinant reason*: it states that nothing ever comes to pass without there being a cause or at least a reason determining it, that is, something to give an *a priori* reason why it is existent rather than non-existent, and in this wise rather than in any other. This great principle holds for all events, and a contrary instance will never be supplied: and although more often than not we are insufficiently acquainted with these determinant reasons, we perceive nevertheless that there are such.[12]

Even if something is determined, Leibniz insists, if it is not demanded by the principle of contradiction, then it is 'contingent', and so not 'absolutely' necessary: hence there is a distinction between absolute and hypothetical necessity. Our actions are hypothetically but not absolutely necessitated. Kant endorses Crusius's attack on this distinction, agreeing that 'the distinction obviously has no power at all to break the force and effective power of necessity' (*NE* 1: 399):

---

[11] I am indebted here to Jeremy Byrd, 'Kant's Compatibilism in the New Elucidation of the First Principles of Metaphysical Cognition', *Kant-Studien*, 99/1 (2008), 68–79 (p. 68).

[12] Leibniz, *Theodicy*, 147–8, §44.

What is at issue is the necessitating principle: namely, *whence* the thing is necessary... the distinction, which everyone recites parrot-fashion, does little to diminish the force of the necessity or the certainty of the determination. For just as nothing can be conceived which is more *more true* than *true*, and nothing *more certain* than *certain*, so nothing can be conceived which is *more determined* than *determined*. (*NE* 1: 400)

In 1755 Kant's compatibilism is more thoroughgoing than Leibniz's, in that he makes no attempt to escape the conclusion that, 'in the case of the free actions of human beings', in so far 'as they are regarded as determinate, their opposites are indeed excluded' (*NE* 1: 400), and so that in no sense is our action genuinely contingent. Kant considers that this does not threaten human freedom, because the alternatives are not 'excluded by grounds which are posited as existing outside the desires and spontaneous inclinations of the subject', where the agent is 'compelled to perform his actions against his will, so to speak, and as a result of a certain ineluctable necessity':

On the contrary, it is in the very inclinations of his volitions and desires, in so far as that inclination readily yields to the blandishments of his representations, that his actions are determined by a fixed law and in a connection which is most certain but also free. (*NE* 1: 400)

In this way, human action follows the pattern laid down for all events:

There is nothing in that which is grounded which was not in the ground itself. For nothing is without a determining ground; accordingly, there is nothing in that which is grounded which does not reveal its determining ground. (*NE* 1: 406)

This chain of grounding takes us back to God:

And thus, by tracing one's way along the inexorable chain of events which... once and for all snakes its way along and weaves its path through the eternal series of consequences, one eventually arrives at the first state of the world. And this state immediately reveals God, the Creator, the ultimate ground of events, and the fertile ground of so many consequences. Once this ultimate ground is posited, other grounds follow, in accordance with an ever constant law. (*NE* 1: 399)

God... as Creator, is, so to speak, the well or bubbling spring from which all things flow with infallible necessity down an inclined channel. (*NE* 1: 403)

Human freedom, for Kant in 1755, just is the product of our determined volition. There is a difference between those actions that can be ascribed to non-rational animals, and those that can be ascribed to our freedom, but this is 'not a difference in the nature of the connection or the certainty' that attaches to the determination (*NE* 1: 400). Free action, just as much as physical events or animal behaviour, is predetermined, and contained entirely within its antecedent ground. Rather, it is the 'way in which the certainty of... actions is determined by their grounds' that 'gives us all the room we need to affirm that they bear the characteristic mark of freedom' (*NE* 1: 400). What matters here is that, 'whereas in the case of brute animals or physico-mechanical actions everything is necessitated in conformity with external stimuli and impulses and without there being any spontaneous inclination of the will', with human freedom the human being's 'actions are called forth by nothing other than motives of the understanding applied to the will' (*NE* 1: 400). Both animal and human actions are determined, but what marks our freedom is that the antecedent grounding cause consists of conscious desires and inclinations, which are themselves in turn antecedently grounded, in a chain of causes that takes us back to God:

> For what is being pleased if it is not the inclination of the will in one direction rather than another, according to the attraction exercised by the object. Thus, your 'it pleases' or 'it causes pleasure' signifies that the action is determined by inner grounds. (*NE* 1: 401)

So much for Kant's engagement with Leibniz. Kant also distinguishes his position from Crusius. Crusius argues that with human actions, there are sufficient grounds in terms of the agent's volition combined with circumstances, but that these do not amount to determining grounds, meaning that the human agent is able to do otherwise.[13] In the *New Elucidation* Kant sets up a dialogue between Titius, 'the champion of the determining ground', and Caius, 'the advocate of the indifference of equilibrium' (*NE* 1: 401), where Cauis ventriloquizes Crusius's demand for sufficient but not determining grounds of free actions. Cauis insists that an act is only 'freely performed' if we 'eliminate everything which is in the nature of a connected series of reciprocally determining grounds occurring in a fixed order', and admit instead 'that in a free action', when faced with alternatives, a person 'is nonetheless able to choose one thing over another, no matter what' (*NE* 1: 402). In response, Titius sets out Kant's position that the determination of the will, 'far from eliminating spontaneity, actually makes spontaneity more certain, provided that "spontaneity" is taken in the right sense': 'For *spontaneity* is action which issues from *an inner principle. When this spontaneity is determined in conformity with the representation of what is best it is called freedom*' (*NE* 1: 402). Here we see that, although the binding-together of morality and freedom occurs paradigmatically with divine freedom, it is also held to apply to human freedom: human beings are fully free when they follow the norms of reason. This principle could get Kant into difficulties, as an implication would seem to be that when one does not follow the moral law, one is not free, and where one is not free, one cannot be held responsible for an

---

[13] See Christian August Crusius, *Entwurf der notwendigen Vernunfwahrheiten* (1745), in *Die philosophischen Hauptschriften,* ed. G. Tonelli (Hildesheim: Olms Verlag, 1964–), vol. 1, §§29, 38, 63, 64, 68. For helpful discussions of Crusius, to which I am indebted, see Watkins, *Kant and the Metaphysics of Causality*, 81–100, and Hogan, 'Three Kinds of Rationalism', 361–5.

action. Kant's answer, here and later on, involves envisaging freedom as having degrees of instantiation:

The more certainly it can be said of a person that he submits to the law, and thus the more that person is determined by all the motives posited for willing, the greater is that person's freedom. (*NE* 1: 402)

A person is minimally but culpably free, and so responsible, in all his or her rational actions—'when motives of the understanding' are 'applied to the will'—whether or not he or she follows the moral law. Although following the law increases our freedom, Kant/Titius is clear that we are guilty (because free) when we fail to do so:

It does not follow from your line of argument that the power belonging to antecedently determining grounds impairs freedom . . . your action was not *unavoidable,* as you seem indeed to think, for you did not seek to avoid it; it was, however, *bound to happen,* given the inclination of your desire relative to the situation as it was constituted. (*NE* 1: 402)

Things get worse still for the miscreant. The insight that the action was 'bound to happen' in fact even 'increases your guilt': 'For the eagerness of your desire was such that you were not to be distracted from your purpose' (*NE* 1: 402). An implication of the shift in Kant's conception of freedom is that he becomes unhappy with the notion that our free actions are 'bound to happen', desiring for human beings the Crusian ability, as Cauis puts it, 'to choose one thing over another, no matter what' (*NE* 1: 402). This is a significant shift, as in 1755 Kant goes as far as to insist that the notion of a contingent being enjoying anything other than determined freedom involves incoherence and contradiction:

A contingent thing is never sufficiently determined, if you abandon the antecedently determining ground, and, hence . . . a contingent thing cannot exist without such a determining ground . . . a being will remain indeterminate and, indeed, incapable of being determined, until, in addition to that which belongs to its inner existence, concepts are deployed which are capable of being thought independently of its existence . . . It follows from this with complete clarity that, without an antecedently determining ground, there can be no kind of determination of a being, which is conceived of as having come into being; and hence, there can be no existence. (*NE* 1: 397)

KANT READS ROUSSEAU

Up until around 1762–3, Kant seems to be content with his 1755 compatibilist analysis of freedom, whereby we are determined by the chain of determining grounds that rests ultimately in God. All that is needed for 'freedom' is that we consciously want to do that which we do: it does not matter if our wanting to do this comes downstream of the divine mind, and is determined for us. From the early 1760s onwards, however, Kant begins to reach for a more demanding form of freedom.

As we have seen above, Kant was familiar with incompatibilist conceptions of freedom from his reading of Crusius. Furthermore, Kant would have been culturally familiar with such conceptions given his early upbringing in Pietist circles, where Leibnizian compatibilism was regarded with some hostility.[14] Although we cannot be sure what precipitates Kant's shift from compatibilism, his reading of Rousseau's *Émile* and *On the Social Contract* in the early 1760s seems to have been a factor.[15] Rousseau, Kant writes, enjoys the 'noble impetus of genius', and has an importance in the moral realm that is equivalent to Newton's in the physical (*Ob.* 2: 219–20).

We might speculate as to whether the category of political and social freedom that is set out in Rousseau's notion of the general will—where a people governs itself rather than being ruled by an external authority—is something that Kant begins to apply to the micro-level, to the human individual. Kant does not put it in these terms, and it is easier in his observations on Rousseau to detect the influence of the novel *Émile*. In *Émile* Rousseau sets out a programme of ideal moral education for the young. Rousseau is suspicious of rooting morality in the passions and sentiment, as the passions bring about an enslavement of the human being. Kant takes from Rousseau a concern for the human creature to take his or her proper place in the created order. This must be neither too high nor too low: 'the greatest concern of the human being is to know how he should properly fulfil his station in creation and rightly understand what one must be in order to be a human being' (*Ob.* 2: 216). If the human being 'learns gratifications that are above or beneath him', then it will

---

[14] For an extensive treatment of this background, see Manfred Kuehn, *Kant: A Biography* (Cambridge: Cambridge University Press, 2001), 24–60.

[15] For more extensive treatments of Rousseau's influence on Kant, see the following: Richard L. Velkley, *Freedom and the End of Reason: On the Moral Foundation of Kant's Critical Philosophy* (Chicago and London: University of Chicago Press, 1989); Ernst Cassirer, *Rousseau–Kant–Goethe: Two Essays* (Princeton: Princeton University Press, 1947). Velkley reads Kant as responding to a 'crisis in modern individualism' (p. 46), where Kant 'fully assents to the most basic premises of that individualism', and where Rousseau shows the way for Kant to emancipate 'human strivings from a restrictive natural order', leading to a 'consequent endorsement of "diversity" in ideas of the good' (p. 46). Prior to reading Rousseau, the suggestion is, Kant was unable properly to ground his assent to 'modern individualism'. In my view, Velkley neglects the strength of Kant's rationalist intellectualism, both prior to and after he had read Rousseau. What matters about freedom is not self-expression or individualism, but the ability to conform to the structure of reason and the moral law, in a way that can be imputed to the agent. Cassirer construes Rousseau's importance for Kant as teaching Kant that 'the only road to knowledge of God leads through conscience, and that here lies the key to all religious truth', such that 'the only theology either can admit and recognize is ethical theology' (p. 48). The supposed 'reduction' of religion to morality will be discussed in Chapter 10.

'conflict with the arrangements that nature has made for him' and he 'will himself disturb the beautiful order of nature and only be ready to damage it':

> He will have left his post . . . since he is not content to be that for which he is destined, where he has left the sphere of a human being he is nothing, and the hole that he has made spreads its own damage to the neighbouring members. (*Ob.* 2: 216)

For this reason the 'science that the human being needs' is 'that which teaches him properly to fulfil the position that has been assigned to him in the creation, and from which he can learn what one must be in order to be a human being' (*Ob.* 2: 217), where 'freedom in the proper sense (moral not metaphysical) is the supreme *principium* of all virtue and of all happiness' (*Ob.* 2: 212–13).

The human being finds his or her proper place in the creation through the exercise of a freedom that tracks morality. Obstacles to freedom come in the form of 'many external things', including 'his concupiscence' and 'nature':

> But what is harder and more unnatural than this yoke of necessity is the [*crossed out*: dependence] subjection of one human being under the will of another. No misfortune can be more terrifying to one who is accustomed to freedom, who has enjoyed the good of freedom, than to see himself delivered [*crossed out*: under] to a creature of his own kind who can compel him to do what he will (to give himself over to his will). (*Ob.* 2: 230)

The thought of 'servitude' is 'terrifying', involving a 'certain ugliness and a contradiction', as it is 'absurd and perverse' that a 'human being should as it were need no soul himself and have no will of his own', and that 'another soul should move my limbs' (*Ob.* 2: 230). Freedom, in that case, would not 'elevate me above the cattle', but would 'place me beneath them':

> Such a person is to himself as it were nothing but the houseware of another. I could just as well indicate my respect to the boots of the master as to his lackey. In short, the person who is dependent in this way is no longer a person, he has lost his rank, he is nothing but a belonging of another person. (*Ob.* 2: 230)

Even 'a small degree of dependency is much too great an evil for it not to be naturally terrifying' (*Ob.* 2: 230). The 'greatest perfection' for human beings is 'to subordinate everything to the free capacity for choice' (*Ob.* 2: 244–6).

The problem of subjugation has not yet taken its sharpest theological form, as Kant distinguishes between subjection to other humans, which is harmful to freedom, and subjection to God, which is not. Although 'the ground of the *potestatis legislatoriae* presupposes inequality, and causes one person to lose a degree of freedom to another', when the human being is subject to the '*potestatis legislatoriae divinae* [divine legislative power]' then 'he is in accordance with nature' (*Ob.* 2: 222–3). This differentiation between dependence upon human beings, and dependence upon God, is most striking, and will be significant again in further chapters.

It is not hard to frame an initial challenge to Kant's distinction between inequality between humans, on the one hand, and the inequality between God and the human creature, on the other. In setting out this challenge, I do not thereby endorse it. The challenge would run along the following lines. What matters, in Kant's own words, is that 'one must not perform actions from obedience to another person that one could do out of internal motivating grounds' such that it makes '*slaves*' to 'do everything out of obedience where it could have been done from internal motivating grounds' (*Ob.* 2: 222–3). Given that this is what matters, subjugation to the will of God might still seem a form of slavery; indeed all the more so because of the greater asymmetry between divine and human power. Subjugation does not become less severe because it becomes more total. In fact, Kant's thought seems to go in this direction later on in the 1760s and 1770s, when he worries about how a being created by God can be free from divine control. In the late 1770s and 1780s there is evidence that Kant goes back to the thought first expressed here, that there is a qualitative difference between subjugation to other created beings and subjugation to God, where the latter does not damage our freedom, and that, in doing so, Kant aligns himself with a more subtle account of the relationship between divine and human action.

KANT ON CREATED FREEDOM IN *THE ONLY POSSIBLE ARGUMENT* (1763)

In *The Only Possible Argument* (1763), there is an intriguing if inconclusive passage where Kant begins to turn over the issue of created human freedom.[16] The context of this discussion reflects the main themes of *The Only Possible Argument* as outlined in Chapter 3, where Kant limits the role of divine intervention in nature, while supporting the notion that a lawful and ordered nature is sustained by the divine understanding. God does not need to 'correct the course of events by direct intervention' (*OPA* 2: 110), because the 'effects of things' are not 'contrary to the will of God':

---

[16] For a discussion of the same passage (*OPA* 2: 110–11), see Hogan 'Kant's Theory of Divine and Secondary Causation', pp. 18–21, manuscript. Hogan focuses less on the implication for human freedom in relation to God, and more on Kant's (grudging) concession that miraculous divine action might be required in order to achieve certain ends.

The contingent connection of those things depends upon the will of God, while their essential relations, as the grounds of what is necessary in the order of nature, derive from that in God which harmonises most fully with His properties in general. (*OPA* 2: 110)

All the 'changes which take place in the world' that are 'mechanical in character' are 'necessary in virtue of the initial order of the universe and of the laws of nature, both general and particular' (*OPA* 2: 110). At this point, Kant makes a move that would not occur to him in 1755. He makes an exception for 'actions which arise from freedom', which he says possess 'an inadequately understood contingency', in contrast to the 'alternations which occur in the world' that are 'necessary in virtue of the initial order of the universe and of the laws of nature' (*OPA* 2: 110). Such actions, 'in so far as they appear to have about them an indeterminacy in respect of determining grounds and necessary laws, harbour within themselves a possibility of deviating from the general tendency of natural things towards perfection' (*OPA* 2: 110–11).

Kant's following discussion is not entirely transparent. Kant concedes that such 'changes in the world', where freedom is the only example given, might mean that 'the course of nature . . . may, on occasion, run contrary to the will of God' (*OPA* 2: 111). Immediately after this, Kant qualifies this remark:

However, even the forces of freely acting beings are not, in their connection with the rest of the universe, entirely emancipated from all laws. They are always subject, if not to necessitating grounds, yet to such grounds as render their execution certain, albeit in a different fashion and in accordance with the rules governing the power of choice. (*OPA* 2: 111)

Kant points to the 'general dependency of the essences of things upon God', and suggests that this is a 'major ground for regarding consequences as on the whole appropriate and in harmony with the rule of the best' (*OPA* 2: 111). The way in which this seems to work is in terms of global overall outcomes, which can ensure that the 'course of nature' is uninterrupted, even if there is some interruption at a more local level: 'The consequences occur in accordance with the course of nature (and there is no need to be misled by apparent deviations in particular cases)' (*OPA* 2: 111). This means, Kant argues, that 'it is only rarely that the order of nature needs to be improved or supplemented by immediate divine intervention', such that 'even revelation only mentions such interventions as occurring at specific times and among specific nations' (*OPA* 2: 111). Kant takes the example of marriages: 'Contingent as the decision to marry may be, it is nonetheless found that in a given country the proportion of marriages to the number of those living is fairly constant, provided that one operates with larch numbers' (*OPA* 2: 111). Similarly, although 'man's freedom contributes to the lengthening or shortening of life', nonetheless: 'Even these free actions must be subject to a greater order, for, on average, if one operates with large numbers, the number of mortalities stands in a very exact and constant ratio to the number of the living' (*OPA* 2: 111). On the basis of these 'few proofs' Kant suggests that 'even the laws of freedom do not, in respect of the rules of the general order of nature, involve any such indeterminacy':

Such an indeterminacy would imply that the ground, which in the rest of nature establishes in the very essences of things themselves an inevitable relation to perfection and harmoniousness, would not, in the natural course of free behaviour, produce at least a greater tendency to delight the Supreme Being, without the assistance of numerous miracles. (*OPA* 2: 111)

In this section of *The Only Possible Argument* we see Kant putting out tendrils towards a possible resolution of the problem of how to relate God, created freedom, and determined nature. He does this by suggesting that a certain level of indeterminacy at the created micro-level is not incompatible with determined order at the macro-level. If the macro-level order becomes precarious, God can intervene with miraculous action. At the same time, Kant qualifies this considerably, stating that 'miracles will either not be necessary at all or only occasionally so, for it would be improper to admit that such imperfections, needing miracles to correct them, should naturally occur' (*OPA* 2: 112). Elements of this solution can perhaps be seen in Kant's 1786 *Conjectures on the Beginning of Human History*, where events at the micro-level, including 'impulses which are blamed as the causes of vice', bring about progress at the macro-level (*CHH* 8: 107–23), which is taken as a sign of 'providence' in the 'course of human affairs as a whole' (*CHH* 8: 107–23).

Even if successful, this solution addresses only the question of how to reconcile general laws of nature with the 'inadequately understood contingency' that makes up human freedom. It does not tell us how human freedom is possible. Kant says as much, reflecting that at this point in his discussion he is concerned not so much with how free action is possible as with 'the course of natural events, in so far as they owe their necessity to laws which are implanted in them' (*OPA* 2: 112). The central question of how the contingency of such free actions can be adequately understood metaphysically, given that every event has determining grounds that flow from God, has not been approached. It is this problem that Kant struggles with in *Reflexionen* from the 1760s.

In a *Reflexion* from around 1764–8 Kant writes that for significant freedom the human being must have ultimate responsibility for beginning the chain of causation:

In human beings the chain of determining causes is in every case cut off, and thus one also distinguishes what is immaterial as a *principium* of life from what is material. Among human beings the spirit is free and wills the good; the animal is an *automaton*; now if only this spirit would always be efficacious on the animal spirit and not get mixed up with the forces of the latter, we would find more proofs of freedom. (*R* 3855; 17: 314)

Towards the end of the 1760s Kant adds to this reflection:

Liberty is independence from external necessitation. Liberty is either original or derivative. The will however is either sensible or intellectual; it is either animal or free. (R 3855; 17: 314)

Other reflections from the period similarly link freedom, imputability, and the requirement that we are in some sense ultimately responsibility for a causal series, by virtue of being its first cause rather than a caused member:[17]

For freedom I. *spontaneity simpliciter and as such (automaton); independence from subjectively necessitating causes (stimuli)* is required, so that determination can be imputed to the subject as his *actions. (R 3860; 17: 315)*

The free will is as it were isolated. Nothing external determines it; it is active, without being passive . . . *Freedom consists in the capacity* to act *independently of external* determining grounds in accordance with the intellectual power of choice. All sensibility is subordinated to this . . . His power of choice as an animal is really always determined by *stimuli*; yet his will is still free insofar as his reason is capable of altering these determinations of the power of choice. (*R* 3872; 17: 319)

THE SILENT DECADE: THE 1770S

The 1770s are called the 'silent decade', with little in the way of publications in the run-up to the first *Critique*. Fortunately, we can hear Kant's thought clearly in his private *Reflexionen*, and in lecture notes taken by students during the period. Although, in general, notes on Kant's lectures need to be used with some caution, these lectures from the 1770s can with some confidence be taken as a guide to Kant's trajectory of thought: first of all, we have corroborating evidence from Kant's *Reflexionen*; secondly, different note-takers report the same patterns of thought; and, thirdly, many of the issues that Kant grapples with are distinctively his own, departing from his earlier philosophy and feeding into his later thought, rather than being a rehearsal of traditional positions.

There is a knotty interpretative question, which I will avoid, as to whether Kant, beginning in the 1770s and running into the 1780s, has a metaphysically less ambitious notion of 'practical freedom' running alongside 'transcendental

---

[17] For other passages in the 1760s which struggle towards a more ambitious conception of freedom, see the following: *R* 3857, *R* 3858, *R* 3922, *R* 3928, *R* 3929, *R* 3984, *R* 3988, *R* 4000, *R* 4006, *R* 4033, and *R* 4180; 17: 313–445.

freedom'.[18] We can remain uncommitted on this question.[19] Even if Kant does have a metaphysically less ambitious conception of practical freedom up and running, and even if this concept of freedom is sufficiently stable not to collapse into a straightforward compatibilism (both of which are contested questions), what matters is that Kant does *also* insist upon the necessity of transcendental freedom.

In these lectures Kant criticizes his earlier compatibilist analysis of what is involved in human freedom. Kant now insists that unless the actions of human beings are not determined by antecedent states of affairs, there is no proper sense in which our action can be imputed to us. To be free, we must enjoy ultimate responsibility for our actions. Transcendental freedom involves 'absolute spontaneity', with Kant setting out the distinction between absolute and qualified spontaneity in the following terms:

> Absolute spontaneity . . . is self-activity from an *inner principle* according to the power of free choice. Spontaneity is either absolute or without qualification, or qualified in some respect. Spontaneity in some respect is when something acts spontaneously *under a condition*. So, e.g., a body which is shot off moves spontaneously, but in some respect. This spontaneity is also called automatic spontaneity, namely when a machine moves itself according to an inner principle, e.g., a watch, a turnspit. But the spontaneity is not without qualification because here the inner principle was determined by an external principle. The internal principle with the watch is the spring, but the external principle is the artist who determines the internal principle. The spontaneity which is without qualification is an absolute spontaneity. (*ML₁* 28: 267)

The shift in Kant's position becomes clear when we consider that in 1755 Kant could have granted that, although our choices enjoy only a 'turnspit spontaneity' in relation to the divine designer who creates and sustains us, they are nonetheless still fully free. More than this, and as we have seen above, in 1755 Kant affirmed that the very notion of a contingent being enjoying anything

---

[18] Relevant texts, where Kant discusses 'practical freedom', include *ML₁* 28: 255–7, 267; *R* 4225–7; *R* 6067–7; A799/B827–A804/B832; *GW* 4: 446–8.

[19] Commentators tend to divide into three groups on the relationship between practical and transcendental freedom. Subscribers to the so-called patchwork theory consider that 'practical freedom' is a poorly integrated remnant of Kant's earlier compatibilism. See Lewis White Beck, *A Commentary on Kant's Critique of Practical Reason* (Chicago: University of Chicago Press, 1960), 190. Another group of commentators argue that Kant is attempting to articulate a type of freedom sufficient for morality that is not as ambitious or absolute as 'transcendental freedom'. See Ameriks, *Interpreting Kant's Critiques*, ch. 6, and Allison, *Kant's Theory of Freedom*, ch. 3. A third group of scholars consider practical freedom to be identical to transcendental freedom, where the distinction between 'practical' and 'transcendental' freedom reflects our perspectival interest in the question. Our interest is 'practical', where we are concerned to impute responsibility. To do this, it is not necessary to speculate on the metaphysical grounding of such freedom and responsibility. Our interest is metaphysical, where we attempt to articulate the fundamental conditions of possibility for practical imputation. See Wood, 'Kant's Compatibilism', 76 ff.

other than antecedently determined freedom involves incoherence and contradiction (*NE* 1: 397).

During the 1770s, the crisis reaches a particularly explicit intensity. Kant just cannot account for how a created being, in relation to God, can be free:

We can very well understand and have insight into divine freedom, but not human freedom. If the human power were merely intellectual, then we could have insight into his power of choice through reason; likewise if he were a *brutum*. But not as a sensible and rational being, since his action is subsequently a *phaenomenon*, but antecedently a *noumenon* under practical laws. (*R* 4788; 17: 728)

Freedom is the capacity to produce and effect something originally. But how original causality and an original capacity for efficient causation obtain in a created being is not to be comprehended at all. (*R* 4221; 17: 462)

Between 1776 and 1778 Kant describes this as the 'only unsolvable metaphysical difficulty' (*R* 5121; 18: 98), which he attends to at length in his metaphysics lectures:

But it is asked: do the actions of the soul, its thoughts, come from the inner principle which is determined by no causes, or are its actions determined by an external principle? If the latter were [the case], then it would have only spontaneity in some respect, but not without qualification, and thus no freedom in the transcendental sense. If it is assumed . . . that the soul has a cause, that it is a dependent being, is an effect of another, then the question here is: whether absolute spontaneity can be attributed to the soul, as a being which has a cause. This is a difficulty which detains us here. Were it an independent being, then we could in any event think in it absolute spontaneity. But if I assume: it is a being derived from another, then it appears to be quite probable that it is also determined by this cause in all its thoughts and actions, thus has only spontaneity in some respect; that it indeed acts freely according to the inner principle, but is determined by a cause. Now the question is: whether I can think [of myself] as soul? Do I have transcendental spontaneity or absolute freedom? (*ML₁* 28: 268)[20]

Earlier in these lectures, Kant sets out a metaphysics of causation that does indeed make human possession of such an ambitious conception of freedom 'difficult to comprehend' (*ML₁* 28: 270). In continuity with his earlier thought, he writes that all 'necessary universal laws' and the 'connection of substances among one another' consist in their constant dependence on the 'unity of the primordial being' (*ML₁* 28: 215), with God being the source of the determining grounds of all events, including the (problematically) 'free' actions of human beings.

We saw that in Kant's discussion of Rousseau in the 1760s, he does not regard subjugation to God as a threat to freedom, in the way that he does

---

[20] For other passages from the 1770s where Kant struggles to reconcile transcendental freedom with our createdness, see the following: *R* 4229, *R* 4338, *R* 4787, *R* 5440, and *R* 5441; 17: 463–18: 183.

subjugation to other creatures. This no longer seems to be Kant's view. Kant worries that if the human being is 'derived from another', then it will be 'determined by this cause in all its thoughts and actions', and so will only enjoy 'spontaneity in some respect', being 'determined' by a (divine) 'cause'. In another *Reflexion* from the 1770s Kant articulates a similar theological anxiety. He writes that freedom consists in 'complete self activity of the will', such that any determination by '*stimuli* or anything else that affects the subject' will eliminate this freedom, even if God is the determining cause:

> Since freedom is a complete self-activity of the will not to be determined by *stimuli* or anything else that affects the subject, in its case it comes down only to the certainty of personality: that it is, namely, conscious that it acts from its own power of choice, that the will is active and not passive, that it acts neither through *stimulos* nor through foreign impressions. Otherwise I must say: I am driven or moved to act in such and such a way, which is the same as to say: I am not acting but being passive. If God rules the determinations of the power of choice, then he acts; if the charms of things necessarily determine it, they they necessitate; in both cases the action does not *arise* from me, rather I am only the means of another cause. (*R* 4225; 17: 464)

According to this picture, there is only activity and passivity. Although they can both occur in the same temporal sequence, where one occurs, the other is eliminated: 'Freedom cannot be divided. The human being is either entirely free or not free at all, since he can either act from an independent *principio* or is dependent on conditions' (*R* 4229; 17: 467). Kant is clear about the importance of this question, writing that the 'question whether freedom is possible' is 'identical with the question whether the human being is a true person and whether the I is possible in a being of external determinations' (*R* 4225; 17: 464).

By the 1770s, our being ultimately responsible (UR) for our free actions has become vital for Kant, leading him to search—as we have seen in the passages above—for an 'inner principle which is determined by no causes', a 'self-activity from an inner principle', a 'capacity to produce and effect something originally'. There are passages in the 1770s that indicate that Kant also considers the ability to do otherwise (AP) to be a feature of any 'absolute spontaneity' that we might enjoy, although not of absolute spontaneity as such, as God does not have this ability to do otherwise (see Chapters 2 and 3). In 1769–70 Kant writes that if human beings 'were completely intellectual', then 'all of their actions would be actively determined but still free' (*R* 4227; 17: 466). In such a case, human beings would be determined by the law of reason, but still free, as freedom is the capacity of reason to follow the moral law. But human beings are not entirely intellectual: they are 'in part sensible, in part intellectual', in such a way that 'the sensible certainly cannot make the *intellectuale* passive, yet the intellectual also cannot overpower the actions except by a certain measure of preponderance over the sensibility' (*R* 4227; 17: 466). 'If everything were determined by reason,' Kant writes, 'then everything would be necessary but also good. If it were determined by sensibility, then there would be neither evil nor good, in general nothing practical at all' (*R* 5611; 18: 252).

We will see in Chapter 6 that in the 1780s and 1790s Kant distances himself from this explanation of our ability to do otherwise (that we are 'in part sensible'), although he continues to think that we do have such an ability. What is significant for us at this point is Kant's differentiated sense of what is required respectively for human and divine freedom, where human beings have ultimate responsibility for their actions and the ability to do otherwise, but where God has ultimate responsibility without being able to do otherwise:

Contingently preferred actions (the freedom of human beings) are those that are not determined through any rules. Necessarily preferred actions (divine freedom) are those that are determined only in accordance with the rule of the good power of choice. (*R* 4337; 17: 510)

Human beings do indeed have the ability to do otherwise, which incompatibilist analyses of freedom try to protect; but this ability is not necessary for freedom as such, as God's actions are necessitated through the 'rule of the good power of choice'. This will lead us to ask the question below (see pp. 79–84) as to why Kant makes the ability to do otherwise a requirement for transcendental freedom at all, given that God does not enjoy such an ability.

In the 1750s not only were Kant's metaphysics of causation and analysis of freedom compatible, but one led ineluctably to the other. By the 1770s it seems that Kant does not quite know how to reconcile divine and human freedom, except to insist that differentiated versions of transcendental freedom must be somehow accessible both to us and to God. By the time of the first *Critique* Kant considers that he has resolved the issue. As we will see in the following chapters, the answer emerges as the possibilities inherent in transcendental idealism unfold; in a sense, God is not (directly, at any rate), the creator and sustainer of space, time, or causation. This claim has a precise sense for Kant, and is not as theatrical and guilty of Titanism as it might sound: God is still the creator and sustainer of substances, and therefore of us, with our forms of intuition (space and time), and categories of understanding. That said, it is important to Kant that he puts the claim in just these terms: that God is not the creator of space, time, or causation. He is not speaking loosely or inattentively here, and to understand what Kant means will reveal what I argue is a central theological issue in Kant's account of the relationship between divine and human action.

Kant's own solution to the problem of how we can say we are free given that we are created by God will be explored in the following chapters. There should be no surprise that this solution has an irreducibly theological dimension, when one considers that the problem to which it is the answer itself has such an explicit theological form. As we have seen above, Kant cannot understand how 'absolute spontaneity' can be attributed to a 'dependent being', who is the 'effect of another'.

KARL AMERIKS'S 'ARGUMENT FROM RESTRAINT'

Karl Ameriks makes the suggestion that in the 'Metaphysik Herder' (1762–4) lectures, Kant comes up with a 'restraint argument' that 'restrains us from ascribing *all* activity and reality to God', so balancing 'Kant's early insistence on ascribing the *ultimate* source of all interaction . . . to God'.[21] It is important to investigate this claim, because, on one construal of Ameriks's interpretation, it might be that Kant had already found a solution in the 1760s to the problem of relating divine and human action. The relevant section of the lectures is where Kant claims that every action is a mixture of spontaneity and reaction:

> If a substance suffers, then it must contain *in itself* by its own power the ground of the inherence of the accident, because otherwise the accident would not inhere in it. But the ground of this must also be *in the efficient power of the substance*, because otherwise it would not act. Consequently the *powers of the substance are harmonious*. In relation to the powers of the others one contains the ground of the inherence of the accident. (*MH* 28: 51–2)

> *Each subject* in which *an accident inheres must itself contain a ground of its inherence*. For if, e.g., God could produce a thought in a soul merely by himself: then God, but not a soul, would have the thought: because there would be no connection between them. (*MH* 28: 52)

This, Ameriks suggests, enables us to say that it is 'we rather than God who have the thought'.[22] This is true, as far as it goes: Kant hopes to avoid a Spinozistic monism, whereby everything is a property of the single divine substance. Ameriks goes on to say that this is a 'very significant claim', which 'balances Kant's early insistence on ascribing the *ultimate* source of all inter-action, all true community, to God', which means that 'God *cannot* be solely responsible for that which we know is going on just in us and which is, at least in some significant part, due to us'.[23]

Ameriks expresses the 'Restraint Argument' in two ways, which perhaps need to be separated out. At one point, Ameriks writes that the argument tells us that God is not *solely* responsible 'for what we know is going on in us', and at another point that God is not *ultimately* responsible. If by God not being *solely* responsible we mean to indicate that human beings have an identity

---

[21] Ameriks, *Interpreting Kant's Critiques*, 125.
[22] Ameriks, *Interpreting Kant's Critiques*, 125.
[23] Ameriks, *Interpreting Kant's Critiques*, 125–6.

distinct from God, and are culpable for their actions, this is indeed part of Kant's meaning. If this is Kant's claim, then he is shoring up a commitment that he already had in 1755, rather than setting out a new position.

It is debatable, though, whether we can affirm, on the basis of what Ameriks has drawn our attention to, that Kant has found a way to say that God is not *ultimately* responsible for human actions. This would have been an exciting result for Kant, as he might have been able to reconcile (restrained) divine action and human freedom without resorting to transcendental idealism. The problem with this purported solution is that both the spontaneity and passivity remain entirely dependent and *determined* by God. That each substance contains the '*ground of its inherence*' is no less constantly dependent upon the interconnecting ground of the divine mind than any other reciprocal connection. Although not everything is identical with God, it is still the case that God is the ultimate source of all interaction and community. God determines that there is an active and a passive moment in each substance, and determines the grounds within substances that enable them to receive an action. That something happens to or in us, rather than in God, is itself determined by God. Immediately before the passage where Ameriks finds the 'Restraint Argument', Kant repeats unambiguously his claim that God is required for all interconnection:

> To the connection of the things in the whole belong *not merely the existences of things . . .* Thus for a connection *something special, reciprocal action,* is still required. For it is not possible for two substances without connection to effect one another.—For without connection nothing that takes place in A can have a consequence in B . . . their *connection still requires a special ground: a special action still* of the creator, since he connected them. Thus *the state of diverse substances that each acts on and suffers from the others* (interaction) has *a special ground in God,* who *willed that they should depend upon one another. (MH 28: 51)*

Inasmuch as there is any 'restraint', it might serve to explain why there are things in the universe that are not just a part of God; but it does not explain how any of those things could enjoy an incompatibilist freedom. This is the problem that Kant faces. God and the human creature are not identical, and so actions can be ascribed to the creature; but the creature still depends entirely upon God inasmuch as God determines all their actions.

IS TRANSCENDENTAL FREEDOM NECESSARY FOR PERFECT FREEDOM?

We saw in the previous two chapters that, for Kant, God enjoys perfect freedom even though God can act only rationally. The rational factor that matters in particular for Kant is 'the good'. It is a mainstay of rationalist and Kantian thought that being influenced by reasons (rather than causes) does not threaten perfect freedom. Indeed, it constitutes it. Accordingly, if this were universalized for all agents, we could say that an agent is free, if that agent is determined by good reasons. If there are no non-rational factors influencing the agent's decision, he or she is free, regardless of whether or not the agent could have done otherwise, or of whether or not the agent is ultimately responsible for his or her actions. As Derk Pereboom puts it, what is important in Kant's conception of perfect freedom (which will feed into the Kantian conception of autonomy) is that one has 'a capacity to commit oneself to certain principles of conduct as rationally binding, principles that are not adopted to satisfy any contingent desires, but necessarily imposed on oneself as rational agent'.[24]

Given this, a question arises as to why Kant is at all concerned that we are ultimately responsible for our actions, or that we have the ability to do otherwise. It seems that what really matters is the quality of the motivation for the action (that it is rational), rather than its causal genealogy (that it not be causally determined).[25] Pereboom's suggestion is that from the point of view of preserving the possibility of perfect freedom—the ability to follow the moral law—we can have perfect freedom without ultimate responsibility or the ability to do otherwise. Regardless of the success of Kant's proposed transcendentally idealist *solution* (about which, more in the following chapters) to the problem of how we can have transcendental freedom (involving UR and AP), we should question first of all why Kant should be interested in such a conception at all, given what is important to Kant.

Pereboom's observations to this effect are a relatively brief aside in his larger argument. It will repay us to develop this aside more fully, given our theological interest in the emergence of Kant's new demands upon freedom. The challenge is nicely put by Pereboom, as Kant does indeed move from a position where we can enjoy perfect freedom—following the good, and wanting to do so for rational reasons—even though whether or not we enjoy perfect freedom is determined for us by God. The sharp edge of the question is this: why does Kant think that we need transcendental freedom in order to sustain the creature's access to perfect freedom? In what follows, I set out the range of relationships to perfect freedom that might be enjoyed by the creator and by creatures, in terms that could be recognized by Kant. After doing this, we will be in a better position to evaluate Pereboom's suggestion.

---

[24] Derk Pereboom, 'Kant on Transcendental Freedom', *Philosophy and Phenomenological Research*, 73/3 (2006), 537–64 (p. 562). Pereboom is himself drawing on Thomas Hill at this point, *Dignity and Practical Reason* (Ithaca, NY: Cornell University Press, 1993), 76–96.
[25] Pereboom, 'Kant on Transcendental Freedom', 562.

In my formulations below I take the term 'perfect freedom' to cover specific actions: an action is done according to perfect freedom if it is done for the sake of the good, and if there are no non-rational factors influencing the decision. The state of 'being perfectly free' applies with respect to an action taken by an agent. This opens up the conceptual possibility of both uncreated and created perfect freedom.

(1) Divine freedom (DF—uncreated perfect freedom). Divine freedom involves necessarily acting according to perfect freedom (PF); further-more, God is ultimately responsible for all God's actions (UR), where there are no external causes to God. Because God necessarily always chooses the best, God could not have done otherwise (AP). So with divine freedom (DF): PF, UR, but not AP.

(2) Created Freedom 1 (CF 1—created perfect freedom). A creature has CF 1 just if God determines that he or she will always choose to act according to perfect freedom (PF). The created being has limitations (because that is what it is to be created), but these limitations do not impact upon the creature's perfect freedom (creatures could be less than omniscient and omnipresent without damaging their perfect freedom). With such a created rational being (CF 1): PF, but not UR, and not AP.

(3) Created Freedom 2 (CF 2—Kant's 1755 position). A creature has CF 2 just if God determines whether or not his or her actions will be in accordance with perfect freedom (PF). Some of the creatures, some of the time, will be determined by God to act according to PF, and others will not. The creature does not have the ability to do otherwise, and is not ultimately responsible for his or her actions. With such a created rational sensuous being (CF 2): PF or not PF, not UR, and not AP.

(4) Created Freedom 3 (CF 3—'transcendental freedom'): a creature has CF 3 just if God determines that he or she is capable of acting from perfect freedom, but can also be sufficiently influenced by non-rational factors and causes, such that it is really possible that he or she does not choose—at all, or for rational reasons alone—the action that rational reasons would recommend (AP); whether or not the creature acts according to perfect freedom in a particular instance is determined not by God, but by the creature, who is ultimately responsible (UR) for whether he or she acts according to PF. So Kant writes 'the human power of choice is not determined by any grounds. Its actions *could all* have occurred in accordance with reason. Hence it is free' (*R* 4226; 17: 465). With such a created being (CF 3): capable of PF, but also capable of not acting according to PF (hence AP), on the basis of his or her UR.

On only one of these models of created freedom (CF 3) does the human being's ability to participate in perfect freedom (PF) require the ability to do otherwise (AP) and our being ultimately responsible (UR). It is perhaps an interesting and attractive result that the most ambitious aspect of transcendental freedom—the demand for ultimate responsibility (UR)—actually arises because of our creaturely limitations and needs: if we were sheerly rational created beings on the model of Created Freedom 1, we would not need the ultimate responsibility condition (UR) to be perfectly free. Our 'imitation' of aspects of divine freedom (specifically UR) is required because of our distance from divine freedom in another respect, when it comes to our ability to do otherwise than the good. Transcendental freedom arises in us because of a lack and a loss; it is a remedial measure, rather than a crowning glory. Kant seems to indicate something along these lines when he writes in 1783–4 that, 'although the human being...can always decide something else', it is 'precisely this which is a lack of freedom in the human being, since he does *not always* act according to his reason', whereas it is 'true freedom in God that he decides only what is in conformity with his highest understanding' (*LPR* 28: 1068). In a similar vein, in 1786 Kant reflects that the 'history of *freedom*', in the sense of human freedom, 'begins with evil', and 'represented a loss' (*CHH* 8: 107–23). This captures that Created Freedom 3 (CF 3) involves being capable of perfect freedom (PF), but also being capable—because of the AP and UR conditions—of not acting according to perfect freedom (PF). So both the alternative possibility (AP) and ultimate responsibility (UR) conditions arise because of a lack of perfect freedom, where such perfect freedom is enjoyed paradigmatically by God alone.

Where does this put us with regard to Pereboom's suggestion that Kant could have protected perfect freedom (PF), without the twin requirements of transcendental freedom, that we be able to do otherwise (AP), and that we be the ultimate source of our actions (UR)? We can now see that there are two possible ways in which Kant could have explored this possibility: Created Freedom 1 (CF 1) and Created Freedom 2 (CF 2). I deal with each of these respectively.

Kant would find two significant problems with claiming that God could have brought about Created Freedom 1 (CF 1), where God creates rational beings who always choose the good. First of all, in terms of the account of real ₊possibility given in Chapter 2, it might be that such a situation is not really possible, even if it is logically possible. At the very least, we might not be able to tell whether Created Freedom 1 (CF 1) picks out a real possibility. Kant does not explicitly rule on this possibility. In lectures from the 1780s he manages to imply two different positions in the course of one paragraph. On the one hand, Kant writes that 'God could have created beings who, although limited, have "overriding reasons" for choosing the good' (*LPR* 28: 113). If Kant really means this—that is, if the reasons really are 'overriding'—this would suggest that it is really possible that God could have created creatures who are limited, but not with respect to their enjoyment of perfect freedom (PF). On the other hand, in the same paragraph, Kant writes that the 'possibility of deviating from the moral law must adhere to every creature', as it is 'unthinkable that any creature could be without needs and limits. God alone is without limitations': 'If every creature has needs and deficiencies, then it must also be possible that impulses of sense (for these derive from the needs) can seduce it into forsaking morality' (*LPR* 28: 113; see also *LPR* 28: 1075). Similarly in *Metaphysik Mrongovious* in the 1780s Kant writes that 'every created being', no matter 'however perfect it may be', has 'needs which certain stimuli provide', with which it must 'struggle', meaning that a human being does not ever have 'holiness, but virtue' (*MMr.* 29: 898).

Perhaps Kant did not spend too much time on this issue, because, even if the situation envisaged in Created Freedom 1 (CF 1) is judged really possible, a second objection to CF 1 arises. Even if CF 1 envisages a really possible world, it is manifestly not the really possible world that God did in fact create, as it is obvious that we do not always choose the good: whatever the theoretical possibilities, this is the pressing reality. Further theoretical implications might cascade from this, depending on how we interpret Kant's rationalist theology in 1770s and the 1780s. We can run though each of the possible interpretations set out in Chapter 3. On one construal, God in perfect freedom will always choose the best really possible world, and so this world must be the best really possible world that God could create. So, in truth, God could not have created a world where creatures enjoyed CF1, even if such a world is really possible. On another construal, by the time Kant writes the third *Critique*, he considers that the only really possible world is the actual world, in which case a world where created beings enjoy CF1 is not even really possible. Alternatively, we can ascribe to Kant the view that God necessarily creates a world that achieves the highest good, although there might be other really possible worlds that also achieve this. Perhaps one of these worlds could have featured CF 1: but still we come back to the point that it is not this one.

The only two viable options for Kant, when it comes to protecting the possibility of perfect freedom in the world that God did in fact create, are Created Freedom 2 (CF 2—the 1755 position) and Created Freedom 3 (CF 3— transcendental freedom). Created Freedom 2 (CF 2) describes Kant's position in 1755, and Created Freedom 3 (CF 3) describes the position that Kant moves to when he articulates the demand for transcendental freedom for human beings. There is no sense though in which CF 2—the position that protects the possibility of PF without the UR or AP conditions—is a neglected alternative. Kant endorses CF 2 in 1755, but increasingly distances himself from this position in the 1760s and 1770s. If there is a result here, it is perhaps a rather negative one. Having tracked in some detail the passages from the 1760s and 1770s where Kant moves from CF 2 to CF 3, are we any closer to answering the question of what, for Kant, is *wrong* with CF 2, as an account of created freedom?

Pereboom's suggestion gives us a sharper version of the question: given that what matters for Kant is perfect freedom, and given the extent to which Kant is prepared to allow divine freedom to be shaped by rational consider-ations, what, for Kant, is wrong with CF 2? It is not enough to say that what is wrong with CF 2 is that it is not true. This is trivial and question begging, and would provoke a reposing of the question: why is CF 2, as an account of what is required for human participation in perfect freedom, not a true account? As this is a shift in what is required conceptually for freedom to be possible, it is not obviously motivated by any 'discoveries' about society or the physical universe. It is a sheer conceptual shift. Kant does not, for example, discover that not all causal series are determined by God, and then find a new conception of freedom; he first arrives at the new conception of freedom, and then struggles to find a way of holding that not all causal series are determined by God.

I would suggest that the passages dealt with above (see pp. 67–78) give at best a suggestive answer to this question. We have a cluster of reactions, fears, and aspirations. In relation to Rousseau, there is a horror of enslavement, and an epiphany about the dignity of the common man, although our obedience to God does not yet seem to threaten our dignity. There is a concern about culpability and punishment, where, if we are determined by God, we are not ultimately responsible for our actions and not to be held accountable. There is also a concern about our created distinctness from God, about how to prevent everything collapsing into a Spinozistic monism. We might perhaps have expected theodicy to play a larger role: if we can be held ultimately responsible (UR) for wrongdoing, such that we have alternative possibilities in front of us (AP), this would seem to exonerate God from responsibility for non-natural evil. Nonetheless, in the 1760s and 1770s this does not seem to be an important consideration for Kant. Even in the 1750s, when Kant endorsed the broadly Leibnizian principle that God creates the best really possible world (while objecting to Leibniz's formulation of the principle), Kant nonetheless criticizes the application of this principle to theodicy (*R* 3703–6; 17: 229–39). In his later thought Kant is hostile to the project of theodicy as such, finding that it founds 'morality on faith' rather than 'faith on morality' (*MPT* 8: 267). It is striking perhaps that this particular sheer conceptual shift in Kant's thought, so important in the development of his critical philosophy, manifests itself more by assertion and sympathy than argument.[26]

---

[26] This recognition of Kant's lack of explicit reasons for shifting to his incompatibilism perhaps finds a secular expression, when even sympathetic commentators express a wish that Kant had advanced his moral theory within a broadly compatibilist framework, which would not require noumenal transcendental freedom: see Allen W. Wood, *Kantian Ethics* (Cambridge: Cambridge University Press, 2008), 135–41, and Karl Ameriks, *Kant and the Fate of Autonomy* (Cambridge: Cambridge University Press, 2000), 19.

PATRICK KAIN ON THE COHERENCE OF KANT'S ACCOUNT OF DIVINE AND HUMAN FREEDOM

Regardless of whether or not Kant explains the grounds for his conceptual shift, the question remains as to the coherence and justification of Kant's claim, that human beings require transcendental freedom (satisfying the AP and UR conditions). Patrick Kain sets out a defence of the coherence of Kant's account of human freedom in relation to divine freedom. Looking at Kain's defence will help us to identify the sharp edge of a theological problem with Kant's account of the relationship between divine and human action. Kain notices that Kant comes to think that 'human freedom requires that humans can do otherwise' but that 'divine freedom precludes the possibility of God doing otherwise'.[27] Kain puts this down to Kant's concern that if a soul is derived from another, then it is determined by another (ML_1 28: 268). Kain finds that the 'presence of "alternative possibilities"' is 'needed to defend the possibility of genuine creaturely self-control and responsibility in this theological context'.[28] This certainly picks up some of Kant's demonstrable concerns. Kain quotes from Kant's *Lectures on the Philosophical Doctrine of Religion*:

If the human being is to be a free creature and responsible for the development and cultivation of his abilities and predispositions, then it must also be within his power to follow or shun the laws of morality. His use of his freedom has to depend on him, even if it should wholly conflict with the plan God designed for the moral world. (*LPR* 28: 1113)

According to this line of thought, Kain reflects, 'creatures endowed with only one principle of action, were that possible, would fail to meet the relevant "control" condition for freedom and responsibility, and this would be so regardless of the content of that single principle of action'.[29] This has the following result:

The presence of creaturely needs and their significance within a creaturely agent's practical reasoning help to satisfy a necessary condition of free and responsible creaturely agency. For a creature, self-control, agency, and responsibility are made possible by the room left for us to choose our character, to choose to prioritize our dignity and our 'own nature' (or 'proper self') or to prioritize our needs and wants instead.[30]

From this, Kain concludes that 'there need be nothing incoherent in having such a differentiated account of divine and human freedom', as 'underlying both' is the view that 'a free rational agent has the capacity, within its own control, to be an efficient cause, independently of all "alien causes", through its

---

[27] Kain, 'The Development of Kant's Conception of Divine Freedom', 28, manuscript.
[28] Kain, 'The Development of Kant's Conception of Divine Freedom', 29, manuscript.
[29] Kain, 'The Development of Kant's Conception of Divine Freedom', 29, manuscript.
[30] Kain, 'The Development of Kant's Conception of Divine Freedom', 29, manuscript.

representations of the good or of the moral law'.[31] Where there is a difference between divine freedom and 'the freedom of a creature', this is 'a reflection of the way that the requirement of self-control must be satisfied differently in the cases of creator and creature':

> In the divine being, freedom requires, and is thus compatible with, complete and ultimate determination; in a creature such as a human being, freedom requires the absence of complete and ultimate determination . . . How such beings may be thought to coexist raises many further questions that must be left for another occasion.[32]

This question, about how such beings may coexist, is of course the guiding enquiry of this book. Kain's account of the difference between divine and human freedom resonates with a line of thought set out in the previous chapter. There we explored Wierenga's claim that only in the case of God could genuinely free actions be determined by perfect goodness in such a way that God could not do otherwise, as only with God can one be confident that there are no *external* determining causes. God's perfect goodness is an *internal* determination of the divine will. Kain's suggestion is that only with God is freedom compatible with there being no temptation to do otherwise than the good. This is because in God there are no sensuous creaturely needs, as there are with human beings. In Chapter 6, I investigate the plausibility of Kant's account of our noumenal ability to do otherwise than follow the moral law. As Kain correctly says, it is not 'creaturely needs' in themselves that lead us astray, but their 'significance within a creaturely agent's practical reasoning', where the free noumenal self chooses to prioritize these needs rather than the moral law.[33] This will lead to the difficult question of why or even how the noumenal self would make this choice, given that the choice to prioritize creaturely needs is not itself caused by these needs, but by an atemporal free action. At this point I will focus on Kain's ascription to Kant of the view that we need to have the ability to do otherwise, and so be ultimately responsible for our actions, in order that we can be considered to be independent of all 'alien causes'.[34]

THE FUNDAMENTAL THEOLOGICAL QUESTION: IS GOD AN ALIEN AND EXTERNAL CAUSE?

Everything depends on what we consider to be an 'alien cause'. In particular, we need to know whether God is or is not an 'alien cause'. The problem that

---

[31] Kain, 'The Development of Kant's Conception of Divine Freedom', 30, manuscript.
[32] Kain, 'The Development of Kant's Conception of Divine Freedom', 30, manuscript.
[33] Kain, 'The Development of Kant's Conception of Divine Freedom', 29, manuscript.
[34] Kain, 'The Development of Kant's Conception of Divine Freedom', 30, manuscript.

the ascription of the ability to do other than the good solves, according to Kain, is the problem of how a being 'derived from another' can be independent of God. From a particular theological perspective, though, this way of conceiving the problem is itself the problem: it is a version of a mistake that becomes more predominant in the modern period, where divine and human freedom are placed in a competitive relationship, and where the scope of action for one can be secured only by limiting the other.

As we will see in Chapter 9, nearly all medieval theistic philosophers would challenge the notion that God can ever be really *external* and *alien* to the creature. In recent literature, an objection to a 'competitive' conception of human freedom and 'alien' divine action is expressed in the main (but not exclusively) by those who style themselves as theologians rather than philosophers of religion, possibly with a suspicion among the former group that much Anglophone philosophy of religion is conducted with a problematic model of divine and human freedom. David Burrell expresses a typical set of misgivings here when he complains of the 'endemic tendency of philosophers treating divinity to assign God a place in the universe, albeit the largest or the first or the most significant';[35] he writes this in the context of underlining the unique and non-competitive relationship between divine and human action that should arise when we contemplate God's status as creator, where God cannot be an alien cause for the creature.

As Kant's thought on the issue becomes more intricate and nuanced, I will go into more depth on this issue in later chapters, untangling precisely what is at stake on both sides of the dispute. As the first stage in this conversation, in the remainder of this section I set out Aquinas's account of why God— uniquely—is not an alien cause for the creature. Kant is not drawing upon Aquinas (except indirectly through Leibniz, about which more in Chapter 8), but Aquinas provides a theological model through which we can interrogate some of the conceptual options negotiated by Kant.

For Aquinas, human freedom emerges from the proper functioning and relationship between the intellect's apprehension of the good, and the will's desire for the good, informed by the intellect. As Eleonore Stump puts it, for Aquinas, the 'will's relations to and interactions with the intellect are the source of the freedom in the will'.[36] A voluntary act, for Aquinas, is a 'special case of being moved by an intrinsic principle', where 'whatever is moved by an intrinsic principle in such a way that it acts for an end which it cognizes as an end has within itself the principle of its action'.[37] For Aquinas it is 'not an

---

[35] David Burrell, 'Divine Action and Human Freedom in the Context of Creation', in *The God Who Acts: Philosophical and Theological Explorations* (University Park, PA: Pennsylvania University Press,1994), 103–9 (p. 104).
[36] Eleonore Stump, *Aquinas* (London and New York: Routledge, 2003), 285.
[37] Stump, *Aquinas*, 285.

empirical claim but a conceptual one' that 'anything external to the agent which acted coercively on the agent's will would thereby destroy voluntariness', such that 'the voluntary movement of the will' from an 'extrinsic principle' is impossible:

> If something extrinsic to the agent were to act on the will with efficient causation, then the tie of the will to the intellect, from which acts of will get their voluntary character, would be broken, and so the act of the will would not be voluntary—or to put it more nearly as Aquinas seems to think of it, in such a case it would not be a real act of the will at all.[38]

Significantly, for our purposes, Stump identifies that God constitutes an 'exception to this claim about extrinsic principles'. God alone 'can be an extrinsic cause without removing voluntariness' just because God is 'the extrinsic cause creating the will with its inclinations and its connections to the intellect': 'this is the one sort of extrinsic principle which not only does not remove voluntariness but is essential for producing it.'[39]

Aquinas tells us that 'it belongs properly to God to move the will', as 'the will is moved by its object, the good, and by him who has created the power of willing', where God is both the object and source of the will.[40] Aquinas draws out an important distinction, derived from Aristotle, between violent and non-violence causation. Violent causation occurs when something is 'coerced', 'moved in a way that is contrary to its own leaning'. A will that is 'moved by another in such a way' would act 'utterly without self-movement', and would not be free.[41] In the case of God, though, the 'resource within' from which we move of our 'own accord' *can* be derived from an 'outward source', as—uniquely with the relationship between creator and creature—'there is no contradiction between being moved of one's own accord and being moved by another':

> Anything that is moved by another is said to be coerced if it is moved in a way that is contrary to its own leaning. It is not said to be coerced if it is moved by one that confers this natural bend upon it; e.g., a heavy body is not coerced in having a downward pull deriving from the cause that produces it. So it is that in moving the will God does not force it, since he gives the will its natural leaning.[42]

Although 'external' to the creature, God 'acts interiorly in all things', for 'God is properly the universal cause of *esse* [being], which is innermost in all things': 'For this reason in sacred Scripture the workings of nature are referred to God as to the one who works within it. *Thou hast clothed me with skin and flesh; thou hast put me together with bones and sinews.*'[43] When Kant worries about the question of how a being who is 'derived from another' can be free, he takes

---

[38] Stump, *Aquinas*, 285.   [39] Stump, *Aquinas*, 536, n. 49.

[40] Aquinas, *Summa Theologiae*, 1a.105.4.   [41] Aquinas, *Summa Theologiae*, 1a.105.4.

[42] Aquinas, *Summa Theologiae*, 1a.105.4.   [43] Aquinas, *Summa Theologiae*, 1a.105.5.

the view that God is an alien cause on the creature. That Kant takes this view is in some ways puzzling, when one considers his approach to perfect freedom. In Kain's account set out above, we saw that 'in a creature such as a human being, freedom requires the absence of complete and ultimate determination'; but, Kain concedes, this does not extend to the absence of determination by reason, which itself constitutes freedom. If one adopts such a conception of freedom, then the principle is already accepted that something in a sense 'external' to the agent—in that it is not identical or co-extensive with the agent and is not brought about by the agent's will—is nonetheless not an alien or violently determining cause. If the principle of 'external' but non-alien determination is permitted in the case of reason, then it provokes the question of 'why not also in the case of God?', especially given that, for Kant, God and reason are so closely identified. It is trivially true that 'alien causes' or 'external *control*' violate freedom for Kant. The question, when considering any x in relation to freedom, needs to be whether x is an 'alien' and controlling/coercive cause, or whether, like reason, it is a determining cause that itself constitutes freedom. Kant changes his mind, not about whether alien causes threaten freedom (of course they do), but about God's status as an alien cause. Kant shifts from considering that determination by God (unlike, for example, determination by random processes) constitutes freedom, to considering that determination by God violates freedom.

Kain's account of divine action as 'alien' to human freedom is likely to be widely comprehensible and attractive to contemporary readers, unless they have been exposed directly or indirectly to pre-modern philosophical theology, or recent systematic theology informed by such pre-modern texts. The notion that divine and human freedom must be to some degree competitive tracks fairly pervasive intuitions about what human freedom would be in relation to (a purported) divine freedom, where it is 'natural' to assume that human freedom can be present only where God 'backs off' from the creature. The issue is a complex one on both sides, and we have not begun to plumb the depths yet. In the terms set out by Kain above, the objective of the book is precisely to explore 'how such beings', that is the free creator and the free creature, 'may be thought to coexist'.[44]

Before we are in a position to do this, there will be further twists in the tale. In the 1770s, as set out above, Kant seems to envisage our dependence upon God as threatening our freedom. Chapter 8 relays the first twist. In contexts where Kant considers that transcendental idealism has solved the difficulty of the relationship between divine and human action, Kant turns (or returns) to a less competitive conception of the relationship between divine action and human freedom, which theologians might find surprising and attractive.

---

[44] Kain, 'The Development of Kant's Conception of Divine Freedom', 30, manuscript.

5

The Solution

The guiding question of this book is how, for Kant, can it be said that we are free, given that we are created by God? In the previous chapter, we saw that Kant's 1755 answer to this question breaks down in the 1760s and 1770s, as the philosopher moves towards a conception of human freedom that requires us to be ultimately responsible for our actions, and to have the ability to do otherwise.

The solution that Kant moves towards in the late 1770s, and sets out extensively in the 1780s, is that we can be said to be free to the extent that we regard ourselves as intelligible beings, capable of noumenal first causation. 'Noumenal first causation' involves being ultimately responsible (UR) for the series of (determined) spatiotemporal empirical events that appear in the phenomenal realm, in such a way that we are able to do otherwise (AP). Kant's solution belongs in the context of the strand of his mature philosophy known as 'transcendental idealism'. It will be essential for the subsequent discussion to set out, in the opening section of the chapter, what I understand 'transcendental idealism' to involve. I do this in stages. First of all, I set out what seems to be relatively uncontroversial; then I locate myself in relation to some of the more controversial interpretative issues in this area.

In the subsequent discussion in this book, I will make a number of wider interpretative claims about Kant that ascribe to him a position that would be incompatible with a 'Kantian' position, on some interpretations of transcendental idealism. So, for example, I will ascribe to Kant the view that God creates and conserves noumenal substances, and that noumenal substances act and bring about consequences (this latter view is described in the literature as 'noumenal affection'). Such claims would be in principle inadmissible in Kantian terms, if transcendental idealism involves the view that we cannot use the category of causation—in any form—beyond the spatial and temporal parameters of our experience. It will be important to explain in the first section of this chapter why I do not consider transcendental idealism, for Kant, to rule out such claims as inadmissible. In any case, as we will see, Kant himself makes such claims, and we should prefer an exegesis of transcendental idealism that is able to support Kant's application of his own theory, even if on philosophical grounds we might prefer Kant to have framed a different theory.

Many of the difficulties that surround the interpretation of transcendental idealism arise because commentators wish to defend Kant's philosophy, or a strand of it. Where they find some passages and claims that are indefensible or implausible, these are judged to be 'against the spirit' of Kant's wider intentions. My task is made easier by virtue of the fact that I attempt merely to set out what the parameters of Kant's theory actually are, by his own self-understanding, even if we might prefer it to be otherwise. I do this with reference to relevant primary texts, and by drawing upon a well-developed secondary literature. My aim is not to evaluate the epistemic merit or otherwise of transcendental idealism, nor to offer a new interpretation of this doctrine, but to understand how transcendental idealism, properly interpreted, is shaped by Kant's struggle with the theological issue of created freedom.

Having set out the parameters of Kant's transcendental idealism, we will be in a position in the second section to set out Kant's account of intelligible freedom, which involves our capacity to be a 'noumenal first cause'. To do this, I go back again to the 1760s. In Chapter 2 I quoted Kant's claim from the 1770s that 'divine freedom is easy to comprehend', with the difficulty arising in the case of human freedom. This was not always Kant's position, or not consistently so. I set out passages from the 1760s and 1770s where Kant describes a problem in conceptualizing divine freedom. The specific problem is how to conceptualize the ability of a (divine) being to initiate a chain of causes without itself being acted upon, when according to the principle of succession, every change that occurs in a substance requires external action. Kant considers his transcendentally idealist account of space and time in the *Inaugural Dissertation* (1770) to solve the difficulty with divine freedom, which enables God to be an unmoved (noumenal) first cause. A solution becomes available because space and time, and the principles of succession and coexistence that govern spatial and temporal reality, are features of our experience of the world, not of the world as it is in itself. We will see that this provides Kant with a model that he applies to our situation in the first and second *Critiques*: determined causal chains belong to the realm of appearances, which leaves open a conceptual space for transcendental freedom. This is a conceptual space that practical reason will be able to exploit. We will also see that there are parallels between the first causation traditionally ascribed to God, and our noumenal first causation. These parallels help Kant to explain why causal determinism is a complete explanation at the phenomenal level, and why our noumenal freedom can never in principle appear in the phenomenal realm. In the third section I discuss Kant's critical distinction between pure and phenomenal substance. This discussion enables me to dispatch a potential objection that talk of God creating noumenal substances illegitimately projects a pre-critical conception of substance into the critical period.

The task in this chapter is largely descriptive and exegetical: to set out the parameters of Kant's critical account of the possibility of noumenal/intelligible freedom. For some readers this will involve traversing familiar and well-explored territory in Kant studies: on the interpretation of transcendental idealism, the status of the thing-in-itself, and the category of intelligible freedom. Nonetheless, it is essential to set out how I am interpreting Kant's claims in this area, and to orient familiar material to our less familiar theological framework, where we ask not only how freedom is protected, given that the physical universe is deterministic, but how freedom is secured, given that we are created by God. In the next chapter I deal with the claim that the notion of noumenal atemporal freedom is so implausible and/or incoherent that we should avoid ascribing it to Kant in any significant sense. In Chapter 7, I look more closely at the precise sense in which Kant would say that he 'believes' in both noumenal freedom and in God.

THE INTERPRETATION OF TRANSCENDENTAL IDEALISM

The precise interpretation of Kant's transcendental idealism is notoriously difficult. Not everything is equally contested, though, and in the first part of this section I set out some relatively non-controversial and low-ramification parameters for interpreting Kant's position. I move on to more controversial interpretative questions after this, which bring with them more specific commitments.

The Copernican Revolution

In two places in the first *Critique* Kant defines transcendental idealism.[1] The first definition occurs in the first edition version of the 'Fourth Paralogism', where Kant is keen to distinguish his *transcendental* idealism from the 'empirical' idealism of Descartes ('all we know of reality are ideas in the mind'), which Kant fears leads to scepticism:

I understand by the *transcendental idealism* of all appearances the doctrine that they are all together to be regarded as mere representations and not things in themselves, and accordingly that time and space are only sensible forms of our intuition, but not determinations given for themselves or conditions of objects as things in themselves.

[1] I am indebted here to Henry Allison, 'Kant's Transcendental Idealism', in Graham Bird (ed.), *A Companion to Kant* (Oxford: Wiley-Blackwell, 2010), 111–24 (p. 111).

To this idealism is opposed *transcendental realism*, which regards space and time as something given in themselves (independent of our sensibility). (A369)

The second definition is offered in the context of the 'Antinomy of Pure Reason':

All objects of an experience possible for us, are nothing but appearances, i.e., mere representations, which, as they are represented, as extended beings or series of alterations, have outside our thoughts no existence grounded in itself. This doctrine I call *transcendental idealism*. (A491/B518–19)

Again the contrast is drawn with 'transcendental realism', which makes 'these modifications of our sensibility into things subsisting in themselves, and hence makes mere representations into things in themselves' (B518–19). The first passage is concerned with the ideality of space and time, and the second passage with the ideality of objects, but as Allison comments, 'they really come to the same thing, since the ideality of the latter is entailed by that of the former', in that objects, for us, are always spatial and temporal.[2] It is important for Kant to distinguish 'transcendental' idealism from the 'dogmatic' or 'material' idealism of Berkeley ('reality just is a systematically ordered series of ideas'), and the 'sceptical' or 'empirical' idealism of Descartes ('all that we know of the world are ideas in our minds') (*Pr.* 4: 293, 373–5). Kant explains that transcendental idealism is 'formal', in the sense that 'it is a theory about the a priori "forms" or conditions under which objects can be cognized by the human mind'.[3]

Kant himself did not intend transcendental idealism to deliver anything less than 'objective' cognition of space, time, and spatio-temporal objects, although commentators have not always found that Kant is successful here. Nonetheless, for Kant, transcendental idealism is 'critical', rather than 'sceptical', because, as Allison puts it, it is 'grounded in a reflection on the conditions and limits of discursive cognition rather than on the contents of consciousness or the nature of ultimate reality'.[4] Kant writes that his study of 'transcendental cognition' is 'occupied not so much with objects', and with the 'nature of things in general', but rather with 'our a priori concepts of objects in general' (A11–12/B25).

Our knowledge of the world, shaped by these a priori concepts, exhibits, as Hogan puts it, 'non-trivial constraints to which objects *must* conform', if we are to experience them, where we 'could not know such necessity to apply to wholly mind-independent entities' (A26/B 42; A32–3/B49; A48/B65; B127;

---

[2] Allison, 'Kant's Transcendental Idealism', 111.
[3] Allison, 'Kant's Transcendental Idealism', 111.
[4] Allison, 'Kant's Transcendental Idealism', 112.

B166–7).[5] In this sense, Kant's 'Copernican Revolution' is motivated by an epistemic humility about the sort of access that discursive human cognition could have to the world. We do not have a God-like access to things in themselves, delivering perfect, total, and unmediated knowledge of the world. Rather, all our knowledge is mediated through the forms of our experience:

Up to now it has been assumed that all our cognition must conform to the objects; but all attempts to find out something about them *a priori* through concepts that would extend our cognition have, on this presupposition, come to nothing. Hence let us once try whether we do not get farther with the problems of metaphysics by assuming that the objects must conform to our cognition. (Bxvi)

In the 'Transcendental Aesthetic' Kant attends to space and time. Kant argues that only if space and time are considered to be the a priori conditions of all our experience, rather than residing in the world independent of our cognition, can we guarantee a priori cognition of the geometrical form of all objects of experience. This delivers the conclusion, for Kant, that space and time are features not of things in themselves, but of our reception of the world. In the 'Transcendental Analytic' Kant attends to certain concepts that shape any experience of objects—cause and effect, substance and accident—finding that they also are not derived from experience, but are applied by the understanding to our experience. Such concepts are 'self-thought a priori first sources of cognition' that 'contain the grounds of the possibility of all experience in general from the side of the understanding' (B167–8). As with space and time, we could not know these necessities to apply to reality as it exists in itself (B126; B167–8; *Corr.* 11.41).

Noumenal Affection

At this point, we enter an area of some interpretative controversy.[6] Kant repeatedly claims that we are somehow affected by noumenal things in themselves, where the effects (but not the causes) of this process manifest themselves in our empirical knowledge. In Kant's own words, the 'constant contention of the *Critique*' is that

it posits this ground of the matter of sensory representations not once again in things, as objects of the senses, but in something super-sensible, which *grounds* the latter and

---

[5] I am indebted here, and in the following, to Demond Hogan, 'Kant's Copernican Turn and the Rationalist Tradition' in *The Cambridge Companion to Kant's* Critique of Pure Reason, ed. Paul Guyer (Cambridge: Cambridge University Press, 2010), 21–40 (p. 26).

[6] For my account of this controversy, including bibliography, I am indebted to Desmond Hogan, 'Noumenal Affection', *Philosophical Review*, 118/4 (2009), 501–32 (pp. 501–5).

of which we can have no cognition. It says that the objects as things-in-themselves *give* the matter to empirical intuitions (they contain the ground by which to determine the faculty of representation in accordance with its sensibility), but they *are* not the matter thereof. (*OD* 8: 215)

The early nineteenth-century commentator Vaihinger dismissed 'any so-called Kantian with the nerve to assert, in the face of a hundred passages, that Kant never really said that there are unknown things in themselves which affect us'.[7] Plenty of Kantians, as we will see, have found this nerve, and not infrequently out of charity to Kant, as Kant's position on noumenal affection can seem to be flatly incoherent. As put originally by Jacobi, but repeated many times since, the problem is this: how can the mind be affected by 'unknowable' objects, when the first *Critique* limits the use of the categories (such as cause and effect) to that which is empirically knowable, which is to say, to that which appears within space and time?[8]

Two broad responses to the doctrine of 'noumenal affection' have dominated the literature. We can accept that Kant holds to the doctrine, but criticize him sharply for doing so.[9] Alternatively, we can adopt a 'deflationary strategy' where we claim that in some sense Kant does not really mean the claim to be taken literally or in a way that is problematic.[10] Whatever the independent philosophical merits of the deflationary strategy, I agree with traditional commentators such as Adickes and Vaihinger, and recent commentators such as Ameriks, Adams, and Hogan,[11] that it is difficult to sustain as an interpretation of Kant's intentions, in the light of Kant's repeated insistence on the importance of noumenal affection. Fichte was one of the first commentators to suggest that Kant—or the spirit of Kant's system—was better served without the claim that the human mind is affected by unknowable noumena.

---

[7] Hans Vaihinger, *Commentar zu Kant's Kritik der reinen Vernunft*, 2 vols (Stuttgart: W. Spemann und Union Deutsche Verlagsgesellschaft 1881–92), 2: 5, 21.

[8] F. H. Jacobi, *David Hume über den Glauben; oder Idealismus und Realismus* (1787), repr. in F H. Jacobi, *Werke* (Leipzig: Gerhard Fleischer, 1815), 2: 303. See also G. E. Schulze, *Aenesidemus* (Helmstadt, 1792).

[9] This is the approach taken by Vaihinger, *Commentar zu Kants Kritik der reinen Vernunft*, 2: 5, 21, 35, and Adickes, *Kant und das Ding an Sich*, 1. More recently, the charge of inconsistency has been made by Strawson, *The Bounds of Sense*, 235–45.

[10] For early treatments of Kant along these lines, see Beck and Fichte: J. S. Beck, *Erläutender Auszug aus den kritischen Schriften des Herrn Prof. Kant, auf Anrathen desselben* (Riga, 1795); and J. G. Fichte, *Erst Einleitung in die Wissenschaftslehre* (1797), in *Fichtes Werke*, ed. I. H. Fichte, Band 1 (Berlin: Bruno Cassirer, 1906), 543, 598. This interpretation was continued in the Marburg school of Neo-Kantianism: see Paul Natorp, 'Kant und die Marburger Schule', *Kant-Studien*, 17 (1912), 193–221. For more recent interpretations along these lines, see Prauss and Allison: Gerard Prauss, *Kant und das Problem der Dinge an Sich* (Bonn: Bouvier, 1974); and Allison, *Kant's Transcendental Idealism*.

[11] For a survey of passages referring to affection by noumenal entities, see Adickes, *Kant und das Ding an Sich*, 4–12, 28–37. See also Ameriks, 'The Critique of Metaphysics: Kant and Traditional Ontology'.

Kant publicly refuted this service, reacting to a review in which it was claimed that 'Fichte has realized what the *Critique* projected',[12] in that Fichte denied the positive theory of things in themselves affecting the sensibility. About this suggestion Kant writes:

Since the reviewer finally maintains that the *Critique* is not to be taken *literally* in what it says about sensibility and that anyone who wants to understand the *Critique* must first master the requisite *standpoint* (of Beck or Fichte), because *Kant's* precise words, like Aristotle's, will destroy the spirit, I therefore declare again that the *Critique* is to be understood by considering exactly what it says. (*DFW* 12: 371)

We can give a flavour of some of the passages from the first *Critique* where Kant refers to things in themselves affecting us:

How things in themselves may be (without regard to representations through which they affect us) is entirely beyond our cognitive sphere. (A190/B235)

Bodies are not objects in themselves that are present to us, but rather a mere appearance of who knows what unknown object. (A387)

Meanwhile we can call the merely intelligible cause of appearances in general the transcendental object, merely so that we may have something corresponding to sensibility as a receptivity. To this transcendental object we can ascribe the whole extent and connection of our possible perceptions and say that it is given in itself prior to all experience. But appearances are, in accordance with it, given not in themselves but only in this experience, because they are mere representations. (A494/B522)

For the existence of appearances . . . demands that we look around us for something different from all appearances, hence for an intelligible object. (A566/B594)

If, on the other hand, appearances do not count for any more than they are in fact, namely, not for things in themselves but only for mere representations connected in accordance with empirical laws, then they themselves must have grounds that are not appearances . . . the intelligible cause, with its causality, is outside the series; its effects, on the contrary, are encountered in the series of empirical conditions. (A537/B565)

Kant seems to be committed to noumenal affection in two contexts. First of all, the notion of noumenal affection has a role in his theoretical philosophy, where the understanding structures that which is given to us in sensation, which comes to us from an unknown ground. As Robert Adams sets it out, 'the actions that thus determine the content of our experience can hardly be identified with the causal actions of objects of our experience' as 'the latter actions are part of the causal structure supposedly imposed on experience by our understanding'; so 'it seems to follow that these actions are accomplished outside of experience, by things as they are in themselves rather than as they

---

appear in experience'.[13] We know then that there must be such a ground of appearances, without knowing any more about it than this:

The transcendental object that grounds both outer appearances and inner intuition is neither matter nor a thinking being in itself, but rather an unknown ground of those appearances that supply us with our empirical concepts of the former as well as the latter. (A380)

Karl Ameriks sets out a helpful account of why such a picture would seem plausible to Kant:

Kant starts [in early works] by going along with the common thought that there are things distinct from us. Then he subtracts from the intrinsic characterization of those things whatever features turn out not to be able to be consistently ascribed to them in that way. Finally, he concludes *not* that there is nothing, but rather that... 'something or other out there' still exists, and it is such that it cannot in itself have the specific spatio-temporal 'forms' that our experience manifests. There is nothing absurd in saying all this while continuing to believe that distinct thing(s) in themselves definitely exist in contact with us, but that theoretically 'we know not what' they are like otherwise in a positive way... The main point here is that there is nothing in any of Kant's arguments about the ideality of spatio-temporality that ever involves *taking back* the most fundamental aspect of his starting position, which is simply the metaphysical claim that we are receptive to other things and there is something more than our individual finite being.[14]

As Hogan observes, this fits well with Kant's statement in the *Prolegomena* about the mind-independent world that 'it never even occurred to me to doubt this' (*Pr.* 4: 293). In a letter to Beck, Kant expresses his dismay with a sceptical reading of the critical philosophy, which took the view that 'we really cannot know whether anything at all corresponds to our representation (as its object)', that is 'whether a representation really *is* a representation (i.e. represents *something*)' (*Corr.* 11: 395). On the contrary, Kant insists, '"representation" means a determination in us that we relate to something else (the former, as it were, substituting in us for the latter)' (*Corr.* 11: 395).

Whether or not Kant's position so construed is ultimately defensible, Kant's philosophy is not *incoherent* on this point in the way claimed by Jacobi and others. It is true that Kant tells us that 'the pure concepts of the understanding can *never* be of *transcendental* but *always* only of *empirical* use' (A247/B303). Crucially, though, when Kant restricts the category of causation to the empirical in this way, the restriction is relevant to what we can claim to *cognize* (*Erkennen*), rather than what we can claim to *think* (*Denken*).[15] By his own lights at least, Kant's epistemic discipline *does* allow us to think of causal

---

13 Adams, 'Things in Themselves', 803.
14 Ameriks, *Interpreting Kant's Critiques*, 29.
15 Hogan, 'Noumenal Affection', 503–4.

relations beyond the bounds of possible experience. There is an 'escape clause',[16] which Kant is able to exploit when thinking about practical reason. Whatever we think about it philosophically, Kant is quite clear here:

The categories are not restricted in *thinking* by the conditions of our sensible intuition, but have an unbounded field, and only the *cognition* of objects that we think, the determination of the object, requires intuition; in the absence of the latter, the thought of the object can still have its true and useful consequences for the use of the subject's reason, which, however, cannot be expounded here, for it is not always directed to the determination of the object, thus to cognition, but rather also to that of the subject and its willing. (B166n)

In this connection, Hogan draws attention to an important asymmetry between what Kant says about the forms of intuition (space and time), and what he claims about the categories of the understanding (such as cause and effect).[17] In the 'Transcendental Aesthetic' Kant moves from the spatial and temporal character of our reception of the world, to the 'notorious and puzzling' claim that things in themselves are non-spatio-temporal. So Kant writes that, 'if we remove our own subject or even only the subjective constitution of the senses in general, then all constitution, all relations of objects in space and time, indeed space and time themselves, would disappear' (A42/B59; see also A26/B42; A32–3/B49). This has provoked a perennial challenge to Kant's thought, known as the problem of the 'neglected alternative'. The alternative that is thought to be neglected is that the world as it is in itself might be spatial and temporal, or have analogous or isomorphic properties, which our forms of intuition are tracking. We receive the world spatially and temporally, the suggestion is, because that is how the world is; our forms of intuition are as they are, because they are suitable for discerning the structure of the world as it is in itself. I say something about Kant's grounds for denying the neglected alternative in Chapter 7. What matters here is that Kant does deny that things in themselves are spatio-temporal. Significantly, Kant does not draw a parallel inference when it comes to the categories of the understanding (such as cause and effect). These categories, Kant writes, are 'not restricted in *thinking* by the conditions of our sensible intuition [space and time], but have an unbounded field' (B166n; A88/B120; A254/B309).

On this account of transcendental idealism, where we know that there are noumenal things in themselves that affect us, there is still plenty of bite to Kant's critical epistemic discipline, because we also know that we always receive things in themselves through our forms of intuition, and 'through

---

[16] This phrase is taken from James Van Cleve, *Problems from Kant* (Oxford: Oxford University Press, 1995), 137.

[17] In my discussion of this asymmetry I am indebted to Hogan, 'Kant's Copernican Turn', 29.

sensibility we do not cognize the constitution of things in themselves merely indistinctly, but rather not at all' (A44/B61–2). It is still the case that we are in principle unable to cognize any of the properties—either intrinsic or relational—of things in themselves, although we may have relatively uninteresting analytical knowledge about them. Chignell and Stang have argued persuasively that our inability to cognize the properties of things in themselves is symptomatic of a more fundamental ignorance about the *real* possibilities that govern things in themselves, in terms of the real/logical distinction set out in Chapter 2.[18] As Chignell puts it, for Kant, 'our theoretical faculties cannot reliably "track" the "real" or metaphysical modality of things without appealing to facts about experience'.[19] In the terms set out in Chapter 2, when it comes to things in themselves, we cannot know what is really possible, or what is really repugnant. So Kant tells us that, 'to *cognize* an object, it is required that I be able to prove its possibility (whether by the testimony of experience from its actuality or a priori through reason)' (Bxxvin.), where it is clear that Kant has real—and not just logical—possibility in mind (see also A232/B284; *Pr.* 4: 333; *BL* 9: 91).[20]

This promises a coherent way in which Kant can insist on noumenal affection, while also upholding our ignorance about the real modalities that govern things in themselves, as 'the possibility of a thing can never be proved merely through the non-contradictoriness of a concept of it, but only by vouching for it with an intuition corresponding to this concept' (B308):

In a word: it is only possible for our reason to use the conditions of possible experience as conditions of the possibility of things; but it is by no means possible for it as it were to create new ones, independent of these conditions, for concepts of this sort, although free of contradiction, would nevertheless also be without any object. (A771/B799)

The connection of all real properties in a thing is a synthesis about whose possibility we cannot judge a priori because the realities are not given to us specifically. (A602/B630)

In any case, whether or not Kant is *justified* in making a positive and theoretical use—albeit minimal and disciplined—of the category of things in themselves, there is no doubt that he does in fact do so. Our discussion of pure

---

[18] Andrew Chignell, 'Real Repugnance and our Ignorance of Things-in-Themselves: A Lockean Problem in Kant and Hegel', in F. Rush, K. Ameriks, and J. Stolzenberg (eds), *Internationales Jahrbuch des Deutschen Idealismus* 7 (Berlin: Walter de Gruyter, 2010); and 'Real Repugnance and Belief about Things-in-Themselves: A Problem and Kant's Three Solutions', in Benjamin Lipscomb and James Kreuger (eds), *Kant's Moral Metaphysics: God, Freedom and Immortality* (Berlin and New York: De Gruyter, 2010), 177–209; Stang, 'Did Kant Conflate the Necessary and the A Priori?'.

[19] Chignell, 'Real Repugnance and our Ignorance', 136.

[20] For these references, I am indebted to Lorne Falkenstein, *Kant's Intuitionism: A Commentary on the Transcendental Aesthetic* (Toronto: University of Toronto Press, 2004), 43.

and phenomenal substance below treats a particular strand of Kant's theoretical commitment to things in themselves.

Even if one finds the details of Kant's philosophy implausible when it comes to noumenal affection, it is not so difficult to understand what Kant is trying to protect with this notion. Any account of the relationship between mind and world is likely to want to say something about two 'moments' in our encounter with the world.[21] Somehow, in some way, there is a resistance from the world, a giveness to the way things are, which provides some friction in relation to our beliefs about the world. On the other hand, the world is rendered intelligible to us by being received, processed, and interpreted. Epistemologies can gravitate more towards one or the other moment, or attempt to hold the balance. But even a heavily empiricist epistemology that attends to the giveness of the world will say something about how we receive it; and the most thoroughgoing constructivist idealism will implicitly concede that it is a non-negotiable given that our minds construct reality (and that this is not itself an idealist construct). In this case, the 'friction' from the universe takes the form of the insight that the universe is a mind-dependent construct, whether we 'like it or not'. Kant's commitment to the thing in itself can be seen to track the plausible intuition that there is a moment of resistance and giveness from the world; while our ignorance about the shape of the world in itself tracks the equally plausible intuition that we receive the world in a certain way, and our knowledge is always on 'this side' of our conceptual skin, demanding an epistemic humility about the world as it is in itself.

The reader who remains unconvinced by Kant's invocation of the notion of the thing in itself will have even less time for Kant's second positive use of this notion, which occurs in the context of his practical philosophy, and will be of great importance to us in the following discussion. As we will see in Chapter 7, Kant is convinced that pure practical reason can give us grounds to believe certain metaphysical claims that cannot be justified on theoretical grounds alone.[22] In particular, there are two claims of particular interest to us: first of all that as a moral agent, I am free from mechanical causal determinism, and enjoy noumenal first causation; and, secondly, that there is a God, the highest good and *ens realissimum*, who is the guarantor that being moral will lead to happiness. This is consistent with Kant's opening statement that he intends to set 'aside *knowledge* [*Wissen*] in order to obtain room for *faith* [*Glaube*]' (Bxxx). The first *Critique* establishes that theoretical reason cannot know whether or not there is a God, or whether or not we are free, which leaves

---

[21] For this way of conceiving the issue, I am indebted to John McDowell, *Mind and World* (Cambridge, MA: Harvard University Press, 1996).

[22] For this way of putting it, and for the subsequent discussion, I am indebted to Adams, 'Things in Themselves', 804 ff.

the field open to practical reason to exercise its own authority on these questions (about which, more in Chapter 7).

It would seem clear that Kant attempts to uphold both noumenal affection and noumenal ignorance, and that he talks of noumenal things in themselves as (unknown) substances that do indeed affect us. Commentators who are suspicious of such claims attempt to interpret all passages referring to noumena in a deflationary way, claiming that the category of 'noumena' has a merely negative and limiting role, where we consider the object as it is independently of our epistemic faculties, or at most that such language has a merely regulative role, where we proceed *as if* there are noumenal objects, without really believing in such realities. The approach to transcendental idealism that I recommend here is at an advantage, as it is able to acknowledge that there are indeed passages where talk of 'noumena' has a purely negative and limiting role, standing merely for what it is that our experience is *not* of (that is, things in themselves as seen by a reality-constituting 'intuitive' divine intellect).[23] Similarly, such an approach can acknowledge that in places a reference to the 'noumenal' might indeed have a merely regulative role, akin to the advantage that Kant considers can be obtained to empirical investigations of accepting-as-true (for heuristic purposes) that the world is the product of a intelligent designer.

The epistemic status of Kant's claims about noumenal freedom and God is a complex and substantial interpretative issue, which I deal with extensively in Chapter 7. At this point, it is sufficient to note that the negative and regulative uses of noumenal language would be consistent ways of speaking, if it is the case that Kant attempts to maintain both noumenal affection and ignorance. If we cannot know what the real modalities of things in themselves are, then they will play a limiting negative role, shading out the space of what it is we *cannot* know; similarly, the category of the noumenal could also play a regulative role, standing for that which affects us, although we know that we know not how. There is considerably more work to do if we go in the other direction, and use the categories of a merely limiting or regulative concept to attempt to make sense of passages that talk about noumenal affection, and our ignorance of the real modalities of things in themselves. If the concept of the noumenal thing in itself is really *no more than* a way of saying what it is our knowledge is *not* of, with no sense that there is an inaccessible 'fact of the matter' beyond what we know,[24] then it is hard to understand the sense from Kant that there really is *something that is not known* by us, that impacts upon us, and *about which we can make claims that might theoretically be wrong, but that can be warranted by practical reason*. In our discussion of noumenal freedom and the existence

[23] See Allison, *Kant's Transcendental Idealism*, 237.
[24] For the claim that the notion of the 'fact of matter' must be abandoned by the transcendental idealist, see Allison, 'Kant's Transcendental Idealism', 121.

of God in Chapter 7, we will see that Kant seems to be genuinely agnostic on these issues, from a theoretical point of view, while thinking that there is nonetheless a fact of the matter, which is inaccessible to our theoretical knowledge. Deflationary approaches tend to claim that, for Kant, there is no 'fact of the matter' at all on some fundamental ontological issues. In contrast, the 'noumenal-affection-and-ignorance' approach will concede that 'the fact of the matter' on fundamental ontological issues can never be known to us, precisely because there is an ontological fact of the matter that is beyond our experience. The more metaphysically committed interpretation of transcendental idealism is able to cope better with a wider range of Kant texts than interpretations that attempt to deflate Kant's notion of the thing in itself, or to restrict it to a merely negative category. This in itself is a mark in its favour.

Interpretations that work within the parameters of noumenal affection and noumenal ignorance are able to contextualize and place into a perspective a debate as to whether Kant's transcendental idealism is committed to one or two realms of objects: that is, is Kant committed to a distinct supersensible realm of 'things in themselves', or is the language of 'things in themselves' a way of describing the objects of our experience, but abstracted from the epistemic conditions that attach to our cognition of them? Theological discussions of Kant are distinctively, although not uniquely, beholden to this way of agonizing over the interpretative options.[25] Here I agree with Adams that 'the emphasis that has been laid on this question' is 'misleading':

A Kant who would offer us one world instead of two, with things in themselves that are somehow identical with the familiar objects of experience, may have seemed to some philosophers less bizarre, or ontologically more economical. But the issue of identity hardly has foundational importance for the theory of noumena. Any answer to it must be derivative in relation to Kant's more fundamental commitments.[26]

The resolution to this question—'one or two realms?'—is, in one sense, straightforward and, in another sense, impossible to resolve, but for perfectly straightforward reasons. In places it is clear that Kant conceives of phenomena and noumena as the same object, considered as it appears to us, and in abstraction from this appearance: 'the distinction between things as objects of experience and the very same things as things in themselves' (Bxxvii). There is one clear example of identity between phenomena and noumena that will be of central importance to us, and that is ourselves, considered as phenomenal

---

[25] See, for example, Firestone, *Kant and Theology at the Boundaries of Reason*, ch. 2, and Anderson and Bell, *Kant and Theology*, ch. 1. My own earlier work shares this preoccupation: *The Realist Hope: A Critique of Anti-Realist Approaches in Contemporary Philosophical Theology* (Aldershot: Ashgate Press, 2006), chs 6–8. Henry Allison is typically cited as representative of the one-realm interpretation, and Peter Strawson as representative of the two-realm interpretation.

[26] Adams, 'Things in Themselves', 821.

and noumenal selves. Elsewhere, Kant does not seem to envisage an identity. For example, when he writes that 'although beings of understanding certainly correspond to the beings of sense...there may even be beings of understanding to which our sensible faculty of intuition has no relation at all' (B308–9). God would be such a being, as God is not an object of experience, but a supersensible reality that is not identical with any of the objects of our cognition. In other cases—for example, in the case of corporeal spatio-temporal entities such as bodies or trees—we simply could not know whether there was some sort of one-to-one correspondence between the objects of experience and things in themselves. Given our noumenal ignorance, how could we know this? We know that our experience of a tree is somehow answerable to and determined by a supersensible reality, but the mechanism of this grounding is in principle inaccessible to us: that is the whole point, we might say. The claim that there *must* be a one-to-one correspondence between the objects of experience and things in themselves risks violating the very epistemic discipline that one-realm interpretations value so highly.

In summary, I agree with those commentators who argue that by his own lights, at least, Kant thought that a commitment to noumenal affection was consistent with the noumenal ignorance that underpins his mature epistemic discipline. The discussion of transcendental idealism in this chapter proceeds within this interpretative context both when discussing pure and phenomenal substance, and when discussing noumenal freedom. As well as gaining support from this interpretative context, supported by Kant texts already cited here, and ably and extensively defended in the secondary literature referred to, my discussion itself offers further support for this interpretation, or at least supplements the interpretation, helping to fill in some of the stranger textures of Kant's account.

As the various implications of transcendental idealism unfold in our subsequent discussion, we will find that transcendental idealism has three aspects for Kant. First of all, it limits our *knowledge* to the realm of experience, which is the realm of spatio-temporal appearances. Secondly, within those limitations, our knowledge is rendered entirely secure and stable. Thirdly, and of most significance to us, possibilities for thinking open up beyond the boundaries of our knowledge: if the spatio-temporal causally determined series that we experience are features of our reception and cognition of the world, rather than being in the world in itself, then it is possible at least that the way things are in themselves is fundamentally different from the way in which we experience them. Epistemic humility brings both security within its parameters, and a conceptual freedom about that which we do not know.

NOUMENAL FIRST CAUSATION

This conceptual freedom, of exploring possibilities for rational thought that go beyond the limits of knowledge, is used by Kant to develop the concept of noumenal first causation. Whatever the status one eventually ascribes to this conception, it cannot be denied that Kant spends some time developing the notion, and this section documents the evolution of this concept in Kant's thought. I begin with a problem that Kant grapples with in the 1760s, of how God can be an unmoved first cause, when the principle of succession tells us that every change must itself be moved by another. We will see that by 1770 Kant is satisfied that he has solved this problem. The solution is that the principle of succession applies only within the bounds of our understanding, rather than applying to the world as it is in itself. I then show how Kant uses this solution to open up the possibility of created transcendental freedom, where human beings enjoy ultimate responsibility for their actions and the ability to do otherwise. From Kant's point of view, this solution has some elegant features: it enables us to postulate noumenal first causation, while upholding the explanatory completeness of causal determinism in the phenomenal realm, which means that in principle we can expect never to experience such freedom in the realm of appearances. Having set out how this works in Kant's first *Critique*, I review some related passages in the second *Critique*.

The Problem of Divine First Causation in the 1760s

In some *Reflexionen* from the 1760s Kant sets out considerations that are similar to those explored in *Living Forces* (1749) and the *New Elucidation* (1755):

Life is the capacity to initiate a state (of oneself or another) from an inner principle. The first is not a complete life, since that whose state is alterable itself always requires something outer as its cause. Bodies may well have an inner *principium* for affecting one another (e.g., interconnection), also for preserving an externally imparted state, but not for initiating anything on their own. Thus is proven all alteration, all origin of a first beginning, and hence freedom. (R 3855; 17: 313)

The nexus of reciprocal causation needs to be grounded by a being who is not part of that nexus, as 'bodies' are unable to initiate 'anything on their own': here we see at work something like the principle of succession. This being, who is not part of the nexus of reciprocal causes, cannot itself be antecedently determined or grounded, but must be independent of antecedent determination, enjoying 'freedom' as the ultimately responsible source of an action.

Kant struggles with two related problems with such a conception of freedom. First of all, as we saw in the previous chapter, Kant has difficulties accounting for how a contingent created being can be free, given his or her involvement in created chains of causation. Secondly, and more surprisingly, there are passages where Kant seems to be unable to account for how God can enjoy such freedom:

A substance that is not externally determined to produce something that previously did not exist acts freely, and this freedom is opposed to the internal or external natural necessity. It acts from the free power of choice insofar as the causality of the action lies in its preference and is not passive. The difficulties concern only the first idea of freedom, and it is incomprehensible in the case of the necessary being as well as in the case of contingent beings, but from different grounds, because the *former cannot initiate* but the latter cannot *first* initiate. (*R* 3857; 17: 314–15)

It is easier to understand what the problem might be for created freedom, given the antecedent determining grounds that are an intrinsic part of our finitude. But why does Kant also state that there is a difficulty with conceiving how 'the necessary being' can 'initiate'? The answer is suggested in comments that Kant appends to another *Reflexion*:

It is difficult to conceive of a beginning in the series of all things, which everything else succeeds, as a *creation*. It is likewise equally difficult to conceive of an infinite series that has passed. It seems to be false to use the idea *all* of an infinite series, and yet the necessity of the *causa prima* is based on that, for otherwise *everything* would be *causatum*. (*R* 3922; 17: 347)

The *Reflexion* itself, to which this is an addition, reads as follows:

Material principles seem to be: whatever happens, must have a ground. Every successive series has a beginning (and every series of subordinated things has a first member). The former proposition implies the latter: for since the beginning is a coming-to-be or event, there must in turn be a ground for it. The idea of freedom designates a coming-to-be without an antecedent determining ground. The nature of our understanding entails in accordance with this rule that nothing contingent is conceivable without a connection to grounds, and that a consequence (in time) without a ground and an occurrence of something without a connection to its ground cannot be conceived, because then the understanding would be entirely unusable. (*R* 3922; 17: 346)

We have an anticipation of a problem set out in the 'Third Antinomy' of the first *Critique*: how can we conceive of a first cause, given that every event and being must have a cause? The principle of succession, which elsewhere has led Kant to posit a first cause, now jeopardizes the coherence of the very same notion, as it is hard to conceive of something with 'a connection to its ground' where the ground is itself 'ungrounded':

For in accordance with the former ['everything that happens has a determining ground'] in the series of causes determining one another we always see into higher grounds, and in accordance with the latter ['everything had a first ground'] we acknowledge that this series is bounded. It is, however, just as impossible to represent a series of subordinate grounds that has no beginning as it is to conceive how it begins. Nevertheless the proposition that everything that occurs has a determining ground is the proposition that makes an infinite series necessary, the *principium* of the form of all our rational judgements about real connection. (*R* 3928; 17: 350–1)

The difficulty in comprehending human freedom lies in the fact that the subject is dependent and yet ought to act independently of other beings.
The necessary being cannot begin to act, the contingent being cannot act in a first beginning. (*R* 4219; 17: 462)

The Solution to the Problem of Divine First Causation

In 1769, the 'year of great light' when Kant moves towards transcendental idealism, Kant finds the solution to the problem of divine first causation: 'the proposition that all series of subordinate things and all successive series have a first member' is 'abstracted more from the boundaries of our understanding than from the object of cognition' (*R* 3928; 17: 350–1). Here we have an early indication that 'antinomies' in metaphysical thought will be removed by the insight that space and time belong only to the form of our experience, rather than to the world in itself. Although 'the idea of undetermined freedom cannot be thought at all in accordance with the laws of our understanding; it is not, however, for this reason false' (*R* 3988; 17: 380), because 'the *philosophia pura* concerning rational concepts is only subjective . . . the proposition that nothing comes from nothing, and the proposition that everything has a ground, make the same mistake, that they are expressed rationally although they are only empirically valid' (*R* 3988; 17: 380). Kant will remain content with this answer throughout his career: that the problem of whether a spatial and temporal series are bounded or infinite takes on its paradoxical form only when we forget that 'some things hold *obiective* under an arbitrary condition, others *subiective* under a condition given through the understanding' (*R* 4000; 17: 381–2):

These given conditions are appearances (space and time are always the basis). Thus, although if the concepts of ground and consequence were objective, then one of the two propositions that there is a first cause or that there is not would have to be true, since neither of them is objective, both may be true at the same time as subjective laws. (*R* 4000; 17: 381–2)

Towards the late 1770s Kant begins to apply this notion of first causation to human freedom, asserting that our noumenal actions are the ultimate source of phenomenal events, but that they do not 'appear' in the phenomenal world as the first event in the series. A first event in a sequence is still in time, and so not a proper 'first cause', in the sense of being a cause that generates the whole series of events without any determining grounds:

Reason is not in the chain of appearance and is with regard to all of that free with regard to its own causality (the actions of reason themselves are also not appearances, only their effects are) . . . The understanding itself is not an object of sensible intuition. (*R* 5611; 18: 252)

Although the 'actions of the free power of choice' appear as phenomena, 'their connection with a self-active substance and with the capacity of reason is intellectual; accordingly the determination of the free power of choice cannot be subjected to the *legibus sensitivus*' (*R* 4225; 17: 464). Any action that appears in the phenomenal realm is treated 'in accordance with the laws of nature of the human being', but 'we do not thereby cognize them as determined', as 'otherwise we would not regard them as contingent and demand that they could and must have happened otherwise' (*R* 5612; 18: 253). The position that Kant outlines is one where 'reason has influence not merely as a comprehending but also as an effecting and driving *principium*'. Reason somehow 'fills the place of a natural cause', although Kant admits that 'we have no insight' into how it does this (*R* 5612; 18: 253). What matters is that we 'regard future actions as undetermined through everything that belongs to the *phaenomenis*' (*R* 5612; 18: 253). In one of his most confident passages from the 1770s, worth quoting at length, Kant sets out the full shape of 'the solution' of how to reconcile our being determined with freedom:

The solution is this. The interconnection of reason with the *phaenomenis* with which it is to stand in *commercio* cannot be understood at all (they are *heterogenea*). The true activity of reason and its effect belong to the *mundo intelligibili*. Hence we do not know to what degree we should impute. Nevertheless we know that the influencing power of reason is not determined and necessitated by any *phaenomena*, rather that it is free, and (in the case of imputation) we judge the action merely in accordance with rational laws. The actions here in the world are mere *Schemata* of the intelligible [actions]; yet these appearances (this word already signifies 'schema') are still interconnected in accordance with empirical laws, even if one regards reason itself, in accordance with its expressions, as a *phaenomenon* (of the character). But what the cause of this may be we do not discover *in phaenomenis*. Insofar as one cognizes one's own character only from the *phaenomenis*, one imputes it to oneself, although it is, to be sure, itself determined by external causes. If one knew it in itself, then all good and evil would not be ascribed to external causes but only to the subject alone, together with the good and the disadvantageous consequences. In the intelligible world nothing happens and nothing changes, and there the rule of causal connection disappears. (*R* 5612; 18: 253–4)

Noumenal First Causation in the First Critique

By the time Kant writes the first *Critique* he is ready for his confident assertion that transcendental idealism protects the possibility of transcendental freedom: 'For if appearances are things in themselves, then freedom cannot be saved. Then nature is the completely determining cause, sufficient in itself, of every occurrence' (A536/B564).[27] The 'freedom' that cannot be saved, if appearances are things in themselves, is of the 'transcendental' variety, involving the ability to do otherwise, and our ultimate responsibility for our actions:

> Freedom must, in relation to the appearances as events, be a faculty of starting those events from itself (*sponte*), i.e., without the causality of the cause itself having to begin, and hence without need for any other ground to determine its beginning. (*Pr.* 4: 344)

In his discussion of the 'Third Antinomy' Kant describes 'transcendental freedom' as the assumption of a 'causality' through 'which something happens without its cause being further determined by another previous cause, i.e. an *absolute* causal *spontaneity* beginning *from itself*' (A446/B474). In presenting the 'antithesis' to this position, Kant sets out the concerns that he has been grappling with throughout the 1770s:

> Every beginning of action, however, presupposes a state of the not yet acting cause, and a dynamically first beginning of action presupposes a state that has no causal connection at all with the cause of the previous one, i.e., in no way follows from it. Thus transcendental freedom is contrary to the causal law, and is a combination between the successive states of effective causes in accordance with which no unity of experience is possible, which thus cannot be encountered in any experience, and hence is an empty thought-entity. (A446–7/B474–5)

This difficulty is now resolved, as transcendental idealism reveals that such determining chains of causation belong only on the side of appearances, and are features not of the world in itself, but of our subjective but universal reception and cognition of the world. It is the 'understanding' that 'brings the manifold of intuition under concepts and through them into connection' (A305–6/B362). When concerned with series in time and space we are concerned only with 'the exposition of *appearances*' (A416).

---

[27] For other passages from the 1770s where Kant reinforces the connection between transcendental idealism, freedom, and morality, see the following: *R* 4723, *R* 4724, *R* 4742, and *R* 5082. For passages from the 1780s see: *R* 5964, *R* 5975, *R* 5977, *R* 5978 and *R* 5979. For an extensive treatment of the role played by freedom in Kant's defence of transcendental idealism, see Desmond Hogan 'Three Kinds of Rationalism and the Non-Spatiality of Things in Themselves', and 'How to Know Unknowable Things in Themselves'.

As we saw above (p. 103), within the limits of experience our knowledge is placed upon a secure footing, by virtue of the insight that we experience the world not as it is in itself, but as it is received by our spatio-temporal forms of intuition. While securing our knowledge within these boundaries, Kant's transcendental idealism opens up the possibility that the world as it is in itself is quite different from the world as we experience it. We cannot *know* about that which is not an appearance, but which lies beyond and behind appearances; but it is at least possible that there is behind appearances that which grounds appearances, but which is not itself subject to the determining chains of causation. Such a being would be an unconditioned cause of causation, a genuine first mover in a theological sense. It is just such a possibility that Kant considers we are warranted in exploiting, in order to be able to ascribe transcendental freedom to human beings, although 'among *appearances*' understanding 'does not permit' us the notion of a 'condition that is itself empirically unconditioned' (A531/B559):

If an intelligible condition, which therefore does not belong to the series of appearances as a member, may be thought for a conditioned (in appearance), without thereby interrupting in the least the series of empirical conditions, then such a condition could be admitted as *empirically unconditioned*, in such a way that no violation of the empirically continuous progress would occur anywhere. (A531/B559n)

Such an intelligible self would enjoy 'freedom in the cosmological sense', the faculty of 'beginning a state *from itself*', the 'causality of which does not in turn stand under another cause determining it in time in accordance with the law of nature' (A533/B561).

Kant explains how our being determined according to our phenomenal appearance would be compatible with our noumenal freedom. As Allen Wood puts it, the picture that emerges is one where our 'empirical causality regarding human actions is an effect of intelligible causality, which (on the theory Kant is proposing) is transcendentally free'.[28] With respect to phenomenal appearances, the 'law of nature' holds that 'everything that happens has a cause', and so that 'all occurrences are empirically determined in a natural order' (A543/B571). So human beings regarded as 'appearances in the world of sense' are to that extent 'also one of the natural causes whose causality must stand under empirical laws', and 'like all other natural things' the human being must have 'an empirical character' (A546/B574). As this 'empirical character' is 'drawn from appearances as effect', if 'we could investigate all the appearances of his power of choice down to their basis, then there would be no human action that we could not predict with certainty, and recognize as necessary given its

---

[28] Wood, 'Kant's Compatibilism', 86.

preceding conditions' (A549/B577), so that 'in regard to this empirical character there is no freedom' (A550/B578).

Only if we 'give in to the deception of transcendental realism' do we conclude from this that 'there is solely a chain of causes' (A543/B571). Transcendental idealism ensures that it is 'possible to regard the same occurrence, which on the one hand is a mere effect of nature, as on the other hand an effect of freedom' (A543/B571). According to this conception, 'the causality of reason in the intelligible character *does not arise* or start working at a certain time in producing an effect' and is 'not subject to the conditions of the temporal sequence' (A551/B579), which enables us to see that, 'if reason can have causality in regard to appearances, then it is a faculty *through* which the sensible condition of an empirical series of effects first begins' (A552/B580).

We saw above that Kant works out this solution first of all with respect to God's relationship to spatial and temporal series; his solution with respect to human beings has some parallel features. So the 'first cause' in a theological sense is *not* the first temporal cause in a sequence, but the unconditioned cause of the whole sequence, which is equally present to each part of the series. Even an infinite series—as Kant himself argues, following the theological tradition, mediated to him through Baumgarten—needs a first cause in the latter sense (ML_1 28: 198–9).[29] Equally a first temporal cause of a series, where there is one, is conditioned by the unconditioned timeless cause. Furthermore, because the unconditioned first cause is quite distinct from the temporal first cause in a series, it does not appear at any particular point in the series, but underlies and sustains the whole of it.

Kant does not understand the relationship between our noumenal/intelligible selves (the first cause), and our empirical selves (the caused series) in terms of a domino model: a one-off first cause that unleashes a series of events in time, whereby more distant events become increasingly remote from the first cause. The first cause of our intelligible action—as with originary timeless divine causation—is just as effective and present at every stage of the temporal sequence. Each stage of the temporal empirical sequence depends equally and constantly on our intelligible (noumenal) action. Just such a conception of the omnipresence of our timeless intelligible action is articulated by Kant in passages such as the following:

Reason is thus the persisting condition of all voluntary actions under which the human being appears. Even before it happens, every one of these actions is determined beforehand in the empirical character of the human being. In regard to the intelligible character, of which the empirical is only the sensible schema, no *before* or *after* applies, and every action, irrespective of the temporal relation in which it stands to other

---

[29] Alexander Baumgarten, *Metaphysika*, 4th edn (Halle: Carl Hermann Hemmerde, 1757), §380.

appearances, is the immediate effect of the intelligible character of pure reason. (A553–4/B581)

For this reason, intelligible freedom can never *appear* in the determined chain of cause and effect, although it does ground the entirety of the appearances that constitute the determined chains of cause and effect. The invisibility of freedom is a theme that Kant returns to repeatedly.[30] If a 'transcendental faculty of freedom' is to be 'conceded', then such a faculty would 'have to be outside the world', 'in order to begin alterations in the world' (A451/B479); if this faculty were to be ascribed to phenomenal substances, 'nature could hardly be thought any longer, because the laws of the latter would be cease-lessly modified' rendering 'confused and disconnected' the 'play of appear-ance' that 'in accordance with mere nature would be regular and uniform' (A451/B479). In the 'temporal succession' all natural causes 'are themselves in turn effects, which likewise presuppose their causes in the time-series', and an '*original* action, through which something happens that previously was not, is not to be expected from the causal connection of appearances' (A544/B572).

It is because the intelligible cause operates outside the chains of nature entirely that natural patterns of causation for all empirical events are left undisturbed. There is a certain elegance to Kant's solution here: the solution made possible by transcendental idealism is noumenal first causation. If this solution is accepted (the sense in which it is 'accepted' is explored further in Chapter 7), then we would indeed expect never to experience or observe noumenal first causation. The very thing that was previously conceived of as a threat to our freedom—our experience of unrelenting and unremitting series of causes—becomes what we would expect if we were free. If freedom is possible, it will be invisible.

Noumenal First Causation in the Second Critique

In the second *Critique* Kant further unfolds the relationship between freedom and transcendental idealism, highlighting the role of God in this relationship. Kant draws out the relationship between freedom and transcendental idealism along the lines set out in the first *Critique*, commenting that in order to resolve the 'apparent contradiction between the mechanism of nature and freedom in one and the same action', one must 'recall what was said in the *Critique of Pure Reason*':

---

[30] As well as the passages discussed here, see also *R* 4548, *R* 5413, *R* 5441, *R* 5608, *R* 5612–14, *R* 5616, *R* 5618–19, and *R* 5978.

Natural necessity which cannot coexist with the freedom of the subject attaches merely to the determinations of a thing which stands under conditions of time and so only to the determinations of the acting subject as appearance. (*CPrR.* 5: 97)

The 'very same subject' considering himself as a 'thing in itself' will view 'his existence *insofar as it does not stand under the conditions of time*', and regard 'himself a determinable only through laws that he gives himself by reason':

In this existence of his nothing is, for him, antecedent to the determination of his will, but every action . . . is to be regarded in the consciousness of his intelligible existence as nothing but the consequence and never as the determining ground of his causality as a *noumenon.* (*CPrR.* 5: 97–8)

A little further on, God is drawn into the discussion. Kant comments that, even 'after all the foregoing has been agreed to', there is a 'difficulty' that 'threatens freedom with complete destruction' (*CPrR.* 5: 100). The difficulty is God:

That is to say: if it is granted us that the intelligible subject can still be free with respect to a given action, although as a subject also belonging to the sensible world, he is mechanically conditioned with respect to the same action, it nevertheless seems that, as soon as one admits that *God* as universal original being *is the cause also of the existence of substance* . . . one must admit that a human being's actions have their determining ground in *something altogether beyond his control*, namely in the causality of a supreme being which is distinct from him and upon which his own existence and the entire determination of his causality absolutely depend. (*CPrR.* 5: 100–1)

Kant is convinced that 'regarding space and time as determinations belonging to the existence of things' would also lead to a 'fatalism of actions' (*CPrR.* 5: 102), where the 'last and highest' source of the 'long series' of 'determining causes' is 'found entirely in an alien hand' (*CPrR.* 5: 101).

The solution is again transcendental idealism, as this 'difficulty' presents itself only when we make the transcendentally realist assumption that 'existence determinable in time and space is held to be the existence of things in themselves' (*CPrR.* 5: 100). There is a lot going on here in these sections of the second *Critique*, which I will explore further in Chapter 8. As we will see, Kant thinks that transcendental idealism enables us to speak unproblematically of our dependence upon God; he also considers himself to have an independent theological argument for transcendental idealism from divine impassibility.

PURE AND PHENOMENAL SUBSTANCE

A potential criticism of my reading of Kant might involve the accusation that I illegitimately project a pre-critical conception of substance into the critical period. Talk of noumenal substances that are created by God would seem to be just the sort of substantive and speculative metaphysical claim that Kant's critical thought makes impossible. Such a concern is ambiguous between two sorts of claim: that this is the sort of talk that ought to have been abandoned, by the lights of Kant's own better judgement; or that, as a matter of fact, Kant did in fact abandon such talk, so that any references to 'substance' have to be reinterpreted as references to the phenomenal substances that make up the realm of appearances.

The first more normative claim, that Kant ought to have given up such talk, depends upon what one thinks Kant's critical discipline amounts to. We note that the interpretation of transcendental idealism recommended above (pp. 92–104) would expect and condone Kant's references to a noumenal category of 'substance', which we know must exist, because all properties must inhere in a substance, while knowing that we can never experience substance in the noumenal sense, just because we can only experience phenomenal properties.

In any case, we can give a more emphatic response to the second claim: that Kant as a matter of fact does not talk in the critical period about noumenal substances as created by God. Whatever we think about it, Kant does in fact talk in this way. In the second *Critique*, Kant writes that '*God* as universal original being *is the cause of the existence of substances*' (*CPrR.* 5: 100). It becomes immediately clear that Kant means that God is the creator of substances, *rather* than of appearances, as he goes onto claim that 'it would be a contradiction to say that God is the creator of appearances' (*CPrR.* 5: 102). This is a claim that I will investigate fully in Chapters 8 and 9. What is significant for us here is that Kant must mean by 'substance' something that is *not* an appearance. In this section I explicate what this conception of substances amounts to, and how it relates to the 'critical discipline' of Kant's mature epistemology.

I present a range of passages from his critical work where Kant employs a notion of substance that is in continuity with his pre-critical thought, which runs alongside the new critical usage of 'phenomenal substance', and which Kant explicitly defends and disciplines in the light of this critical usage. I then set out passages where Kant applies this distinction to our selves, and where he identifies the concept of 'pure substance' with intelligible/noumenal substances. In the 'Paralogisms' of the first *Critique*, Kant demolishes the claims of rational psychology to establish that we have immortal and immaterial souls. I agree with commentators such as Ameriks and Wuerth that although Kant 'clearly rejects the rationalists' conclusions' about the soul,[31] he does so

---

[31] Ameriks, *Kant's Theory of Mind*, chs 6–7; and Wuerth, 'The Paralogisms of Pure Reason'. I am indebted to Ameriks and Wuerth in the following discussion of the noumenal self.

on a fairly narrow front. As Wuerth argues, Kant 'himself believes that the soul is a simple, identical substance in on ontologically significant sense';[32] what Kant objects to is the way in which rationalists put this to use, in order to establish theoretical knowledge about the immortality of the soul. We will see that the fundamental distinction between noumenal and phenomenal selves is vindicated rather than challenged in the 'Paralogisms', and in other texts from the 1780s and 1790s.

Schematized and Unschematized Conceptions of Substance

In a range of passages from the critical period Kant clearly uses the term 'substance' to represent intelligible objects.[33]

The substantial is the thing in itself and unknown. (*R* 5292; 18: 145)[34]

That which is as such (in all respects) (in itself, not logically) the subject, the last subject, and which does not as a predicate further presuppose another subject, is substance. (*R* 5295; 18: 145)[35]

The pure concept of substance would mean simply a something that can be thought only as subject, never as predicate of something else. (A147/B186)

Substances in general must have some intrinsic nature, which is therefore free from all external relations. (A274/B330)

We begin with the category of substance, whereby a thing in itself is represented. (A344/B402)[36]

Substance is the first subject of all inhering accidents . . . Of no thing can we intuit the substrate and the first subject. (*ML₁* 28: 226)

This pure unschematized concept of substance has no application in experience (A147/B186). The concept can be applied only to experience when it is mediated through time (and space as an aspect of our temporal experience of external phenomenal objects), which constitutes the 'phenomenal' concept of substance:

---

[32] Wuerth, 'The Paralogisms of Pure Reason', 210.

[33] In this discussion of the distinction between pure and phenomenal substance I am indebted to Michael Radner, 'Substance and Phenomenal Substance', in Kenneth F. Barber and Jorge J. E. Gracia (eds), *Individuation and Identity in Early Modern Philosophy* (Albany, NY: State University of New York Press, 1994), 245–66; and Langton, *Kantian Humility*, ch. 3.

[34] My translation.

[35] My translation.

[36] My translation. Curiously, this line is not translated in the Cambridge edition: 'so werden wir . . . hier von der Kategorie der Substanz anfangen, dadurch ein Ding an sich selbst vorgestellt wird' (A344/B402).

The schema of substance is permanence of the real in time, that is, the representation of the real as a substratum of empirical determination of time in general, and so as enduring when all else changes. (A143/B183)

With that which is called substance *in appearance* things are not as they would be with a thing in itself which one thought through pure concepts of the understanding. The former is not an absolute subject, but only a persisting image of sensibility, and it is nothing but intuition, in which nothing unconditioned is to be encountered anywhere. (A525–6/B553–4)

In the realm of appearances, 'phenomenal substance' represents the 'enduring' in that which appears, the 'substratum of all change' (A182/B224). In the 1790s Kant tells us that we should distinguish an explanation that pertains to 'the intelligible world', where we 'understand by substances things as they are in themselves', from an explanation that pertains to the 'sensible world', where we 'understand by substances the perduring in appearances' (*MMr.* 29: 849).

Michael Radner is correct in saying that 'the original substance concept is now distributed over both sides of the appearance/thing-in-itself distinction'.[37] When applied to things in themselves, 'substance' represents the 'absolute subject, the last subject', which does not 'as predicate further presuppose another subject' (*R* 5295; 18: 145); in the realm of appearances, 'phenomenal substance' describes that which has 'permanence and temporal causality'.[38] Kant informs us that the latter is not properly speaking 'substantial', in the sense of not presupposing another subject: 'a phenomenon that is a substratum for other phenomena is not thereby a substance, or is only a substance comparatively speaking' (*R* 5312).

Right into the 1790s Kant has no hesitation linking the category of 'substance' with the notion of noumenal things in themselves:

A phenomenon is in itself no substance, with respect to our senses we call the appearance of substance itself substance. But this phenomenal substance must have a noumenon as substrate. This can be called transcendental idealism. (*MD* 28: 682)

Notable here is that the concept of substance as noumenon is explicitly defended as an aspect of transcendental idealism. We cannot cognize the noumenal substance, or know much more about it than that it exists, as 'all substances are cognized by us' and can only be 'considered as they can be determined in space and time' (*MV* 29: 1005). In the passage above Kant says that 'phenomenal substance must have a noumenon as substrate'. This is not untypical of the way in which Kant speaks about noumenal substances: as something that we presuppose must exist, but about which we can know very little, except for analytical truths, and that every appearance is in some way the effect of a noumenal substance.

---

[37] Radner, 'Substance and Phenomenal Substance', 251.
[38] Radner, 'Substance and Phenomenal Substance', 251.

The Noumenal Self as Unschematized Substance

In numerous texts Kant relates the notion of the self, as a thing in itself, to the category of noumenal substance. In the first *Critique* Kant distinguishes the human being considered as noumenon from the phenomenal self:

This intelligible ground [the noumenal self] does not touch the empirical questions at all, but may have to do merely with thinking in the pure understanding; and, although the effects of this thinking and acting of the pure understanding are encountered among appearances, these must nonetheless be able to be explained perfectly from their causes in appearance, in accord with natural laws, by following its merely empirical character as the supreme ground of explanation; and the intelligible character, which is the transcendental cause of the former, is passed over as entirely unknown, except insofar as it is indicated through the empirical character as only its sensible sign. (A545–6/B573–4)

Although the human being is 'in one part phenomenon', in another part, 'in regard to certain faculties he is a merely intelligible object' (A546–7/B574–5). Wuerth draws attention to the unique nature of our relationship with the noumenal thing-in-itself that is ourself: 'in our relation to all other things . . . we deal only with the *effects* of the things on us, which as such are coloured by our manner of actively receiving these effects'.[39] This is the familiar conceptual space carved out by transcendental idealism. In 'only one case', that is, 'our relation to ourselves, we stand in the relation to an existing thing of *being* the thing in itself'.[40] The conceptual thinkability of ourselves as noumenal substances does not, though, give us any determinate knowledge about ourselves as noumenal substances.

This reading is consistent with the progression of ideas that Kant sets out in the 'Paralogisms', where Kant critiques the ambition of rational psychology to derive knowledge of an immaterial and immortal soul, from the claim that the soul is—in a less metaphysically freighted sense—a simple substance. Kant defines a 'paralogism' as 'an inference that is false as far as its form is concerned', but that is 'correct' with respect to 'its matter (the major premise)' (R 5552; 18: 218–21). The 'I think', Kant says, is the 'sole text' of rational psychology (A343/B401). This enables a legitimate application of the concept of substantiality with reference to the self:

That the representation of which is the *absolute subject* of our judgements, and hence cannot be used as the determination of another thing, is *substance*. I, as a thinking being, am the *absolute subject* of all my possible judgements, and this representation of Myself cannot be used as the predicate of any other being. (A348)

---

[39] Wuerth, 'The Paralogisms of Pure Reason', 222.
[40] Wuerth, 'The Paralogisms of Pure Reason', 222.

Using the category of substance for talking of the self, as the 'constant logical subject of thinking' (A350), is not itself mistaken. One can 'quite well allow the proposition *the soul is substance* to be valid' (A350), as long as we realize that it 'cannot teach us any of the usual conclusions of the rationalist doctrine of the soul', such as 'the everlasting duration of the soul through all alterations', even 'the human being's death' (A350–1). When we do this, we in fact use categories that pertain to the phenomenal concept of substance, and so ascribe 'outer appearances to a transcendental object'; although this substance is the 'cause of this species of representations', it is a 'cause' with which 'we have no acquaintance at all, nor will we ever get a concept of it' (A393). As Kant explains in the *Prolegomena*, the self as absolute subject 'cannot be itself a predicate of any other thing; but just as little can it be a determinate concept of an absolute subject' (*Pr.* 4: 334).

As Wuerth explains, by 'determinate concept' Kant means a concept such that 'of at least one pair of opposed predicates, one of the predicates in the pair is included in the concept to the exclusion of the other'.[41] A concept is 'thoroughly determinate' when it 'includes one predicate from each of all possible pairs of opposed predicates' (A358/B314).[42] In order to have a determinate concept we need to experience an object under the forms of space and time. It is part of our human cognitive condition that 'understanding and sensibility can determine an object only in combination' (A358/B314). The same epistemological restraints apply to our experience of ourselves, as 'the inner intuition, in which alone my existence can be determined, is sensible' (Bxln.). Any intuition of myself is mediated through the forms of space and time, 'through which I determine this thought' (B158).

When these restraints are violated, the rationalist makes the mistake of using empirical and phenomenal concepts to make claims about our noumenal substantiality, arriving at 'flawed, inflated', and 'determined versions' of the claim that I am a simple substance.[43] The rationalist begins with the claim that, 'as thinking being (soul), I am *substance*' (A348), but incorrectly infers from this the determinate claim that 'I, as a thinking being, *endure* for myself, that naturally *I neither arise* nor *perish*' (A349), and that I am simple (without parts) (A351–61), a continuous person over time (A362–6), and identical with an immaterial mind, rather than a body (A367–80).

In the 'Transcendental Aesthetic' Kant considers that he has 'undeniably proved that bodies are mere appearances of our outer sense, and not things in themselves' (A358). It is because of this 'we can rightfully say that our thinking subject is not corporeal', in that 'it could not be an appearance in space'

---

[41] Wuerth, 'The Paralogisms of Pure Reason', 213. In this paragraph I am indebted to Wuerth's formulation of the issue.

[42] Wuerth, 'The Paralogisms of Pure Reason', 213.

[43] Wuerth, 'The Paralogisms of Pure Reason', 230.

(A357). We are permitted to speak of a 'Something that grounds outer appearances', a 'Something, considered as noumenon (or better, as transcendental object)' (A358), and we can know that 'this Something is not extended, not impenetrable, not composite, because these predicates pertain only to sensibility and its intuition':

These expressions, however, do not give us cognition of what kind of object it is, but only that, since it is considered in itself...these predicates of outer appearances cannot be applied to it. (A358–9)

As long as claims are put in this negative key, where we know what the self as a 'noumenal Something' *cannot* be, then a series of further insights follow. It is because of what we know that the soul is not that we need not be troubled by the relationship between matter and soul/mind. Both matter and 'inner sense' (A379) are differences in the modes of appearance, rather than differences in things-in-themselves, and the '*transcendental* object' that 'grounds both outer appearances and inner intuition is neither matter nor a thinking being in itself, but rather an unknown ground of those appearances that supply us with our empirical concepts of the former as well as the latter' (A 379–80). Matter, therefore, is not a distinct type of substance from mind, but is itself a phenomenal appearance (A385), no more nor less an appearance than the 'inner sense' of our thinking. The 'expression that only souls (as a particular species of substances) think' should be dropped and instead it should 'be said, as usual, that human beings think', that is 'the same being that as outer appearance is extended is inwardly (in itself) a subject' (A359). This offers Kant a 'liberation' (A388) from the problem that arises when our souls are thought to be bound up in mechanical chains of causation: bodies are not objects in themselves, but 'a mere appearance of who knows what unknown object' (A387). If matter is not a thing in itself, Kant reasons, dualism is not possible, thus avoiding both a souless materialism and a 'spiritualism' (B420–1). Mind–body dualism is ruled as inadmissible, in that it claims to have cognition about 'the constitution of our soul', where we claim to know that the soul has a 'separate existence' to that which grounds matter (B420).

Even here, in one of the most critical and challenging passages of the first *Critique* for using the notion of substance to talk about our 'noumenal selves', we find that the limitations on our knowledge about the 'soul' occur within a precisely delineated account of what we can *know* is not true about ourselves considered noumenally. Our ignorance has a shape, and there are limitations to our ignorance as well as to our knowledge. We *know* that certain things are not true of ourselves considered noumenally, and that we can acknowledge our non-negotiable rational need to employ the category of ourselves *qua* not being an appearance. Given this, certain assumptions about the self as noumenal substance become theoretically permissible, and will become required after practical reason has done its work (about which, more in Chapter 7). The

'Paralogisms' do not challenge our central claim that Kant continues to employ a category of noumenal substance, which has some continuity with his pre-critical usage, within the restraints of his epistemic discipline.[44]

At the head of this section, I asked what exactly Kant has in mind when he writes that '*God* as universal original being *is the cause of the existence of substances*' (*CPrR*. 5: 100), when it is clear in what follows that Kant does not mean 'phenomenal substances'. In the first section of the chapter (pp. 92–103) I argued that it is consistent with Kant's own understanding of his epistemic discipline to permit talk of noumenal affection, without implying theoretical knowledge of what this involves, and without importing spatial and temporal categories into the intelligible realm. In a parallel way, Kant can speak of God 'causing' the existence of substances, without implying theoretical knowledge of this causation, and without importing spatial and temporal categories into the intelligible realm. In 1797 Kant offers an explicit reflection along these lines. Kant concedes that there would be a 'contradiction' in the notion of a divine '*creation of free beings*', if the '*temporal condition*' that attaches to the phenomenal category of causation 'is also introduced in the relation of super-sensible beings' (*MetM*. 6: 280n.). If we were to claim theoretical 'objective reality' for our claims about the supersensible realm, Kant admits, then the 'temporal condition would have to be introduced here too' (*MetM*. 6: 280n.), as we can have theoretical knowledge only about that which is given in spatio-temporal experience. The solution, therefore, is to use only the 'pure category' of causation, 'without a schema put under it'—that is, without the 'temporal condition'—when talking about the 'concept of creation with a morally prac-tical and therefore nonsensible intent' (*MetM*. 6: 280n.).

A QUESTION OF PLAUSIBILITY

In this chapter I have set out Kant's account of the limitations of our theoretical knowledge to that which we experience within space and time, and shown how this opens up possibilities for thought. In our thinking we are permitted to frame the conception of noumenal first causation. This is a category that Kant arrives at first of all when protecting the possibility of divine first causation, but in the 1770s and 1780s he extends it to ground the possibility of human freedom. We can regard ourselves as noumenally free inasmuch as we regard ourselves as noumenal substances, created by God. I have argued that Kant does indeed use the category of noumenal substance, and that he does not consider this to violate his critical epistemic discipline.

---

[44] Further relevant Kant texts, cited by Wuerth, from the 1780s and 1790s include the following: *MMr*. 29: 912; *R* 6334; *ML₂* 28: 563, 590; *MV* 29: 1005, 1025.

Even if Kant permits us to employ the categories of noumenal freedom and God in our thinking, many commentators have wanted to say that Kant's commitment to these concepts is heavily circumscribed. The suspicion can be that in some sense Kant does not *really believe* in noumenal freedom, or in God, but preserves these concepts in his system as heuristic devices, where we proceed 'as if' we were noumenal beings, and 'as if' there exists an omnibenevolent creator. In Chapter 7 I consider the epistemic status of Kant's claims about freedom and God, and defend the claim that Kant really does believe, without theoretically knowing, that we are noumenally free, and that there is a God. The 'deflationary' readings of Kant on God and freedom, which I spend the next two chapters arguing against, can be motivated by a sense that commitments to noumenal freedom and God are just too extravagant and implausible, so that charity to Kant in these areas requires an interpretation that avoids ascribing to him a full-scale belief-in-the-truth. In the next chapter I take this motivation for deflationary readings head on. I argue that belief in noumenal freedom and God would not be implausible for Kant, and that, although there is a degree of incoherence in his notion of noumenal freedom giving rise to evil actions, Kant is in fact aware of this incoherence, and considers it to be unavoidable, or even important.

6

Incoherence

For some commentators the strand of Kant's transcendental freedom outlined in the previous chapter—noumenal first causation—is one of the most extravagant, and least attractive, elements of Kant's critical philosophy. In a recent work, Allen Wood concedes that Kant ('unfortunately') wants 'to make positive use of noumenal freedom', but complains that this is an '*outrage*', a 'disgraceful supernaturalism' that offends 'enlightened people everywhere'.[1] In particular, there can be bafflement at the notion that an *atemporal* 'act' of noumenal freedom gives rise to a spatio-temporal series of events. Even if it is not *automatically* and in principle ruled as inadmissible by Kant's transcendental idealism, the complaint is that there is something incredible and unbelievable about such a conception. So Derk Pereboom complains of 'this sort of atemporalist line' that it is 'at best insignificantly more credible than an overt contradiction'.[2] Perhaps rather hopefully, Pereboom adds that it is 'far from clear that this is Kant's considered position, rather than a view he experiments with in just one place'.[3] It is not clear which 'one place' Pereboom has in mind, as he himself offers two sources for the concept in Kant, with one reference to the second *Critique* (*CPrR*. 5: 95), and another to *Religion within the Boundaries of Reason Alone* (*Rel*. 6: 32–48). In any case, Pereboom insists that 'it is not clear that this is his position in the *Critique of Pure Reason*'.[4]

If Pereboom is correct that Kant is not really committed to the notion of atemporal noumenal first causation, then I am wrong to claim that Kant answers the question of how we can be free, by postulating that we are capable of noumenal first causation. This is centrally relevant to our guiding question of how Kant reconciles divine action and human freedom, and so demands attention.

In the first section of this chapter I ask whether the notion of atemporal first causation would be in Kant's eyes so extravagant as not to be a serious

---

[1] Wood, *Kantian Ethics*, 138, 296.
[2] Pereboom, 'Kant on Transcendental Freedom', 556.
[3] Pereboom, 'Kant on Transcendental Freedom', 557.
[4] Pereboom, 'Kant on Transcendental Freedom', 557.

possibility. I do not offer an opinion on whether the atemporalist line is fundemantally credible 'to us'; all sorts of positions might be credible or incredible to different readers. We can be more confident, though, on the question of whether such a picture could be credible for Kant. In the second section I investigate the claim that the position is not only implausible, but incoherent, when it comes to explaining the origin of 'evil'. Such incoherence might also challenge the confidence with which we ascribe atemporal first causation to Kant. I accept that there is a degree of incoherence in Kant's account of the origin of evil, but suggest that Kant is aware of it, and considers the insuperable incomprehensibility of his position to be in some sense important. Theologians working within an Augustinian tradition might consider this to be a studied and valued incoherence demanded by the subject matter itself.

THE PLAUSIBILITY OF ATEMPORAL FIRST CAUSATION

Kant's Extensive Use of the Notion of Atemporal First Causation

The sort of claim that Pereboom and others find so extravagant as to be scarcely more plausible than a contradiction is exemplified in the following passage from the second *Critique*:

> But the very same subject, being on the other side conscious of himself as a thing in itself, also views his existence *insofar as it does not stand under conditions of time* and himself as determinable only through laws that he gives himself by reason; and in this existence of his nothing is, for him, antecedent to the determination of his will, but every action—and in general every determination of his existence changing conformably with inner sense, even the whole sequence of his existence as a sensible being—is to be regarded in the consciousness of his intelligible existence as nothing but the consequence and never as the determining ground of his causality as a *noumenon*. So considered, a rational being can now rightly say of every unlawful action he performed that he could have omitted it even though as appearance it is sufficiently determined in the past and, so far, is inevitably necessary; for this action, with all the past which determines it, belongs to a single phenomenon of his character, which he gives to himself and in accordance with which he imputes to himself, as a cause independent of all sensibility, the causality of those appearances. (*CPrV.* 5: 97–8)

Pereboom suggests that Kant's discussion of atemporal causation is limited to a few isolated instances. We saw in Chapter 5 that this is not true. In the early 1770s Kant first develops the notion of atemporal noumenal first causation in relation to God (*R* 3298; *R* 3988; *R* 4000). In the late 1770s Kant extends the notion to human beings (*R* 4225; *R* 5611; *R* 5612), further developing this application extensively in the 1780s (A445–51/B473–9; A531–57/B559–86; *Pr.* 4: 343–4; *CPrR.* 5: 95–102).[5]

Kant continues to be comfortable with talking of atemporal freedom in the 1790s. Kant employs this category in *Religion within the Boundaries of Mere Reason*, where he tells us that 'the propensity to evil' in human beings is an 'intelligible deed, cognizable through reason alone apart from any temporal condition' (*Rel.* 6: 31), which appears as a 'deed contrary to law', which is 'sensible, empirical, given in time' (*Rel.* 6: 31). As Wood puts it, Kant 'employs the notion of our noumenal "disposition" or "attitude" (*Gesinnung*) as a sort of timeless analogue or substitute both for moral striving and moral progress'.[6] Only because 'we can form no positive notion of timeless eternity' we 'think of ourselves as striving and morally progressing in time'.[7]

Nothing remains for us but to think of an endlessly progressing change in the constant progress toward our final end, through which our *attitude* remains always the same. (But our attitude is not, like this progress, a phenomenon; rather it is something supersensible, and so does not alter in time). (*EaT* 8: 334)[8]

Echoing Augustine, Wood expresses Kant's thought nicely: 'Temporal striving and moral progress are the moving images of our eternal moral attitude, which we cannot conceive directly but to which we can relate only through such temporal images or parables.'[9] The notion of atemporal first causation appears again in the late 1790s. In the *The Metaphysics of Morals* (1797) Kant resolves the problem of how to conceive created human freedom, by resorting to the non-temporality of our freedom. Kant sets up the familiar problem:

No concept can be formed of how it is possible for *God to create* free beings, for it seems as if all their future actions would have to be predetermined by that first act, included in the chain of natural necessity and therefore not free. (*MetM.* 6: 280n.)

That we are 'still free' the 'categorical imperative proves for morally practical purposes', although we are not able to 'make this relation of cause to effect comprehensible for theoretical purposes' (*MetM.* 6: 280n.). 'All that one can require of reason here', Kant continues, is 'to prove that there is no contradiction in the concept of a *creation of free beings*' (*MetM.* 6: 280n.). Kant resolves

---

[5] Pereboom cites just one text from the first *Critique* that could be taken as supportive of the notion of noumenal first causation (A548/B576), 'Kant on Transcendental Freedom', 557. Pereboom finds that the text is capable of more than one interpretation. But, as we have seen in Chapter 5, there are many more texts that support the notion of noumenal first causation.

[6] Wood, 'Kant's Compatibilism', 98.

[7] Wood, 'Kant's Compatibilism', 98.

[8] Here I use the translation given by Wood in his article 'Kant's Compatibilism' (p. 98), rather than the translation, also by Wood, in the *Cambridge Edition*.

[9] Wood, 'Kant's Compatibilism', 99.

the difficulty here, as he does elsewhere, by the claim that the appearances that constitute deterministic series are not things in themselves, so that the 'category of causality', where we refer to a *temporal condition*, is not introduced 'in the relation of supersensible beings' (*MetM*. 6: 280n.).

Whether we like it or not, it seems that we must concede that Kant resorts to the notion of atemporal first causation frequently and systematically, from the 1770s into the 1790s. I will offer three considerations as to why such a view can be ascribed to Kant, without also ascribing to Kant a credulous enthusiasm for claims that he should have found implausible. First of all, we need to consider the plausibility of the notion of noumenal first causation against Kant's rationalist framework. Secondly, Kant's claim is in fact epistemically modest, according to the interpretation of Kant's critical epistemic discipline set out in Chapter 5. Finally, some of the more extravagant implications that have been ascribed to atemporal first causation could be dreamt up only if we ourselves violate Kant's critical strictures.

Atemporal Agency and the Rationalist Mindset

Pereboom complains that the notion of atemporal agency does not 'fit well with the moral life as we understand it', where 'moral conversion' seems to imply 'an actual change in one's moral disposition'.[10] This is undoubtedly true, and even a sympathetic commentator such as Wood concedes that Kant's theory 'cannot permit us to conceive of ourselves', that is, our noumenally morally free selves, as '*trying* or *striving* to produce a certain result over a period of time'.[11] The empirical appearance of a change in moral disposition can be thought of only as 'results or products of (timeless) agency, and not as the actual exercise of it'.[12] This might be a significant obstacle for our adopting Kant's notion of timeless agency, but it is not clear that it would be such a serious concern for Kant himself.

The advantage of tracking the emergence of Kant's mature position from his early thought, as we have done in Chapters 4 and 5, is that we can see for ourselves that the offered solution (noumenal first causation) is a hard-won result, which comes at the end of a process of adapting rationalist metaphysics, with its fundamental ingredients of created substances (including human beings) and the uncreated first cause, God. We saw that Kant struggles with the problem of how God can initiate a series of causes without himself being acted upon. Kant solves this conceptual difficulty by discovering that space and time, and the principles of succession and coexistence that govern spatial

---

[10] Pereboom, 'Kant on Transcendental Freedom', 556–7n.
[11] Wood, 'Kant's Compatibilism', 98.
[12] Wood, 'Kant's Compatibilism', 98.

and temporal events, are features of our experience of the world, not of the world in itself. This solution Kant then applies to human first causation. To the rationalist mindset, there is nothing extravagant as such about the fundamental elements of this account: God, created substances, and space and time, as 'well-founded phenomena', rather than as fundamental realities.

It is a structural feature of rationalist patterns of explanation that well-founded phenomena can have an explanatory source that is radically different in its nature from that whose appearance it grounds. That the noumenal reality that underlies the appearance of a moral conversion is quite different from the empirical appearance is as we might expect on a rationalist mindset, which seeks the fundamental grounds for phenomena: consider, for example, the fundamental non-spatial and non-temporal monads that ground Leibniz's universe. Although Kant's critical discipline leads him to make only minimal and disciplined inferences about the fundamental furniture of the universe, it remains an important source of hope for Kant that the noumenal reality that grounds appearances is radically distinct in its properties from that which it grounds. This makes it possible to believe, on practical grounds, that freedom is really possible.

Atemporal First Causation and Kant's Critical Discipline

Kant himself would admit that we cannot *know* using theoretical reason that noumenal first causation does occur. In Chapter 5 (pp. 92–103) I agreed with commentators who argue that Kant's critical discipline instructs us that our judgements about what is 'really possible' are limited to the realm of phenomenal appearances; we cannot know what is 'really possible' for things in themselves.[13] As will be more fully explored in the next chapter, Kant does not claim theoretical knowledge of noumenal first causation. From a theoretical point of view, all that he says in the first *Critique* is that it is *possible* that noumenal first causation is *really possible*, in that there is no contradiction with theoretical knowledge: 'nature at least *does not conflict with* causality through freedom' (A558/B586). Wood correctly cautions us that Kant's intention is 'not positively to establish that we are free or morally responsible for our actions and consequences', but 'only to suggest one possible way in which the moral responsibility we ascribe to ourselves may be reconciled with the mechanism of nature'.[14] Only through practical reason do we gain warrant for

---

[13] See Chignell, 'Real Repugnance and our Ignorance', and 'Real Repugnance and Belief'; and Stang, 'Did Kant Conflate the Necessary and the A Priori?'.

[14] Wood, 'Kant's Compatibilism', 92–3. Wood's own attitude towards the status of such a 'possible' account has hardened in more recent work. In *Kantian Ethics*, Wood calls such an account a 'pure fiction', on a par with stories peopled by 'fairies and witches', believed in by 'contemptibly superstitious people' (p. 137). My claim here is not that Kant *is* epistemically

assenting to the possibility held open by theoretical reason. That Kant, consistent with the strictures of his critical philosophy, is epistemically nuanced in terms of the status that he is prepared to give noumenal first causation does not reflect negatively upon how fundamentally credible he considers such a picture. Indeed, it sits rather comfortably with Kant's wider account of noumenal substances (things in themselves) with causal and modal properties that are in principle unknowable to us. Because it is possible that noumenal first causation is really possible, it is quite strictly 'credible'; and because practical reason finds that it cannot do without the belief in noumenal first causation in order to sustain morality, such a conception is not only 'believable' but 'to be believed' (about which, more in Chapter 7).

Atemporal First Causation and Extravagant Consequences

Reflecting on the epistemic discipline that frames Kant's belief in noumenal first causation enables us to deal with a further criticism of the same concept. Ralph Walker finds that the notion of timeless noumenal choices has hugely extravagant consequences. If the world is in part the product of my timeless noumenal choices, then 'I can be blamed for the First World War, and for the Lisbon earthquake that so appalled Voltaire. Gandhi is no less guilty than Amin of the atrocities of the Ugandan dictator'.[15] Wood is right to respond that on Kant's theory 'what my intelligible choice fundamentally decides is my empirical character, the kind of person I will be',[16] so that Kant could reasonably hold us responsible only for 'those events which must belong to the actual course of things because I have the empirical character or fundamental maxim that I do'.[17] Although Kant 'must admit' that 'this may include events that happen at places and even times remote from my life history in the temporal world', Kant could reply that, because in principle we know nothing about how our timeless choices operate on the temporal world, 'it must be impossible for us to say with confidence which events these may be', such that it 'seems open to Kant to suppose that they correspond to those events for which we normally regard ourselves as morally responsible'.[18] Only if we violate Kant's epistemic humility can we confidently derive extravagant consequences from the concept of noumenal first causation.

---

justified in his commitment to noumenal freedom, according to his mature epistemic discipline, but that Kant thinks he is, for reasons that are not implausible (for Kant) given what he thinks this discipline amounts to.

[15] Ralph Walker, *Kant* (London: Routledge and Kegan Paul, 1978), 149.
[16] Wood, 'Kant's Compatibilism', 92.
[17] Wood, 'Kant's Compatibilism', 92.
[18] Wood, 'Kant's Compatibilism', 92.

THE ORIGIN OF EVIL AND THE INCOHERENCE OF NOUMENAL FIRST CAUSATION

How Can our Noumenal Selves Choose other than the Good?

Even if I am correct that Kant himself would not regard noumenal first causation as 'flatly implausible', there is a more damaging immanent criticism of Kant's model of noumenal first causation that might trouble Kant. This criticism is that such a model, even if it adopted, fails to provide an explanation, or even a coherent conceptual space, that can account for why or how our atemporal noumenal selves ever freely choose evil. This problem emerges precisely because our empirical character is conceived of as an effect of a timeless decision, rather than a cause, or part of the cause, of this decision. This does not allow us to explain moral corruption in terms of a 'struggle' between our sensuous nature and our moral character, as any such 'struggle' would itself be the moving image, representing we know not quite how the textures and subtleties of a timeless free choice. The noumenal self making the timeless free choice could not *itself* be mired in sensuous impulses and temptations. The question that emerges is this: given that a rational being would choose the good, and given that the noumenal free self is not subjected to any interfering sensuous impulses, why would a rational noumenal being ever choose to do otherwise than the good?

Just as God's rationality entails that he will always choose the good, it is hard to understand even the real possibility of our choosing less than the good. If the noumenal self is an atemporal first cause, then it is not subjected to sensuous impulses, in which case it is perfectly rational (that is, there are no non-rational or irrational factors that interfere with it or press upon it). The idea that a noumenal self would be entirely 'free' of law is for a Kant a 'contradiction', 'absolutely impossible': 'To think of oneself as a freely acting being, yet as exempted from the one law commensurate to such a being (the moral law), would amount to the thought of a cause operating without any law at all' (*Rel.* 6: 35). As we saw in Chapter 2, the perfect freedom enjoyed by God is not a freedom from rationality, but is rather the inability to do otherwise than that which is rational. Being determined by sensuous impulses is contrary to such freedom, but being determined by the moral law constitutes it.

If the noumenal self is perfectly rational, it cannot do otherwise than the good, as 'the determination according to natural law is abolished on account of freedom' (*Rel.* 6: 35); but, if the noumenal self can do otherwise than the good, then it would seem that it is not perfectly rational, in which case it must be subjected in some way to sensuous and irrational impulses, in which case it is not an atemporal free first cause. It would seem that, conceptually speaking, we are either noumenal and so perfectly rational, and so not able to do otherwise than the good; or we are able to do otherwise than the good, and so not perfectly rational and noumenally free. The 'explanatory space' that Kant is aiming for requires our assent to the proposition that the noumenal free self (who is perfectly rational) is also able to do otherwise than the good; but it is hard to see why or how this can be.

In *Religion within the Boundaries of Mere Reason* Kant engages with this precise problem. Kant begins by setting out that 'every propensity is either physical, i.e., it pertains to a human's power of choice as natural being', or it is 'moral', pertaining 'to a human being's power of choice as a moral being' (*Rel.* 6: 31). A 'propensity to evil' can 'only attach to the moral faculty of choice', an 'intelligible deed, cognizable through reason alone apart from any temporal condition' (*Rel.* 6: 31). There is no need to offer a 'formal proof' that 'there must be such a corrupt propensity rooted in the human being', given the 'multitude of woeful examples that the experience of human *deeds* parades before us' (*Rel.* 6: 32–3), where these examples are the phenomenal effects of intelligible deeds.

The propensity to evil is an intelligible free act: but what could be the 'motivation' or grounds for the noumenal free self to choose evil? Kant eliminates various candidates as the 'ground of this evil' (*Rel.,* 6: 34–5). The ground of evil 'cannot be placed, as is commonly done, in the sensuous nature of the human being, and in the natural inclinations arising from it'. Sensuous impulses, Kant explains, 'bear no direct relation to evil', rather giving the 'occasion for what the moral disposition can demonstrate in its power, for virtue' (*Rel.* 6: 35). Furthermore, with sensuous impulses we cannot 'presume ourselves responsible for their existence', because 'natural inclinations do not have us for their author', whereas we 'are responsible for the propensity to evil' found in the subject as a 'freely acting being' (*Rel.* 6: 25). We cannot 'inquire into the origin in time' of free deeds but 'must inquire only into its origin in reason' (*Rel.* 6: 41). '*Sensuous nature*' contains 'too little to provide a ground of moral evil in the human being': 'For to the extent that it eliminates the incentives originating in freedom, it makes of the human a purely *animal* being' (*Rel.* 6: 35). Neither can we impute to human beings 'an *evil reason* as it were (an absolutely evil will)' (*Rel.* 6: 35). This would contain 'too much, because resistance to the law would itself be thereby elevated to incentive', rendering the human subject a '*diabolical* being' (*Rel.* 6: 35). Human beings are neither animal nor diabolical, and their choosing evil is caused neither by sensuous impulses nor by a desire to usurp the moral law. This only serves to underline the difficulty of the question as to why and how human beings, as noumenal first causes of their actions, can choose to do otherwise than that which is rational, given that the freedom they enjoy 'abolishes' determination according to natural (non-moral) laws.

Sensuous Impulses and the Origin of Evil

There are passages in Kant's writings that might seem to suggest that the explanation, for why we fail to follow the moral law, is that we are overcome by sensuous impulses. To consolidate our account of the incoherence in Kant's account of noumenal freedom, we need to address these passages.

In 1769–70 Kant writes that, if human beings 'were completely intellectual', then 'all of their actions would be actively determined but still free' (*R* 4227; 17: 466). In such a case, human beings would be determined by the law of reason, but still free, as freedom is the capacity of reason to follow the moral law. But human beings are not entirely intellectual: they are 'in part sensible, in part intellectual', in such a way that 'the sensible certainly cannot make the *intellectuale* passive, yet the intellectual also cannot overpower the actions except by a certain measure of preponderance over the sensibility' (*R* 4227; 17: 466). 'If everything were determined by reason,' Kant writes, 'then everything would be necessary but also good. If it were determined by sensibility, then there would be neither evil nor good, in general nothing practical at all' (*R* 5611; 18: 252).

Similarly in *Metaphysik Mrongovious* in the 1780s Kant writes that 'however perfect' a 'created being' may be it will have 'needs which certain stimuli provide, with which they have to struggle', meaning that a human being does not ever have 'holiness, but virtue' (*MMr.* 19: 897–898). In a similar vein, in the *Lectures on the Philosophical Doctrine of Religion* Kant tells us that God 'created the human being free, but gave him also animal instincts; he gave the human being senses to be moderated and overcome through the education of the understanding', where the human being 'struggles with his own limits, with his animal instincts' (*LPR* 28: 1078). Similarly, in the *Danziger Rationaltheologie*—a different note-taker, but on the same part of the lectures—there is a passage about cultivating our reason, so that we will not be led astray by our 'animal instinct [*tierische Instinkte*]' (*DR* 28: 1287).

These passages taken in themselves are suggestive of the view that our animal instincts lead our freedom astray, rather than being a problem that arises from our (motiveless) misuse of freedom. It might be that Kant is just inconsistent here. Nonetheless, it has to be acknowledged that in all the more fully worked-out passages, including all those that feature in works published by Kant after 1780, he denies that our sensuous instincts are the cause of our evil-doing. Given this, we cannot consider the view that our evil actions are caused by sensuous temptations to be Kant's considered view.

It is also worth reflecting on the immediate context of some of the passages about our 'animal instincts'. In the *Lectures on the Philosophical Doctrine of Religion* and the *Danziger Rationaltheologie*, Kant is reflecting on the emergence of evil in human history. In the same passage Kant is concerned to relate his account, for example, to the 'mosaic story' and the notion of 'progress' in the 'earthly world', where evil 'can be regarded as *incompleteness in the development of the germ toward the good*' (*LPR* 28: 1078). It is possible to read the references to our historical 'animal instincts' as compatible with the more fundamental metaphysical account. In this case, the history of our overcoming of our animal instincts is the phenomenal appearance and manifestation of the noumenal fall and conversion. This would be similar to the way in which the feeling of 'respect' for the moral law is the phenomenal appearance of our noumenal free choice to obey the categorical imperative, rather than our obedience being subsequent to the feeling of respect (*CPrR*. 5: 72–73). In this way, Kant's detailed interest in human history, social conditions, culture, and anthropology (*Rel.* 6: 27, 93–4; *APV* 7: 119–20, 285–6, 293–5, 321–33) would not be in contradiction with his fundamental metaphysical account, any more than a detailed study of Newtonian principles is undercut by Kant's conviction that these principles do not apply at a fundamental noumenal level.[19]

This reading is compatible with other accounts that Kant gives, where the underlying noumenal decision appears in the empirical realm either as our being overwhelmed by sensuous impulses, or as our being in control of our sensuous impulses. When we fail to follow the moral law, we are overcome by sensuous impulses: but the latter is a consequence, rather than a cause. The free action that determines 'whether the human being is good or evil' fundamentally lies in how the noumenal self orders two principles: the principle of the moral law, and the principle of self-love. One of these principles must be subordinate to the other, and the difference between good and evil lies in '*which of the two he makes the condition of the other*' (*Rel.* 6: 36). The human being is evil when he reverses the proper order and 'makes the incentives of self-love and their inclinations the condition of compliance with the moral law', whereas 'it is this latter that, as *the supreme condition* of the satisfaction of the former, should have been incorporated into the universal maxim of the power of choice as the sole incentive' (*Rel.* 6: 36).

Kant's considered account of the origin of evil actions is that they are not caused by our being overwhelmed by sensuous impulses, but that our being overwhelmed by sensuous impulses is itself the effect of our noumenal self choosing the principle of self-love over the principle of the moral law. But now the question of the origin of evil simply repeats itself in a different key: why and how would the noumenal self choose the principle of self-love over the principle of the moral law, given that they are in a state of freedom, and not under pressure from sensuous impulses or other external influences? Kant

---

[19] This would be my answer to Allen Wood's observation that ascribing noumenal freedom to Kant 'contradicts' Kant's interest in these matters, *Kantian Ethics*, 136. I am indebted to Wood for these references to *APV*.

acknowledges the problem, telling us simply that 'we are incapable of assigning a further cause for why evil has corrupted the very highest maxim in us, though this is our own deed' (*Rel.* 6: 32). Further down, Kant writes that we cannot doubt the 'propensity to evil in human nature', as this is 'established through experiential demonstrations of the actual resistance in time of the human power of choice against the law' (*Rel.* 6: 35); nonetheless, these 'demonstrations still do not teach us the real nature of that propensity or the ground of this resistance' (*Rel.* 6: 35). The 'disharmony in our power of choice', whereby we make 'lower incentives' (the principle of self-love) our 'supreme' principle, remains 'inexplicable to us' (*Rel.* 6: 43). Furthermore, there is something principled and systematic about this inexplicability, which cannot be overcome by either a posteriori investigation or a priori reflection:

Evil can have originated only from moral evil (not just from the limitations of our nature); yet the original predisposition (which none other than the human being himself could have corrupted, if this corruption is to be imputed to him) is a predisposition to the good; there is no conceivable ground for us, therefore, from which moral evil could first have come in us. (*Rel.* 6: 43)

Kant receives the account of the fall given in Genesis as the expression of 'this incomprehensibility in a historical narrative', where the 'absolutely *first* beginning of all evil' (in the serpent) is 'represented as incomprehensible to us (for whence the evil in that spirit?)', and where the human being is 'represented as having lapsed' only '*through temptation*, hence not as corrupted *fundamentally*', so that 'there still remains hope of a return to the good from which he has strayed' (*Rel.* 6: 44).

A Theological Appreciation of Kant: Evil as 'Systematically Inexplicable'

What are we to make of this difficulty, and of Kant's principled admission that it cannot be addressed? Where there seems to be a real difficulty for Kant is that belief in noumenal first causation was warranted by practical reason because it was, Kant told us, the (only) way that we can sustain a belief in transcendental freedom for human beings, given the mechanism of nature. We do not have, and could not get, independent evidence for the belief; all the warrant that we have arises from its explanatory power in grounding our freedom, if it is assumed. The freedom that needs explaining involves our being ultimately responsible for our actions *and* our being able to do otherwise than that which is morally good. But now it seems that we have lost that warrant, as we cannot see *how* noumenal first causation could guarantee our ability to do otherwise than the good. Some commentators have become exasperated with Kant at this point. So Gordon Michalson complains that 'it is simply not clear that [Kant] has any reason for claiming that freedom is the ground of moral evil other than his own systematic need to salvage individual accountability and culpability in moral matters'.[20] Michalson concludes that Kant can 'no more explain the "fall" than could Augustine, his long-windedness in the matter notwithstanding'.[21]

If a theological defence of Kant's position were to be attempted, I think it would begin by probing the appropriateness of the demand that the fall should be 'explained'. The admission that 'we cannot see *how*' the fall occurs—how a free being created by the ground of good chooses evil—is itself ambiguous between a stronger and a weaker claim. On a strong reading we might mean 'we can see that noumenal first causation could not guarantee our ability to do otherwise than the good', in which case the transcendentally idealist solution to the problem of human freedom is in real trouble. A weaker reading would instead claim that 'although *we* cannot see *how* noumenal first causation could guarantee our ability to do otherwise than the good, nonetheless we can neither know that this is really possible, nor that it is not possible'. The second weaker reading fits with Kant's systematic and principled insistence that the limits of the really possible are not coextensive with the limits of our experience or understanding. If we experience something, we know that it is actual, and so really possible; but we do not know the noumenal grounds of this really possible experience, and we do not know the scope or limitations of that which is really possible in itself. On this basis, we could still be asked to assent to noumenal first causation, if it is the only possible grounding for our freedom, *even if* we cannot know whether or not it is in itself really possible at all, and even if we have some—not definitive but troubling—grounds for doubting that it is. The fundamental incomprehension that attaches to the possibility of noumenal first causation also helps to account for Kant's extreme caution in the first *Critique*; after setting out the model for noumenal first causation, he is clear that he has not only failed to establish 'the *reality* of freedom' (A557–8/B585–6), but also that he has 'not even tried' to 'prove the *possibility* of freedom', because 'from mere concepts a priori we cannot cognize anything about the possibility of any real ground or any causality' (A558/B586).

The extent to which one will go along with Kant here will depend upon one's attitude to practical reason as an independent source of warrant for belief (see Chapter 7), and also on how comfortable one is with allowing incomprehensibility and our cognitive limitations to do *positive* as well as negative work: where, just because we cannot comprehend something, it does not mean that we cannot posit or hope for the incomprehensible reality. Indeed, the significance of the reality being *in principle* incomprehensible is that, for

---

[20] Michalson, *Fallen Freedom*, 65.
[21] Michalson, *Fallen Freedom*, 65.

all we know, the mystery could be a function of our limited access to real possibilities, rather than due to a real contradiction or 'repugnance' (in Kant's terms) in the thing itself.

It might also be that there are some theological grounds for regarding human freedom as a particularly appropriate place for systematic explanation to break down. There is an Augustinian theological tradition that would support Kant. In *De Libero Arbitrio* Augustine addresses a similar problem to the one discussed above, of why a will disposed towards the good, because created so, would ever turn away from this good:

> Perhaps you are going to ask what is the source of this movement by which the will turns away from the unchangeable good toward a changeable good. This movement is certainly evil, even though free will itself is to be counted among good things, since no one can live rightly without it. For if that movement, that turning away from the Lord God, is undoubtedly sin, surely we cannot say that God is the cause of sin. So that movement is not from God. But then where does it come from? If I told you that I don't know, you might be disappointed; but that would be the truth. For one cannot know that which is nothing.[22]

Augustine's response here is framed within an account of evil as a *privatio boni*: a deprivation in reality and goodness, where created beings are inexplicably, but by their own free will, disordered and disoriented in relation to God. Kant would have been familiar with broad Augustinian themes from his pietist upbringing;[23] and he could have been familiar with this specific Augustinian teaching on 'nothingness' as the source of evil from Leibniz. In a *Dialogue on Human Freedom and the Origin of Evil* (1695) Leibniz explicitly endorses and ascribes to Augustine the view that evil arises from 'nothingness or non-being'.[24]

The theologian Karen Kilby recommends Augustine's position here, not so much because it is a solution, but because it knowingly fails to be one ('I don't know'). Kilby argues that. when it comes to evil, there is something theologically appropriate about this 'systematic inexplicability'.[25] Its inexplicability is what makes evil *evil*, rather than comprehensible suffering to a worthy end. Comprehensible suffering to a worthy end is not so much evil as 'an initially challenging good'. There is an intrinsic grammatical link between incomprehensibility and evil. Kant does not offer this argument, instead resting his case

---

[22] Augustine, *De Libero Arbitrio. On Free Choice of the Will*, trans. Thomas Williams (Cambridge and Indianapolis: Hackett Publishing Company, 1993), bk.II.20.

[23] See F. Ernest Stauffer, *German Pietism during the Eighteenth Century* (Leiden: E. J. Brill, 1973).

[24] Gottfried Wilhelm Leibniz, *Dialogue on Human Freedom and the Origin of Evil* (25 January 1695), in *Philosophical Essays*, ed. Roger Ariew and Daniel Garber (Indianapolis and Cambridge: Hackett, 1989), 111–17.

[25] Karen Kilby, 'Evil and the Limits of Theology', *New Blackfriars*, 84/983 (2003), 13–29 (p. 25).

for incomprehension on a more general doctrine about our inability to know the real possibilities of things in themselves; but it might be that theologians will find this apophaticism attractive for other reasons, related to instincts that could be called 'Kantian', where we should not attempt to comprehend that which is in principle beyond comprehension.

Kant does not flinch from the mysterious nature of our ability to do other than the good, and then our ability to turn away from evil back to the good. Kant acknowledges our lack of comprehension, and exhorts us to live without resolving it. It is enough that we are called to the good life through the moral law, and 'it is presumptuous to require that more be made manifest to us' (*Rel.* 6: 145). 'Regarding these mysteries,' he writes, 'God has revealed nothing to us, nor can he reveal anything, for we would not *understand* it':

It would be as if from the human being, through his freedom, he wanted to *explain* and *make comprehensible* to us what happens; regarding this God has indeed revealed his will through the moral law in us but has left the *causes* whereby a free action occurs or does not occur on earth in the same obscurity in which everything must remain for human investigation; all this ought to be conceived, as history, according to the law of cause and effect yet also from freedom. Regarding the objective rule of our conduct, however, all that we need is sufficiently revealed (through reason and Scripture), and this revelation is equally understandable to every human being. (*Rel.* 6: 144)

My aim in this chapter has not been to argue that Kant's account of noumenal causation is plausible and coherent; rather it has been to show why Kant might regard it as plausible, and why the element of incoherence might be expected and permitted by theologians working in a broadly Augustinian tradition. It is correct to say that, in some sense of the verb 'believe', Kant believes in noumenal first causation, and in God having created us with this freedom. At the same time, Kant's concept of 'belief' has different textures. In the next chapter I ask in what sense precisely Kant believes in noumenal freedom and God.

7

Belief

The central exegetical claim of this book is that Kant struggles with the irreducibly theological problem of how it can be said that human beings are free, given that they are created by God. In Chapter 4 I demonstrated that Kant wrestled with this problem in the 1760s and 1770s. In Chapter 5 I set out Kant's solution to this problem: noumenal first causation, made possible by transcendental idealism.

After setting out the shape of this solution, I have been involved in a rearguard action of defending the claim that this could indeed be Kant's position, against a series of objections. First of all, there was the objection, dealt with in Chapter 5, that the concepts required for noumenal first causation (the noumenal self and substance as thing-in-itself) are in principle ruled out by Kant's transcendental idealism. Secondly, there was the claim, dealt with in Chapter 6, that the notion of noumenal first causation is so wildly implausible that, even if it is in principle 'thinkable', we should avoid ascribing it to Kant.

In this chapter I deal with a related but distinct set of objections to my central exegetical claim. There are different facets to this set of objections, but what they amount to, putting it briskly, is this: Kant could not be said to have the 'theological problem' that I ascribe to him after the 1770s, because, in his critical philosophy, Kant does not really believe in God. That is to say, Kant does not believe in God in the way that he would need to, in order to have anything that constitutes a 'theological problem'. If Kant does not really believe in God, in the relevant sense of 'believe', this would indeed punch a hole under the waterline of the book. For this reason, I need to defend the claim that Kant really does believe in God, in such a way that he could have a theological problem relating divine and human freedom. This is the purpose of this chapter.

As with the discussion of transcendental idealism, this involves engaging with well-rehearsed issues in Kant studies. As before, it is essential that I do this, if I am to avoid an unacceptable lacuna in the overall argument of the book. The central exegetical and theological claims of the book require us to defend the claim that Kant continues to believe in God. I also need to orient these well-rehearsed debates in Kant studies to what will be the less familiar agenda of Chapters 8–10.

In the first section, we see that Kant thinks that it is impossible to have theoretical knowledge of the existence or non-existence of God. Kant's settled position after 1785 is that it is also impossible to have theoretical knowledge about the existence or otherwise of noumenal freedom. Nonetheless, as I explore in the second section, for the purposes of practical reason, it is both permissible and required (on the basis of morality) to believe in noumenal freedom, and (on the basis of belief in morality and freedom) to believe in God and immortality. I agree with commentators who find that Kant even claims to enjoy a form of knowledge (*wissen*) in the case of noumenal freedom, albeit that the knowledge is grounded upon practical reason. In the third section we see that belief in God, although not grounded upon theoretical reason, is able to serve theoretical reason in some of its rational tasks. The concept of God is able to do this, because of continuities with the rationalist conception of God that Kant explored in his early philosophy. These continuities are set out in the fourth section. In the fifth section, I argue that the way in which Kant thinks about God and freedom is most plausibly construed as realist, in that the propositions 'there is a God', and 'we are noumenally free', are true or false independently of our most epistemically disciplined beliefs, even though we cannot have theoretical knowledge about God (or freedom).

We cannot have theoretical knowledge about God and freedom, but this leaves open the question of whether or not we can have true beliefs about God and freedom. The remaining sections of this chapter engage with this question. Kant's insistence that we must believe (*glauben*) in God and freedom can be taken in one of two quite different ways. We might interpret Kant as saying that we should 'accept-as-true' judgements about God and noumenal freedom, whilst bracketing out the question of their truth or falsity; on this account, Kant does not 'believe-in-the-truth' of propositions about God and noumenal freedom. In the sixth section, I set out the distinction between 'acceptance-as-true' and 'belief-in-truth', drawing upon work in recent epistemology. I explore what impact an interpretation of Kant as merely 'accepting-as-true' the proposition that God exists would have on the central exegetical claim of the book, that Kant struggles with the theological problem of how it can be said that we are free given that we are created by God. I submit that there could still be some interest in the exegetical question, but that its importance would be reduced.

The task of interpretation is slightly more straightforward with freedom, as in this case Kant does claim a form of (practical) knowledge, which suggests that Kant 'believes-in-the-truth' of judgements about freedom. In the case of judgements about God, the situation is more ambivalent. Kant never claims knowledge (*wissen*) of God, but rather 'belief' (*glauben*). In the seventh section I explore the significance of the category of *glauben* for Kant, as he distinguishes it from 'knowledge' (*wissen*) and 'opinion' (*meinen*). In the eighth section I argue that some forms of *Glaube* are indeed merely 'accepted-as-true' by Kant, but that *Glaube* in God on moral–practical grounds is more plausibly read as a case of 'belief-in-truth'. In the ninth section I refute the most serious objection to this interpretation, which draws attention to the way in which belief in God is described by Kant as voluntary and 'subjective'. I show that faith, according to the tradition upon which Kant is drawing, is always understood as involving a voluntary aspect, without this deflating the commitment that underlies the belief.

In the final section of the chapter I concede that there are hints of doubt about the existence of God in Kant's critical philosophy. Such doubt is not really 'acceptance-as-true', I argue, but the possibility of genuine unbelief. Fragmentary texts in the *Opus Postumum* (1800–3) indicate that these shards of doubt become more significant in the last years of Kant's life. I accept that, by the end of his life, Kant has ceased to believe-in-the-truth of the proposition that God exists, as traditionally understood. What is interesting, I suggest, is that he now believes-in-the-truth of a different quasi-theological proposition, that we are divine, inasmuch as we give ourselves the moral law. This sets us up with an intriguing interpretative question as to why Kant makes this shift, not from belief to unbelief, but from (broadly) orthodox traditional theological belief, to heterodox quasi-theological belief. The final three chapters of the book help us to answer this question.

THE IMPOSSIBILITY OF THEORETICAL KNOWLEDGE ABOUT GOD AND NOUMENAL FREEDOM

Kant is clear that we cannot have theoretical knowledge about whether or not God exists. Kant states that there are 'only three kinds of proof for the existence of God possible from speculative reason' (A590/B618): those that attempt to derive theoretical knowledge of a highest being from the concept of God, those that proceed from the fact that there exists something contingent, and those that draw theistic conclusions from the appearance of order and design in the universe. Kant refutes all three strategies (A590/B618–A642/B670). The success or otherwise of Kant's criticisms of these arguments does not concern us here, where we are concerned just to understand the epistemic status of his remaining commitment to God.[1] What matters for our purposes is that Kant is 'certain' that we can never discover a demonstration sufficient

---

[1] For an extensive discussion of Kant's criticism of natural theology, see Byrne, *Kant on God*, chs 2 and 3; and Wood, *Kant's Rational Theology*, ch. 2.

for theoretical knowledge that 'there is a God' and 'a future life': 'For whence will reason derive the ground for such experience and their inner possibility?' (A742/B770). Theoretical knowledge requires a spatio-temporal experience, and Kant thinks that in principle we cannot have a spatio-temporal experience of God. This principled impossibility of theoretical knowledge about the existence of God cuts two ways, as a *lack* of experience of God does not constitute grounds to doubt the existence of God. So Kant is 'apodictically certain' that 'no human being' will ever be able to assert that there is no God (A742/B770): 'The same grounds for considering human reason incapable of asserting the existence of such a being, when laid before our eyes, also suffice to prove the unsuitability of all counter-assertions' (A641/B669). When it comes to the battleground between theoretical theists and atheists, Kant insists that 'this ground will bear no warrior in full armor and equipped with weapons that are to be feared' (A743/B771). Instead, there is only 'ridicule and boasting, which can be laughed at like child's play' (A743/ B771). Kant finds this a 'comforting' thought, as it offers reason 'peace and tranquil possession' and 'courage' (A743/B771), where practical reason will be able to deliver 'firm belief' (*Glaube*) justified 'by the sharpest reason', even though you must surrender the claim 'of knowledge' (A744/B772).

The case of freedom is slightly more complicated. Although there are some passages from 1781 to 1785 (discussed immediately below) where Kant does imply a theoretical knowledge of freedom, his settled critical position seems to be that we have no theoretical knowledge of the existence of intelligible freedom. In the first *Critique* Kant tells us that he has not been 'trying to establish the *reality* of freedom'. He also says that 'we have not even tried to prove the *possibility* of freedom', as 'this would not have succeeded either, because from mere concepts a priori we cannot cognize anything about the possibility of any real ground, or any causality' (A558/B586). The 'one single thing' that theoretical reason can establish is that 'nature at least *does not conflict with* causality through freedom' (A558/B586).

This seems to be in tension with other comments from the first *Critique*, where Kant writes that the human being 'knows [*erkennt*] himself also through pure apperception' to be a 'merely intelligible object' (A546/B574). There is also a section in the *Groundwork* where Kant implies theoretical grounds for asserting our transcendental freedom, where the 'human being finds in himself' a 'pure self-activity', a 'spontaneity so pure' that 'proves its highest occupation in distinguishing the world of sense and the world of understanding from each other' (*GW* 4: 452). It might be possible to render these two moments in Kant's thought consistent. For example, Ameriks and Hogan suggest that we might achieve consistency by saying that, although we have theoretical grounds for asserting our freedom, we cannot theoretically explain our possession of this freedom;[2] or we could follow Wood, who argues that the considerations in the *Groundwork* should be understood as practical rather than theoretical (see *GW* 4: 448), with the 'fact of reason' of the second *Critique* acting as a 'summary' of the practical arguments of the *Groundwork*.[3] In any case, by the time Kant writes the second *Critique* he has abandoned (if he ever held them) *theoretical* proofs of our transcendental freedom,[4] grounding a commitment to freedom on the 'fact of reason' that is morality (*CPrR.* 5: 29–31), where 'consciousness of this fundamental law . . . forces itself upon us . . . as a synthetic a priori proposition that is not based on any intuition' (*CPrR.* 5: 31).

The 'concept of a *causa noumenon*' does not 'contradict itself', as long as the concept is 'applied to things as beings of the pure understanding' (*CPrR.* 5: 55). At the same time 'I do not now claim *to know theoretically* by this concept the constitution of a being *insofar as* it has a *pure* will':

It is enough for me to thereby only designate it as such a being and hence only to connect the concept of causality with that of freedom (and with what is inseparable from it, the moral law as its determining ground); and I am certainly authorized to do so by virtue of the pure, not empirical origin of the concept of cause, inasmuch as I consider myself authorized to make no other use of it than with regard to the moral law which determines its reality, that is, only a practical use. (*CPrR.* 5: 56)

PRACTICAL WARRANT FOR KNOWLEDGE OF FREEDOM AND BELIEF IN GOD

Although we cannot have theoretical knowledge about freedom, Kant considers that freedom is a precondition for the possibility of morality, where morality is an a priori 'fact of reason' (*CPrR.* 5: 31).[5] In the preface to the second edition of the first *Critique* Kant writes that, when evaluating the 'real possibility' of a 'concept' (such as freedom), we do not need to look only to the 'theoretical sources of cognition', but we can also look to 'practical ones' (Bxxvin.). In the margin to his copy of the first *Critique* Kant writes:

---

[2] See Hogan, 'Three Kinds of Rationalism', 379–82, and Ameriks, *Kant's Theory of Mind*, ch. 6.

[3] Wood, *Kantian Ethics*, 134.

[4] For accounts of Kant's shift here, see Ameriks, *Kant's Theory of Mind*, 209–20; and Bernd Ludwig 'Die "consequente Denkungsart der speculative Kritik": Kants radikale Umgestaltung seiner Freiheitslehre im Jahre 1786 und die Folgen für dir Kritische Philosophie als Ganze', *Deutsche Zeitschrift für Philoosphie*, 58/4 (2010), 595–628.

[5] In this section I am indebted to Hogan, 'Three Kinds of Rationalism', 379–80, Ameriks, *Kant's Theory of Mind*, ch. 6, and Sebastian Gardner, 'The Primacy of Practical Reason', in Graham Bird (ed.), *A Companion to Kant* (Oxford: Wiley-Blackwell, 2010), 259–74.

'Morality is that which, if it is correct, positively presupposes freedom. If the former is true, then freedom is proved' (A558/B586; E. clxxvi; 23:42). Practical reason, or reason in as much as it is concerned with the good, is able to provide a 'non-theoretical warrant for knowledge of freedom'.[6]

> In the concept of a pure will there is contained the concept of a causality with freedom, that is, a causality that is not determinable in accordance with laws of nature and hence not capable of any empirical intuition as proof of its reality, but that nevertheless perfectly justifies its objective reality a priori in the pure practical law, though not (as is easily seen) with a view to the theoretical use of reason but only to its practical use. (*CPrR.* 5:55)

That which practical reason claims to establish must not be in contradiction with the deliverances of theoretical reason. If theoretical reason 'had proved that freedom cannot be thought at all' then '*freedom* and with it morality' would 'have to give way to the *mechanism of nature*' (Bxxix). But theoretical reason has shown us that our experience of spatio-temporal determinism in nature is a feature of our reception of the world, which leaves open the possibility that things in themselves might not be determined.

Practical reason is, therefore, not impeded by speculative reason, and is able to work through the implications of the insight that freedom 'is the condition of the moral law, which we do know' (*CPrR.* 5:4). On this basis we can claim to '*know* a priori' (*wissen*) about the possibility of 'freedom', albeit on practical grounds (*CPrR.* 5: 4; see also *CPrR.* 5: 105).[7] Similarly, in the third *Critique*, Kant writes that 'the idea of freedom' as a 'particular kind of causality' is the 'only one among all the ideas of pure reason whose object is a fact [*deren Gegenstand Tatsache ist*] and which must be counted uniquely amongst the *scibilia* ['things that can be known']' (*CJ* 5: 468). This is surprising perhaps when we consider that Kant has just limited the realm of the 'factual' to 'objects for concepts the objective reality of which can be proved . . . in all cases by means of intuitions corresponding to the concepts' (*CJ* 5: 468). Belief in freedom is to be given the status of the factual. Although this would be 'excessive from a theoretical point of view' (*CJ* 5: 468), it 'can be established through practical laws of reason' (*CJ* 5: 468). Whatever we think about it, we seem to have a type of 'knowledge' (*wissen*) of freedom, although this is from *practical* rather than *theoretical* reason.

As we have seen in Chapters 4 and 5, Kant is convinced that if things in themselves are spatio-temporal, then we could not be free. If we do indeed have practical knowledge that we are free, then this entails that things in themselves are not spatio-temporal. This suggests a possible

---

[6] Hogan, 'Three Kinds of Rationalism', 379.

[7] For my discussion of Kant's use of *wissen* in relation to freedom, I am indebted to Hogan, 'Three Kinds of Rationalism', 379–82.

response to what is sometimes known as the 'neglected-alternative' objection to Kant's transcendental idealism. Kant claims to *know* that space and time are features of our experience of the world *rather than* being features of the world as it is in itself (A26/B42). The alternative that is considered by some critics to be neglected by Kant is that things in themselves might *also* be spatial and temporal, or, at least, have isomorphically structural properties that ground our spatio-temporal forms of intuition.[8] As Hogan shows, if we have (practical) knowledge that we are free, we do indeed have grounds for denying that things-in-themselves could be determined in spatio-temporal ways, which would also explain our inability to attain theoretical knowledge of things-in-themselves, as we only have knowledge of spatio-temporal reality.[9] Kant's claim to practical *knowledge* of freedom provides a 'more unified picture of his theoretical philosophy', giving credence to his own claim that 'the origin of the critical philosophy is *morality,* with respect to the imputability of action' (*N.* 20: 235).

The concepts of God and immortality 'attach themselves' to the concept of freedom 'and with it and by means of it get stability and objective reality, that is, their *possibility* is *proved* by this: that freedom is real, for this idea reveals itself through the moral law' (*CPrR.* 5: 4). Belief in God and immortality do not have the same status of *Wissen* as belief in freedom, even from a practical point of view. 'Freedom' is required by the 'moral law', but 'the ideas of *God* and *immortality* . . . are not conditions of the moral law but only conditions of the necessary object of a will determined by this law' (*CPrR.* 5: 4).

In order to reach the concepts of God and immortality, Kant invokes a principle known as the 'priority of practical reason', that, 'in the union of pure speculative with pure practical reason in one cognition, the latter has primacy' (*CPrR.* 5: 121).[10] Kant explains that the union between the practical postulate

---

[8] For criticism of Kant along these lines, see Falkenstein, *Kant's Intuitionism,* 304–7. See also Guyer, *Kant and the Claims of Knowledge,* 333–44. For a fuller discussion of the 'neglected alternative', see my 'Kant's Transcendental Idealism, Freedom and the Divine Mind', 628–32.

[9] Hogan, 'Three Kinds of Rationalism', 379–82. I am indebted to Hogan in my account of a possible response to the neglected alternative. Hogan cites other references from the 1760s and 1770s where we find 'the idea of a practical warrant for upholding transcendental freedom' (p. 380n.): *ML₁* 28: 332–3; *R* 4156, 17: 437. Hogan also draws attention (p. 380n.) to a moral proof for freedom in Christian August Crusius, *Anweisung, Vernünftig zu Leben* (Leipzig: J. F. Gleditsch, 1767), §42.

[10] Although our commitment to freedom is grounded by practical reason, Sebastian Gardner argues persuasively that it is less clear that Kant invokes the *principle of the priority* of practical reason to defend his conception of freedom. In the second *Critique,* freedom is grounded directly upon the 'fact of reason' that is morality (*CPrR.* 5: 42–50). This comes before Kant's discussion of practical primacy (*CPrR.* 5: 119). Also, there is no discussion of the practical primacy principle in the *Groundwork.* This opens up the possibility of defending practical primacy on the basis of what we know about freedom, rather than defending freedom on the basis of the principle. See Gardner, 'The Primacy of Practical Reason', 262–4. On the other hand, as Gardner concedes, freedom is described as a postulate (*CPrR.* 5: 132, 5: 134; *JL* §38), where postulates are 'linked intimately' with the category of practical primacy (Gardner, 'The Primacy of Practical Reason',

and that which it grounds must be 'not *contingent* and discretionary but based a priori on reason itself and therefore *necessary*' (*CPrR.* 5: 121). That is to say, the commitment must be necessary in grounding something that itself commands our assent. In this case, morality is an a priori 'fact of reason', and morality cannot be grounded, Kant argues, without belief in God and immortality. As Chignell puts it, Kant does not write a 'blank check that would allow *any* old non-epistemic merit to count'.[11] For the priority of practical reason to be activated, the 'goals, interests and needs in question must somehow arise from what Kant thinks of as our rational nature (in our drive for unified knowledge, or its need for moral coherence)'.[12]

In the 'Dialectic' of the second *Critique*, Kant sets out his moral argument for the existence of God, which turns on his conception of the highest good. 'The highest good' is separated into two elements: one a demand and the other a promise. Kant tells us that 'the concept of the *highest* . . . can mean either the supreme (*supremum*) or the complete (*consummatum*)' (*CPrR.* 5: 110). The 'supreme principle' is the bindingness of the moral law as such, the 'condition which is itself unconditioned . . . not subordinate to any other (*originarium*)'. Our duty is to obey those universalizable laws of self-legislating practical reason that are categorical imperatives. More controversial is Kant's insistence that this supreme condition is 'not yet . . . the whole and complete good . . . for this, *happiness* is also required'. And this happiness cannot be Stoic self-content, merely present in 'partial eyes', but must even be present 'in the judgment of the impartial reason' (*CPrR.* 5: 110). Such a belief in completion is a 'demand' of practical reason just because 'to need happiness, to be also worthy of it, and yet not to participate in it cannot be consistent with the perfect volition of a rational being that would at the same time have all power' (*CPrR.* 5: 110).

Belief in God is required, not optional, as *only* a 'supreme cause of nature having a causality in keeping with the moral disposition' (*CPrR.* 5: 125) can bring about this distribution of happiness in proportion to virtue. If we are unable to believe that worthiness to be happy will be met with proportionate happiness, then we will be caught in a practical antinomy. The desire for happiness (*CPrR.* 5: 108–11) would be set against the demands of virtue in such a way that the moral law would lead to a practical absurdity (*CPrR.* 5: 111–14). Belief in the existence of God (and immortality) is not only warranted, Kant insists, but 'necessary', as the 'highest good' is 'possible only under the condition of the existence of God', which connects 'the presupposition of the existence of God inseparably with duty' (*CPrR.* 5: 125).

---

262). We do not need to take a stand on this issue. What matters is that (practical) knowledge of freedom is established on the basis of morality, and that Kant uses the priority of practical reason to establish belief in God and immortality.

[11] Andrew Chignell, 'Kant's Concepts of Justification', *Noûs*, 41/1 (2007), 33–63 (p. 53).

[12] Chignell, 'Kant's Concepts of Justification', 53.

As with Kant's refutations of theoretical proofs for the existence of God, the success or otherwise of Kant's moral-practical proof does not concern us.[13] What matters is that Kant himself is convinced that it provides warrant for belief in God. Furthermore, Kant suggests that it should not be a cause of regret that belief in God can be grounded only upon practical reason, writing that we should not 'worry about the good cause (of practical reason), for that never comes into play in a merely speculative dispute' (A744/B772). There is even the suggestion that it is providential that claims about God and immortality are beyond the realm of our knowledge (A743/B771). In a related vein, Kant comments in the *Lectures on the Philosophical Doctrine of Religion* that we should 'thank heaven' [*Heil uns!*] that 'our faith [*Glaube*] is not knowledge':

For divine wisdom is apparent in the very fact that we do not know but rather ought to believe that a God exists [*daß ein Gott sei*]. For suppose we could attain to knowledge of God's existence through our experience or in some other way . . . In his every action the human being would represent God to himself as a rewarder or avenger; this image would force itself involuntarily on his soul, and his hope for reward and fear of punishment would take the place of moral motives; the human being *would be virtuous from sensible impulses*. (*LPR* 28: 1084)

NON-MORAL GROUNDS FOR DOCTRINAL BELIEF IN GOD

We cannot have theoretical knowledge of the existence of God; nor can we have the sort of knowledge on practical grounds that we can claim in the case of freedom. Kant consistently uses the term *Glaube* (usually translated as 'faith' or 'belief') in the context of religious commitments; although, he also uses this term in other contexts, both moral and theoretical. This brings us to a further application of 'belief [*Glaube*] in God', where Kant considers that theoretical reason can also gain benefits from belief in God. These benefits are manifested in a circumscribed role for belief in an intelligent designer in the first *Critique*, and in the third *Critique*, where the amenability of the world to our cognitive capacities evokes a sense of there being a teleology immanent within nature, where the assumption of an intelligent designer helps us to track and to be responsive to teleological features of the world.

In the 'Dialectic' of the first *Critique*, after denying that we can have theoretical proofs of the existence of God, Kant nonetheless writes that the 'thesis of the existence of God belongs to doctrinal belief [*Glaube*]', where

---

[13] See Byrne, *Kant on God*, chs 5 and 6. For my interpretation of Kant's moral proof, see 'The Irreducible Importance of Religious Hope in Kant's Conception of the Highest Good', *Philosophy*, 83/325 (2008), 333–51.

'purposive unity' is 'so important a condition of the application of reason to nature that I cannot pass it by', where there is 'no other condition for this unity that could serve me as a clue for the investigation of nature except insofar as I presuppose that a highest intelligence has arranged everything in accordance with the wisest ends' (A826/B584). Kant concludes that 'the presupposition of a wise author of the world is a condition of an aim which is, to be sure, contingent but yet not inconsiderable, namely that of having a guide for the investigation of nature' (A826/B854).[14] This reflection is sketched only briefly in the first *Critique*. In the third *Critique* Kant dwells more extensively on the non-moral 'doctrinal' beliefs that are warranted in relation to two rational needs of the scientist.

First of all, the scientist has an interest in constructing a unified and elegant system of empirical laws, whereby lower-level laws can be derived from a small number of higher-level laws (*CJ* 20: 209). Secondly, the scientist has an interest in understanding the self-regulating and self-reproducing characteristics of biological organisms (*CJ* 5: 362–415). In both cases, Kant considers that the scientist can serve these rational interests and needs only by approaching nature as a teleological system, designed by a divine intelligence. At the same time, Kant is clear in the third *Critique* that it is 'absolutely impossible from a theoretical point of view' for 'human reason' to have 'any theoretical proof of the existence of the original being as a divinity or of the soul as an immortal spirit' (*CJ* 5: 466). Nonetheless, as Chignell puts it, although the presupposition of a divine designer does not constitute theoretical knowledge, the presupposition of 'intelligent design' provides 'an opportunity for her to discover many *other* truths that have predictive and descriptive value, and also to "unify" her various assents about goal-directed systems in nature'.[15]

THE RATIONALIST CONCEPTION OF GOD IN KANT'S CRITICAL PHILOSOPHY

Even sympathetic commentators have been puzzled by this category of 'doctrinal belief'. Leslie Stevenson, for example, complains that it is an unstable hybrid between theoretical and practical reason.[16] Stevenson comforts himself that Kant does not appeal to this category after the first *Critique*, but the evidence from the third *Critique* suggests that this is not correct. I discuss the category of 'doctrinal belief' further below (pp. 143–149), but if we were to

[14] I am indebted here to Chignell, 'Kant's Concepts of Justification', 50–1.
[15] Chignell, 'Kant's Concepts of Justification', 50–1.
[16] Leslie Stevenson, 'Opinion, Belief or Faith, and Knowledge', *Kantian Review*, 7 (2003), 72–101 (pp. 94–5).

attempt a sympathetic explanation of why Kant invokes this category, we should look to the continuity of the rationalist conception of God in Kant's critical philosophy.

In both the first *Critique* and his *Lectures on the Philosophical Doctrine of Religion*, Kant returns to the proof offered for the existence of God in 1763 (discussed in Chapter 3), and remains positive about its role in providing the *content* for the concept of God, whatever we might say about the status of the belief in the *existence* of God. In the first *Critique* Kant describes the concept of the 'All of reality' as a need of reason, as 'all concepts of negations are . . . derivative' upon the 'thoroughgoing determination of all things', a 'transcendental substratum', 'nothing other than the idea of an All of reality [*omnitudo realitatis*]' which 'contains as it were the entire storehouse of material from which all possible predicates of things can be taken': 'All true negations are then nothing but *limits*, which they could not be called unless they were grounded in the unlimited (the All)' (A575/B603–A576/B 604). At the same time, Kant is clear that this does not deliver knowledge that there is such a being 'conforming to the ideal' of the 'All of reality'. Rather there is 'only the idea of such a being, in order to derive from an unconditioned totality of thoroughgoing determination the conditioned totality, i.e., that of the limited' (A577–8/B605–6). What we have secured is not the 'objective relation of an actual object to other things', but 'only that of an *idea* to *concepts*', where we remain in 'complete ignorance' about the 'existence of a being of such pre-eminent excellence' (A579/B607).

In his *Lectures on the Philosophical Doctrine of Religion* Kant explicitly refers back to his 1763 proof, announcing that 'this proof can in no way be refuted, because it has its ground in the nature of human reason' (*LPR* 28: 1034). Even sympathetic commentators have found this pronouncement 'surprising'[17] or 'hardly transparent',[18] going beyond his more circumspect treatment in the first *Critique*. I would suggest that if this is read in context, there is no obvious tension with the line pursued in the first *Critique*. It is true that Kant states in the *Lectures* that it is 'necessary for me', in that it satisfies a demand of reason, 'to assume a being which is the ground of everything possible, because otherwise I would be unable to know what in general the possibility of something consists in' (*LPR* 28: 1034). But, just before this, Kant has written that 'the absolute necessity which we indispensably need as the final ground of all things is the true abyss for human reason':

One can neither resist nor tolerate the thought of a being represented as the highest of all possible things, which may say to itself, 'I am from eternity to eternity, and outside me there is nothing except what exists through my will; *but whence then am I?*'—Here

---

[17] Chignell, 'Kant, Modality, and the Most Real Being', 159.
[18] Wood, *Kant's Rational Theology*, 73.

everything falls away beneath us, and the greatest perfection, as much as the smallest, hovers without any support before speculative reason, and it costs reason nothing to let them both disappear, nor is there the least obstacle to this. In short, an absolutely necessary thing will remain to all eternity an insoluble problem for the human understanding. (*LPR* 28: 1033)

This is a remarkable passage, with the concept of God, which we can neither 'resist' nor 'tolerate', hovering between reality and nothingness, curiously paralleling a traditional theistic world view, where the whole of the creation is suspended and protected from annihilation only by the constant action of God. The passage represents strikingly the difference between Kant's critical position and his account in 1763, where Kant offers a similar ventriloquizing of the thought of God: '*I am from eternity to eternity: apart from me there is nothing, except it be through me*' (*OPA* 2: 151). In his *Lectures* Kant appends to this line '*but whence then am I?*' (*LPR* 28: 1033), indicating that we no longer have theoretical knowledge about the existence of God. This lack of knowledge about the *existence* of God, alongside ongoing confidence in the *concept* of God, is in fact compatible with Kant's observation in the first *Critique* that 'the concept of an absolutely necessary being is a pure concept of reason, i.e., a mere idea', where 'the objective reality' of this idea is 'far from being proved by the fact that reason needs it' (A592–3/B620–1). The oscillation between 'resisting' and 'tolerating' the idea of God is also expressed in this section of the first *Critique*, where Kant writes that 'the inference from a given existence in general to some absolutely necessary being' is 'strange and paradoxical', seeming both 'urgent and correct', while at the same time, when 'framing a concept of such necessity, we have all the conditions of the understanding entirely against us' (A592–3/B620–1).

In a *Reflexion* from 1785–6, Kant again endorses the rationalist proof from possibility:

The possibilities of things, which can only be regarded as determinations of a single universal possibility, namely of the highest being, prove the existence of the *realissimi* as a sum-total [of realities], consequently, if understanding is a reality, they prove that it is intelligent. (*R* 6278, 18: 544–6)

Once again, when read in context, this passage can be aligned with the first *Critique* without much difficulty. Just before this passage, Kant writes that 'absolute necessity is a boundary-concept, by means of which we must always necessarily arrive at some first-thing, which can only be assumed for the sake of its consequences, but which itself cannot be understood or comprehended' (*R* 6278, 18: 544–6). The 'consequences' would seem to be the 'completeness' brought to reason by thinking of each particular determination as a limitation of the 'All of reality'. Although our reason regards all possibilities in this light, Kant is clear that this does not deliver to us knowledge of 'a reality'. Immediately after the passage cited above, Kant distinguishes an insight into what our reason requires from an insight into how reality must be: 'All error consists in our taking our way of determining concepts or deriving them or dividing them to be conditions of things in themselves' (*R* 6278, 18: 544–6).[19]

Reason has certain immanent needs, organizational and structural tasks and exercises for which the concept of God as the harmonious 'All of reality' is indispensable, without this establishing grounds for belief in the existence of God. Pure theoretical reason has an important but limited task in relation to the concept of God, 'purifying it of everything that might be incompatible with the concept of an original being, and of all admixture of empirical limitation', even though we cannot from this idea alone attain 'to the existence of a supreme being' (A639–40/B667–8). In *Metaphysiks Vigilantius* (1794–5), Kant even talks of our attaining a *cognition* (*Erkenntnis*) of the concept of God through pure speculative reason, albeit that we cannot thereby establish the existence of the God described in this concept.[20]

Metaphysical cognitions must therefore be cognitions simply of reason, they arise a priori through pure concepts of reason, i.e., the principles or grounds of cognition are so constituted that one connects the necessity of what one cognizes with the cognition itself, and the concepts are directed at objects that are not only cognized independently of all experience, but that also can never *possibly* become an object of experience. E.g., God, freedom, immortality. (*MV* 29: 945)

In a telling passage from the first *Critique* Kant makes it clear that the God whose existence is postulated by moral-practical reasoning, is the same God who is conceptualized and understood by pure theoretical reason:

Accordingly, despite all its inadequacies, transcendental theology retains an important negative use, and is a constant censor of our reason when it has to do merely with pure ideas, which for this very reason admit of no standard but the transcendental one. For if in some other, perhaps practical relation, the *presupposition* of a highest and all-sufficient being, as supreme intelligence, were to assert its validity without any objection, then it would be of the greatest importance to determine this concept precisely on its transcendental side, as the concept of a necessary and most real being, to get rid of what is incompatible with the highest reality, what belongs to mere appearance (anthropomorphism, broadly understood), and at the same time to get out of the way all opposed assertions. (A640/B668)

---

[19] See also *R* 5492, *R* 5502, *R* 5508, *R* 5522, *R* 5525, *R* 6278. For these extra references, I am indebted to Wood, *Kant's Rational Theology*, 73.

[20] For my discussion of this use of the concept of cognition, I am indebted to Firestone, *Kant and Theology at the Boundaries of Reason*, 36, 38, 46. In drawing upon Firestone, I do not therefore accept the claim made by Firestone and Jacobs that 'pure cognition is perhaps the most important new element of his philosophy of religion' (*In Defense of Kant's Religion*, 233). For a critique of this claim, see Pamela Sue Anderson, 'The Philosophical Significance of Kant's Religion: "Pure Cognition" or "Belief" in God', *Faith and Philosophy*, 29/2 (2012), 151–62.

In this passage Kant tells us that practical moral reason leads us to presuppose a 'highest' and 'all-sufficient' being, both categories from Kant's rationalist heritage. Later on in the first *Critique* Kant tells us that practical reason 'inexorably leads to the concept of a *single, most perfect*, and *rational* primordial being' (A814/B842). This identity between the God of rationalist theology, and the God postulated by practical reason, receives confirmation in the second *Critique*, where Kant explains how the concept of God can be filled out on the basis of practical reason:

When I now try to bring this concept into relation with the object of practical reason, I find that the moral principle admits it as possible only on the presupposition of an author of the world possessed of the *highest perfection*. He must be *omniscient* in order to cognize my conduct even to my inmost disposition in all possible cases and throughout the future, *omnipotent* in order to bestow results appropriate to it, and so too *omnipresent, eternal*, and so forth. Thus the moral law, by means of the concept of the highest good as the object of a pure practical reason, determines the concept of the original being as the *supreme being*. (*CPrR*. 5: 140)

Kant relates this to the critical strictures of the first *Critique*. Although we can have '*theoretical cognition* only in application to *empirical* objects', practical reason is able to bring about a '*determined thought of the supersensible*', to the extent that 'this is determined merely through such predicates as necessarily belong to the pure *practical purpose* given a priori and to its possibility' (*CPrR*. 5: 141). What we in fact find is that moral–practical reason demands a being of the 'highest perfection', which brings back in the traditional properties that attach to the mere concept of God, before we have established grounds for believing in the existence of the reality described by this concept.[21]

---

[21] Peter Byrne argues that Kant's critical conception of God is framed only for practical purposes, in a way that does not give us any sort of 'description' of God (*Kant on God*, 66–8). All that practical–moral reasoning gives us, Byrne claims, is the 'assurance *that* there is a source of moral teleology in the world' (p. 67). If this is correct, there is no continuity of rationalist theology in Kant's critical philosophy, and no identity between the 'All of Reality' or speculative reason and the God postulate of practical reason. Byrne writes that there is 'nothing to be done' with the *Lectures* (pp. 67–8), which clearly set out a substantial conception of God, because they are 'wholly at variance with the clear messages gleaned from other Critical writings' (p. 73). Byrne does not discuss the wide range of passages cited above that also indicate a rich and rationalist conception of God (A575/B603–A578/B606; A592–3/B620–21; A639–40/B667–8; A814/B842; *CPrR*. 5: 137–8, 141; *R* 6278, 18: 544–6; *MV* 29: 945). In support of his minimalist position, Byrne takes other passages out of context (*CJ* 5: 483; *WRP* 20: 304; and *CPrR*. 5: 137–8). It is true that, in these passages, Kant warns against the inappropriate ascription of predicates to God. But, in each case, Kant's warnings have a much more specific target in view than Byrne allows, and are consonant with the 'purifying' role of theoretical reason unpacked above (A639–40/B667–8). Kant's particular targets for criticism, in each of the sections cited by Byrne respectively, are as follows: attempts to construe God as a first cause in space and time (*CJ* 5: 483); attempts to establish the existence of God on the basis of the concept of an 'absolutely necessary thing' (*WRP* 20: 304); and attempts to ascribe to God 'predicates drawn from our own nature', where we add to the concept of God 'psychologically', drawing upon the exercise of our empirical faculties (*CPrR*. 5: 137). In none of these instances is Kant criticizing the process of

This procedure for arriving at the traditional properties of God is confirmed also in lectures given by Kant in 1784–5. The 'very concept' of morality 'brings us to belief in God', a 'supreme being, who is holy in His laws, benevolent in his government, and just in His punishments and rewards' (*Coll.* 27: 306). Contemplation of these moral attributes brings us to see that God must enjoy 'omniscience, omnipotence, omnipresence and unity':

> The most holy and benevolent being must be omniscient, so that He may perceive the inner morality that resides in his disposition. Hence He must also be omnipresent; and the wisest will can only be a single one. Hence His unity, since without this condition the *principium* of morality might be fabricated. (*Coll.* 27: 396)

As we have interpreted it in Chapter 5 (pp. 92–104), a central plank of Kant's transcendental idealism involves the claim that we are ignorant about the *real* possibilities that govern thing in themselves. In this chapter so far we have received further confirmation that God and noumenal freedom are among those things about which we are ignorant, with respect to theoretical knowledge. It is precisely such ignorance, I will argue in the next section, that makes it plausible to consider Kant a realist about God and freedom (at least according to one useful stipulation of what could be meant by 'realism').

KANT'S REALISM ABOUT GOD AND NOUMENAL FREEDOM

'Realism' and 'anti-realism' are not natural kinds, but philosophical terms of art. There is no single thing that is 'realism'. Rather, there are more or less apt ways of distinguishing a position one calls 'realism' from a position called 'anti-realism', in order to capture a particular conceptual texture, difference, or similarity in a particular area. In this studiedly artificial way, I offer the following as an apt-for-purpose distinction between realism and anti-realism, where our purpose is to understand the precise epistemic texture of Kant's commitment to belief in God. We are realist about a proposition if we consider that the truth or falsity of the proposition is independent of our epistemic practices for forming beliefs.[22] We are anti-realist if we deny this claim, such

---

ascribing *appropriate* predicates to God, which are demanded by the concept of 'a *single, most perfect*, and *rational* primordial being' (A814/B842).

[22] For a fuller discussion see my *The Realist Hope*, and 'Realism and Anti-Realism' in *The Oxford Handbook to the Epistemology of Theology*, ed. Richard Aquino (Oxford: Oxford University Press, forthcoming). See also Patrick Kain, 'Realism and Anti-Realism in Kant's Second *Critique*', *Philosophy Compass*, 1 (2006), 449–65.

that the truth or falsity of a proposition is considered to be dependent upon our epistemic practices. Most people, unless they have read too much (and perhaps not enough) philosophy, will think that the proposition 'Mars has two satellite moons' should be given a realist analysis. Similarly, most people would find it a strain to offer a realist analysis of the claim that 'Tony Hancock is extremely funny': it would be a heroic ontologist who insisted that a person's 'funniness' is independent of whether or not people find that person funny. In other areas, such as God, freedom and morality, it is more difficult to know what to think.

We have seen that, for Kant, God and noumenal freedom are among things-in-themselves, about which we cannot have theoretical knowledge, because we do not know the real possibilities that govern things-in-themselves. Another way of putting this is that the truth or falsity of propositions about the real possibilities that govern things-in-themselves is independent of our epistemic practices. This is realism, on my construal, in that the truth about God and noumenal freedom (whether they exist and in what way) is independent of our beliefs about either.

Kant's realism, on this construal and on these issues, can hardly be in any doubt, when we review what has been discussed above (pp. 137–149). We saw, in the first *Critique*, that Kant insists that we will never be able to demonstrate either that there 'is a God' or that there is not, as reason has no way 'to derive the ground' for the 'inner possibility' of either (A742/B770). Even having framed a complete conception of God, Kant insists we are ignorant 'as to the existence' of such a being (A579/B607). If the truth or falsity of propositions about the existence of God were not independent of our epistemic practices, there could be no conceptual space for such critical scepticism. It is in fact Kant's critical scepticism (on the front of theoretical knowledge) about God's existence that indicates Kant's realism. We saw this take a striking form in his *Lectures*, where Kant ventriloquizes God's own reflections, 'I am from eternity to eternity, and outside me there is nothing except what exists through my will' (*LPR* 28: 1033). Kant uses this formulation in 1763 (*OPA* 2: 151), but then supplements it here: 'but whence then am I?' (*LPR* 28: 1033). Kant describes the concept of God as 'hovering' between existence and non-existence, 'an insoluble problem for the human understanding' (*LPR* 28: 1033).

Similarly with freedom, Kant insists that he has failed, by theoretical reason alone, to 'prove the possibility of freedom', not because there is no truth or falsity independent of our epistemic practices, but because 'we cannot cognize anything about the possibility of any real ground' (A558/B586). This renders implausible Allison's claim that when it comes to the question of whether we are *really* free, there is no 'context-independent "fact-of-the-matter"' for Kant.[23] It is true that there is no context-independent *access* to the fact-of-the-matter,

---

[23] Allison, 'Kant's Transcendental Idealism', 121.

but it is only because there is a fact-of-the-matter that is independent of our spatio-temporal experience that practical reason is permitted to postulate such freedom at all. If the bounds of reality were coextensive with our contextual (spatio-temporal) experience of it, then freedom would not be really possible, and we would not be able to presuppose it, in which case 'morality' would 'have to give way to the mechanism of nature' (Bxxvii–xxix).

That we can have no theoretical knowledge about the truth of things as they are independent of our epistemic practices impacts upon our access to knowledge about the truth, but it does not affect a realist account of truth about things-in-themselves, as realism is construed here. I do not deny that there are other useful ways of carving up the realist/anti-realist distinction. It might be apt for other purposes to stipulate that it is criterial for realism that we can have knowledge about the truth that is independent of our epistemic practices. If we stipulate that the possibility of theoretical knowledge is criterial for 'epistemological realism', as Merold Westphal does, Kant does indeed end up a form of epistemological anti-realist about God and freedom, in that he denies the possibility of theoretical knowledge about the truth.[24] At the same time, Westphal concedes that Kant is a 'metaphysical realist' in that 'the world or God exists independently of our thinking about them'; indeed 'that is what the thing in itself is all about'.[25] A construal of 'epistemological realism' that links realism to the possibility of theoretical knowledge would seem too rigorous if our purpose is to distinguish competing positions in philosophical theology. The philosophical tradition will insist that we can have true beliefs about God, based on revelation, faith, and (perhaps) some evidence; but theoretical knowledge about God will often be denied by the orthodox theologian, because of the mystery of the divine nature, where only God can *know* the divine nature. And indeed, having framed 'epistemological realism' in this way, Westphal finds that most orthodox philosophical theologians, including Augustine, Aquinas, Karl Barth, and Kant, are 'epistemological anti-realists'.[26] Such an account of epistemological realism turns out to be apt for the rhetorical purpose of bringing to light that if Kant is an 'anti-realist' about God, in denying theoretical knowledge, then so too is much of the orthodox theological tradition.

A more divisive construal of 'epistemological realism' would require not the possibility of theoretical knowledge but the possibility of *true belief*, which could be delivered by faith or practical reason. Such a construal has the advantage of separating out the field more: the theological tradition would insist on the possibility of true beliefs about God, and God's action, on the

---

[24] Merold Westphal, 'Theological Anti-Realism', in *Realism and Religion: Philosophical and Theological Perspectives* (Aldershot: Ashgate Publishing, 2007), 131–45.
[25] Westphal, 'Theological Anti-Realism', 131.
[26] Westphal, 'Theological Anti-Realism', 141.

basis of God's own self-revelation received by faith. The sharp question to put to Kant, therefore, is whether he considers *true belief* about God and freedom to be possible, on the basis of practical reason. It is to this question that I turn in the remainder of the chapter.

BELIEF AND ACCEPTANCE

In recent work on epistemology a distinction has been drawn between 'acceptance-as-true' and 'belief-in-truth'. Drawing out aspects of this distinction will help us to take a precise interpretative question to Kant's texts.[27] First of all, I set out a version of the distinction, followed by some explanation and examples.[28]

Acceptance-as-true
I accept a proposition as true, when I presume that it is true for the purposes of a specific project or activity. I bracket the question of whether the proposition is ultimately true or false, and do not stake myself on the ultimate truth or falsity of the proposition. I could even 'accept-as-true' a proposition—for the purposes of making possible a particular project or activity—while believing the proposition to be false.

Belief-in-truth
I believe a proposition is true, when I affirm that the proposition is true. Even though my warrant for believing the proposition might come from practical reason, I affirm that it is true independently of its usefulness for practical purposes. I could not 'believe-in-the-truth' of a proposition— even for practical purposes—whilst regarding the proposition as false.

Acceptance-as-true is a common and important texture in our ordinary epistemology. For example, well-trained store workers 'accept-as-true' that 'the customer is always right'; but they will not, if they are rational, believe this. Customers return items as faulty that they have broken themselves, or invent defects in products that they return. The judge accepts-as-true that the accused is innocent until proven guilty, although she might believe the accused to be guilty. The doctor urgently needs to treat a patient, and is torn between two equally likely diagnoses. Because treatment must proceed if there is to be any

---

[27] Here I am indebted to Andrew Chignell, whose work alerted me to the value of applying this contemporary debate to Kant exegesis: see Chignell, 'Kant's Concepts of Justification', and Andrew Chignell, 'Belief in Kant', *Philosophical Review*, 116/3 (2007), 323–60.

[28] In the way I set out this distinction, and in the following examples and explanation, I am indebted to Edna Ullman-Margalit and Avishai Margalit, 'Holding True and Holding as True', *Synthese*, 92/2 (1992), 167–87 (pp. 170–2). Ullman-Margalit and Margalit also have a helpful section where they apply this distinction to Kant (pp. 172–4).

chance of a successful outcome, the doctor accepts-as-true one of the diagnoses, without believing that it is true. Acceptance-as-true need not involve belief in the truth of the proposition, but it is not therefore anti-realism: the judge believes there is a truth of the matter about whether the accused is guilty or innocent, independently of the epistemic practices of the court. Belief-in-truth, on the other hand, occurs where we stake ourselves on the veracity of the proposition. This is not the same thing as having strong evidence for the proposition: I might have weak evidence, and I might know that it is weak, but still invest in its truth.

This distinction between acceptance-as-true and belief-in-truth involves creating terms of art where ordinary language tends to use the more blanket term 'belief'. There are other ways in which the distinction could be drawn, and the same distinction could be drawn in more detail.[29] Typically, in the literature, the distinction is mapped onto a further distinction between assents that we hold voluntarily ('acceptance-as-true'), subject to our choosing to adopt the practice for which the assent is a required presumption, and assents that we cannot help but hold ('belief-in-truth'), because we just consider that they are true. This particular further detail is potentially misleading for our purposes, for reasons that will become clear. Although it is certainly the case that there is always a voluntary dimension to 'acceptance-as-truth', it does not follow that a voluntary dimension is inconsistent with belief-in-truth, especially in the area of religious faith. 'Acceptance-as-true' is also sometimes characterized as pertaining to practical reason, rather than to reason in its more theoretical endeavours. It is better for our purposes if we use the more neutral phrasing, where a proposition is accepted-as-true for the purpose of a 'specific project or activity', as Kant will apply a notion of 'acceptance-as-true' in theoretical as well as practical contexts.[30]

The distinction as drawn out above is sufficient for our purposes of setting out meaningful interpretative options when treating Kant. The question is: what is the precise epistemic status of Kant's 'belief' (*Glaube*) in God (and freedom): 'acceptance-as-true' or 'belief-in-truth'? All the commitments that I have so far ascribed to Kant are compatible with either 'acceptance-as-true' or 'belief-in-truth': a lack of theoretical knowledge, commitment to the

---

[29] For more detail, with contrasts to other natural epistemic textures, see Ullmann-Margalit and Margalit, 'Holding True and Holding as True'. Other commentators use the category of 'acceptance' to cover a wider class of propositional attitudes. For example, Stalnaker distinguishes passive from active acceptance, where the latter involves 'belief-in-truth' with a degree of voluntariness to this belief: see Robert Stalnaker, *Inquiry* (Cambridge MA: Bradford Books, 1984). Audi similarly describes a 'duality' in the use of acceptance language, where 'on one use, acceptance entails belief', but not on another: see Robert Audi, 'Belief, Faith and Acceptance', *International Journal for Philosophy of Religion*, 63/1 (2008), 87–102 (pp. 90–1).

[30] Here I depart from Ullmann-Margalit and Margalit, who restrict the category of acceptance to practical contexts ('Holding True and Holding as True', 177–8). In this I am closer to Jonathan Cohen, who uses the category of 'acceptance' in theoretical as well as practical contexts ('Belief and Acceptance', *Mind*, 98/391 (1989), 367–89 (p. 368)).

propositions on practical grounds, a traditional rationalist conception of that which is accepted/believed-in, within the framework of a realism about the ultimate truth or falsity of the propositions that are accepted/believed-in.

Accounts of Kant's belief in God that treat it as a case of 'acceptance-as-true', where the question of truth is bracketed, are sometimes called 'deflationary accounts', in that they deflate any seemingly substantial metaphysical commitments.[31] A reader attached to a deflationary reading, who remains unconvinced by the eventual conclusions of this chapter, could continue to engage with this book even without being converted to a more metaphysically committed reading. An account of Kant that is deflationary still has to consider, in some way, the content of texts where Kant discusses the relationship between divine and human action. The guiding question of how it can be said that we are free, given that we are created by God, would still have some purchase, but it would have reduced importance. On a deflationary account we would be dealing with a demythologized construal of the question, which now puts the emphasis on the '*how can it be said*' clause in 'how can it be said that we are free, given that we are created by God?'. The question now means: 'how can we accept-as-true the claim that we are free, given that we also accept-as-true the claim that we are created by God?' In the opening of this chapter, I commented that if Kant is not committed to belief in God, this puts a hole under the waterline of the book. If Kant's commitment to belief in God is a case of mere acceptance-as-true, I think we lose some of the wind in our sails, if not a sail or two. For this reason, I take the challenge of the acceptance-as-true interpretation head on.

OPINION, BELIEF OR FAITH, AND KNOWLEDGE

In a number of places Kant distinguishes three ways of holding a proposition to be true (*das Fürwahrhalten*): *meinen*, *glauben*, and *wissen*

---

[31] For examples of such interpretations, see Paul Guyer, *Kant on Freedom, Law, and Happiness* (Cambridge: Cambridge University Press, 2000); Patrick Frierson, *Freedom and Anthropology in Kant's Moral Psychology* (Cambridge: Cambridge University Press, 2003); Byrne, *Kant on God*, chs 4–5. The debate around how to interpret Kant's 'belief' in God is sometimes framed in terms of whether we have a case of 'belief that' there is a God, or 'belief in' God. See Anderson and Bell, *Kant and Theology*, and A. W. Moore, *Noble in Reason, Infinite in Faculty: Themes and Variations in Kant's Moral and Religious Philosophy* (London: Routledge, 2003), 155–8, 188–9. The conclusion of these commentators is that Kant's belief in God is a case of 'belief in' rather than 'belief that', where the latter is a form of theoretical knowledge appropriate to empirical cognition, and 'belief in' is 'characterized by what it enables us to do' (Moore, *Noble in Reason*, 189. The question resurfaces as to whether 'belief-in' God is a case of 'belief-in-the-truth' or 'acceptance-as-true'. As I read Moore, and Anderson and Bell, their position gravitates closer to 'belief-in-truth', in that 'genuine agnosticism' about God is ruled out: 'if we really do have no alternative except to believe in them [the postulates], then we have no alternative but to *believe* them' (Anderson and Bell, *Kant and Theology*, 66).

(A820/B848–A831/B859).[32] These are usually translated as 'opinion', 'belief' or 'faith', and 'knowledge'. This was a standard way of classifying the field in Kant's context, and has its origins in medieval theology (about which, more below). Kant's discussion of the trio features some interpretative knots,[33] but for the most part we can avoid these for our purposes of determining whether *Glaube*, in the case of God, is a form of acceptance-as-true or belief-in-truth.[34]

Kant distinguishes between these various epistemological textures in terms of a further distinction between the 'objective sufficiency' and 'subjective sufficiency' that we have for our beliefs:

> Taking something to be true [*fürwahrhalten*] ... has the following three stages in relation to conviction ... : having an opinion, believing and knowing. Having an opinion [*meinen*] is taking something to be true with the consciousness that it is subjectively as well as objectively insufficient. If taking something to be true is only subjectively sufficient and is at the same time held to be objectively insufficient, then it is called believing [*glauben*]. Finally, when the taking something to be true is both subjectively and objectively sufficient it is called knowing [*wissen*]. (A822/B850)

Kant explains that we have 'objective grounds' (A820/B 848) for a judgement, if the judgement is valid for everyone 'merely so long as he has reason'. In this passage, Kant seems to contrast this with 'subjective' grounds for a judgement where it 'has its ground only in the particular constitution of the subject' (A821/B848). Such a judgement with subjective grounds has a mere 'private validity', which 'cannot be communicated' (A821/B849). Taken in isolation, this distinction suggests a familiar distinction between the individual subject's own assessment of his or her epistemic justification, and a publicly available evaluation of this justification.[35] This would give us a quantitive distinction between different degrees of the same sort of epistemic justification: inadequate (subjective) and adequate (objective). Kant is notoriously unclear about his subjective/objective distinction, but from other passages we can at least tell that by 'subjective grounds' he does not simply mean the individual's own (perhaps idiosyncratic) assessment of his or her epistemic justification. In other places where Kant uses the category of the 'subjective', he uses it where judgements are universal for all human beings, *given* the constitution of the human subject, with experiences (of space and time, or of beauty) and

---

[32] This trio also appears in lecture notes based on Kant's 'Logic Lectures': see *BL* 24: 148, 228.; *VL* 24: 850; *DL* 24: 732; *JL* 9: 66. I am indebted to Stevenson, 'Opinion, Belief or Faith, and Knowledge', for these references.

[33] These are explored fully in Stevenson, 'Opinion, Belief or Faith, and Knowledge', Chignell, 'Belief in Kant' and 'Kant's Concepts of Justification', and Wood, *Kant's Moral Religion*, 13–25.

[34] In this section I am indebted to Chignell, 'Belief in Kant' and 'Kant's Concepts of Justification'; Stevenson, 'Opinion, Belief or Faith, and Knowledge'; and Wood, *Kant's Moral Religion*, 13–25.

[35] Stevenson, 'Opinion, Belief or Faith, and Knowledge', 84.

practical projects (morality) that are non-negotiable for us. Space and time are 'subjective', in that they are dependent upon the forms of intuition of the human subject (A42/B59). Judgements of taste, in the third *Critique*, are universally valid for all human beings, and so are 'subjectively' but not 'objectively valid' (*CJ* 5: 215). Just as people can think that they have objectively sufficient grounds, but fail to, so people can think that they have subjectively sufficient grounds, but fail to; indeed, the 'subjective grounds' discussed above that have only a 'private validity' (A821/B848) would seem to be insufficient in this way. Both *wissen* and *glauben* are based on universally valid grounds, reasons that compel the judgement of any rational person:[36] in the case of *wissen* we have universal grounds that are objectively valid (irrespective of our commitment to a particular project), but in the case of *glauben* we have universal grounds that are subjectively valid (for all rational human agents committed to the project for which the *Glaube* is required).

We have *wissen* where we have a logical proof, or a spatio-temporal experience. The example given above of space being 'subjective' should not confuse us here: space is 'subjective' only in the sense that it is dependent upon our forms of intuition. Our judgements about the Euclidean properties of space are 'objective', in that we are compelled to make these judgements simply by virtue of the fact that we receive the world according to Euclidean principles, and regardless of any rational commitments, such as the commitment to follow the moral law. In the case of *wissen* we have 'conviction' (*Überzeugung*). *Meinen* ('opinion') is a lesser grade on the same qualitative scale as *wissen*, involving speculations about matters of fact where we have insufficient evidence. Where we know that we have insufficient evidence, 'opinion' is a perfectly respectable epistemic attitude; we make an epistemic mistake, though, when we confusedly think that we have objective grounds sufficient for 'conviction' (*Überzeugung*), when we do not. As *meinen* and *wissen* are different grades on the same scale, one can become the other through the accretion of evidence: 'opining [*meinen*] can be gradually supplemented by the same kind of grounds and finally become a *knowing* [*wissen*]' (*OIT* 8: 141).

Glauben is distinct from both *wissen* and *meinen*. It is distinct from *wissen* in that we do not have objective grounds, in the sense of logical proofs or spatio-temporal experience. It is distinct from *meinen* in that we hold to beliefs generated through *glauben* with the conviction (*Überzeugung*) that is usually appropriate only to *wissen*, where we might have empirical evidence appropriate only to *meinen*, or no empirical evidence at all. Here we seem to have a 'subjectively' grounded form of conviction, where 'subjective sufficiency is called conviction (for myself)' (A822/B850). We have the 'subjective' (and universally valid) grounds to do this, when a particular rational human project

---

[36] See Stevenson, 'Opinion, Belief or Faith, and Knowledge', 85; and Wood, *Kant's Moral Religion*, 14–16.

permits or requires us to hold the belief. At this point, we can pose our precise question to the category of *Glaube*: when we believe (*glauben*) a proposition to be true, on the basis that it is required for a particular rational project, is this a case of 'accepting-as-true' or 'belief-in-truth'?

THE CASE FOR BELIEF-IN-TRUTH

As we have seen above, Kant considers that our assent to the proposition that we are noumenally free has the status of *wissen*, albeit based on practical grounds, and not amounting to theoretical knowledge. Given this, it seems only plausible to apply the category of 'belief-in-truth' in the case of noumenal freedom. Kant's belief (*Glaube*) in God, though, is different. Kant never uses the category of *wissen* in this context. When he describes belief in God as 'morally necessary', he explains that this 'moral necessity *is subjective*, that is, a need, and not *objective*', relative to the binding human moral project of 'striving to produce and promote the highest good in the world' (*CPrR.* 5: 125–66).

In the discussion of 'noumenal affection' in Chapter 5, I suggested that it was clear from Kant's texts that he was committed to some notion of our being affected by things-in-themselves, even if some commentators do not find this consistent with Kant's wider philosophy. In the case of the status of 'belief in God'—acceptance-as-true or belief-in-truth—the textual evidence is more ambivalent, reflecting perhaps Kant's own ambivalence. Nonetheless, I do consider that it is more plausible to read Kant as subscribing to belief-in-truth about God, for reasons I set out in this section. In the next section, I address some of the considerations that lead commentators to ascribe a more deflationary reading to Kant's belief in God, along the lines of 'acceptance-as-true'.

At this point, we need a more precise differentiation of the different ways in which Kant uses the category of *Glaube*. Across his work, Kant distinguishes between three different types of *Glaube*: 'pragmatic', 'doctrinal', and 'moral'. As we will see, the first two categories are cases of 'acceptance-as-true', but the last category is an example of 'belief-in-truth'.

Kant gives an example of a 'pragmatic belief' (*pragmatische Glauben*) in the first *Critique* (A824/B852). A doctor makes a diagnosis, as a basis for giving urgent treatment. The doctor might not believe-in-the-truth of the diagnosis. There might be an equally probable alternative diagnosis, nonetheless, a decision must be made for practical purposes, and the diagnosis must be accepted-as-true. Kant also gives the example of a businessman who, 'in order to strike a deal', needs 'not just to opine that there will be something to be gained thereby, but to believe it, i.e., to have his opinion be sufficient for an undertaking into the uncertain' (*JL* 9: 67–8n.)[37] Kant explains that in this case we have belief, rather than opinion, not because of the 'degree' of evidence, but because of the 'relation that [the belief] has as cognition to action' (*JL* 9: 67–8n.).

'Doctrinal belief' (see pp. 143–144) arises from the human project of acquiring systematic theoretical knowledge about nature. It remains a species of *glauben*, in that it is dependent upon a specific human rational project, even though the project in this case is not a practical or moral one.[38] In the first *Critique* Kant explains that 'the thesis of the existence of God belongs to doctrinal belief' (A826/B854). It arises in that the presupposition of the 'purposive unity' of the universe is a 'condition of the application of reason to nature', where there is no 'other condition for this unity' than the presupposition of 'a highest intelligence' (A826/B854). Kant is clear that the word 'belief' in this context 'concerns only the direction that an idea gives me' (A827/B855). It is 'contingent' upon my need to have a 'guide for the investigation of nature', where the 'outcome of my experiments' confirms the 'usefulness of this presupposition' (A826/B854). Such doctrinal belief in God is a specific case of what Kant calls 'regulative ideas', where 'concepts of reason' that have 'no object in any sort of experience' are 'thought problematically', that is, without affirming or denying their existence: 'In order to ground regulative principles of the systematic use of the understanding in the field of experience in relation to them (as heuristic fictions)' (A771/B799). Both pragmatic and doctrinal beliefs are more plausibly construed as examples of 'acceptance-as-true' rather than 'belief-in-truth'. This applies also to the doctrinal belief in the existence of God, which serves as a regulative idea that directs the course of our investigation into nature. If this were all Kant had to say about God, we could conclude that Kant's belief in God is a case of 'acceptance-as-true'. In fact, though, Kant has quite a lot more to say about other types of belief in God. Kant explicitly distinguishes between merely regulative doctrinal belief in God, and moral belief in God. Doctrinal/regulative belief in God must 'not be called practical' (A827/B855). Kant concedes that 'there is something unstable about merely doctrinal beliefs', because of 'difficulties that come up in speculation', but that 'it is entirely otherwise in the case of moral belief':

For there it is absolutely necessary that something must happen, namely, that I fulfill the moral law in all points. The end here is inescapably fixed, and according to all my insight there is possible only a single condition under which this end is consistent with all ends together and thereby has practical validity, namely, that there be a God and a future world; I also know with complete certainty that no one else knows of any other

[37] For this reference, I am indebted to Stevenson, 'Opinion, Belief or Faith, and Knowledge', 92.

[38] For my discussion of doctrinal belief, I am indebted to Stevenson, 'Opinion, Belief or Faith, and Knowledge', 94–5, and Chignell, 'Belief in Kant', 345–54. Chignell is more positive about this category than Stevenson.

conditions that lead to this same unity of ends under the moral law. But since the moral precept is thus at the same time my maxim (as reason commands that it ought to be), I will inexorably believe in the existence of God and a future life, and I am sure that nothing can make these beliefs unstable, since my moral principles themselves, which I cannot renounce without becoming contemptible in my own eyes, would thereby be subverted. (A829/B857)

A similar distinction between the theoretical–doctrinal and practical–moral needs of reason to presuppose the existence of God is drawn by Kant in his essay *What Does It Mean to Orient Oneself in Thinking?* (1786). The theoretical and doctrinal need of reason is 'only conditioned': 'We must assume the existence of God *if we want to judge* about the first causes of everything contingent, chiefly in the order of ends which is actually present in the world' (*OIT* 8: 139). 'Far more important', Kant explains, 'is the need of reason in its practical use':

Because it is unconditioned, and we are necessitated to presuppose the existence of God not only if we *want* to judge, but because we *have to judge* . . . reason *needs* to assume . . . a supreme intelligence as the highest *independent* good . . . in order to give objective reality to the concept of the highest good, i.e. to prevent it, along with morality, from being taken merely as a mere ideal, as it would be if that whose idea inseparably accompanies morality should not exist anywhere. (*OIT* 8: 139)

In the second *Critique* Kant goes well beyond anything that acceptance of a regulative idea would deliver, and claims that practical reason grounds the 'objective reality' (*die Objektive Realität*) of God and immortality, as well as freedom, even claiming that theoretical cognition thereby is extended:

Thus by the practical law that commands the existence of the highest good possible in the world, the possibility of those objects of pure speculative reason, the objective reality which the latter could not assure them, is postulated; by this the theoretical cognition of pure reason certainly receives an increment, but it consists only in this: that those concepts, otherwise problematic (merely thinkable) for it, are now declared assertorically to be concepts to which real objects belong, because practical reason is thereby justified in assuming them. (*CPrR.* 5: 134)

Theoretical reason is 'forced to grant *that there are such objects*' as God and immortality, 'though it cannot determine them more closely and so cannot itself extend this cognition of the objects' (*CPrR.* 5: 135). In this sense, Kant keeps himself within the limits of his epistemic discipline, as he understands these limits, as there is 'no extension of the cognition *of given supersensible objects*' (*CPrR.* 5: 135), beyond cognition of their existence, sufficient for the purposes of morality. When we believe God to have certain properties, it is because of what we 'cognize' about the concept of the highest perfection (see pp. 144–149), rather than because of an extension of our theoretical knowledge of 'supersensible objects'.

Kant reiterates this view in his essay *What Real Progress Has Metaphysics Made in Germany?* (1793). After the familiar denial of the possibility of 'theoretical knowledge beyond the objects of the senses' (*WRP* 20: 296), Kant stipulates that the 'modality of our assent' to the proposition that there is a God is a case of neither opinion nor probability (*WRP* 20: 297). The 'super-sensible differs in its very species from the sensuously knowable', so that there is 'no way at all of reaching it by those very same steps whereby we may hope to arrive at certainty in the field of the sensible': 'Thus there is no approximation to it either, and therefore no assent whose logical value could be called probability' (*WRP* 20: 299). In the case of God, we must have '*belief*' (*WRP* 20: 297). Such belief is 'not a prudential doctrine' along the lines of 'better to believe to profess too much than too little', because 'in that case the belief would not be sincere' (*WRP* 20: 298). Belief in God, freedom, and immortality are 'necessary' in 'a moral sense', whereby we 'voluntarily grant them objective reality' (*WRP* 20: 299).

This capacity of practical reason to inform theoretical reason makes sense when one considers the importance that Kant attaches to the unity of reason: that theoretical and practical reason are not two distinct 'faculties', but a single reason engaged with the questions '(1.) What can I know? (2.) What should I do? (3.) What can I hope?' (A805/B833). When discussing the primacy of practical reason in moral contexts, Kant writes about 'the union of pure speculative with pure practical reason in one cognition', where theoretical reason 'must accept' propositions that '*belong inseparably to the practical interest* or pure reason' (*CPrR.* 5: 121).

As Sebastian Gardner explains,[39] the 'authority of practical reason' for Kant is 'due to theoretical reason's recognition of their *shared nature* or *essence*': 'It is still only one and the same reason which, whether from a theoretical or a practical perspective, judges according to a priori principles' (*CPrR.* 5: 121). This theme of the unity of reason is also picked up in the *Groundwork*, where Kant writes that 'there can, in the end, be only one and the same reason, which must be distinguished merely in its application' (*GW* 4: 391). The unity of reason, and the priority of reason in its practical application, undergird Kant's whole conception of the critical philosophy. In the first *Critique* Kant states that 'the entire armament of reason' is 'directed only at the three prob-lems ... *what is to be done* if the will is free, if there is a God, and if there is a future world' (A800/B828). 'Theology and morality', Kant writes, 'were the two incentives, or better, the points of reference for all the abstract inquiries of reason' (A853/B881). In the second *Critique* Kant affirms that 'speculative reason is only conditional and is complete in practical use alone' (*CPrR.* 5: 121), and in the third *Critique* Kant affirms that '*God, freedom,* and *immortality of the*

---

[39] Sebastian Gardner, 'The Primacy of Practical Reason', 267. In my discussion of the unity of reason, I am indebted to Gardner, pp. 261–9.

soul are those problems at the solution of which all the apparatus of meta-physics aims as its final and sole aim' (*CJ* 5: 473). The patterns of mutual support between parts of Kant's system are complex. Theoretical reason provides to practical reason a purified 'cognition' of the concept of God; practical reason informs reason in its theoretical aspect of the existence of God (according to this concept); and then, in the third *Critique*, theoretical reason is assisted in its rational task of understanding nature, by assuming teleological patterns of order in nature, dependent upon a divine intelligence. Kant is explicit about the way in which this rational interest in teleology ('physical ends') can then feed back into, and further support, our moral interest in God, because of the unity of reason:

Now the objective reality of the idea of God as the moral author of the world cannot of course be established by means of physical ends *alone*; nevertheless, if the cognition of those ends is connected with that of the moral end, then the former, because of the maxim of pure reason to seek unity of principles as far as possible, is of great significance for assisting the practical reality of that idea by means of the reality that it already has for the power of judgment from a theoretical point of view. (*CJ* 5: 456)

Finally, in this connection, I would submit that the subsequent discussion in Chapters 8–10 will itself offer implicit support for interpreting Kant's belief in God as 'belief-in-truth'. In the final three chapters, I will present material where Kant worries about fairly technical issues in relating God to the creation. Kant will claim that God is not the creator of appearances (*CPrR*. 5: 102), that space is 'not a thing as a divine work' (*R* 6057; 18: 439), that God does not concur with natural events, but that God does concur with free human action, although not in a sense that would be recognized by the medieval tradition. This sort of discussion is itself suggestive of belief-in-truth rather than acceptance-as-true. The question of the precise causal joint between God and the creation is significant and important, if the claim that 'God exists' is true independently of its usefulness for practical purposes, even if the warrant I have for the belief comes from practical considerations. It is less easy to see why such technical issues matter if I am presuming the truth of 'God exists' for practical purposes, bracketing the question of whether the proposition is ultimately true or false, such that I do not stake myself on the ultimate truth or falsity of the proposition. It is hard to understand why Kant continues to worry about fairly technical questions in philosophical theology, to do with the precise scope of divine action, if his God-talk has a merely heuristic ('look at it this way, but don't concern yourself with the truth'), or morale-boosting function.

THE CASE FOR MERE ACCEPTANCE-AS-TRUE

Belief in God as Incompatible with the 'Copernican Revolution'

Before looking at a more compelling exegetical reason for claiming that Kant intends to 'accept-as-true' only the proposition that God exists, I deal first of all with a not unusual (but nonetheless unsatisfactory) way of putting the claim that Kant cannot believe in God (or even noumenal freedom) in the sense of 'belief-in-truth'.

One can find the attitude that Kant cannot possibly believe in God or freedom, because it contradicts what we *already know about transcendental idealism*. What is known about transcendental idealism is that it inaugurates a Copernican Revolution, which involves denying extravagant metaphysical claims about the structure of reality independent of our cognition, because we now understand that 'all objects without qualification are to be considered as having to "conform to our cognition"' (Bxvi).[40] Although responses along these lines have a seeming force, they prejudge the issue in an unhelpful way, as they have already decided what 'transcendental idealism' itself involves. 'Transcendental idealism' cannot be invoked as a straightforward objection to an interpretation, when it is the interpretation of transcendental idealism that is itself at issue.[41]

In Chapter 5 I set out an interpretation of transcendental idealism whereby Kant's claim to restrict knowledge to 'make room for faith [*Glaube*]' has real bite (Bxxx). The category of theoretical knowledge is a subset of the wider category of reason. It is not the case that the point of transcendental idealism is to make 'all objects' conform in a Copernican way to our cognition. Such Copernicanism applies just to the spatio-temporal objects of theoretical knowledge. Theoretical knowledge is secured by virtue of being limited to the realm of spatio-temporal experience. Transcendental idealism, I argued, limits theoretical knowledge to the spatio-temporal, secures knowledge within those limits, *and* opens up a space for reason beyond these limits, precisely because we are now assured that the limits of experience are not coextensive with the way in which things-in-themselves must be.

The 'Subjective' and Voluntary Nature of Belief in God

We will need more precise textual grounds to doubt that Kant believes-in-the-truth of the proposition that God exists. These grounds might be found where

---

[40] For a sensitive and nuanced ventriloquizing of this position, see Gardner, 'The Primacy of Practical Reason', 270–3 (p. 271).

[41] For this way of putting the response to the critic, I am indebted to Hogan, 'How to Know Unknowable Things in Themselves', 60.

Kant underlines the element of voluntariness that is involved when it comes to believing in the existence of God. Beliefs that are 'subjective' are, as we have seen, not beliefs with inadequate or idiosyncratic justification, but beliefs that we choose to assent to, inasmuch as we are committed to certain human rational projects. Although it is 'morally necessary' to believe in 'the existence of God', this 'moral necessity *is subjective*, that is, a need, and not *objective*, that is, itself a duty' (*CPrR.* 5: 125). Belief in God guarantees one aspect of the 'highest good', the promise of 'happiness in thorough conformity with . . . worthiness' (*CPrR.* 5: 144):

The way in which we are to think such a harmony of the laws of nature with those of freedom has in it something with respect to which we have a *choice*, since theoretical reason decides nothing with apodictic certainty about it. (*CPrR.* 5: 145)

Further down, Kant writes that the 'manner' in which we render the promotion of the highest good possible 'rests with our choice', where a 'free interest of pure practical reason decides for the assumption of a wise author of the world' (*CPrR.* 5: 146). Belief in God, therefore, is 'not commanded', but is a 'voluntary [*freiwillig*] determination of our judgement, conducive to the moral (commanded) purpose and moreover harmonizing with the theoretical need of reason to assume that existence and to make it the basis of the further use of reason' (*CPrR.* 5: 146). In his 1793 essay *What Real Progress?*, this voluntary dimension to belief is again underlined, with Kant telling us that we 'voluntarily' grant 'objective reality' to 'God, freedom in its practical aspect, and immortality' (*WRP* 20: 299).

Certainly then, for Kant, there is an important voluntary element to belief in God. This can seem to tip the interpretative scales towards acceptance-as-true, rather than belief-in-truth.[42] If we believe in the truth of something, we would usually regard this as something over which we have no choice: we simply have to believe this, because it seems to us to be the truth. We might even prefer not to have to believe it. Only if we bracket the question of truth, in the way permitted by 'acceptance-as-truth', can we really have the sort of voluntary control over our assents presupposed by Kant. In the contemporary epistemological literature, the distinction between the involuntary and voluntary is used almost as a litmus test for whether we have a case of 'acceptance' or 'belief'.[43]

---

[42] See, e.g., Byrne, *Kant on God*, 'belief in God exists for the Critical philosopher as a result of human reason's need to orient itself . . . But it is still a need and not a fact about reality independent of us' (p. 77). Byrne bases this on the passage from *What is Orientation in Thinking?* discussed above (*OIT* 8: 138–9). Byrne does not pay sufficient attention to Kant's own distinction in this passage between the theoretical and practical needs of reason.

[43] See Ullmann-Margalit and Margalit, 'Holding True and Holding as True', 179–80.

Our response to this consideration comes in two stages. First of all, we need to frame Kant's language of the 'voluntary' within other comments that he makes about the rational obligation to believe in God. Although there is work for the will to do when it comes to believing in God, we need to consider Kant's insistence that the will *ought* to assent to the existence of God, if morality is to be given a secure foundation. In that sense the 'choice' presented to the will is between that which it ought to do if it is to achieve rational stability, and that which it ought not to do. The person who attempts to be moral, but chooses not to believe in God, is a 'scoundrel' in that he generates an 'inconsistency in judgements', by pre-supposing in his moral actions that virtue leads to happiness, while under-mining the possibility of this in his propositional assents (*LPR* 28: 1083). In the context of a discussion about Spinoza, Kant seems to concede the possibility of a different type of atheism, not for scoundrels who dogmatic-ally deny the existence of God. In the case of this more virtuous atheism the person can be 'well-meaning', but unable to assent to belief in God on theoretical grounds. Such a person can be moral, while saying 'there is no God', but, as John Hare puts it,[44] there is still something 'rationally unstable about such a state': 'The end, therefore, which this well-inten-tioned person had and should have had before his eyes in his conformity to the moral law, he would certainly have to give up as impossible' (*CJ* 5: 452). Secondly, and more fundamentally, we need to question the way in which the category of the 'voluntary' has been fused in the contemporary discussion to the category of 'acceptance-as-true', rather than belief. As it is a term of art, the distinction between acceptance and belief can be usefully carved up in different ways. Nonetheless, there is a danger of historical blindness creeping in, where voluntariness is taken as an automatic indi-cation that an assent is accepted-as-true rather than believed-in. The danger is that we are not sensitive to a historical tradition that treats religious belief as *sui generis* and unique, with elements of the voluntary running alongside a purported certainty about, and vulnerability to, the truth of the matter. To set this out, I look at Aquinas's account of belief in God.

Aquinas on the Voluntary Nature of Belief in God

When discussing the nature of faith, Aquinas follows the twelfth-century Parisian theologian Hugh of St Victor by placing faith in God 'midway

---

[44] John Hare, 'Kant on the Rational Instability of Atheism', in Chris L. Firestone and Stephen R. Palmquist (eds), *Kant and the New Philosophy of Religion* (Bloomington and Indianapolis: Indiana University Press, 2006), 62–78 (p. 63).

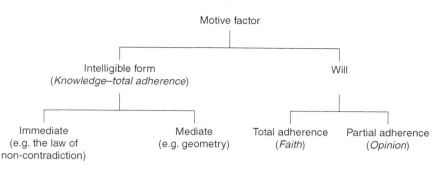

Fig. 1. Knowledge, opinion, and faith according to Aquinas

between science and opinion'.[45] For Aquinas, when the intellect comes to know something, it moves from being in a state of potential with respect to that knowledge (the 'possible intellect'), to being in a realized state of knowledge. When the 'possible intellect' is faced with two alternatives, Aquinas considers that it is 'determined towards one of them only by some motive factor'.[46] There are only two such motive factors. We can be moved by the 'proper object' of the intellect, which is to say by 'an intelligible form, i.e., an essence'. When this happens, no act of will is needed, as the intellect simply locks onto the nature of the thing understood. In other cases, the will is involved, as 'the mover of all other human powers';[47] in such cases, there is an element of decision. Although not conceptually difficult, the taxonomy becomes rather intricate, and may be clarified by Fig. 1 above.

There are two ways, epistemically speaking, that the intellect can attach itself to a truth claim: with either total or partial adherence. Cases where the intellect 'is determined in such a way as to adhere totally to one alternative' can occur in either of the two ways outlined in Figure 1: either 'by an intelligible form or by the will'. The total adherence that arises through an 'intelligible form' can in turn be either immediate or mediate. It is immediate 'when from the very things known the truth of the mind's propositions is infallibly clear'. This occurs 'with one who understands principles' such that, 'once the terms are known', they 'are themselves known immediately'. So the law of non-contradiction would be such a principle. A determination of the will occurs 'mediately' when we are dealing, not just

[45] Aquinas, *Summa Theologiae*, 2a2ae.2.2. Hugh of St Victor wrote that 'faith is a form of mental certitude about distant realities that is greater than opinion and less than science', in *De sacramentis* I.10.2, quoted in Aquinas, *Summa Theologiae*, vol. 31, appendix 4, pp. 205–15; see also p. 11n.

[46] Aquinas, *De Veritate*, XIV, I, trans. T. C. O'Brien, in Aquinas, *Summa Theologiae*, vol. 31, appendix 4, p. 210.

[47] Aquinas, *De Veritate*, XIV, I.

with first axioms, but with truths established deductively on the basis of such axioms. In the case of geometry, for example, 'the intellect is determined' when the definitions of terms are known and the principles are correctly applied. Such a form of knowledge is what Aquinas means by a 'science', and one who arrives at truths mediately through the intelligible forms is in 'the condition of one having science'.[48]

When we understand the properties of a triangle, we do not *choose to believe* that the internal angles add up to 180 degrees: because this conclusion is necessary, we have no choice but to believe it. An opinion arises when we are dealing with contingent matters, about which there is no necessity. In such cases, there is a degree of volition involved, in that we choose to believe one thing rather than another. When the intellect cannot be determined to one alternative by necessity, then the will becomes involved, 'which chooses assent to one determined side', from a 'motive that is sufficient to move the will, but insufficient to move the intellect, e.g., that it appears good or appropriate to assent to the one alternative'.[49] Opinion is an instance of 'assent to one of two opposite assertions, with fear of the other, so that the adherence is not firm'.[50]

Although faith concerns eternal truth, it is not a truth whose necessity we can see. Because we cannot see the necessity, it resembles opinion, in that there is a volitional element to faith. We choose to believe one thing and not the other, without being compelled by necessity. But, because the object of faith is eternal truth, it resembles science, in its orientation to necessary truths; accordingly, faith involves an absolute certitude, which is usually appropriate to science, in relation to the truth that is its object. For this reason, faith 'holds a middle place, for it surpasses opinion because its adhesion is firm' while it 'falls short of science, because it lacks vision'.[51] So, although faith is 'imperfect as knowledge', because it is 'without clarity or vision',[52] when we believe with faith, we believe with certainty, not in a hypothetical or doubtful way.

When drawing his distinction between knowledge, opinion, and belief, Kant is working within this tradition. We can say this without knowing the exact route by which it is delivered to Kant. What is significant is that belief in God has a unique status within this tradition, combining a voluntary element that goes beyond the theoretical evidence, with a certain attachment to the truth. For this reason, a literate and historically informed reading of Kant's discussion of the voluntary and 'subjective' aspect of belief in God draws him closer to the medieval tradition, rather than pulling him towards a contemporary anti-realism or a deflationary strategy. If Kant were to expound the category of

---

[48] Aquinas, *De Veritate*, XIV, I.
[49] Aquinas, *De Veritate*, XIV, I.
[50] Aquinas, *Summa Theologiae*, Ia2ae.67.3.
[51] Aquinas, *Summa Theologiae*, Ia2ae.67.3.
[52] Aquinas, *Summa Theologiae*, Ia2ae.67.3.

belief in God in a traditional way, we would expect him to say that such belief involves a voluntary moment, where the certainty that we attach to the belief is not proportionate to the theoretical evidence that we can cite in support of the belief. And this, we find, is what he does say.

BELIEF IN GOD 'CAN THEREFORE OFTEN WAVER': TOWARDS THE *OPUS POSTUMUM*

In the second *Critique*, after setting out that belief is a 'voluntary determination of our judgement', arising from the 'moral disposition', Kant writes that belief 'can therefore often waver even in the well-disposed but can never fall into unbelief' (*CPrR.* 5: 146). Taken in itself, this passage supports a 'belief-in-truth' reading. If assent to the proposition that 'God exists' were merely 'acceptance-as-truth', there is less conceptual space for an anxiety about the fundamental truth of the proposition. Such wavering has its natural home where there is a truth-vulnerable belief in the proposition, such that, if there is no God, the proposition would have to be abandoned, regardless of how useful it might be. The possibility that such wavering opens up for Kant at this point is not 'mere acceptance', but 'unbelief'. This is perhaps closer to the bone for Kant.

Although Kant commits himself to belief-in-truth that there is a God, there are hints throughout his critical work that he is able to understand genuine existential doubt on this front. There is the reference cited above to the wavering in our belief that 'can never fall into unbelief'. There is the passage discussed in the previous chapter, where Kant talks of the thought of God hovering 'without any support before speculative reason', an 'insoluble problem for the human understanding' (*LPR* 28: 1033). In the first *Critique* Kant talks of being able to 'speak the language, justified by the sharpest reason, of a firm belief' (*die vor der schärfsten Vernunft gerechtfertigte Sprache eines festen Glaubens zu sprechen*) (A744/B772), which might suggest a slightly detached or uncertain attitude to the statements that we affirm when we speak this language of 'firm beliefs'. Perhaps there is a similar detachment in Kant's distinction between the 'logical certainty' in God, which he does not have, and the 'moral certainty', which he does: 'I must not even say "*It is* morally certain that there is a God", etc., but rather "*I am* morally certain" etc. (A829/B857). Just as in the second *Critique* Kant insists that such belief cannot fail, so also he write here that he is 'in as little danger of ever surrendering' belief in God, as he is worried of losing his 'moral disposition' (A829/B857). It is significant that Kant thematizes the possibility of unbelief; although he denies the possibility, unbelief threatens as a live option, with perhaps a sense that Kant needs to reassure himself.

In his final and unpublished work, the *Opus Postumum*, this threatened unbelief seems to ripen. Running repeatedly through the fragmented discussion of God and morality in the *Opus Postumum* is the reiterated and unresolved question: 'Is there a God?' (*OP* 21: 9, 13, 17, 23).

The extent to which a decline in Kant's mental powers can be detected in the *Opus Postumum* is debated, but it can at least be taken as an indication of some trajectories in Kant's latest thought. In the *Opus Postumum* Kant keeps returning to the suggestive notion that the concept of God arises wherever moral–practical reason is at work, making 'freedom under the law into the ground of the determination of one's actions', such that one's duties are also one's commands:

> The idea of such a being, before whom all knees bow, etc., emerges from this imperative and not the reverse, and a God is thought necessarily, subjectively, in human practical reason, although not given objectively: Hereupon is founded the proposition of the knowledge of all human duties *as* divine *commands*. (*OP* 22: 122)

We find this idea, Kant writes, 'in the mind of man', as a 'principle of moral–practical reason' (*OP* 22: 121). Although, in this sense, 'there exists a God' (*OP* 22: 122), God is a 'principle' that is 'morally law-giving' (*OP* 22: 122). We no longer have the assurances of the second *Critique* that practical reason postulates 'the objective reality' (*die Objektive Realität*) of God, so that 'the theoretical cognition of pure reason' receives an 'increment' (*CPrR*. 5: 134). Now Kant writes that God is not a '*substance* outside myself, whose existence I postulate as a hypothetical being' (*OP* 22: 123), and that 'I, man, am this being myself—it is not some substance outside me' (*OP* 21: 25).

On the basis of the *Opus Postumum*, it would be difficult to sustain the view that Kant continues to believe-in-the-truth of the existence of God, independently of the usefulness of this concept for practical reason. The suggestion here seems to be that our own commanding of the moral law to ourselves has the mark of divinity, 'the spirit of man, under a compulsion which is only possible through *freedom*' (*OP* 21: 25). From this divine activity 'emerges' 'a God' thought 'in human practical reason'. While 'all expressions of moral–practical reason are divine', in that they 'contain the moral imperative', 'it is not God in substance whose existence is proved' (*OP* 21: 26). 'The commanding subject', Kant writes, 'is God', where 'this commanding being is not outside man as a substance different from man' (*OP* 21: 21).

It is hard to resist Eckart Förster's claim that in the *Opus Postumum* the concept of God is reduced to being a 'thought object', where '"God exists" means . . . that he exists in practical reason'.[53] These fragments where Kant

---

[53] Eckart Förster, *Kant's Final Synthesis: An Essay on the Opus Postumum* (Cambridge, MA, and London: Harvard University Press, 2000) ch. 5 (p. 142). For a similar claim that the *Opus Postumum* marks a discontinuity with Kant's position in the 1780s and mid-1790s, see Keith

discusses the existence of God within our moral–practical reason are dated to the very last years of Kant's life (1800–3). As such, they do not fundamentally threaten the claim that in Kant's critical work in the 1780s through until the mid-1790s, Kant is more plausibly read as recommending belief-in-the-truth of the proposition that there is a God. Nonetheless, on the basis of the evidence presented in the *Opus Postumum*, it looks likely that by the end of his life, Kant does not believe any more in the truth of the proposition that there is a God, independently of human moral–practical reason.

This suspicion of a late decline in Kant's religious beliefs, or at least in their traditional form, receives some biographical support. A friend of Kant's in old age, Pörschke, reported of Kant that 'he often assured me even when he had been *Magister* for a long time, he did not doubt any dogma [*Satz*] of Christianity. Little by little, one after the other, they broke off.'[54] Watching Kant's coffin lowered into the earth, another friend, Scheffner, says: 'You will not believe the kind of tremor that shook my existence when the first frozen clumps of earth were thrown on his coffin—my head and heart still tremble.'[55] According to a recent biographer of Kant, Scheffner's unease owed much to his awareness that, although in Kant's philosophy 'he had held out for eternal life and a future state', in his personal life he had become 'cold to such ideas'.[56]

What these narratives of decline in religious belief perhaps miss is that, although Kant in his last years no longer believes or even accepts-as-true traditional religious doctrines, he now seems to believe-in-the-truth of a *different* set of at least quasi-theological propositions: that our giving to ourselves the moral law has the mark of divinity, such that, in a sense, we are God-like in this function. We have a sort of *theosis*, where human beings

---

Ward, *The Development of Kant's View of Ethics* (Oxford: Blackwell, 1972), 160. Guyer, on the other hand, makes a case for continuity from the earlier critical works to the *Opus Postumum*, arguing that Kant has always considered belief in God to be 'merely heuristic': a 'representation without theoretical force', which nonetheless 'plays an essential role in making our conduct coherent', in 'Beauty, Systematicity, and the Highest Good: Eckart Förster's *Kant's Final Synthesis*', *Inquiry*, 46/2 (2003), 195–214. See also Paul Guyer, 'The Unity of Nature and Freedom: Kant's Conception of the System of Philosophy', in Sally Sedgwick (ed.), *The Reception of Kant's Critical Philosophy: Fichte, Schelling, and Hegel* (Cambridge: Cambridge University Press, 2007), 19–53. Byrne (*Kant on God*, 126) agrees with Guyer. My argument across this whole chapter favours Förster and Ward over Guyer and Byrne. Stephen Palmquist (*Kant's Critical Religion*, 360) argues in relation to the *Opus Postumum* that, although 'God may be present *in* our reason ... our reason is not coextensive with God's nature'. This is correct, I think, of Kant's critical philosophy in the 1780s and 1790s, but does not seem to be the position that he sets out in the *Opus Postumum*, as we see above.

[54] Kuehn, *Kant: A Biography*, 138; the reference is Johann Friedrich Abegg, *Reisetagebuch von 1798* (Frankfurt: Insel Verlag, 1976), 184.

[55] Kuehn, *Kant: A Biography*, 2; the reference is Scheffner to Lüdeck, 5 March 1804, in Arthur Warda and Carl Driesche *Briefe von und an Scheffner*, 5 vols (Munich and Leipzig: Dunker and Humblot, 1916), 2: 443.

[56] Kuehn, *Kant: A Biography*, 3.

become transformed in the image of God; but where God disappears into the human being as this happens. If there are latent gestures towards the possibility of unbelief in Kant's critical thought, there are also latent hints of this element of *theoisis* through freedom and the moral law. These strands are quite tightly controlled and censored in his critical work. Within his lifetime Kant was faced with the suggestion that his philosophy involved a form of 'religious mysticism', with C. A. Wilmans writing a Latin doctoral dissertation *On the Similarity between Pure Mysticism and the Kantian Religious Doctrine* (Halle, 1797).[57] Kant endorsed Jachmann's critical reply to Wilman's thesis. In a preface to Jachmann's work Kant insists that mysticism is 'the opposite of all philosophy', and that it should be eliminated (*PJ* 8: 441). Kant calls the view that 'wisdom is *infused* into a person from above (by inspiration)' a 'chimaera', because the 'possibility of a *supersensible experience*' is a 'direct self-contradiction' (*PJ* 8: 441). But experiencing supersensible objects, and being 'infused from above', are not necessarily the only or the most important things going on in the tradition known as 'mysticism'. As important is the interior transformation of the person, as he or she enters into a deeper union with the divine. Although I have nothing invested in the (fraught) category of the 'mystical' for the purposes of this book, it should be said that this aspect of what becomes called 'mystical' does find expression in the *Opus Postumum*:

'There is a God,' namely, in human, moral–practical reason, [as] a determination of one's actions in the knowledge of human duties *as* (as if) divine commands—'we are originally of divine race' with regard to our vocation and its dispositions. (*OP* 21: 30)

The human moral subject is raised 'to the rank of a single, powerful being': 'We may infer as [if] there were such a being [God]—with the same force as if such a being were combined in substance with our being' (*OP* 21: 20). In this momentum towards the interiorizing of divinity, we have a *theiosis* that eclipses God, rather than being an increasing participation in God, as would be more usual in a theology that is heavily marked by the notion of *theiosis*. Kant warns that it would be 'enthusiasm' to represent 'that which is in man [the idea of God]' as 'something which is outside him . . . as thing in itself (substance)' (*OP* 21: 26).

The *Opus Postumum* presents us with a suggestive interpretative question: why does Kant shift from his position in his critical works, where he affirms belief in God as an independently existing reality, to his final position, that God/divinity resides within our law-giving capacity, rather than outside this

---

[57] For a recent interpretation of Kant's thought as 'mystical', see Palmquist, *Kant's Critical Religion*. Palmquist is correct to complain that 'Kant's conception of mysticism is rather too narrow', such that Kant 'equates "mystical" with "magical"' (*Rel.* 6: 120). Palmquist (*Kant's Critical Religion*, 308–9) applies the term 'mystical' to Kant, because of Kant's use of the idiom 'voice of God' to describe our participation in practical reason (*Rel.* 6: 153).

capacity? I submit that the final three chapters of the book help to suggest an answer to this question. Part of the answer will be that Kant is not able to explore a conceptual texture such as participation in God, as he is unable to account for how God can act in our free acts. This relates to a competitive element in Kant's conception of divine and human action, which will come to light in Chapters 8–10: where God acts, then we are not free. The non-rigorous but suggestive momentum of thought that leads Kant to the strange mixture of unbelief and *theiosis* that we find in the *Opus Postumum* might be this: if the moral law is 'divine'—either as a command, or as grounded in the divine understanding—and if the divine is external to us, then the moral law might also become external to us in a way that threatens our freedom, unless perhaps divinity is rendered entirely immanent to human reason, as seems to happen in the *Opus Postumum*. The traditional theologian could agree that God is radically interior to each creature, closer to that creature than any created reality, including the creature itself; but the theologian would ground this interiority in God's utter transcendence, which is what makes it possible for God to be immanent to all of the creation, because of God's transcendence to any part of the creation. God is not located in a part of the creation, but is equidistantly central to all of it, as its first cause and final end. It will be Kant's denial of *concursus*, uncovered in Chapters 9 and 10, that will make such a conception of the creator–creature relation impossible for Kant.

8

Creating the Kingdom of Ends

In Chapter 5 I explored the shape of Kant's solution to the problem of created freedom. I found that we can be said to be free, given that we are created by God, to the extent that God creates us as noumenal substances who enjoy atemporal first causation. Chapters 6 and 7 have addressed serious challenges to this interpretation of Kant: I have argued that although Kant denies theoretical knowledge in these areas, he does believe in the truth of the propositions that God exists, and that we are noumenally free.

At this point in the book, I have completed the rearguard action of defending the notion that the critical Kant could have a theological problem at all. Now we need to become more precise about what the shape of this theological problem is for Kant. It is time to drill down on some passages where Kant insists that although God is the creator of substances, God is not the creator of space and time, or of appearances. These passages will turn out to be of central importance in understanding Kant's precise position on the question of the relationship between divine and human action. On first blush, such passages might suggest a certain degree of 'Titanism', where space is 'our creation' rather than God's. In this chapter I argue that this is a misleading impression: by establishing some distance between God and the creation of space (and time), Kant is able to explore a more theologically nuanced model of divine–human interaction than the one he employed in the 1760s and the 1770s (as set out in Chapter 4). This is not to say that there are not theological problems with Kant's account of God not being the creator of space and time: these are explored in the final two chapters of the book.

In the first section of the chapter I set out the texts where Kant makes the claim that 'God is not the creator of appearances' and that space is 'not a thing as a divine work', where Kant draws connections between these claims and the possibility of genuine human freedom. In the context of insisting upon a distance between the creator and created space and time, Kant presents a distinctive and independent argument for transcendental idealism, from considerations pertaining to divine impassibility. I outline this argument in the second section. I argue that even if we accept the argument from divine impassibility to transcendental idealism, this would not warrant us in saying that God is not the creator of space and time. The more plausible thing to say would be that God is the creator of space and time, in that God is the creator of the spatio-temporal forms of human intuition. It is puzzling that Kant does not say this, given that God creates us, and the forms of our intuition, and therefore space and time, inasmuch as these have any reality at all.

In the third section of the chapter I reflect on how, for Kant, substances—including our noumenal selves—are still dependent upon God, in a way that no longer seems to trouble Kant. This opens up the possibility of a more nuanced account of divine–human interaction in Kant, where he makes a distinction between dependence upon other created substances (which threatens freedom), and dependence upon God (which does not threaten freedom). In Kant's account of the 'Kingdom of Ends', he describes our noumenal selves as dependent upon God alone, which enables reciprocal and non-dependent interaction with other noumenal selves. In the fourth section I outline the way in which this insight is taken up by Schleiermacher in his later thought. Schleiermacher is explicitly meditating on Kantian themes when offering his account of absolute dependence upon God, the other side of which is absolute independence from all created substances. This leads us to the decisive and final question about the relationship between divine action and human freedom in Kant's thought, taken up in the final two chapters.

APPEARANCES ARE NOT CREATIONS

In this section I draw explicit attention to a dimension of Kant's transcendental idealism that has appeared a number of times in our discussion, but not received much sustained discussion, here or elsewhere in the literature. In the second *Critique*, in the context of explaining that freedom can 'be saved' (*CPrR*. 5: 101) only by regarding the human subject as a noumenal self, Kant insists that we should regard ourselves as created only with respect to our noumenal existence, but *as appearances* we should not regard ourselves as created, because God is not the creator of appearances:

> If existence *in time* is only a sensible way of representing things which belongs to thinking beings in the world and consequently does not apply to them as things in themselves, then the creation of these beings is a creation of things in themselves, since the concept of a creation does not belong to the sensible way of representing existence or causality but can only be referred to noumena. Consequently, if I say of beings in the sensible world that they are created, I so far regard them as noumena. Just as it would be a contradiction to say that God is the creator of appearances, so it is also a contradiction to say that as creator he is the cause of actions in the sensible world and thus of actions as appearances, even though he is the cause of the existence of the acting beings (as noumena). (*CPrR*. 5: 102)

Kant is explicit that when it comes to our existence in space and time, it no longer makes 'the slightest difference that the acting beings are creatures' (*CPrR.* 5: 102). Our createdness 'has to do with [our] intelligible but not [our] sensible existence and therefore cannot be regarded as the determining ground of appearances' (*CPrR.* 5: 102). The 'separation of time (as well as space) from the existence of things in themselves', and so from the sphere of divine creation—as God creates things in themselves—is therefore of 'such great importance' (*CPrR.* 5: 102–3), because 'if the beings in the world as things in themselves existed *in time*', then 'the creator of substance would also be the author of the entire mechanism in this substance' (*CPrR.* 5: 102).

If God is not the creator of appearances, then God is not the creator of space and time. God remains the creator of those noumenal substances (human beings) who are themselves the source of space and time: '*God* as universal original being *is the cause of the existence of substances*' (*CPrR.* 5: 100). In that sense we might speak of God 'indirectly' creating space and time; I will say more about this direct/indirect distinction in the next chapter. Here it is sufficient to acknowledge that Kant wants to say that in some sense God is directly the creator of things in themselves, whilst the appearances that arise from things in themselves are not the direct result of divine creation. Kant anticipates this striking claim, that God is not the creator of space (and time), in a number of *Reflexionen* from around 1778–80:

Whatever God did is good, but it does not lie in the sensible world as a mere schema of the intelligible world. Thus space is nothing in itself and is not a thing as a divine work, but rather lies in us and can only obtain in us . . . The appearances are not actually creations, thus neither is the human being; rather he is merely the appearance of a divine creation. His condition of acting and being acted upon is an appearance and depends on him as bodies depend on space. The human being is the *principium originarium* of appearances. (*R* 6057; 18: 440)

There is one passage—and only one that I know of—from the critical period where Kant talks of God being 'to an extent' the creator of space. This passage does not present difficulties for our interpretation of Kant, although it does threaten the cogency of aspects of Kant's solution to the problem of relating divine and human freedom, as it puts pressure on the implied distinction between direct and indirect creation. In his *Lectures on the Philosophical Doctrine of Religion* (1783–4), Kant states that as space is only the appearance of relations, the 'relation between things themselves' is only possible inasmuch as God 'determines the place of each through his omnipresence': 'To this extent', Kant tells us, 'God is the cause of space', and space is the 'phenomenon of his omnipresence' (*LPR* 28: 1108–9). The issue that Kant is addressing here is that, for things-in-themselves to be in connection with one another, there must be a medium of reciprocal connection, although this medium of reciprocal connection cannot be space, as space pertains only to the sensible/

phenomenal realm. Space is the form by which we experience the world, and so can only be the medium through which causation—as we experience it— occurs. But space, and the causation that it makes possible, are not features of the world in itself. In fact, the medium for the reciprocal connection of noumenal selves can be regarded as the 'divine omnipresence'. Space is, therefore, the 'phenomenon of omnipresence'—the appearance of connectivity—because, as Kant puts it in the *Metaphysik Mrongovius*, 'the concept of space accomplishes in the sensible world what the divine omnipresence does in the noumenal world' (*MMr.* 29: 866). That is to say, space connects substances, such that one can 'therefore call it [space] as it were a phenomenon of the divine omnipresence': 'Perhaps God wanted thereby to make his omnipresence sensibly cognizable to us...Perhaps space is also the only sensibility that belongs to all rational beings other than God' (*MMr.* 29: 866). This apparent concession to God's creative role with respect to space does not challenge our interpretation of Kant's stated intentions. In his discussion of space as 'phenomenal omnipresence' we continue to find God distanced from the *direct* creation of space, because, as phenomenon, space is dependent directly on the human noumenal mind, albeit that the form our 'making' can take is constrained by the work already done by divine omnipresence. It could still be said of space, as the phenomenon of divine omnipresence, that it 'lies in us', 'depends on us', and that we are the *principium originarium* of space. Kant's intentions cannot be in any doubt when we line up the claims documented above that space is 'not a divine work', that God is not the 'determining ground' of space, and that it would be a 'contradiction' to say that that God is the creator of space.

Kant's qualified claim—that space is 'to an extent' created by God—does not present a problem for our claim that Kant intends to render God's creative relationship to space an indirect one. Although it is clear that Kant intends to distance God from the creation of space—in order to protect both divine impassibility and the possibility of human freedom—it is less than clear how successful Kant is, given all the qualifications that he himself puts in: in particular, that God creates things-in-themselves (including us), and creates us as the makers of space, where our making is constrained by divine omnipresence. Furthermore, if things-in-themselves (including us) are still related by the divine omnipresence, does not the whole problem of freedom in relation to God re-emerge?[1] Why is it sufficient for freedom to render space the human-mind dependent 'phenomenal appearance' of this 'noumenal' relationality, given the implication that as the 'phenomenon of divine omnipresence', space still comes downstream of divine noumenal omnipresence? In terms of the problem that troubles Kant in the 1760s and 1770s, it would seem

---

[1] Laywine, in *Kant's Early Metaphysics and the Origins of the Critical Philosophy*, 141–2, notices a similar problem.

that the question still stands of how 'absolute spontaneity can be attributed to the soul, as a being which has a cause', and of how a 'being derived from another' can avoid being 'determined by a cause' *(ML₁* 28: 268). Kant does have an answer to this question, which is set out in the third section of this chapter (pp. 178–186).

KANT'S ARGUMENT FROM DIVINE IMPASSIBILITY TO TRANSCENDENTAL IDEALISM

In contexts where Kant distances God from the direct creation of space and time, he insists that this is essential not only for protecting human freedom, but also for preserving the impassibility of the divine nature. This section looks at Kant's arguments in this area. I follow Kant by focusing upon space, although Kant considers that structurally similar arguments apply in the case of time also (see *CPrR,* 5: 102; *R* 5962, 18: 401). I argue that even if Kant is correct that divine impassibility requires space to be a form of human intuition, rather than a thing in itself, this does not justify the claim that God is not the creator of space (as a form of intuition). Kant seems to consider that if space is not dependent upon the human mind, the features of space, in particular that it is infinite and one, mean that it will threaten God's impassibility. The implication is that, by moving space and time over to the human noumenal mind, God is protected from spatiality and temporality. We see this in a note in Kant's copy of the first *Critique*, where Kant sets out the view that space is 'attributed to things only insofar as they appear to us' (A27/B43): '*Fields of space and of time*. I. Both cannot extend further than to objects of the senses, thus not to God' (E. xx, 17; 23: 44). If space is a condition 'of all existence in general', Kant worries, then it would also have to be a condition 'of the existence of God' (B 72).[2] We might object that there are other ways in which we could prevent space being a 'condition of all existence in general'. Perhaps we could say that space is not a necessary feature of all possible worlds, such that God could have done without space, if God had wanted to. Even if space is conceived of as a condition of created existence, it is not clear why such spatiality would be contagious for the divine nature. The existence of space would still be dependent directly upon the divine will to create, with space having no existence independent of God's decision to create.

Nonetheless, whatever we think about it, Kant seems to be convinced that if God is (directly) the creator of space, space will become an unacceptable condition of God's own existence. It is not enough that space is not a necessary emanation of the divine existence; space must also not be a direct product of

---

[2] See Paul Guyer's discussion of this passage, *Kant and the Claims of Knowledge*, 352–4.

the divine creation. When Kant insists that 'space is nothing in itself and not a thing as a divine work' (*R* 6057; 18: 439), we find Kant explicitly putting in place a protective buffer between the creator and created space. In *Reflexion* 6285 from the mid/late-1780s Kant writes that:

Things in space are all bound a priori to the conditions of space. Were space something in itself, it would be necessary, and even God in his being would be bound to it. God must be present to things in themselves and so therefore to thinking beings, and therefore, God must make the idea of space a necessary determination of the outer intuition of thinking beings. (*R* 6285; 18: 552–3)[3]

At the heart of Kant's difficulty is his view that if space and time are things in themselves, then such realities would be problematically infinite and absolute in a way that would threaten their distinctness from God. This problem arises acutely for Kant from 1768 onwards, when Kant becomes convinced that space and time must be conceived of as infinite and absolute, rather than as properties that are derivative upon the relations between substances (*DS* 2: 375–83). Two thinkers in particular trouble Kant: Spinoza and Newton. In relation to Spinoza, Kant writes that, if the 'ideality of time and space is not adopted, nothing remains but Spinozism':

In which space and time are essential determinations of the original being itself, while the things dependent upon it (ourselves, therefore, included) are not substances but merely accidents inhering in it; for, if these things exist merely as its effects *in time*, which would be the condition of their existence itself, then the actions of these beings would have to be merely its actions that it performs in any place and at any time. (*CPrR.* 5: 100–2)

This presents a further threat to our freedom, distinct from the threat offered by a conception of God as the 'supreme artist'. On a Spinozistic conception of God, the problem is not that our actions are controlled by God; rather, it is that we are not even distinct from God.

In relation to Newton, and Newton's supporter Clarke, Kant considers that 'infinite space', regarded as a thing in itself, becomes a 'property or attribute of God' (*R* 6285, 18: 552). Kant has in mind the view expounded by Newton and Clarke that space is the divine *sensorium*, which is to say, a 'necessary emanation' of the existence of God, where space, as an uncreated aspect of the divine nature, is the means by which God is present to objects that he wills into existence. Both the Spinozistic and the Newtonian anxieties present an intriguing set of interpretative and conceptual issues, some of which I explore elsewhere.[4]

---

[3] My translation.
[4] See my 'Kant's Transcendental Idealism and Newton's Divine *Sensorium*', *Journal of the History of Ideas*, 72/3 (2011), 413–36.

For our purposes here, we do not need to evaluate Kant's claim that space and time must be forms of our intuition, if the divine nature is to be protected from inappropriate spatialization and temporalization. There is a more pressing issue, which arises even if we grant the success of Kant's argument from divine impassibility to transcendental idealism. We can grant, for the sake of argument, that space and time are forms of human intuition, rather than things in themselves, and we can allow that putting space and time on this footing is the only way to protect divine impassibility. Within Kant's theistic framework, this amounts to the claim that space and time are created by God as the forms of human intuition. So why say that space and time are 'not creations', to the extent of insisting that it would be a 'contradiction' to say that God is the creator of appearances? God is the creator of human noumenal minds, creating minds in such a way that 'God must make the idea of space a necessary determination of the outer intuition of thinking beings' (*R* 6285; 18: 552–3).[5] Given this, it seems odd to deny that God is the creator of space and time, understood in this transcendentally idealist sense: God creates our spatial and temporal form of receiving the world, and this is what it is to create space and time. Our reasons for adopting a transcendentally idealist conception of space and time might be various: they could include epistemic considerations, as well as theological considerations about divine impassibility. But *still* it is hard to see why God is not the creator of the appearances of space and time, inasmuch as God creates the human noumenal mind and its forms of intuition.

THE KINGDOM OF ENDS

At the end of the first section of this chapter, I set out an immanent difficulty with Kant's resolution of the relationship between divine and human action. The original threat to human freedom came about because of our created status, where all created series originate in God. Kant's solution to this problem was to say that space and time are not divine creations; rather, space and time arise from our way of receiving of the world. Nonetheless, Kant still requires that we consider ourselves to be noumenal selves *created* by God. Kant presents this picture as his account of what would resolve the problem of human freedom. The difficulty is this: as God is still the source of the reciprocal relations between created noumenal selves, the question about how we can be both free and created seems to re-instate itself, albeit at a noumenal level.

---

[5] My translation.

We have seen above that Kant tells us that 'God is the cause of space' to the extent that the 'relation between things themselves' are possible only inasmuch as God 'determines the place of each through his omnipresence' (*LPR* 28: 1108–9), and that 'the concept of space accomplishes in the sensible world what the divine omnipresence does in the noumenal world' (*MMr.* 29: 866), in that space connects substances. In the second *Critique* we saw that Kant claims that God, as 'the universal original being', is the cause 'of the existence of substance' (*CPrR.* 5: 100). Among the substances created are our noumenal selves as 'finite things in themselves' (*CPrR.* 5: 101). In the *Inaugurual Disserta-tion* where Kant first makes systematic use of the phenomena/noumenal distinction, he tells us that at the noumenal level '*substances*' are 'related to one another as complements to a whole', in relationships that are 'reciprocal' (*ID* 2: 390). These relationships can be provided only by 'the ground of the universal connection, in virtue of which all substances and their states belong to the same whole which is called *a world*' (*ID* 2: 398). Kant goes on to write that this interaction between substances requires 'a special ground', which is God (*ID* 2: 407). The fundamental metaphysics of this account, set out in 1770, involves God creating and relating dependent substances. This account is consistent with Kant's position in the 1750s, where Kant's account of freedom is compatibilist, as substances, and the relations between substances, depend entirely upon God. In Kant's later philosophy, when it comes to the noumenal realm, we seem to have the same situation: God creates inter-related dependent substances. The question is, therefore: why does transcendental idealism make any difference, in a way that enables an incompatibilist account of human freedom?

In the first part of this section I will suggest that Kant does in fact have an answer to this question, and that it lies in his distinction between a created community and a created series. Transcendental idealism makes it possible for us to hold, on the basis of practical reason, that God creates us as rational beings *in community* with other rational beings, rather than in causal series, where we are subordinated to other (rational and non-rational) beings. To be in reciprocal community—the Kingdom of Ends—with other created rational beings does not violate freedom. Nor, it seems, does it violate our freedom to depend upon God as such. What threatens our freedom is a particular type of mediated dependence upon God, where we depend upon God *mediately* through being acted upon by other created substances, which are themselves parts of causal series, which in turn depend upon God. Direct or immediate dependence upon God, it seems, does not threaten freedom, but rather makes possible community and freedom. Although Kant is not very expansive or explicit on this issue, I consider that there is enough textual evidence to recommend this interpretation of Kant; or, at least, that it is a view that Kant gravitates towards at certain points. Kant considers us to be, with respect to our noumenal selves, dependent upon God for our existence, and for whatever community of reciprocal connection there might be in the noumenal realm, in a way that does not threaten our freedom; our subordination within causal spatio-temporal series that are grounded in God *would* threaten our freedom if these deterministic series were things in themselves, but transcendental idealism gives us the conviction that spatio-temporal causation does not apply to things in themselves.

If all this is correct, then it nuances our discussion in Chapter 4, where a strand of evidence from the 1760s and 1770s seemed to indicate a conceptual shift in Kant's thought, where God becomes an alien and violent cause to the creature. The precise nuance Kant moves towards in the late 1770s and 1780s is that direct dependence upon God does not threaten freedom in the way that mediated dependence upon God does. This is a more subtle conception than the 'competitive' relationship between divine and human freedom envisaged in the 1760s and 1770s.

Stepping back from the details of Kant's texts, I conclude this section by suggesting that the theologians who had cause to be suspicious of Kant's 'competitive' conception of divine and human freedom, as set out in Chapter 4, might approve of Kant's distinction between direct and mediated dependence upon God. Kant himself does not do much to develop his ideas against a traditional theological canvass, but we can find in Aquinas support for the claim that dependence upon *God alone* does not threaten freedom in the way that dependence upon other created substances does. Kant's implicit solution, I will suggest, is arguably developed at length by Schleiermacher, who is himself immersed in Kant's struggle to preserve a space for transcendental freedom.

First of all, we turn to the distinction between created communities and created series. In our discussion so far, we have engaged extensively with Kant's anxieties around determined causal series, where parts of the series are 'subordinated' to one another, and determined 'unilaterally' (B112), in a way that leads back to the first cause, God. Kant draws out another way in which substances are connected with one another. This is by being a 'community' where a 'whole is divided into parts', but where 'none can be contained under any other': 'They are thought of as *coordinated* with one another, not *subordinated*, so that they do not determine each other *unilaterally*, as in a *series*, but *reciprocally*, as in an *aggregate*' (B112). With 'causality' one can 'ascend from the effect as the conditioned to the causes as conditions' (A414/B441–2), whereas in the 'entirety of things' that constitutes a community:

One is not subordinated, as effect, under another, as the cause of its existence, but is rather coordinated with the other simultaneously and reciprocally as cause with regard to its determination (e.g., in a body, the parts of which reciprocally attract yet also repel each other), which is an entirely different kind of connection from that which is to be found in the mere relation of cause to effect (of ground to consequence), and in which the consequence does not reciprocally determine the ground and therefore does not constitute a whole with the latter (as the world-creator with the whole). (B112)

Anything that we experience in the spatial and temporal nexus is part of a subordinated series. Kant is clear that appearances in phenomenal space are as much a manifestation of the series-style subordination as appearances in phenomenal time. With respect to 'spaces', Kant writes that their 'boundaries' are 'determined . . . always through another space' (A414/B441), and so to this extent are 'exponents of a series', as they are 'subordinated to one another as conditions of their possibility' (A414/B441). Just as phenomenal cause-and-effect patterns of succession have a noumenal analogate of ground and consequence, so phenomenal patterns of coexistence in space have a noumenal analogate, which, as we have seen, Kant suggests might be 'divine omnipresence'. If, as is the case, everything that we experience is part of a subordinated and deterministic series, we cannot have a phenomenal experience of community. This is what Kant suggests when he writes about the difficulty of knowing 'how a community of substances is possible at all' (B428), a question that he tells us 'lies outside the field of all human cognition' (B428).

As with noumenal first causation, where we lack theoretical warrant, we can have practical (moral) epistemic grounds for belief in the possibility of community between substances, and specifically between rational substances. This practical warrant for belief in a community between rational substances is indeed provided, for Kant, by reflection on the moral law.[6] In the *Groundwork* Kant writes that, inasmuch as 'every rational being' must 'regard himself' as 'giving universal laws with respect to any law whatsoever to which he may be subject', then 'it is just this fitness of his maxims for giving universal laws that marks him out as an end in itself' (*GW* 4: 438). This means that 'he must always take his maxims from the point of view of himself, and likewise every other rational being, as lawgiving beings (who for this reason are also called persons)':

Now in this way a world of rational beings (*mundus intelligibilis*) as a kingdom of ends is possible, through the giving of their own laws by all persons as members. Consequently, every rational being must act as if he were by his maxims at all times a lawgiving member of the universal kingdom of ends. (*GW* 4: 438)

The Kingdom of Ends is precisely a non-subordinated community of noumenal first causes, exercising their capacity for transcendental freedom, as set out in Chapters 4–6. Kant considers that such a *community*, as opposed to a series, would be impossible, if the way in which we universally experience the

---

[6] Allen Wood draws attention to the importance of the 'notion of community' in Kant's ethics, which 'corrects a common view of Kant's ethics as essentially individualistic', in 'Kant's Formulations of the Moral Law', in Graham Bird (ed.), *A Companion to Kant* (Oxford: Wiley-Blackwell, 2010), 291–307 (p. 303), and in *Kant's Ethical Thought* (Cambridge: Cambridge University Press, 1999), 274–82, 309–20. See also Lucas Thorpe, who tracks the continuity from the notion of 'a world' in Kant's early metaphysics—interconnected substances—to the 'ethical ideal of a realm of ends', in 'Is Kant's Realm of Ends a *Unum Per Se*?', 479.

world is in fact the way in which the world really is. If this were the case, the
world would be fundamentally spatial, temporal, and causal, dominated by
subordinated and series-shaped patterns that lead back to a determining God.
Practical reason gives us warrant to hold that the world as it is in itself is really
not like this. In the absence of a veto from theoretical reason, the 'fact of
reason' that is the moral law requires us to believe that we relate to each other
as free beings in a community, where the only law that shapes (and constitutes
our freedom) is the 'moral law', the 'fundamental law of a supersensible nature
and of a pure world of the understanding', the counterpart of existing 'in the
sensible world but without infringing upon its laws' (*CPrR*. 5: 43). This
intelligible community of rational free beings, who enjoy created transcendental freedom, Kant calls 'the *archetypal world* (*natura archetypa*)' (*CPrR*. 5:43).
As with belief in God, Kant is careful to insist that we 'cognize' the archetypal
world 'only in reason' (*wir bloß in der Vernunft erkennen*), that is, through a
practical reason that warrants belief ordered to moral ends. The sensible world
that we do experience can be considered, on similar grounds, 'the possible
effect of the idea of' the archetypal noumenal world, which is 'the determining
ground of the will' (*CPrR*. 5:43).

Later on, in the second *Critique*, Kant further develops this concept of the
archetypal community of free rational beings in the context of his moral proof
for the existence of God. Kant uses the concept of a community when
unpacking the 'concept of a highest good', which 'supplements' a lack in the
'moral law of itself' (*CPrR*. 5:128). The moral law of itself does not '*promise*
any happiness' (*CPrR*. 5:128), and happiness cannot be the goal or incentive of
obeying the moral law. Nonetheless, as we saw in Chapter 7, Kant considers
that it ought to be the case that following the moral law leads to happiness,
where it is the Christian 'doctrine of morals' that 'supplements this lack':

> By representing the world in which rational beings devote themselves with their whole
> soul to the moral law as a *kingdom of God*, in which nature and morals come into a
> harmony, foreign to each of them of itself, through a holy author who makes the
> derived highest good possible. (*CPrR*. 5:128)

Although God is sovereign in this Kingdom, the relationship between rational
creatures is a community rather than a subordinated series, and even the
relationship between God and rational creatures, on the moral front, has the
structure of a community, rather than a subordinated series:

> In the order of ends the human being (and with him every rational being) is an *end in
> itself*, that is, can never be used merely as a means by anyone (not even by God)
> without being at the same time himself an end, and that humanity in our person must,
> accordingly, be *holy* to ourselves. (*CPrR*. 5: 131)

We have now come round full circle. In his earliest philosophy, Kant
considered that there were two principles pertaining to the connection of

substances, the principles of coexistence and succession, both aspects of the principle of sufficient reason with respect to the interconnection of substances. The principle of succession, we recall, stated that 'no change can happen to substances except in so far as they are connected with other substances; their reciprocal dependence on each other determines their reciprocal changes of state' (*NE* 1: 410). The principle of coexistence stated that 'finite substances do not, in virtue of their existence alone, stand in relationship with one another', and that the 'divine understanding' as the 'common principle of their existence' is required to maintain the substances 'in a state of harmony in their reciprocal relations' (*NE* 1: 413). In 1755 human freedom was carved out in a conceptual space determined by both these principles. Conforming to the principle of coexistence, Kant writes in 1755 that all substances, including human beings, are 'linked together' in 'the idea entertained by the Infinite Being' (*NE* 1: 415), where the interaction between substances depends entirely upon 'divine support' (*NE* 1: 416). In conformity with the principle of succession, our 'free' actions occur as part of the 'inexorable chain of events' (*NE* 1: 399), where God as creator 'is, so to speak, the well or bubbling spring from which all things flow with infallible necessity down an inclined channel' (*NE* 1: 403).

The fate of these two principles is not the same. In his critical thought, Kant remains committed to the principle of coexistence among things in themselves, albeit holding the principle on practical rather than theoretical grounds. Much more problematic for Kant is the principle of succession. In Chapter 4 we saw evidence of Kant's increasing anxiety about the claim that our 'actions are determined by a fixed law and in a connection which is most certain but also free' (*NE* 1: 400). We saw Kant worrying that it is 'not to be comprehended at all' how an 'original causality and an original capacity for efficient causation obtain in a created being' (*R* 4221; 17: 462). Kant, we recall, was concerned that, if 'it is a being derived from another, then it appears to be quite probable that it is also determined by this cause in all its thoughts and actions' (*ML₁* 28: 268).

By distinguishing a created community from a created series, Kant is now able to conceive that a being who is derived from God can still be free, so long as God creates such a being so that it is independent of, not subordinate to, other created beings. As Kant unpacks his resolution to the problem of created freedom, it seems that what specifically troubles him is not the idea that God creates us, but that God creates us as subordinate parts of a series involving other created substances that act upon us. Transcendental idealism tells us that 'in the intelligible world' the 'rule of causal connection disappears' (*R* 5212, 18: 119–20), and so that freedom is possible, even though we are created. When Kant tells us that 'in the intelligible world nothing happens and nothing changes' (*R* 5612, 18: 253–4), he is telling us that the principle of succession no longer applies in the world in itself, even if the principle of coexistence does. If transcendental idealism is true, then God can create us in a community, where we can enjoy the freedom of a first cause.

There are passages in Kant's critical philosophy that support the interpretation developed here. Consider this reflection from the 1780s, already quoted in part above:

God has not given human beings independence from himself (God), but from the incentives of sensibility, i.e., [*crossed out*: moral] practical freedom. Their actions are appearances and to that extent subject to the merely inner conditions of humanity. Punishments and rewards also belong among these. Whatever God did is good, but it does not lie in the sensible world as a mere schema of the intelligible world. Thus space is nothing in itself and is not a thing as a divine work, but rather lies in us and can only obtain in us. (*R* 6057, 18: 439–40)

We have already drawn on the second part of this passage, when establishing that Kant means to distance God from the creation of space and time ('space . . . is not a thing as a divine work'). We are now in a position to appreciate the importance of the immediate context of this line. The acknowledgement that 'God has not given human beings independence from himself' confirms that Kant no longer has an anxiety about our being created as such, but rather about whether we are created with a capacity to act independently of subordinating and deterministic series of cause and effect. The claim that space (and time and causation) is not a 'thing as a divine work' enables Kant to hold out for the possibility that God has given human beings 'independence . . . from the incentives of sensibility' (*R* 6057). It is not Kant's idiom, but we might say that transcendental freedom, consisting of the ability to do otherwise and enjoying ultimate responsibility for our actions, comes to us as a divine gift; but not a gift that makes us like God, as our created transcendental freedom, unlike God's uncreated freedom, suffers from the ability to do otherwise than follow the moral law.

In drawing a qualitative distinction between the sort of dependence that creatures have on God, as against the dependence they might have on one another, Kant is in line with a theological heritage running through Aquinas, which informs Leibniz and continental rationalism. In the *Summa Contra Gentiles* Aquinas sets out a distinction between types of dependence. Aquinas writes that, 'if the will is moved by some external principle, the motion will be violent', such that it is 'impossible for the will to be moved by an extrinsic principle as by an agent'. The will cannot be moved by 'some external principle which moves in the way of an agent'. It is clear, though, that God is not such an 'external principle', because 'no created substance is joined to the intellectual soul in regard to its inner parts, but only God, Who is alone the cause of its being and Who sustains it in being': 'Therefore, by God alone can voluntary movement be caused.'[7] God can never be a violent external cause, because God is the source of the being and nature of all creatures, and the purpose and end

---

[7] Aquinas, *Summa Contra Gentiles*, 2: 88.5.

of all creatures is found in God, so that 'it is not contrary to nature when created things are moved in any way by God'; indeed it is 'impossible to say that whatever is done in any creature by God is violent or contrary to nature'.[8]

There is no evidence that Kant draws directly on Aquinas, but Kant could have encountered this core distinction between creaturely dependence on God, and creaturely dependence upon other creatures, through the work of Leibniz. Leibniz's pre-established harmony is different from both Aquinas and Kant, in his denial that there are patterns of causal influence between creatures. All intersubstantial causation comes from God to the created monad, rather than between created monads. Leibniz considers this doctrine to give reassurance about the relationship of community between God and creatures. We can fill in some of the background for this from Leibniz's *Discourse on Metaphysics*, although this cannot be more than background, as this text was not available to Kant.[9] Leibniz writes that 'God is our immediate external object and . . . we see all things by him', so that, 'when we see the sun and the stars, it is God who has given them to us', where 'God is the sun and the light of all souls, the light that lights every man that comes into this world'.[10] This has the implication that 'we should have no fear of those who can destroy the body but cannot harm the soul', because 'nothing is capable' of acting upon our souls 'except God alone'.[11] This reflection comes immediately after Leibniz's reflection about 'the Kingdom of Heaven, that perfect republic of minds which deserves the title of the City of God'.[12] A similar reflection concludes the *Monadology*, a text that Kant had studied. Leibniz reflects that 'minds' are 'images of the divinity itself, or of the very creator of nature',[13] and that 'this is what makes it possible for minds to enter into a kind of community with God': 'And from this it clearly follows that the totality of all minds must make up the City of God the most perfect possible state, under the most perfect of monarchs.'[14] The function of this 'City of God' for Leibniz is to 'be a moral world within the natural world',[15] and to establish a 'perfect harmony . . . between the physical realm of nature, and the moral realm of grace; that is, between God considered as designer of the machine of the universe, and God considered as monarch of the divine city of minds'.[16]

---

[8] Aquinas, *Summa Contra Gentiles*, 2: 100.3–4.

[9] See Daniel Garber, 'What Leibniz Really Said?', in Daniel Garber and Béatrice Longuenesse (eds), *Kant and the Early Moderns* (Princeton: Princeton University Press, 2008), 64–78 (p. 65).

[10] Gottfried Wilhelm Leibniz, *Discourse on Metaphysics* (1686), in *Philosophical Essays*, ed. Roger Ariew and Daniel Garber (Indianapolis and Cambridge: Hackett, 1989), 35–68 (p. 60, §28).

[11] Leibniz, *Discourse on Metaphysics*, 59, §27.

[12] Leibniz, *Discourse on* Metaphysics, 59, §27.

[13] Gottfried Wilhelm Leibniz, *Monadology*, in *Philosophical Texts*, ed. Ariew and Garber, 280, §83.

[14] Leibniz, *Monadology*, 280, §84.

[15] Leibniz, *Monadology*, 280, §86.

[16] Leibniz, *Monadology*, 280, §87.

Leibniz must be considered an influence on Kant's similar reflections about the Kingdom of Ends and the Kingdom of Heaven. At the same time, one way of stating Kant's problem with created freedom is in terms of a contrast with Leibniz. Leibniz, unlike Aquinas and Kant, rejects the notion of transeunt forces between substances, so never has to reckon with the problem of a threat posed to created freedom from other created forces. Leibniz insists that 'speaking with metaphysical rigor, there is no real influence of one created substance on another, and . . . all things, with all their reality, are continually produced by the power of God'.[17] The only 'extrinsic principle' that acts upon any monad is God, whose action upon the creature is interior and non-violent. Kant, like Aquinas but unlike Leibniz, is committed to transeunt forces between substances, and so has to reckon with a problem that Leibniz can avoid, of how we can be rationally free (acting according to perfect freedom), given that we are impacted upon externally by created substances.

SCHLEIERMACHER, TRANSCENDENTAL FREEDOM, AND ABSOLUTE DEPENDENCE UPON GOD

We find this strand of Kant's thought taken up in a dimension of Schleiermacher's mature thought. In his earlier works Schleiermacher is critical of Kant's transcendental freedom, preferring a compatibilist account of freedom.[18] Schleiermacher's mature position, expressed in *The Christian Faith*, as interpreted by Jacqueline Mariña (whom I follow here), has something like the following recognizable Kantian shape. Our experience of the world is structured around two principles: on the one hand, we are receptive (to information, external influences, sensuous impulses, and other people); on the other hand, we are active (carrying out projects, manipulating the world, acting upon others). So we could say that our experience of the world is one of 'relative dependence' (to the extent that we are receptive) and 'relative independence' (to the extent that we are active). Consequently, our experience of the world is fragmented: divided into subjects and objects, activity and receptivity. Schleiermacher is convinced that behind this divided subject/object structure, with patterns of relative dependence/independence, is a relationship of *absolute* dependence upon God, the unitary source of that which we encounter as divided (activity and receptivity). Significantly, for our purposes, the 'moment' of absolute dependence upon God is also the moment of absolute *independence* from the world, just because we become

---

[17] Leibniz, *New System*, 143.
[18] For a full account of Schleiermacher's early criticism of Kant, see Mariña, *Transformation of the Self*, ch. 1. I am indebted to Mariña throughout this section.

aware that our spontaneity comes not from the world, but from elsewhere (from God).

Mariña identifies a profound reciprocity in Schleiermacher's thought between absolute dependence upon *God* (and only God), and spontaneity in relation to the world. As Mariña puts it, 'God is the source of whatever freedom the self may possess in relation to the world':

Because the soul is directly receptive to the divine influence, it is not a mere turnspit, reacting mechanically to *outside* influences. The transcendental light of consciousness that opens out into the world is a light preserved in its being in and through spirit's relation to the infinite and absolute.[19]

In Schleiermacher's terms, the transcendental self is analogous to a 'point' that 'cuts a line' but that is 'not part of that line', being 'truly and more immediately related to the Infinite than to the Line, and anywhere along the line you can place such a point'. As the self becomes aware of its relationship 'to the Infinite and Eternal', it 'discovers its creative nature', so that 'the light of God begins to shine . . . banishing far hence the mists in which enslaved humanity strays in error'.[20]

In the pre-cognitive moment behind self-consciousness, where we are grasped by a sense of our absolute dependence upon God, we are not 'part of the world', and so not implicated in the structures of relative dependence and independence. As we approach the moment of absolute dependence upon God, we also approach the ideal and limit of absolute spontaneity (recognizably descended from Kant's transcendental freedom), with Schleiermacher claiming that 'no one can doubt that the results of free activity take place in virtue of absolute dependence', as the 'God-consciousness' (that is, our awareness of absolute dependence) has a 'content which relates exclusively to human freedom and presupposes it'.[21]

Schleiermacher understands sin as a distorted or impaired 'God-consciousness', with a limited grasp of our absolute dependence, employing a Pauline distinction between the spirit and the flesh to describe the successful and the damaged God-consciousness respectively. When we see ourselves as merely receptive, we are subject to our sensuous bodily nature, vulnerable to the corruption and determination that threatens when we are impacted upon by intra-wordly causes.[22] Sin is 'an arrestment of the determinative power of the spirit, due to the independence of the sensuous functions'.[23] In a description

---

[19] Mariña, *Transformation of the Self*, 131.

[20] Mariña, *Transformation of the Self*, 131.

[21] Friedrich Schleiermacher, *The Christian Faith*, trans. H. R. Mackintosh and James Stuart (Edinburgh: T&T Clark, 1928), reprint with a foreword by B. A. Gerrish (Edinburgh: T&T Clark, 1999), §62.2; discussed by Mariña, *Transformation of the Self*, 239.

[22] See Mariña, *Transformation of the Self*, 242.

[23] Schleiermacher, *The Christian Faith*, §66.2, discussed by Mariña, *Transformation of the Self*, 242.

that parallels Kant's discussion of our sensuous nature, Schleiermacher writes
that when 'the predominant factor is not the God-consciousness but the flesh',

every impression made by the world upon us and invoking an obstruction of our
bodily and temporal life must be reckoned as an evil, and the more so, the more
definitely the moment of experience terminates solely in the flesh apart from the
higher consciousness.[24]

On the other hand, 'to see oneself as absolutely dependent on the ground of
being', as Mariña puts it, 'allows one to understand oneself as subject to a
higher destiny and therefore as *free* in relation to the world', so that 'we are no
longer bound to identify ourselves with the body, which has a particular causal
history and particular sensuous desires associated with that causal history'.[25]
As with Leibniz and Kant, this has implications for the possibility of genuine
community between free creatures, also construed in Schleiermacher as the
'Kingdom of God'. As Mariña puts it, the 'identification of the self with that
which transcends the body . . . is a condition of the possibility of genuine love':

In viewing others as one views oneself, as loci of self-transcendence, one values them
precisely because they have the possibility of recognizing their absolute dependence on
the Whence of all that is. As such it is through the higher consciousness that genuine
love of the neighbour is possible.[26]

When the God consciousness is dominant, the 'action of one person' cannot
be a 'hindrance to another's life', as 'in virtue of the God-consciousness that
was supreme in all, each could not but acquiesce in the other's every action'.[27]

The position we have ascribed to Kant is this. Transcendental idealism
resolves the problem of created transcendental freedom in that it reveals
that the deterministic and subordinating causal series that we experience do
not structure things in themselves. Rather they are features of our experience
of the world. As Kant himself puts it, God creates us so that we experience the
world in this way. Space, time, and causation are not features of the world as
created by God, but features of how we are created to experience the world.
This leaves open the possibility (a 'possibility of a real possibility') that we are
created such that we enjoy a noumenal first causation in a community of
rational free beings, a community sustained by God, who is the guarantor of
the practically demanded harmony between morality, worthiness of happiness, and happiness. God does not make us independent of God, but sustains
our freedom in a community of rational creatures. Schleiermacher, I suggest,

[24] Schleiermacher, *The Christian Faith*, §75.1, discussed by Mariña, *Transformation of the
Self*, 242.
[25] Mariña, *Transformation of the Self*, 242–3.
[26] Mariña, *Transformation of the Self*, 245.
[27] Schleiermacher, *The Christian Faith*, §75.1, discussed by Mariña, *Transformation of the
Self*, 245–6.

takes forward this strand of Kant's thought, and systematizes it with less epistemic caution.

A THEOLOGICAL DISTINCTION: CREATION AND PRODUCTION

The account we have given of Kant's conception of created freedom is rather broad brush with respect to one vital detail: although God creates and sustains free rational creatures, and in that sense free rational creatures depend upon God, when these free rational creatures act, what *precisely* is the relationship between divine and human action? The next two chapters are dedicated to this question. The answer to the question ties in with the puzzle uncovered above, as to why exactly Kant insists that appearances are not creations.

In order to put the sharpest possible focus on this question, I will conclude the chapter with a possible theological explanation as to Kant's surprising theological assertion that God is not the creator of appearances. This possible explanation can then be tested fully in the next chapter. There is a fairly technical and entirely orthodox sense in which a scholastically informed theologian might say that God is not the 'creator' of appearances. According to one scholastic way of carving up the semantic field of terms such as creation and conservation, what is distinctive about *creation*—in contrast to conservation (or concurrence, about which, more in the next chapter)—is that it involves bringing into existence an entity *ex nihilo*, rather than God acting on an already existing subject.[28] Suarez, for example, puts it in these terms:

As theologians define it, 'creation' signifies the production of an entity *ex nihilo*. So as to distinguish this action from others, the phrase '*ex nihilo*' rules out any concurrence on the part of a material cause and any dependence of the entity that is created on a subject . . . so that '*ex nihilo*' expresses the same thing as 'out of no subject' (*ex nullo subjecto*). And this is how the action in question is distinguished from the other sort of action, which involves the eduction [of a form] from the potentiality of a subject. For these two sorts of action exhaustively divide all efficient causality; and so just as the phrase '*ex nihilo*' is sufficient to distinguish creation from eduction, so too it is sufficient to convey the nature of creation.[29]

There is a sense, therefore, in which accidents that subsist in a subject are not 'created', as this would involve 'an accident' being 'made by God separate from

---

[28] For this point, I am indebted to Jeffrey K. McDonough, 'Leibniz: Creation *and* Conservation *and* Concurrence', *Leibniz Review*, 17 (2007), 31–59 (p. 35).

[29] Francisco Suarez,, SJ, *On Creation, Conservation and Concurrence: Metaphysical Disputations 20–22*, trans. with introduction by A. J. Freddoso (South Bend, IN: St Augustine's Press, 2002), 20.1.1., p. 2.

a subject', with 'a mode of being similar to subsistence'.[30] An alteration within an existing substance is a case not of creation *ex nihilo*, but of 'what we might call *production* within the order of nature—a leaf's turning from green to red, a pair of rabbits conceiving a bunny, or an artist throwing a flower pot'.[31] As McDonough puts it, 'the production of ordinary effects within the order of nature was taken to necessarily involve acting upon an already existing subject, of realizing some already present potentiality'.[32] This opens up a possible explanation for Kant's talk of our being the source of space and time, as '"creation" of effects in this loose sense was held to be appropriate not only to God but to creatures as well':

> For the scholastics, God's act of creation thus was not viewed as a rival to creaturely production within the order of nature, but rather a necessary condition for it: God's act of creation brings into being the active and passive powers of creatures which then unfold within the order of nature 'producing' effects within the natural world.[33]

Kant could have found this distinction between creation in the strict sense and the production of effects within the order of nature in Leibniz's *Theodicy*:

> As for the so-called creation of the accidents, who does not see that one needs no creative power in order to change place or shape, to form a square or column, or some other parade-ground figure, by the movement of the soldiers who are drilling; or again to fashion a statue by removing a few pieces from a block of marble; or to make some figure in relief, by changing, decreasing or increasing a piece of wax? The production of modifications has never been called creation, and it is an abuse of terms to scare the world thus. God produces substances from nothing, and the substances produce accidents by the changes of their limits.[34]

Is it possible to understand Kant's pronouncements about God not being the creator of appearances entirely in the terms of this traditional distinction? It should be conceded, I think, that the distinction between creation *ex nihilo* and the production of changes within the created realm does some work in Kant's thought. It lies behind Kant's distinction (explored on pp. 114–16) between pure noumenal substances, which are created *ex nihilo*, and phenomenal substances, which are the appearances, the produced accidents, of these noumenal substances. It would follow from this that phenomenal substances are not strictly speaking created *ex nihilo*, in that they are not proper substances, but have more the status of accidents that subsist in substances. Accordingly, in the 'First Analogy' of the first *Critique*, Kant distinguishes

---

[30] Suarez, *On Creation, Conservation and Concurrence*, 20.1.1, p. 2.
[31] McDonough, 'Leibniz: Creation *and* Conservation *and* Concurrence', 35.
[32] McDonough, 'Leibniz: Creation *and* Conservation *and* Concurrence', 35.
[33] McDonough, 'Leibniz: Creation *and* Conservation *and* Concurrence', 35–6.
[34] Leibniz, *Theodicy*, §395; see also §32. McDonough, 'Leibniz: Creation *and* Conservation *and* Concurrence', 36.

'arising and perishing' from 'alterations of that which arises and perishes' (A188/B231), explaining that 'alteration is a way of existing that succeeds another way of existing of the very same object' (A188/B231). As we only ever perceive phenomenal substances, fundamental 'arising or perishing per se cannot be a possible perception', but only 'alteration' (A188/B231), from which Kant derives the conclusion of the first Analogy that 'persistence'—not arising or perishing—is a 'necessary condition under which alone appearances, as things or objects, are determinable in a possible experience' (A189/B232).

Although Kant is aware of the distinction between creation *ex nihilo*, and the production of alterations within the creation, I do not think that his theological pronouncements can be understood entirely within the terms of this distinction. It is suggestive that as well as saying that appearances are 'not creations', Kant uses more expansive expressions, such that space is not a 'divine work', and that with respect to our existence in space and time it no longer makes 'the slightest difference that the acting beings are creatures' (*CPrR.* 5: 102), such that our createdness 'has to do with [our] intelligible but not [our] sensible existence and therefore cannot be regarded as the determining ground of appearances' (*CPrR.* 5: 102). The reason why Kant's position does not fall within the framework of a traditional theological distinction can become clear only when we analyse precisely what role Kant gives to divine action, where this is construed more broadly than the creative act of bringing substances into being *ex nihilo*. This is the topic of the next chapter.

9

Concurrence

We have tracked a trajectory in Kant's thought from the 1750s into his critical philosophy. In the 1750s, Kant considers that human freedom is compatible with God being the creative and sustaining source of our existence, and of our actions. To be free, human beings do not need to enjoy an ultimate responsibility for their actions, and they do not need to enjoy the possibility of doing other than they do. We have seen how in the 1760s and 1770s Kant's position on human freedom shifts significantly. He begins to reach out for a notion of transcendental freedom, whereby human beings enjoy ultimate responsibility for their actions (as God does), and where human beings (unlike God) have the (regrettable) possibility of acting other than they do.

In the 1760s and 1770s, Kant sometimes expresses a distinctively theological problem with transcendental freedom, asking how we can be free if our existence is 'derived from another'. Towards the late 1770s, and in the 1780s, Kant's thought takes a different turn, where Kant distinguishes between our dependence upon other created substances (which does threaten freedom) and our dependence upon God. Dependence upon God does not threaten freedom, as God creates us as (in some sense) the source of space and time, and so also the source of the non-free causal series of appearances. Determinism comes downstream of our reception of the world, rather than us coming downstream of a deterministic world. This leads us to ask about the precise nature of the relationship between divine and human action. In particular, and in the light of Kant's acknowledgement that dependence upon God does not threaten freedom, we want to understand the precise theological significance of Kant's claims, reviewed in the previous chapter, that 'it would be a contradiction to say that God is the creator of appearances' (*CPrR.* 5: 102), that 'space is not a thing as a divine work' (*R* 6057), and that it would be a 'contradiction' to say that God 'is the cause of actions in the sensible world' (*CPrR.* 5: 102).

In this chapter I focus on the precise 'causal joint' between God's creative action and our free actions. I interrogate this issue by focusing on some fairly narrow and technical debates in late medieval and early modern philosophy. We do this because this is the discourse out of which, and in which, Kant's position on the issue is explicitly set out. The narrow and technical discussion is itself motivated by and oriented to a cosmic and perennial question. In short, the issue is how we can relate the claim that God is the creator *ex nihilo*, such that everything that exists is dependent entirely and utterly upon God, with the claim that the creature has an existence that is distinct from God, and is capable of an action that belongs properly to the creature, and is not just an aspect of divine action. The question has a particular pertinence when we are thinking about those actions of creatures that are called 'free', but is not restricted to that issue; the question of the proper and distinct action of the creature covers all the effects brought about by created substances, rational and non-rational, free and un-free.

In this first section of this chapter I set out the conceptual options in the medieval and early modern period for understanding the relationship between divine and human action: occasionalism, mere conservation, and concurrence. We will see that the favoured position among orthodox philosophical theologians was concurrence (including Aquinas, Suarez, and Leibniz), where God not only creates and sustains every creature, but acts directly in every action of every creature, including free human action. I then move into an analysis of Kant's texts. Kant distinguishes between the possibility of concurrence in the contexts of nature and of freedom, and I discuss each in turn. This distinction between concurrence in the case of nature and in the case of freedom is not characteristic of the medieval discussion, where the rational freedom of human beings is understood as a species of divinely-concurred-with-secondary-causation, rather than being a qualitative breach and rupture with the usual weave of divine action. For this reason, when discussing the medieval discussion, I speak only of 'creaturely action', which includes inanimate and animate nature, and the free action of rational creatures. The qualitative distinction between nature and freedom is important for Kant, so it is in this context that I introduce such a distinction.

Kant dismisses the cogency of concurrence in nature, arguing that an effect brought about in nature is brought about either directly and entirely by God, or by the creature, rather than by God (albeit that the creature is created and sustained by God). This makes Kant a 'mere conservationist' about the relationship between divine and creaturely action: God's direct action is restricted to creating and conserving the creature, such that God does *not* act in every action of every creature. In his critique of mere conservationism Suarez sets out some of the implications of adopting this position. We find that Kant understands these implications, and embraces them. This enables us to explain precisely what Kant is driving at in the passages reviewed in the previous chapter, where he insists that God is not the creator of appearances. In the case of special interventions such as miracles, Kant does allow for something that he calls '*concursus*'. I explain why the theological tradition would consider such a case of 'concurrence' still to fall within a 'mere conservationist' frame-work and to be an insufficient account of divine action in nature.

When it comes to free actions, Kant seems more open to the possibility of divine–human concurrence, particularly when talking about the divine assist-ance that is available to human beings when they struggle to be moral. Once again, by drawing on Aquinas, Suarez, and Leibniz, I will show that the traditional theologian would not regard this as a genuine case of concurrence. As before, Kant uses the language of concurrence within a framework of mere conservation. In the fourth section of this chapter I consider how the intro-duction of concurrentism interacts with the distinction between compatibilist and incompatibilist conceptions of freedom. I argue that we need four cat-egories rather than two, distinguishing the relationship between creator and creature, and between creatures. Enriching our set of distinctions helps us to locate where the real conflict lies in some theological debates, and also enables us to map the precise conceptual options taken, and neglected, by Kant. In the next chapter, I explore the wider implications of Kant's denial of concurrence, in terms of Kant's legacy for Christian theology.

OCCASIONALISM, MERE CONSERVATION, AND CONCURRENCE

All medieval and early modern philosophical theists accept that God creates substances *ex nihilo*, and that God also conserves substances for their dur-ation, such that, if God were to withdraw his conserving action, the substances would be annihilated. As St Thomas puts it, 'the *esse* [*being*] of all creatures depends on God in such a way that . . . they would be reduced to nothingness if they were not conserved in being by the action of God's power'.[1] Using a Platonic idiom, Thomas talks of God 'communicating *esse*' to something, by which he means that God brings that thing into existence, and conserves it in its existence, where the thing would cease to exist were God to withdraw the action of sustaining it. As we have seen in the previous chapter, Kant assents to the claims that God creates substances and conserves them in their existence, albeit that he derives epistemic warrant for this claim, not from theoretical knowledge, but from practical reason (in the second *Critique*), and reflective judgement (in the third *Critique*). In the 1780s we find Kant distinguishing along traditional lines between two aspects of God's creative activity: creation, which is 'the actuation of the beginning of the world', and conservation, which

---

[1] Aquinas, *Summa Theologiae*, 1.104.1. Cited by Freddoso, 'God's General Concurrence with Secondary Causes: Pitfalls and Prospects', 142–3.

is 'the actuation of its duration' (*LPR* 28: 1104). In line with the tradition, Kant observes that 'the same divine power which actuated the beginning of the world constantly actuates its duration', so that 'every substance in the world can have duration only through a continuous *actus divinus*' (*LPR* 28: 1104; see also *DR* 28: 1307; *R.* 4792, 17: 729; *R.* 6173, 18: 476).[2] Within this framework of creation and conservation there were three principle medieval and early modern theistic accounts of God's action in relation to nature: occasionalism, mere conservation, and concurrence. In this section I set out these accounts. In my characterization of these approaches, I draw on the work of the philosopher and exegete Alfred Freddoso, who has brought both precision and passion to a set of issues that can otherwise be rather technical and obscure.

According to occasionalism, there are no patterns of inter- or intra-substantial causation in nature.[3] God is the sole cause of all the effects in nature, with created natural substances making no causal contribution. So the gas flame does not heat the water in the kettle; God alone heats the water in the kettle on the occasion of the kettle being presented to the flame: 'in short, there is no creaturely or "secondary" contribution at all to any such effect.'[4] Inasmuch as there are what seem to be regular causal patterns in nature, this is because God acts according to an arbitrary intention to bring about the same effect given the same occasion. As Freddoso puts it, occasionalism is a 'remarkably devout theory of divine causation'.[5] As it manifests itself in Malebranche, it traces its roots back to St Augustine's emphasis upon the centrality of divine action and sovereignty, being 'untainted by Aristotelian naturalism'.[6] Kant was aware of occasionalism through Malebranche and Descartes. We saw in Chapter 4 (pp. 61–67) that the pre-critical Kant rejects occasionalism, insisting that there are genuine patterns of intersubstantial causation in nature; in his critical thought, Kant continues to reject occasionalism, writing that, 'if one assumes occasionalism', then 'everything that is

---

[2] For the references to the *Reflexionen*, I am indebted to Hogan, 'Kant's Theory of Divine and Secondary Causation', 5.

[3] Freddoso defines occasionalism as the denial of transeunt action: 'created substances are incapable of *transeunt* action, i.e., action that has effects outside the agent', in 'God's General Concurrence with Secondary Causes: Why Conservation is not Enough', *Philosophical Perspectives*, 5 (1991), 553–85 (p. 554). This would need to be modified slightly, if Leibniz is not to become an occasionalist by definition. Leibniz does not believe in intersubstantial causation, but does believe in the real causal contribution of secondary agents. As Kant does accept transeunt causation, it is unnecessary to get into the intricacies of applying the distinction between occasionalism, mere conservation, and concurrence to a framework where there is no intersubstantial causation.

[4] Freddoso, 'God's General Concurrence with Secondary Causes: Why Conservation is not Enough', 553.

[5] Alfred J. Freddoso, 'Medieval Aristotelianism and the Case against Secondary Causation in Nature', in Thomas V. Morris (ed.), *Divine and Human Action: Essays in the Metaphysics of Theism* (Ithaca, NY, and London, Cornell University Press, 1988), 74–118 (p. 77).

[6] Freddoso, 'Medieval Aristotelianism', 77.

natural is entirely lost', so that it can be 'presupposed that no one who cares anything for philosophy will assume this system' (*CJ* 5: 422).[7]

Occasionalism denies that any created substance makes a secondary causal contribution to the effects that are seemingly produced by created substances. In terms of relating divine and creaturely action, occasionalism tends to locate all causal activity in God, and has nothing to say about creaturely action. 'Mere conservationism', on the other hand, tends to reduce the role of divine action and to emphasize the integrity of creaturely action. The mere conservationist will hold that when substances directly produce an effect, they alone are the immediate causes of that effect. God is merely an indirect or remote cause. Created substances rely upon God's primary causation to bring them into existence, and to sustain them in existence; but, when the created substances themselves act, it is in some straightforward sense *their own action*, rather than God's, albeit that the action would be impossible without God's creating and sustaining activity. As Freddoso sets it out: 'according to mere conservationism, God contributes to the ordinary course of nature solely by creating and conserving natural substances and their accidents, including their active and passive causal powers.'[8] Mere conservationism will be an important category for understanding features of Kant's thought, so it is worth setting out Freddoso's account at some length:

Created substances are genuine agents that can and do causally contribute to natural effects by themselves, given only that God preserves them and their powers in existence. When such substances directly produce an effect via *transeunt* action (i.e., action that has an effect outside the agent itself), they alone are the immediate causes of that effect, whereas God is merely an indirect or remote cause of the effect by virtue of His conserving action. Consequently, the actions of created substances are their own actions and not God's actions, and their effects are their own immediate effects and not God's immediate effects.[9]

Occasionalism and mere conservation are at opposite ends of a conceptual spectrum in relating divine action and creaturely natural (secondary) causation: occasionalism denies that there is genuine secondary causation, while mere conservationism allows that there is genuine secondary causation, but insists that when there is, God is not directly acting at all, except inasmuch as God sustains the background being (*esse*) of all created substances. As David Burrell describes the position of the mere conservationist (in the course of

---

[7] In my discussion of Kant's attitude to occasionalism in the critical period, I am indebted to Hogan, 'Kant's Theory of Divine and Secondary Causation', p. 23, manuscript.

[8] Freddoso, 'God's General Concurrence with Secondary Causes: Why Conservation is not Enough', 554.

[9] Freddoso, 'God's General Concurrence with Secondary Causes: Pitfalls and Prospects', 133–4.

criticizing it), one thinks of '*existing* as a floor provided by the creator upon which and by virtue of which' the creature then acts.[10]

The majority view of late medieval Aristotelian scholastics, still held by early modern thinkers such as Suarez and Leibniz, was that both occasionalism and mere conservation were 'unseemly extremes'[11] where the theologian needs to find a way to assert that both the creature and God cooperate or *concur* in the production of every natural effect. So 'concurrentism' holds that a 'natural effect is produced immediately by both God and created substances'.[12] Against the occasionalist position, the concurrentist holds that created substances make a genuine causal contribution, but, against the mere conservationist, they

do so only if God cooperates with them contemporaneously as an immediate cause in a certain 'general' way which goes beyond conservation and which makes the resulting cooperative transeunt action to be in all relevant respects the action of both God and secondary causes.[13]

This divine cooperation with genuine secondary causation is called 'concursus', 'general concurrence', or 'concourse'.

We can attempt to capture the distinction between mere conservation and concurrence accounts in both intuitive and technical terms. The more technical descriptions, discussed below, are attempting to track the rule of theological grammar that God is the creator *ex nihilo*, and that everything that is depends upon God entirely for every aspect of its existence. As the contemporary theologian Kathryn Tanner puts it, 'from the general to the most specific features of existence, all that the creature is it owes to God as the creator of the world', where the 'relation of dependence upon God is absolute . . . in its range, manner and efficacy'.[14]

The contrast with the mere conservationist account can be represented in the following terms, set out by Tanner. The mere conservationist understands creatures to be directly dependent upon God for their continued existence, from which basis creatures then perform their proper actions: these actions lead to events and to patterns of order and relation, which are indirectly dependent upon God, and directly dependent upon the causal activity of creatures. The concurrentist, on the other hand, will envisage the plane of

---

[10] Burrell, *Freedom and Creation in Three Traditions*, p. 68.
[11] Freddoso, 'God's General Concurrence with Secondary Causes: Why Conservation is not Enough', 554.
[12] Freddoso, 'God's General Concurrence with Secondary Causes: Why Conservation is not Enough', 554.
[13] Freddoso, 'God's General Concurrence with Secondary Causes: Why Conservation is not Enough', 554.
[14] Kathryn Tanner, 'Human Freedom: Human Sin, and God the Creator', in Thomas F. Tracy (ed.), *The God Who Acts* (University Park, PA: Pennsylvania University Press, 1994), 111–36 (pp. 112–13).

non-divine existence that directly and constantly depends upon divine action as incorporating and including every creaturely action and effect, and so all the events and patterns of order and relation that arise from these creaturely actions and effects. As Tanner puts it, 'everything nondivine, in every respect that it is, is dependent upon God's creative activity, which brings it forth':

God's creative activity calls forth or holds up into being throughout the time of its existence what has its own integrity as a nondivine existence, and this nondivine existence has to be considered the consequence of God's creative calling forth and holding up *as a whole*, in its order and in its entirety, in every detail and aspect.[15]

The technical terms in which concurrence theories have been described and defended should not be allowed to obscure the theological passion that motivates those who defend it. So, for example, Tanner writes about this conception of God that:

This is a vision of a God supremely beneficent, a giver of gifts beyond any human giver's capacities to comprehend, to whom it is fitting to raise one's voice in joyful thanksgiving and without whom, it is appropriate to confess in utmost humility, one is literally nothing.[16]

Similarly, Alfred Freddoso prefaces his defence of the conception of concurrence by drawing on a range of biblical passages that express the 'pervasiveness of God's causal activity'.[17] In a rebuke to Job, Yahweh asks:

> Who has laid out a channel for the downpour
> and for the thunderstorm a path
> To bring rain to no man's land,
> the unpeopled wilderness;
> To enrich the waste and desolate ground
> till the desert blooms with verdure?

> Has the rain a father;
> or who has begotten the drops of dew?
> Out of whose womb comes the ice,
> and who gives the hoarfrost its birth in
> the skies? (Job 38: 25–9).

The total dependence upon God's causal activity extends to the actions of animate nature:

> Do you hunt the prey for the lioness
> or appease the hunger of her cubs
> While they crouch in their dens
> or lie in wait in the thicket?

---

[15] Tanner, 'Human Freedom', 113.
[16] Tanner, 'Human Freedom', 112–13.
[17] Freddoso, 'Medieval Aristotelianism', 74.

> Who puts wisdom in the heart,
> and gives the cock its understanding?
> Who provides the nourishment for the ravens
> when their young ones cry out to God,
> and they rove abroad without food? (Job 38: 39)

Even 'free actions of rational creatures' are described in scripture as 'products of God's ever-present causal influence': 'O Lord, You mete out peace to us, for it is You who have accomplished all we have done' (Isa. 26: 12). In medieval debates about divine causation, a number of passages from the New Testament were thought to command a concurrentist account of divine action, a claim that has been supported in some recent New Testament scholarship.[18]

> There are different works, but the same God who accomplishes all of them in everyone. (1 Cor. 12: 16)

> It is not that we are entitled to ourselves to credit for anything. Our sole credit is from God. (2 Cor. 3: 5)

> He is not far from any of us, since it is in Him that we live, and move, and have our being. (Acts 17: 27–28)

It is important to approach the more technical debates by stepping through this theological hinterland. Only in this way can we understand the determination of some thinkers to defend a concurrentist account of divine and creaturely action, and the dismay—and inflammatory comments—that can arise when concurrentism is neglected or dismissed. As will become clear in the following discussion, it is not easy to *explain* or *elucidate* the precise causal joint between God and creatures required by the concurrentist account. Consequently, the temptation to dispense with concurrentism, or to reconstrue it more 'intuitively', is all too easy to appreciate, and needs less in the way of supporting hinterland. We turn now to more technical characterizations of the distinction between concurrentist and mere conservationist accounts. These slightly more formal characterizations are helpful in providing a finely grained anatomy of the concept, which enables us to identify where and when it is functioning according to a traditional sense, and where the vocabulary of concurrence is being used, but outside the traditional grammatical rules, which attempt to track a relationship of absolute dependence of creation upon God.

The tradition that defends concurrentist accounts distinguishes between immediate causation, on the one hand, and mediate indirect causation, on the other hand. To give a rigorous and non-circular account of this distinction is no easy task, and I do not propose to try. As we saw in the previous chapter,

---

[18] John Barclay, 'By the Grace of God I Am What I Am: Grace and Agency in Philo and Paul', in John M. G. Barclay and Simon J. Gathercole (eds), *Divine and Human Agency in Paul and his Cultural Environment* (London and New York: T&T Clark, 2007), 140–57.

Kant himself relies upon some sort of distinction here, without much precise reflection. It will be sufficient to set out the bones of how the distinction has been understood, again following Freddoso. What any formal account attempts to track is the claim that 'divine involvement with the world' must not be 'partial, nor mediate, nor simply formative', but must be 'equally' and 'directly productive of everything that is in every aspect of its existence'.[19] Suarez describes an immediate efficient cause as a 'cause on which the effect directly depends for the proper *esse* that it has insofar as it is an effect . . . only this sort of cause is a cause properly and absolutely speaking'.[20]

Freddoso puts this more formally:

x is an **immediate** *efficient cause* of *y* at instant *t* if and only if *x*, by acting, directly communicates *esse* to *y* at *t*.[21]

Something is a mediate efficient cause if it makes a causal contribution to an effect without being an immediate cause. There are a number of forms that this might take: *x* might have acted long ago to bring about a causal series, each of which is an immediate cause of the next; *x* might remove an impediment to *y*, or be a cause of a chain of events that removes an impediment; or *x* might enable *y* to act in a certain way. More formally, Freddoso puts this in the following terms:

x is a **mediate efficient cause** of *y* at instant *t* if and only if
for some *z*, distinct from *y*, and for some t*, *x* is an immediate cause of *z* at *t**, and by virtue of being an immediate cause of *z* at *t**, *x* is a cause of *y* at *t*.[22]

Mere conservationists consider that God is only a mediate efficient cause of the secondary actions of created substances; concurrentists insist that God is an immediate cause of all the actions of created substances. It is by no means straightforward to give a coherent account of divine concurrence; although supportive of the notion, Freddoso concedes that there are 'intricate philosophical problems concerned with the nature of cooperative transeunt action'.[23] In some ways, both occasionalism and mere conservationism are

---

[19] Kathryn Tanner, *God and Creation in Christian Theology: Tyranny or Empowerment* (Minneapolis: Fortress Press, 2005), 46.

[20] Francisco Suarez, SJ, *On Efficient Causality: Metaphysical Disputations 17–19*, trans. Alfred Freddoso, in *The Yale Library of Medieval Philosophy*, ed. Norman Ktrezmann, Eleanore Stump, and John Wippel (New Haven, CT: Yale University Press, 1994), 17.2.2.

[21] Alfred J. Freddoso, 'Introduction', in Suarez, *On Creation, Conservation and Concurrence*, p. liv. I have adapted Freddoso slightly here and below, dropping his reference to 'per se' causation. The introduction of the notion of a 'per se' cause does not, for our purposes, contribute anything over and above that which is contained in the category of an 'immediate' cause.

[22] Freddoso, 'Introduction', p. lviii.

[23] Freddoso, 'God's General Concurrence with Secondary Causes: Why Conservation is not Enough', 555.

theoretically preferable, just in the sense that it is fairly clear to see what it is they are asserting, and how what they are asserting might be true. We have fairly uncomplicated analogies that can be derived or abstracted from experience for being the primary or sole cause of something, of things seeming to be causes but not being (a simulated image of a billiard ball hitting another billiard ball), and of indirect dependence (I need oxygen to breath as a supporting condition for writing a book, but the oxygen is not directly a cause of my writing a book on Kant). It is less clear what we are asserting when we talk of the concurrence of God and natural causes. As we will see, some of the more intuitive and tempting analogies for concurrence are generally ruled as inadmissible or misleading. It is important to understand, therefore, that the drive towards concurrence does not primarily arise because of the sense that it is an uncomplicated, elegant, and non-mysterious model of causal influence. It is more that it is perceived as the only *theologically* appropriate model, which is compatible with both divine sovereignty and the distinctness and integrity of the creation. The whole endeavour is a contemplation on the claim, as put by Burrell, that 'God not only causes each thing to be, and thus makes it able to act, but God also acts in its acting by causing it to be the cause that it is'.[24] The determination to make the model of concurrence work, and to defend it from attack, arises not least because of a sense of the theological *inappropriateness* of other models, in terms of what they assert, or what they imply, or fail to exclude.

In the course of our discussion of Kant's approach to concurrentism, I will set out some of the more detailed objections that concurrentists such as Aquinas, Molina, Suarez, and Leibniz raise against mere conservationism. Before this, it is instructive to look at what Suarez describes as his 'best argument', which is that only concurrence does justice to the 'breadth of the divine power', presupposing 'on God's part a perfection untainted by imperfection'. With concurrence 'a perfect and essential ordering intercedes between the First Cause and the secondary cause'. Suarez comments that 'there is nothing' in the 'arguments' of detractors of concurrence that cannot be dealt with, and so that 'therefore, this general influence should not be denied to God'.[25] Freddoso comments that it is an 'overstatement' of Suarez to call this his 'best argument'.[26] Certainly, as a technical explanation of how concurrence works, it does not take us very far. It is perhaps revealing, though, that Suarez

---

[24] Burrell, *Freedom and Creation in Three Traditions*, 68–9; Burrell offers this as a paraphrase of Aquinas, *Summa Theologiae*, 1.105.2.

[25] Suarez, *On Creation, Conservation and Concurrence*, 22. Sect. I, §13, quoted in Freddoso, 'God's General Concurrence with Secondary Causes: Why Conservation is not Enough', 578.

[26] Freddoso, 'God's General Concurrence with Secondary Causes: Why Conservation is not Enough', 577.

ascribes this status to what is essentially a piece of theological grammar rather than theoretical explanation: that, where there is nothing impossible, we should ascribe to God the perfection that conforms to the full breadth of divine power, and seek to reply to arguments to the contrary. This joins up with the discussion earlier in this section, concerning the theological hinterland that motivates a drive towards concurrence. As Freddoso puts it, we find an 'a priori predilection for concurrentism over mere conservationism', where 'the claim is that, in general, theistic naturalists should be antecedently disposed to countenance in nature the maximal degree of divine activity compatible with the thesis that there is genuine secondary causation'.[27] I will return to this claim in the final chapter, after our discussion of Kant's criticism of concurrence.

The early fourteenth-century Dominican bishop William Durandus is described by Freddoso as the 'only theologian whose name is explicitly associated with this doctrine [mere conservationism] by sixteenth-century writers'.[28] Freddoso adds that 'it cannot be emphasized enough that the position . . . that God's action in the ordinary course of nature is exhausted by creation and conservation . . . is regarded as too weak by almost all medieval Aristotelians as well as by the occasionalists'.[29] Freddoso expresses himself at points by claiming that scholastic thinkers regarded mere conservationism 'as in effect a form of deism',[30] describing it as 'weak deism' beyond 'the pale of theistic orthodoxy'.[31] After being convinced by Peter van Inwagen that the term 'deism' is not only 'historically and philosophically inaccurate' but also 'inflammatory', Freddoso 'recants' from the use of this term.[32] Nonetheless he insists that 'the near unanimity of the tradition on this point constrains any contemporary theistic philosopher from simply assuming without argument that Durandus' position is theologically orthodox'.[33] This is, I will argue further down, a revealing series of reactions: the temptation to inflammatory charges of deism, a recanting from this, but a remaining anxiety. I will suggest that this maps onto some of the theological issues that arise from Kant's treatment of the relationship between divine and human action.

---

[27] Freddoso, 'God's General Concurrence with Secondary Causes: Why Conservation is not Enough', 577.

[28] Freddoso, 'Medieval Aristotelianism',77–8n.

[29] Freddoso, 'Medieval Aristotelianism', 77–8n.

[30] Freddoso, 'Medieval Aristotelianism', 77–8n.

[31] Freddoso, 'God's General Concurrence with Secondary Causes: Why Conservation is not Enough', 578–9.

[32] Freddoso, 'Medieval Aristotelianism', 78n.

[33] Freddoso, 'Medieval Aristotelianism', 77–8.

KANT ON CONCURRENCE IN NATURE

A Methodological Justification

Before we investigate Kant's account of concurrence in relation to nature, a methodological justification is in order. It might be suggested that it is anachronistic to apply a distinction that has its home in technical scholastic debates to Kant's critical philosophy. There are several observations to be made here. First of all, even if there were no explicit discussion of this distinction in any of Kant's sources, or in Kant himself, the conceptual question remains a fair one: given that Kant believes that God creates substances (as I have argued in Chapters 5–7), and that these substances enjoy genuine secondary causation, does Kant conceive of the relationship between God and created substances in terms of mere conservation, or concurrence? That is: does God somehow act immediately and directly in the action of the created substance, or does the substance act independently of God, so that the action is only indirectly dependent upon God, inasmuch as God conserves the substance with its capacities for activity? Or does Kant not take a position on this (perhaps because of his epistemic discipline)? In the previous chapter I drew together and reflected upon evidence that Kant is committed to the belief that God creates and sustains free rational creatures in a reciprocal community, the 'Kingdom of Ends'. At the same time, I acknowledged that it remained rather hazy precisely what the relationship was between divine primary action and the secondary action of free rational creatures. Even judged in conceptual terms, the distinction between mere conservation and concurrence helps us to track the precise nature of the relationship conceived by Kant.

Furthermore, Kant would have been familiar with the distinction between concurrence and mere conservation from the German rationalist tradition. Concurrence accounts are explicitly recommended by Wolff, Baumgarten, and Meier.[34] Furthermore, Leibniz supports concurrence, and explicitly denounces mere conservation, in texts that we know Kant to have studied. In his *Theodicy* Leibniz refers to and dismisses Durandus' mere conservationism:

Some have believed, with the celebrated Durand de Saint-Pourçain . . . that the co-operation of God with the creature . . . is only general and mediate, and that God creates substances and gives them the force they need; and that thereafter he leaves them to themselves, and does naught but conserve them, without aiding them in their actions. This opinion has been refuted by the greater number of Scholastic

---

[34] Christian Wolff, *Theologia Naturalis Methodo Scientifica Pertracta* (Frankfurt and Leipzig, 1736), §875; Baumgarten, *Metaphysica*, §954–9; Georg Friedrich Meier, *Metaphysik* (Halle: Carl Hermann Hemmerde, 1757), §§1027–8. For these references, I am indebted to Hogan, 'Kant's Theory of Divine and Secondary Causation', p. 25, manuscript.

theologians . . . apart from the fact that we are obliged ourselves sometimes to maintain that which we conserve, we must bear in mind that conservation by God consists in the perpetual immediate influence which the dependence of creatures demands. This dependence attaches not only to the substance but also to the action, and one can perhaps not explain it better than by saying, with theologians and philosophers in general, that it is a continued creation.[35]

Later on in the *Theodicy* Leibniz again mentions 'Durand de Saint-Pourçain', who, he writes, 'seem[s] to maintain that God, having given to creatures the power to act, contents himself with conserving this power'.[36] Leibniz explicitly locates concurrentism, which he supports, in between Durandus's mere conservationism, and the occasionalism of Bayle, who 'seems to fear lest the creature be not sufficiently dependent upon God', and who 'goes so far as to deny action to creatures'.[37] Elsewhere Leibniz echoes Suarez's 'best argument', as set out above, that we should accept there is 'as much dependence of things on God as is possible, without infringing the divine justice', by which Leibniz means, without involving God in evil actions.[38]

More significant still is that Kant himself explicitly discusses the notion of concurrence in a significant number of texts. These texts, most of which are unavailable in English translation, have not to date received much attention.[39] They repay examination, as they do in fact explain Kant's otherwise perplexing statements about the created status of 'appearances'. In turn, this explanation takes us to the heart of a concern that orthodox theologians might have with Kant's conception of divine and human action. When discussing concurrence, Kant makes a distinction, perhaps following Leibniz[40] and Baumgarten,[41] between concurrence in 'nature' and in 'freedom'. I follow this distinction by asking first of all how Kant conceives of the relationship between divine action and the secondary activity of non-free created substances.

---

[35] Leibniz, *Theodicy*, §27. See also §381 and §392, and *Causa Dei*, §§10–12, in *Die Philosophischen Schriften*, 6: 440. For my discussion of Leibniz, and for these references, I am indebted to Ezio Vailati, 'Leibniz on Divine Concurrence with Secondary Causes', *British Journal for the History of Philosophy*, 10/2 (2002), 209–30 (p. 212n.); Sukjae Lee, 'Leibniz on Divine Concurrence', *Philosophical Review*, 113/2 (2004), 203–48; and McDonough, 'Leibniz: Creation *and* Conservation *and* Concurrence'.

[36] Leibniz, *Theodicy*, §381.

[37] Leibniz, *Theodicy*, §381.

[38] Leibniz, 'Necessary and Contingent Truths' (*c.*1686), in *Philosophical Writings*, ed. and trans. Mary Morris and G. H. R. Parkinson (London: Dent, 1973), 96–105 (p. 102); cited by Lee, 'Leibniz on Divine Concurrence', 214.

[39] Discussion of Kant's account of *concursus* can be found in Kain, 'The Development of Kant's Conception of Divine Freedom', 30; Mariña, 'Kant on Grace: A Reply to his Critics', 385–6, and Hogan, 'Kant's Theory of Divine and Secondary Causation', pp 21–36, manuscript.

[40] Leibniz, *Theodicy*, §§24–27.

[41] Baumgarten, *Metaphysica*, §§481–2.

The Denial of Concursus in Nature

In *Reflexionen* from the 1780s, where Kant draws the distinction between *concursus* with respect to nature and with respect to freedom, he consistently denies that *concursus* applies with respect to nature (the case of freedom, as we will see, is more complex for Kant):

Concursus is in contradistinction to a solitary action. Operating with (concurrence *Mitwirkung*) or operating alone. The (forces of) the world are unified in nature and freedom; in respect of nature God is the sole cause, in respect of freedom, he concurs. (*R* 4748, 17: 696)[42]

Creation; conservation; governance; concursus, not with respect to nature, but freedom. (*R* 6121, 18: 462)[43]

Kant is unable to countenance *concursus* between God and natural effects, in that it seems to ascribe some sort of insufficiency to divine causality, as if the solitary causation of God is not enough:

Now one cannot think that God concurs with natural effects as such (for he is not *concausa* of nature, but *causa solitaria*), i.e., one cannot conceive of the insufficiency of his own causality in the creation. (*R* 6167, 18: 473–474)

Conservation is no concursus, for this is the nexus of cooperating causes with a cause; [so] therefore solitary causes do not concur. (*R* 6169, 18: 474)[44]

The concursus of nature presupposes that nature has a causality that is independent in itself; for, if God is the cause of the same, this means: the solitary cause is not assisting. God concurs therefore only with freedom; because nature is his own work, he cannot concur with that. (*R* 6171, 18: 475)[45]

Of God one cannot say that he concurs with that which occurs according to mechanical laws, insofar as he is the author of this order, for example, that God concurs with the fertility of the season in summer. (*R* 8083; 19: 627)[46]

In his 1795 text *Perpetual Peace*, Kant repeats a similar point, that *concursus* implies some sort of insufficiency in the divine action:

But as for the concept, customary in the schools, of divine *intervention* or collaboration (*concursus*) toward an effect in the sensible world, this must be given up. For to want to pair what is disparate and to let what is itself the complete cause of alterations in the world *supplement* its own predetermining providence (which must therefore have been inadequate) during the course of the world is, *first*, self-contradictory. (*PP* 8: 362n.)[47]

---

[42] My translation.   [43] My translation.   [44] My translation.
[45] My translation.   [46] My translation.
[47] I depart here from the translation in the *Cambridge Edition*, which translates '*gebräuchlich in den Schulen*' as 'current in the academic world'; *gebräuchlich* can mean not just 'current', but 'customary' or 'usual', and *die Schulen* should be permitted to have the connotation of the medieval Schools (of the scholastic theologians), as well as the systems of the German rationalists. As well as being justified in its own right, the revised translation makes more sense; the

In his *Lectures on the Philosophical Doctrine of Religion*, Kant observes that, for *concursus* to occur, the cooperating causes 'must be coordinated with one another and not subordinated one to another':

> For if the causes are subordinated one to another and constitute a chain or series of causes in which each is a particular link, then each link in the chain is the complete cause of the next, even if all together they have a common ground in the first cause. (*LPR* 28: 1105)

When this happens, really we have a *causa solitaria*. Whereas, for a *concursus*:

> Causes have to be united and coordinated with one another; and one cause must make up for what the other fails to produce. Thus the effect is produced only by the causes being unified and working in community with one another. (*LPR* 28: 1105)

We do not need to be cautious in using the *Lectures* here, either out of a concern for the reliability of the transcription, or because of the possibility that Kant might be rehearsing a traditional position, without meaning to endorse it. First of all, similar passages about the impossibility of *concursus* appear in other transcriptions of the same lectures (*NTV* 28: 1207–13; *DR* 28: 1308–11), although the *Pölitz* lecture notes (*LPR*) provide the most nuanced and detailed version. Kant repeats a similar position in lecture notes from the 1790s.[48]

> If God is the Author of the world, so he cannot also concur with himself. The connection of causes with the first cause is concursus. Solitary causes do not concur. God is alone the cause of all natural changes, and do he does not concur. (*MK₂* 28: 811)[49]

> The connection of several causes is called concursus. A cause which does not have a co-cause [*concausam*] is a solitary cause, the solely effective cause, which cause is not concursus. (*MD* 28: 648)[50]

Secondly, the position staked out in these lecture notes is corroborated in other published texts and *Reflexionen*. Thirdly, the position that Kant sets out is a departure from the traditional perspective, reflecting distinctively Kantian concerns, and so cannot be a rehearsal of it.

Previously in the *Lectures*, Kant invokes the division of reality into substances, and accidents, which inhere in substances. Spinoza's definition of substance—'that whose existence does not require the existence of anything else' (*LPR* 28: 1041)—is, for Kant, an unhappy one. It results in the unpromising

---

position Kant is opposing is much older, as he would know, than a 'current' theory in his 'academic world'.

[48] For these references to lecture notes in the 1790s I am indebted to Hogan, 'Kant's Theory of Divine and Secondary Causation', p. 30, manuscript.

[49] My translation.

[50] My translation.

conclusion that 'there is only one substance, God', as 'everything in the world is an *accidens* inhering in this divinity' (*LPR* 28: 1041). Kant uses the term 'substance' to denote anything 'real which *exists for itself, without being a determination of any other thing*', which gives Kant the result that 'all things are substances', which is to say, 'anything which is a subject of predication is a substance' (*LPR* 28: 1042–3). Kant reasons that 'God . . . does not concur in the existence of substances'. This because 'substances contribute nothing to their own duration, and therefore cannot themselves operate in union with God as *concausae* of their own conservation' (*LPR* 28: 1107). Substances depend entirely on God and nothing else, in that they depend upon God's creative and conserving act. Where we are talking about substances, we see 'only a subordination of causes':

> Every substance has its ground in God as the *prima causa*, since the matter of every substance itself is created by him, but just for this reason there can be no *concursus*, for if there were, then the substance would have to be coordinated with God. (*LPR* 28: 1106)

When it comes to the products of the secondary causation of created substances, Kant similarly finds that there is no *concursus*, as in this case—and consistent with mere conservation—God is not the immediate cause of the actions that bring about these occurrences:

> There takes place no *concursus* of God with natural occurrences. For just because they are supposed to be natural occurrences, it is presupposed already that their first proximate cause is in nature itself, and it must be sufficient to effect the occurrence, even if the cause itself (like every natural cause) is grounded in God as the supreme cause. (*LPR* 28: 1106)

When he talks about 'natural occurrences', it seems likely that Kant is talking about *natura* in the sense of 'creation': created (noumenal) substances, rather than nature in the sense of spatio-temporal appearances. Kant states that 'every natural cause' is 'grounded in God as the supreme cause'; but God, as we know, is not the supreme cause of nature in the sense of spatio-temporal appearances, although God is the creator of substances as things in themselves. The 'natural causes' that are grounded in God must, for the sake of consistency, be things in themselves. By the time something has the status of a phenomenal appearance, it is a natural occurrence that arises somehow from the 'first proximate cause', which is the thing in itself. Given this, it is *also* the case that 'natural occurrences' in the sense of phenomenal appearances are such that their proximate and direct causes do not include a concurring divine action. Phenomenal natural occurrences have as their causes other phenomenal events, all of which are grounded ultimately—we know not how—upon noumenal affection.

By his own lights, Kant refutes the notion of divine concurrence with created substances, at least where freedom is not involved. Given this, we would have to say that Kant is a mere conservationist with respect to created substances. This is not only implied in Kant's work, but explicitly set out. Kant follows his criticism of the notion of *concursus* by asking: 'Can it not be recognized how inappropriate it is to use this expression [God's "cooperation"] in place of "divine conservation" (*LPR* 28: 1109). The importance of this result becomes clear only when we think through some of the implications of this denial. To help here, I turn to a criticism of mere conservation set out by Suarez.

Suarez's Criticism of Mere Conservationism

Philosophical criticisms often work by presenting a bullet that is supposed to be so unpalatable to the bite that the interlocutor backs down: 'if you say *x*, you will see that *y* follows', where *y* is considered to be obviously unacceptable in some way. Suarez offers some criticisms of mere conservation, indicating that they lead to consequences that the philosophical theologian is supposed to find obviously unpalatable. These same consequences of mere conservation are seen and understood by Kant, who is prepared to bite the bullet and to endorse mere conservation and its implications. Some of the more extreme expressions that Kant uses for his transcendental idealism are in fact, Suarez would agree, precise and honest implications of his denial of concurrence. Where Suarez would find the implications of this denial beyond the pale of what is theologically seemly, Kant finds that they are the only way to protect a space for created freedom. The suggestion is not that Kant is indebted to Suarez on this point, but that Kant understands the same point that is grasped by Suarez, in relation to the conceptual momentum that is unleashed by his denial of concurrence.[51]

The mere conservationist insists that the action of a substance depends not upon God's immediate and direct cooperation while the action exists, but only on God's remote conservation of the substance with its capacities for action. Suarez worries that if the action really does not depend upon God immediately, 'then there is no basis for insisting that the form or effect *produced* by the agent depends upon God conserving it immediately'.[52] Suarez's concern is that, 'if God does not have an immediate influence on every action of a

---

[51] Although they do not explore the consequences of denying concurrence to the same extent that Suarez does, Baumgarten and Meier explicitly set out that God's concurrence extends to the effects of secondary causes: Baumgarten, *Metaphysica*, §958, and Meier, *Metaphysik*, §1027. For these references to Baumgarten and Meier I am indebted to Hogan, 'Kant's Theory of Divine Causation and Secondary Causation', 29.

[52] Freddoso, 'God's General Concurrence with Secondary Causes: Why Conservation is not Enough', 571.

creature, then a created action itself does not of itself require God's influence essentially in order to exist, even though it, too, is a certain participation in being':

Therefore, there is no reason why the form that comes to exist through such an action should require for *its* conservation an actual influence of the First Cause. For it does not require this influence in order to *come to exist* [*ratione sui fieri*], according to the position in question, since this coming to exist is not itself immediately from God. Nor does it require this influence in order *to exist* [*ratione sui esse*], since [if it did, this would be] mainly because it is a participated being—but this reason is not judged sufficient, according to the position in question, in the case of the action itself; therefore, neither will it be sufficient in the case of the form, i.e., the terminus of the action.[53]

If the action of a secondary cause is its own immediate action, and not God's, then it seems that God does not give being-as-such to the product of that action: God merely supports the substance who brings about the effect. This, I suggest, explains the interpretative puzzle we were left with at the end of the last chapter. If Kant was a mere conservationist, then he would indeed insist that 'appearances'—space, time, and phenomenal causal series—are not 'divine works'; rather, they are the direct result of the (non-free) action of noumenal substances, in this case ourselves, as we receive and cognize representations that are grounded by things in themselves. In this case, we are the direct cause of nature as appearance. Kant agrees with Suarez that, if there is no divine concurrence with created substances, but only conservation, God does not directly bring about the actions of these substances, nor the products of these actions. This, I submit, precisely explains the significance of the passages that we found puzzling in the previous chapter, where Kant insists that 'it would be a contradiction to say that God is the creator of appearances' (*CPrR.* 5: 102), that 'space is not a thing as a divine work' (*R* 6057), and that God is not 'the cause of actions in the sensible world' (*CPrR.* 5: 102).

In the previous chapter (pp. 176–78) I suggested that Kant has difficulty relating space and time to God, once space and time are no longer conceived by him as derived from relational properties between substances. If space and time are in some sense infinite and absolute, as Kant thinks from 1768 onwards, then Kant worries that they will become properties of God, such that God will be spatialized. By Kant's own account, at least, this is one factor, or at least a further rational credential, for a view of space and time as forms of human intuition, rather than absolute and infinite things in themselves. In the previous chapter I argued that even if we accept Kant's theological reasons for

---

[53] Suarez, *On Creation, Conservation and Concurrence*, 22.1, §9. Cited and discussed by Freddoso, 'God's General Concurrence with Secondary Causes: Why Conservation is not Enough', 571–2.

construing space (and time) as forms of intuition, we still could not understand why space (and time) could not be considered as caused by God, where what is caused are space (and time) as forms of our intuition. We now have the answer to this question: God creates and conserves noumenal substances, but the actions and effects of substances, which include the reception of things in themselves through the forms of intuition, are not directly divine actions. Hence, 'space is not a thing as a divine work'.

Kant would find the mere conservationist approach that he sets out explicitly criticized in Leibniz. Leibniz complains that the production of a new reality without divine concurrence 'seems neither appropriate to creatures nor worthy of God'.[54] Leibniz asks, 'who would believe that substances cannot be produced but by God and yet accidents can be produced without divine concurrence, and therefore be more independent?'[55] Leibniz is concerned that if creatures could produce accidents without divine concurrence, then 'pari jure' they would be able to produce substances, 'but then the world would not essentially depend on God, a view which is not only wrong but also leads to irreligion'.[56] Leibniz's position, as set out by Vailati, is that 'all created reality depends on God with the same degree of complete immediacy'.

If creatures could produce accidents without divine concurrence, accidents would depend on God mediately, namely, through their substances, while substances would depend on God immediately... mere conservationism *à la* Durandus makes a part of nature too independent of God.[57]

Here we have the answer to another question raised at the end of the last chapter, as to why Kant's theological assertion that appearances are not created could not be understood within the terms of a traditional theological distinction between creation *ex nihilo* and the production of effects within the creation. Kant's denial of concurrence entails that appearances are not only 'not creations' in the sense that they are not created *ex nihilo*, but that appearances are not *directly* the result of immediate divine action.[58]

---

[54] Leibniz, *De Libertate Fato Gratia Dei*, in *Textes Inédites d'après les manuscrits de la Bibliothèque provinciale de Hanovre*, ed. by Gaston Grua (Paris: Gaston Grua, 1948), 314–15; cited and discussed by Vailati, 'Leibniz on Divine Concurrence with Secondary Causes', 213.

[55] Leibniz, *De Libertate Fato Gratia Dei*, 314–15.

[56] Vailati, 'Leibniz on Divine Concurrence with Secondary Causes', 213.

[57] Vailati, 'Leibniz on Divine Concurrence with Secondary Causes', 216.

[58] Hogan writes that, if presented with Suarez's objection to mere conservationism, 'Kant would simply grant the conclusion, since his official view is that God conserves accidents only mediately, by virtue of an immediate conservation of substances in which they inhere' (Hogan, 'Kant's Theory of Divine and Secondary Causation', pp. 28–9, manuscript). It seems more plausible to say that Kant's 'official view', about the created status of accidents, is itself the *result* of his denial of concurrence, rather than being an independently arrived at commitment. We have found no other good reason for Kant to hold the position that accidents are not 'divine works', a conclusion that we have seen that Kant extends to all spatio-temporal appearances (see pp. 173–76). Kant's distancing of God from the creation (and conservation) of spatio-temporal

Miracles and Concurrence in Nature

Kant is a mere conservationist about the ordinary course of nature. In a few references, Kant seems to hold out for the possibility of a type of concurrence between God and natural events, with respect to miraculous interventions. The references to miracles as a possible form of concurrence are scanty and inconclusive, but nonetheless need to be considered in any systematic exploration of Kant's attitude to concurrence. As we will see, Kant seems to take the view that when miracles occur, God 'concurs' with natural causes. A little more investigation, though, reveals that Kant's account would not be considered as a genuine case of concurrence by the theological tradition.

In a number of *Reflexionen* Kant talks about divine *concursus* as 'the immediate supplementation of a natural capacity, towards the fulfilling of a particular purpose' (*R* 4792, 17: 729),[59] where *concursus* involves a miraculous intervention in the course of nature. 'Divine concursus' is a case of 'extraordinary direction... insofar as the action provides a complement to ordinary action' (*R* 8081).[60] In his *Lectures on the Philosophical Doctrine of Religion*, after denying divine concurrence in the ordinary course of natural occurrences, Kant goes on to say:

> Yet a *concursus* between God and natural occurrences in the world is still not impossible; for it is always thinkable that a natural cause is not sufficient by itself to produce a certain effect. In such a case God might give it a *complementum ad sufficientiam*; but whenever he did this, he would *eo ipso* perform a *miracle*. For we call something a miracle *when the cause of an occurrence is supernatural*, as it would be if God himself operated as *concausa* in the production of such a miracle.—Hence if one ascribes to God special turns and twists of affairs in the world, then one is only predicating so many miracles of him. (*LPR* 28: 1109–10)

Kant's admission of the conceptual possibility of divine concurrence in this sense is perhaps rather grudging. Certainly he is eager to emphasize that it is 'unthinkable that God, who is the *causa prima* of the whole of nature, might also cooperate as a *concausa* in each particular occurrence' (*LPR* 28: 1109–10). The concurrence whose possibility Kant allows is an extraordinary intervention, an '*exception to the rule of nature*'. Kant argues that, were we to say (along with the theological tradition) that God cooperates as a '*concausa* of every particular natural occurrence', then 'every natural occurrence would be an exception to the laws of nature':

---

appearances requires explanation, as it goes beyond anything that is required by any epistemological insights offered by transcendental idealism (see pp. 176–78), and cannot be fully accounted for by the traditional distinction between creation and production (see pp. 189–91).

[59] My translation.
[60] My translation.

Or rather there would be no order at all in nature, because the occurrences would not happen according to general rules, but in each case God would have to give a *complementum ad sufficientiam* to anything which was to be set up according to his will. (*LPR* 28: 1109–10)

Kant concludes this thought by exclaiming 'what imperfection in a world, totally irreconcilable with a wise author!' (*LPR* 28: 1109–10). With warnings throughout his texts, early and late, about the 'lazy reason' that resorts to miraculous divine intervention as an explanation of events (*OPA* 2: 108–12; A691–2/B719–20; A773/B801; *LPR* 28: 997, 1071), it is clear that Kant is reluctant to employ the conceptually 'not impossible' category of divine *concursus* (or 'intervention') in order to explain natural occurrences.

Traditional concurrentists would not find Kant's employment of the category of *concursus* to be appropriate here, and would find his account of miracles to derogate from divine sovereignty over nature. The type of miracle that Kant has in mind is what Aquinas categorizes as a *contra naturam* miracle, where God produces the effect by himself alone, but where secondary agents 'retain their causal tendency to produce an effect directly contrary'.[61] Aquinas writes that a miracle

is said to be *contra naturam* when there remains in nature a disposition that is contrary to the effect which God produces, as when He kept the young men unharmed in the furnace even though the power to incinerate them remained in the fire [Daniel 3], and as when the waters of the Jordan stood still even though gravity remained in them [Josue 3].[62]

Aquinas, Molina, and Suarez agree that God brings about such miracles by omission, rather than commission. God does this by depriving a created thing of its natural action by withholding his concurrence. As Suarez puts it:

Just as God can deprive a created thing of its existence simply by withholding His action, so too He can deprive a created thing of its natural action simply by withholding His concurrence; therefore, just as from the former power one infers evidently an immediate dependence in existing, so too from the latter power one infers an immediate dependence in the action itself. The antecedent (as I certainly concede) is not evident from any natural experience.[63]

---

[61] Freddoso, 'God's General Concurrence with Secondary Causes: Why Conservation is not Enough', 573.

[62] Aquinas, *De Potentia*, 6.2.3, cited and translated by Freddoso, 'God's General Concurrence with Secondary Causes: Why Conservation is not Enough', 573.

[63] Suarez, *On Creation, Conservation and Concurrence*, 22.I, §11. Cited and discussed by Freddoso, 'God's General Concurrence with Secondary Causes: Why Conservation is not Enough', 573.

The concern that concurrentists would have about Kant's notion of miracles is that we seem to have *contra naturam* miracles only when God *opposes* natural causes. Molina expresses precisely this concern:

If God did not cooperate with secondary causes, He clearly would not have been able to bring it about that the Babylonian fire did not burn the three young men except by opposing it, as it were, and impeding its action either (i) through some contrary action or (ii) by placing something around the young men or conferring on them some resistant quality which would prevent the fire's impressing its action upon them. Therefore, since this derogates both the divine power and also the total subjection by which all things submit to and obey that power, one should claim without doubt that God cooperates with secondary causes, and that it was only because God did not concur with the fire in its action that the young men were not incinerated by it.[64]

The concern of the concurrentists, as expressed by Freddoso, is that God should 'not have to counteract His creatures from without in order to make them do His bidding'.[65] Because God 'controls them from within as creator and governor', God should not have to '"vie" with them'.[66] We have what we might call a piece of theological grammar, rather than an elegant theoretical solution. The grammar is that it is theologically inappropriate to have a conception where God must *intervene* and *oppose* creatures in order to bring about miracles. This can be put in a number of ways: that it derogates from God's power and sovereignty over nature; or, if we prefer less authoritarian tropes, that it neglects the *sui generis* and intimate relationship between God and creatures, where God is more at the centre of the creature than the creature is to itself. The concurrentist finds it obvious that we must say rather that 'God can make created agents from within "forgetful of their power"'.[67] Where something is a piece of grammar, rather than an explanation of how the grammar can be understood or applies, it has a non-negotiable quality for those who ascribe to it: this must be respected and held to, whether or not we are able, now or ever, fully to understand and to apply it. It has also therefore a rather arbitrary quality: it is bedrock, the place from which we argue, rather than something argued to. Those not seized of the grammar will, I think, not be easily persuaded that a mere conservationist account of miracles derogates

---

[64] Luis de Molina, *On Divine Foreknowledge: Part IV of the "Concordia"*, trans. with introduction and notes by Alfred J. Freddoso: (Ithaca, NY: Cornell University Press, 1988), II.25, §15. Cited and discussed by Freddoso, 'God's General Concurrence with Secondary Causes: Why Conservation is not Enough', 573–4.

[65] Freddoso, 'God's General Concurrence with Secondary Causes: Why Conservation is not Enough', 573–4.

[66] Freddoso, 'God's General Concurrence with Secondary Causes: Why Conservation is not Enough', 575.

[67] Freddoso, 'God's General Concurrence with Secondary Causes: Why Conservation is not Enough', 576.

from divine power, or from the uniqueness of the relationship between creator and created. They might even think that only God's ability to intervene and oppose secondary agents constitutes or exemplifies such power, or uniqueness. Here we turn our spade. At this point, I share Freddoso's sense that, 'while I myself think that it is obvious enough' that mere conservationism derogates from divine power/uniqueness, 'I see no easy way to convince someone who disagrees'.[68]

In actual fact, one of the arguments given historically for concurrence is that it is the only model that can give a proper account of miracles as a case of God withdrawing the usual intermediate causal chains, which are held in his immediate conserving act as much as any miraculous event. Miracles are, as Aquinas puts it, 'things that are at times divinely accomplished, apart from the general established order in things'.[69] In that miracles occur by omission, rather than commission, we might almost say that a miracle occurs when there is less divine action, or where the divine action sustains less in the way of a mediating causal buffer between God and the event. Kant allows a space for divine *concursus*, in the sense of the miraculous; nonetheless, when we interrogate his concept of the miraculous, we find that it is conceived of as the intrusion of a radically discontinuous principle of action, rather than as the result of God's withdrawing layers of causation. In effect, we have a significant inversion of the understanding of the concurrentist concept of miracle. In sum, although Kant uses the term *concursus*, he does this within a mere conservationist, rather than a concurrentist, framework.

CONCURRENCE AND FREEDOM

As the following texts indicate, Kant seems more positive about using the category of *concursus* with respect to our free actions:

Concursus is in contradistinction to a solitary action. Operating with (concurrence *Mitwirkung*) or operating alone. The (forces of) the world are unified in nature and freedom; in respect of nature God is the sole cause, in respect of freedom, he concurs. (*R* 4748, 17: 696)[70]

The freedom of worldly creatures through divine [wisdom] influence is *concursus*. (*R* 5632, 18: 264–5)[71]

---

[68] Freddoso, 'God's General Concurrence with Secondary Causes: Why Conservation is not Enough', 577.

[69] Aquinas, *Summa Contra Gentiles*, 3.2, 101.1.

[70] My translation.   [71] My translation.

The creation of the world, neither emanation nor of an architect. Subtle atheism. Conservation in time. Concursus with human moral freedom. The end of creation. (*R* 6019, 18: 425)[72]

As concursus providence is called direction, and indeed mainly with respect to freedom. (*R* 6118, 18: 460–1)[73]

Creation; conservation; governance; concursus, not with respect to nature, but freedom. (*R* 6121, 18: 462)[74]

As before, what matters is not that Kant uses the term *concursus*, but what precisely he means. In what sense is there divine *concursus* with human freedom? Several passages point to a fairly straightforward explanation. God can supplement the action of the creature by removing impediments to the creature's free action: 'Moral concursus occurs through the removal of obstacles to our inner morality and not through the determination of our actions' (*R* 4623, 17: 487).[75] If this is correct, then there is still a part of the action, our own moral endeavour, which is solely ours, and not the object of concurrence. This seems to be what Kant has in mind in the following passages:

Thus God cannot concur in the causality of freely acting beings toward his moral ends in the world, for he must not be regarded as *causa* of their free actions. That which gives free actions the *complementum ad sufficientam* toward divine moral ends (holiness) is the spirit of God. This, however, if the actions are still to remain imputable, must also not be *causata* of the holy spirit, but only the removal of obstacles to freedom. The spirit of God is that which gives the moral law motivating force; thus an inner moral life, which is certainly not possible in accord with natural laws, is at work in us. Everything that is morally good in us is an effect of the spirit of God and what is imputed to us is that we make room for this. (*R* 6167, 18: 473–4)

With respect to natural events, God is the author; but not with respect to free human actions; there he is only a concurring cause; for the free actions would not be free if they were determined through a cause. With respect to nature, God is not a concurring cause [*concurrirt nicht*], but he is solitary cause [*causa solitaria*]; but with respect to the actions of creatures God is a concurring cause [*concurrirt Gott*], because the insufficiency of creatures requires a concurrence [*Mitwirkung*]; for all free creatures, however free they are, can produce nothing, except through their limitation, both with respect to nature and physical actions, and also with respect to moral actions. (*ML₁* 28: 347)[76]

Kant seems to have in mind not a single action, with God and the creature cooperating, but two parallel actions: the free action of the creature, and God's assistance to the creature in reaching their goal. This is also suggested in *R* 6171, where Kant writes that God 'concurs only with freedom', insofar as 'freedom has the highest good as its purpose', where God assists in the

---

[72] My translation. [73] My translation. [74] My translation.
[75] My translation. [76] My translation.

'bringing about of the highest good', which involves reconciling worthiness to be happy (following the moral law) with happiness.[77] In this sense, God's concurrence with free actions falls under the broader category discussed above of God's actions to 'supplement' a 'natural capacity' towards 'the fulfilling of a particular purpose' (*R* 4792).

In the Collins lecture notes from 1784–5, Kant explains that 'everything can be imputed to man that is brought forth naturally by him, through his own powers' (*Coll.* 27: 309). Divine assistance comes in when the human being makes 'himself worthy of every supplementation of his frailty' (*Coll.* 27: 310). Only 'our good behaviour makes us worthy of divine assistance' (*Coll.* 27: 310), and 'the man who does not behave as he naturally ought to, can hope for no supernatural assistance', so that the 'supernatural presupposes the natural' (*Coll.* 27: 310). Lecture notes from the 1790s also endorse a notion of divine *concursus* as the supplementation of a discrete human effort:

God concurs towards the moral good, in order to complete, what the human being, with all his striving towards the highest good, cannot achieve. One can think of a divine concursus not otherwise than with respect to freedom, and not with respect to nature. (*MK$_2$* 28: 811)[78]

But, even here, we think of this as *concursus* only 'by analogy' (*ad analogiam*) (*MK$_2$* 28: 811). In *Perpetual Peace*, Kant writes that 'from *a morally practical point of view*' the 'concept of a divine *concursus*', in the sense of supernatural supplementary assistance, 'is quite appropriate and even necessary': 'Belief that God, by means incomprehensible to us, will make up for the lack of our own righteousness if only our disposition is genuine, so that we should never slacken in our striving towards the good' (*PP* 8: 362). At the same time, Kant warns, consistently with his misgivings about 'lazy reason', that 'no one must attempt to *explain* a good action (as an event in the world) by this *concursus*', as to attempt such an explanation would be 'a futile theoretical cognition of the supersensible' (*PP* 8: 362).

Where Kant seems to endorse divine *concursus*, what he has in mind is a conjunction of two cooperating causes: human free action brought about directly by the secondary cause, and assisting divine action brought about directly and solely by God. This conception of two separate causal factors comes across starkly in lecture notes from the 1780s:

We do not ascribe free actions to the course of nature, to the mechanism of nature, that is, when every event has its ground in the preceeding event and is determined through it. In the case of freedom every action is presupposed as if it were not

---

[77] My translation.
[78] My translation. For this reference to *MK$_2$* I am indebted to Hogan, 'Kant's Theory of Divine and Secondary Causation', p. 32, manuscript.

determined.—Moral concursus is, when I presuppose a moral concursus with respect to moral events.—If these events are free, then they do not unfold from the first order, which God set down in the world. These events are therefore not determined through that which God sets down in the creation. It seems that these events ground themselves on a causality, which is distinct from the creation, and which is independent of the divine plan for the creation. If that is the case, we are permitted to think of a concursus, which is two coordinated causes. (*DR* 28: 1311)[79]

Just before this passage, in the same transcript of Kant's lectures, there is an emphatic statement that God cannot be thought of as a concurring cause of the free action of the human, in the way that traditional concurrence accounts would require. That strand of the *concursus* that is human action must be untouched by divine action, if the human act is to have moral worth:

It is not permitted to think of God's concursus with free actions. These actions are events in the world. If God is the determining cause of these actions, then they are not free. But God, however, does not concur; then he would not be a solitary cause. If I say, God concurs with the determination of our willing, then that would be again a miracle. If God concurs with morality, then the human being has no moral worth, because nothing can be imputed to him. (*DR* 28: 1309)[80]

Once again, as with Kant's account of miracles, we find that a conception of *concursus* as the conjunction of two separate causes would be ruled out by traditional concurrentists. On this point Freddoso agrees with Durandas that the conjunction of two separate causes 'is not a version of concurrentism at all':[81] 'For it is one thing to say that God immediately produces something that exists in the creature . . . It is quite another thing to say that God immediately produces each thing that a creature produces.'[82] It is precisely this latter claim that the concurrentist wishes to make. Aquinas denies that 'an effect produced jointly by God and creatures is a conjunction of two independently produced per se [immediate] effects':

It is not the case that the same effect is attributed to a natural cause and to the divine power in such a way that it is effected partly, as it were, by God and partly by the secondary cause. Rather, the whole is effected by both of them according to different modes—just as the same effect is attributed as a whole to the instrument and also as a whole to the principle agent.[83]

<hr>

[79] My translation. [80] My translation.

[81] Freddoso, 'God's General Concurrence with Secondary Causes: Pitfalls and Prospects', 144.

[82] William Durandus, *In Sententias Theologicas Petri Lombardi Commentariorum Libri Quattuor* (Venice, 1571; reprinted at Ridgewood, NJ: Gregg Press, 1964), bk II. dist.1, a.5, §6, cited, translated, and discussed by Freddoso, 'God's General Concurrence with Secondary Causes: Pitfalls and Prospects', 144.

[83] Aquinas, *Summa Contra Gentiles*, 3.1, 70.8. I use the translation provided by Freddoso, 'God's General Concurrence with Secondary Causes: Pitfalls and Prospects', 146–7.

The goal of the concurrentist is to show 'that when God and creatures cooperate they act by means of one and the same action', such that, 'when God concurs with secondary agents', neither 'God's action nor the secondary causes' action can even *exist* in the absence of the other, and so neither can be sufficient to produce the effect in the absence of the other'.[84] In their cooperative actions 'God and secondary causes constitute a single total cause through a single undivided action, a dependence that can be unitary even if the cooperating agents are distinct'.[85]

As with Kant's use of the language of *concursus* in the case of miracles, it turns out that Kant's application of this notion to human freedom occurs also within a mere conservationist framework, and is not what the theological tradition would regard as proper concurrence.

CONCURRENCE AND COMPATIBILISM

Concurrentist accounts of human freedom can cause problems for some of the standard distinctions between compatibilist and incompatibilist approaches. For example, Thomas Flint is not alone in having difficulty in finding a neat category for Thomist approaches to freedom. Flint concedes that Thomists rarely style themselves as compatibilists, in that they reject a 'determinism of circumstances'.[86] This would fit with Stump's characterization of Aquinas's position that 'a decision is free only if it is not the outcome of a causal chain that originates in a cause outside the agent'.[87] Nonetheless, Flint complains that 'the kind of divine activity that the Thomists see as compatible with human freedom would not be deemed compatible by those with libertarian inclinations':

For the heart and soul of libertarianism is the conviction that what an agent does freely is genuinely up to the agent to do freely or refrain from doing freely; no external circumstance, no other agent, does or even can determine what I do freely. Physical determinism, which sees my actions as determined by physical laws and *prior* states of the universe, is clearly at odds with this core insight. But surely the Thomist picture of *simultaneous* divine determinism [Flint's description of concurrentism] will strike the true libertarian as equally destructive of human freedom. And, indeed, if external determination is incompatible with human freedom, does it really make that much difference how much the determination is accomplished? Are the movements of a

---

[84] Freddoso, 'God's General Concurrence with Secondary Causes: Pitfalls and Prospects', 151–2.

[85] Freddoso, 'God's General Concurrence with Secondary Causes: Pitfalls and Prospects', 151–2.

[86] Flint, 'Two Accounts of Providence', 173.

[87] Stump, *Aquinas*, 302.

hand puppet any more under its own control than those of a windup doll? In sum, if we think of compatibilism in the broader sense as the view that a free action *can* be externally determined, does it not appear that Thomism is indeed ultimately rooted in compatibilism?[88]

This is an illuminating passage for drawing out some of the distinctive instincts of the concurrentist. Flint hits the nail on the head when he asks 'does it really make that much difference how much the determination is accomplished?' The concurrentist would answer that it makes *all the difference*, whether it is *God* determining our actions, or something other than God (physical determinism, for example). It is standard to draw attention to the Thomist commitment to *simultaneous* divine action in this context, as being the key to how the Thomist, by his own lights, can avoid the 'determinism of circumstances': divine action is 'present *when* one acts, but not *before* one acts; otherwise, one would have the dreaded determinism of circumstances'.[89] But this would seem less fundamental, theologically, than the fact that it is *God* acting, because—as we have seen in Chapters 4 and 8 (pp. 86–89 and pp. 178–180)—God is the only extrinsic cause who can act upon the creature without being violent or coercive in a way that threatens freedom. When Flint asks 'are the movements of a hand puppet any more under its own control than those of a windup doll?', the concurrentist would agree that the puppet and the doll are under the same sort of determinism. But that is not to the point: the difference that counts is that between a creature moved by another creature or created series of events, and a creature moved by the creator. Here the concurrentist would insist that the movements of the creature moved by the creator are entirely free, in a way that is not true of movements that are caused by another creature or created series.

In the passage above, Flint comments that 'Thomism is indeed ultimately rooted in compatibilism', if we 'think of compatibilism in the broader sense as the view that a free action *can* be externally determined'.[90] Arguably it is not a broader sense of compatibilism that captures the Thomist intuition, but a much narrower one: the *only* form of external determination that is compatible with free action is that which comes from God. Any other form of determination would be a 'determination by circumstances', and the human being is free if only he or she is not determined by 'a causal chain that originates in a cause outside the agent'.[91] The point is that God is not a cause 'outside the agent', at least, not in the sense that could be detrimental to freedom. This is a unique and *sui generis* form of compatibilism. Theologians who defend a concurrentist account are reflectively aware of the

[88] Flint, 'Two Accounts of Providence', 174.
[89] Flint, 'Two Accounts of Providence', 174.
[90] Flint, 'Two Accounts of Providence', 174.
[91] Stump, *Aquinas*, 302.

difficulty in categorizing the relation between God and the creature. Kathryn Tanner comments that, when 'discussion is limited to created causes', then 'talk of two sufficient causes working for the same effect makes no sense', so that theological discourse has to 'violate in a systematic fashion our expectations for talk of sufficient causes'.[92]

Rather than attempting to fit the concurrentist model into the compatibilist/incompatibilist distinction, it is better to expand the conceptual map to four fundamental positions rather than two. The more fundamental distinction from a theological point of view is whether one has a compatibilist or a incompatibilist account of the relation between God and the creature. The concurrentist gives a strong theologically compatibilist answer, insisting not only that God's action on the creature can never violate the creature's freedom, but in fact that God's action on the creature when acting is the source of the creature's freedom. The theological incompatibilist, such as Thomas Flint, insists that God's action on the creature would threaten the creature's freedom.

One can then ask a distinct question, largely untouched by the answer to the theological question, as to whether we need a compatibilist or incompatibilist account of our freedom in relation to causal factors on the created plane. The concurrentist could adopt a compatibilist account of the relation between God and the creature, but insist that we are genuinely free only if we are a first mover with respect to other created causes, enjoying both ultimate responsibility for our actions with respect to created causes, and having the ability to do otherwise. Alternatively, the concurrentist could settle for a compatibilist account of freedom in relation to other created causes, being content that our freedom does not require ultimate responsibility for our actions, or the possibility of doing otherwise. As Kathryn Tanner puts it, the 'idea of God as creator', in a concurrentist sense, 'is compatible with *any* philosophical account of the nature of human freedom short of the theological judgement that human freedom requires freedom from or with respect to God'.[93] The theological claim can be in place 'whatever one's account of the natural and psychological conditions for human choice—however strongly one maintains the freedom of human choice from determination by psychological preconditions, natural circumstances, and so forth'.[94]

We can set out the four positions with respect to human freedom in relation to God below:

---

[92] Tanner, *God and Creation in Christian Theology*, 93.
[93] Tanner, 'Human Freedom', 111.
[94] Tanner, 'Human Freedom', 111.

1. Theological Compatibilism A: compatibilist account of the relation between God and the creature, but incompatibilist with respect to our freedom in relation to other created causes.

2. Theological Compatibilism B: compatibilist account of the relation between God and the creature, and compatibilist with respect to our freedom in relation to other created causes.

3. Theological Incompatibilism A: incompatiblist account of the relation between God and the creature, and incompatiblist with respect to our freedom in relation to other created causes.

4. Theological Incompatibilism B: incompatibilist account of the relation between God and the creature, but compatibilist with respect to our freedom in relation to other created causes.

Setting out the distinctions in this way does not help us to resolve the issue of the correct account of freedom, but it does enable us to set out more clearly what the dispute is. It enables us to locate the instinct of philosophers of religion such as Flint that the concurrentist model is 'ultimately rooted in compatibilism', alongside the judgement of theologians such as Tanner and Burrell that the concurrentist model is neutral with respect to the compatibilism/incompatibilism issue. Both judgements are correct when properly framed. The concurrentist model is fundamentally compatibilist, but need be so only with respect to *one* causal relation: that between God and the creature. Because this is the only relation that needs to be construed in compatiblilist terms, it is true that a concurrentist could also be incompatiblist with respect to created causes.

CONCURRENCE AND THE SHIFT IN KANT'S ACCOUNT OF CREATED FREEDOM

We can track Kant's movement on the issue of created freedom in terms of the four possibilities set out above. In 1755 Kant's position is described by 'Theological Compatiblism B', where Kant has a compatiblist account of the relation between God and creatures, and a compatiblist account of the relation between creaturely freedom and other created causes. This position comes under pressure when Kant begins to want an incompatibilist account of the relation between our freedom and other created causes. This shift could be accommodated either by moving to 'Theological Compatibilism A', or by moving to 'Theological Incompatibilism A'. Kant finds his way to the latter, but has to struggle to do so, as he finds it hard to account for how a 'being which has a cause' can be so independent of God. We might ask: why did Kant not move instead to 'Theological Compatibilism A'? Kant could have moved to Theological Compatibilism A, while still preserving created transcendental freedom with respect to the relation between free created beings and other created causes. The answer tracked in this book to this question, as to why Kant does not move to Theological Compatibilism A, is that he cannot accept a genuinely concurrentist account of the relationship between God and creatures. This means that the only way in which he can protect incompatibilist creature freedom is to move to 'Theological Incompatibilism A'. Kant understands the relationship between his denial of concurrence and his adoption of this position, and this is what lies behind the otherwise puzzling passages where he insists that God is not the creator or cause of appearances.

This is not to say that the pre-critical Kant must, therefore, be read as supporting concurrence theories of divine action. Although any full concurrence account will be a form of 'Theological Compatibilism' (A or B), it is not the case that any version of 'Theological Compatibulism B' will be a form of concurrentism. There is a conservationist version of 'Theological Compatibilism B': God determines human actions, so that human beings do not have the ability to do other than they do, and are not ultimately responsible for their action, although, when the human being acts, it is the human being (deterministically) acting, rather than God. Kant does not offer an explicit discussion of concurrentism in his pre-critical work. Nonetheless, Hogan suggests that there are grounds for considering the pre-critical Kant to prefer mere conservationism over concurrence. Hogan points to the way in which Kant envisages substances being placed in interconnection with each other by God, as discussed in Chapters 3 and 4 (pp. 47–52 and 61–67). 'The notable point' is Kant's 'consistent classification of this divine connecting act with God's *conserving* activity': 'The scheme of the divine understanding, the origin of substances, is an enduring act (it is called *conservation [conservatio]*)' (*NE* 1: 414).[95] This argument from a lack of explicit reference to concurrence cannot be more than suggestive.[96] Concurrence theories are rival theories not to conservationist accounts as such, but only to *mere* conservationist accounts, and a reference to conservation would not rule out a further commitment to concurrence. The crucial question is whether a thinker

---

[95] Hogan, 'Kant's Theory of Divine and Secondary Causation', pp. 14–15, manuscript. This departs slightly from the *Cambridge Edition*, which uses 'preservation' to translate *conservatio*.

[96] To support his claim that Kant probably rejected concurrence in his pre-critical work, Hogan also cites *R* 8083 (quoted on p. 205), which is dated by Adickes to 1760–4, 'Kant's Theory of Divine and Secondary Causation', p. 30, manuscript. Adickes is less than certain, though, about the dating, providing alternative possible dates of 1764–8, and 1773–5. Given that all the other references to concurrence are from the 1770s or later, it is not clear whether *R* 8083 provides evidence for Kant's pre-critical dismissal of concurrence, or whether the lack of corroborating evidence for Kant's pre-critical dismissal of concurrence provides grounds to reject the dating of this *Reflexion* to the 1760s.

considers that there is *more* to divine action than creation and conservation alone. All we can say with certainty is that the pre-critical Kant ascribes to some version of 'Theological Compatibilism A' (concurrentist or conservationist), but shifts over to 'Theological Incompatibilism A' and a clear dismissal of concurrentism. It makes sense that the issue of concurrentism would become a more live question for Kant once he begins to want an incompatibilist account of human freedom (specifically in relation to God). With his compatibilist account of human freedom in the 1750s, there would not perhaps be much at stake for Kant in the question of whether or not mere conservation or concurrence is the correct account of divine action.

We set out on this exploration of Kant's views on divine concurrence in order to answer the question of how precisely Kant envisages the relationship between divine action and human freedom. We saw that Kant acknowledges that noumenal substances are dependent upon God, in that God creates them *ex nihilo*, and God conserves them in existence. Such dependence upon God does not, for Kant, in itself present a challenge to human freedom, in the way in which dependence upon a created causal series would. I suggested that Schleiermacher's conception of 'absolute dependence' on God could be understood as an elaboration of Kant's central insight here. From the analysis of Kant on *concursus*, we have found that he sees no space for conceiving of God concurring with ordinary natural occurrences. Here Kant is a 'mere conservationist': a commitment that explains and illuminates some of his more puzzling comments about the distance between God and the effects of secondary causation (which include all 'appearances'). Kant leaves open the possibility of *concursus* with respect to miraculous interventions, but we saw that this was not of *concursus* as the theological tradition would understand it. Similarly, with respect to free actions, Kant speaks of *concursus*, meaning divine assistance; but again, as with his discussion of miracles, this would not be an understanding of *concursus* that would be recognized by the theological tradition.

In the next chapter I consider the profound difficulties in the debate between supporters and critics of concurrentism: these difficulties are at work, I suggest, in wildly different estimations of Kant's importance, or wholesomeness even, for Christian theology. I suggest that although there is much in Kant that the theologian might find surprisingly illuminating and consoling, this specific issue of the relationship between divine and human action is, and should be, a real stumbling block.

10

Legacy

Even when we have contemplated the parameters of the concurrentist position, I confess it remains difficult to *understand* how our action being free is compatible with it being part of the same unified action that is determined by God's. Rather as with divine simplicity, it can feel as if it is being *asserted* that two hard-to-relate considerations are unifiable, and a name is given to the assertion; but we might worry that the assertion itself has not been explained or defended.

In the first section of this chapter I interrogate some of the deep tectonic plates that underlie the conflict between supporters and detractors of concurrentism. Articulated disputes, in the form of discussions, can be rare between these two groups, as they can find each other's company so frustrating, for reasons that I hope to explicate.[1] Recently there has been a more affirmative trend in receiving Kant's contribution to philosophy of religion and philosophical theology. This has to be a welcome corrective to a previously dominant sense of Kant as implacably opposed to any theological project. Nonetheless, in the second section of the chapter, I argue that, whatever one's attitude to Kant's wider philosophy of religion, Kant's denial of concurrentism should be given a central and explicitly thematized place in any theological reception of his thought. In the third section I show how Kant's denial of concurrence works itself out when Kant does his own constructive philosophical theology. In particular, we notice the work done by the denial of concurrence in areas where we would expect a theologian to have something robust to say about divine action: in particular, grace and atonement. Whatever else we might want to say about Kant, he is not able to say very much about divine action in these areas: and this needs to be faced, one way or another, by any Christian theologian who wants to use Kant as a resource.

---

[1] A notable exception is the collection of essays edited by Thomas F. Tracy, *The God Who Acts* (University Park, PA: Pennsylvania University Press, 1994), where defenders of concurrentism (Burrell and Tanner), and detractors (Tracy and Hasker), articulate the grounds for their mutual disappointment with each other.

I conclude the book, by setting out a final twist in the tale. I attend to some passages in Kant, and some dimensions of his thought, that do seem to leave the door open to genuinely concurrentist accounts of the relationship between divine and human action, along the lines of 'Theological Compatibilism A', as set out in the previous chapter. I do not suggest that Kant himself went through this door, but a Kantian might, while still drawing inspiration from strands of Kant's own thought.

THE DEBATE AROUND CONCURRENTISM: GRAMMARIANS AND THEORETICIANS

When attending to the conflict that surrounds concurrentism, we might distinguish between 'grammarians' and 'theoreticians'. For 'grammarians', the lack of comprehensibility or explanatory power presented by concurrentist approaches might seem entirely appropriate, even laudable. It pertains to the uniqueness of God as creator. Our relationship to divine action *should be* dis-analogous with anything else we know of in the creation. The creator–creature relationship does not resemble the relationship between human beings, who we may think of as free to the extent that their actions are not caused by another. But then it should be true, the grammarian might claim, that the nature of the creator's activity is unique, and to that degree 'systematically inexplicable'. What matters is that we keep within the boundaries of the non-negotiable parameters of what Christian theologians must say about God and the creation: God is good, God is free, God is all-powerful, and we are created free, yet depend upon God entirely and at every moment.

Theoreticians, on the other hand, can be shocked by the willingness of grammarians to assert and name a solution, without explaining how, or much minding, if the solution itself is coherent or utterly mysterious, and without defending it against counter-arguments. Tempers can then become a little frayed when accusations of deism start flying, or where those who deny the concurrentist approach are accused of 'Titanism', and of implying that 'in the most important respects . . . one is not God's creature', as 'some of the greatest attributes of a specifically human existence' are 'exempted' from 'dependence upon God'.[2]

At the very least, grammarians should concede the point that the issue is difficult. Even the theological grammarian who considers that Kant's denial of

---

[2] Kathyrn Tanner makes this accusation in 'Human Freedom', 115; for a spirited and indignant rebuttal, see William Hasker, 'God the Creator of Good and Evil?', in Thomas F. Tracy (ed.), *The God Who Acts*.

concurrence is a problem should be generous enough to concede that if we talk about the 'problem with Kant', we also need to talk about 'the problem with the problem', to which Kant is a powerful and honest witness. It is striking in this regard that a supporter of concurrentism, Suarez himself, is able to state so powerfully the problem with concurrentism, when ventriloquizing an argument for occasionalism, the view that 'created things do nothing, but God brings about everything in their presence'.[3] The 'principal foundation' for occasionalism, Suarez explains, is that 'to whatever extent efficient causality is attributed to the creature, to that extent the divine power of the creator is diminished':

For either God does everything, or He does not do everything; the latter detracts from the divine efficacy, and for this reason we will show below that it is false and erroneous, since it implies that something exists without depending on God. But if God does everything, then I ask again whether He does it immediately and by a power that is sufficient, or only mediately and by a power that is not sufficient. The latter detracts from the divine perfection. But if the former is true, then any other efficient causation is superfluous, since one sufficient and efficacious cause is enough to produce the effect.[4]

Another supporter of concurrentism, Freddoso, acknowledges that this is a 'real challenge' to the '*via media* between occasionalism and the theory on which God contributes to natural effects only *mediately*, i.e., by creating and conserving material substances and their powers':

For if God is an *immediate* active cause of every effect brought about in the realm of pure nature, then nonfree creatures are immediate active causes of natural effects only if some such effects come immediately from *both* God and creatures. But, the argument goes, it is impossible to give a coherent and theologically orthodox account of how an effect might be brought about directly or immediately by both God and a creature—i.e., an account that does not render one of those alleged causal contributions wholly redundant.[5]

The problem of human sin also presents a challenge for thinkers who uphold concurrentist approaches. It seems that the theologian must say that here at least, in the case of sinful human actions, there is an act where God is not acting, but where the human being acts contrary to the will of God. The mere conservationist seems to have less difficulty here: God is responsible only for our existence, but does not act directly in our free actions. Where the concurrentist tradition attempts to deal with this problem, it speaks of sin as a

---

[3] Freddoso, 'Medieval Aristotelianism', 92.

[4] Suarez, *On Efficient Causality. Metaphysical Disputations 17–19*, disp. 18, p. 593. Cited and discussed by Freddoso, 'Medieval Aristotelianism', 92.

[5] Freddoso, Medieval Aristotelianism', 92–3.

lack, or a defect in the proper created order.[6] As Tanner acknowledges, this 'simply pushes the question of the origin of sin back to the question of what brought about the first defect': 'The question has to stop somewhere since, according to our premises, God does not create a world of sin. But wherever one stops, God's will would seem to be behind whatever created activity brings sin about.'[7] After exploring different strategies, Tanner concludes that the theologian 'can offer no account of how sin actually arises that does not imply that God's creative will is directly behind such an eventuality'.[8] The implication that Tanner draws from this is not that concurrentism should be abandoned, but rather that we should abandon the attempt to find an explanation for sin: 'To say that sin is an exception to the premise of God as creator is therefore to say that sin is ultimately *without* explanation; it is what, by all rights, should not exist in a world that God creates. If a good God is the ultimate explanatory principle according to our picture, is not this inexplicable character of the coming to be of sin what one should expect.'[9] In this we have an answer that resembles the recourse to systematic inexplicability discussed in Chapter 6 (pp. 131–134). Significantly, for our purposes, this response does resemble Kant's own approach to the problem of sin, which is to consider it genuinely and systematically incomprehensible. Kant does not use his denial of concurrence to help explain the origin of human sin. I will return to the significance of this point further down.

If the difficulties in understanding divine concurrence overwhelm us, and we are not content to keep the grammar without theoretical explanation, or to consider sin to be systematically inexplicable, then we face a choice: we can render either divine or creaturely action 'wholly redundant'[10] with respect to creaturely secondary causation (over and above the divine action of sustaining the existence of the creature). Which we are prepared to abandon, divine or human action, will depend upon a whole framework of priorities and aspirations. One way of understanding Kant's position is that he considers God's contribution to the action of creatures to be redundant, that is, beyond the (admittedly significant) work of creating and conserving. Most theologians who style themselves as such will be more comfortable with Freddoso's sense of priorities, when he comments that 'God's contribution is on all accounts nonredundant'.[11] If concurrentism cannot be made to 'work' though, and if we are concerned with this inability, the same theologians might be uncomfortable

---

[6] Leibniz explores a solution along these lines. See *Causa Dei,* in *Die Philosophischen Schriften,* 6: 440, and *Dialogue on Human Freedom and the Origin of Evil.* For interpretative controversies surrounding Leibniz's position, see Lee, 'Leibniz on Divine Concurrence', 207–9.
[7] Tanner, 'Human Freedom', 130.
[8] Tanner, 'Human Freedom', 133.
[9] Tanner, 'Human Freedom', p. 133.
[10] Freddoso, 'Medieval Aristotelianism', 92.
[11] Freddoso, 'Medieval Aristotelianism', 92–3.

with Freddoso's admission that this can push us to the view that 'therefore, God is the sole active cause of every effect in nature . . . How, after all, can God be thought to cooperate or concur with creatures without compromising His perfection in general or His omnipotence in particular?'[12] Freddoso observes that 'the scholastics could reach no agreement on this matter', a point that the occasionalist Malebranche 'was especially delighted to emphasize'. This can lead to a situation where a reason for 'embracing' occasionalism is 'the conviction that the only philosophically respectable alternative to it is a view according to which God is not an immediate cause of natural effects'.[13]

We have seen why orthodox medieval and early modern theists reject anything other than a full-blooded concurrence theory, and we have seen what they think is wrong with mere conservation. At the same time, we have seen the difficulties with making a full-blooded conception of concurrence credible or coherent, and we have reflected on a potential stand-off between those who place a higher value on orthodoxy, and those who primarily seek explanatory coherence. It is not clear that these are commensurate values, or that the disagreement between interlocutors can be weighed up against a neutral and commensurate set of intellectual, philosophical, and theological criteria. We reach perhaps one of those bedrocks of philosophical and theological disagreement.

Where one stands on this issue can be predicted by how Wittgensteinian one's instincts are when one is presented with a particular type of intellectual dilemma. The dilemma arises when we have a commitment that we are interested in investigating: for example, belief in the external world, other minds, ethics, aesthetics, God. We then attempt to frame a theoretical account that explains and justifies the commitment. If the theoretical account breaks down, do we abandon the commitment, or the attempt at explanation and justification? Wittgenstein prefers the latter option, presenting a suggestive (if prejudicial) analogy. He imagines a scientist creating a robotic hand in order to model the actions of a natural hand. A philosopher then notices that the robotic hand is unable to do some of the things that the natural hand can achieve. A certain sort of philosopher—for Wittgenstein, the mistaken sort— would then announce that the natural hand must be unable to do some of the things that we thought it could do, because of the failure of the model. It is possible that the chances for concurrence approaches are better than this, and a number of models and partial analogies have been explored in traditional and recent literature.[14] But, even so, the concurrence relation can never in principle have an entirely clear and intuitive analogy. When we find a clear

---

[12] Freddoso, 'Medieval Aristotelianism', 92–3.

[13] Freddoso, 'Medieval Aristotelianism', 92–3.

[14] See, for example, Freddoso, 'God's General Concurrence with Secondary Causes: Pitfalls and Prospects', 148–50.

analogy from the creaturely realm, then we necessarily fail to track the unique concurrence relation between God and the creature, which is unlike any created relation.

RECENT THEOLOGICAL RECEPTION OF KANT: AN 'AFFIRMATIVE' TREND

Understanding Kant's difficulty in relating divine and human action should be a significant factor in how theologians receive Kant. In this section I explore the more 'affirmative' trend in the recent reception of Kant in philosophy of religion and theology. This more affirmative approach is a helpful corrective to the 'standard narrative' of Kant that was dominant for much of the twentieth century, where Kant creates difficulties only for religion and theology, ruling out 'God-talk', eliminating metaphysics, eulogizing verifiable experience, and demythologizing religious language into moral categories.[15] Kant scholarship across the board has taken a more scholarly, holistic, pluralistic, and historically sensitive turn, and theological reception of Kant has benefited from this. Correctly, there is acknowledgement that Kant is a fellow traveller with at least some strands of theology, recognizably on an orthodox spectrum, albeit that these commitments, as with any theological position, could be challenged on immanent theological grounds, as well as secular ones.

Not all theologians and believers will much like rationalist theology, immersed in Platonic and intellectualist categories; nonetheless, as we have seen in Chapters 2, 3, and 7, Kant consistently adheres to such theology, with the only significant shift being the epistemic grounding available for the claims of rationalist theology. In any case, while it is unlikely that Kant's adherence to rationalist Platonizing theology will persuade anyone who dislikes such approaches to adopt them (perhaps because of concerns about divine freedom, set out in Chapter 3), it is equally the case that his adherence to this tradition does not make this style of thought any more or less fraught. In fact, those who dislike the content of rationalist theology are likely to think better of Kant's critical epistemic vehicle, as Kant moves away from theoretical certainties, and towards the category of *Glaube*, which reckons with principled and insuperable limitations to our knowledge, while placing existential and moral needs at the heart of a more textured epistemology. As we have seen in Chapters 5 and 7, Kant is concerned to limit the claims of theoretical knowledge, in order to facilitate a blossoming of other types of epistemic commitment, addressing the deep and universal needs of human reason and morality.

---

[15] For an example of this sort of reception of Kant, see Nicholas Wolterstorff, 'Is it Possible and Desirable for Theologians to Recover from Kant?'.

Kant describes his task in *Religion within the Boundaries of Mere Reason* as one of translation, from the 'outer circle' of historically revealed religion, into the 'inner circle' of that which is revealed to pure reason, governed by the needs and entitlement of practical reason alone (*Rel.* 6:12). Kant envisages, not 'two circles external to one another', but two 'concentric circles', with the '*wider* sphere of faith' including the '*narrower*' sphere of the 'pure *religion of reason*' (*Rel.* 6: 12). This can seem to give a straightforward priority, or at least a veto, to pure practical reason over historical revelation. Recently, some commentators have argued that Kant, or at least the faithful Kantian, could conceive a more complex dynamic between the two concentric circles. In the light of the insuperable limitations upon our knowledge, Firestone and McCammon have emphasiszed the irreducible role of historical examples and symbols in Kant's thought, at least for finite and limited human beings, where historical religion might be able to deliver insights ahead of our rational capacities, with insights coming from the outer circle of faith, which reason would otherwise have no access to.[16]

Affirmative interpreters of Kant's philosophy of religion suggest that the charge that Kant *reduces* religion to morality is less persuasive when one goes beyond the second *Critique*, and consider the suggestive role played by God in the third *Critique*.[17] At least, if there is an identification of God with the moral law, then the category of morality is transformed and enriched by virtue of this identification, becoming, one might say, a 'cosmic' concept, with implications for how we must conceive the very teleological structure of the universe. It is less that religion is reduced to morality, but rather that morality is '*raised* to the status of religion'.[18]

We might also explore, along with Palmquist, the extent to which Kant's conception of our capacity to choose to assent to a binding moral law is itself a capacity to participate in something that is ultimately grounded in the divine understanding.[19] This involves joining themes together more explicitly than Kant himself does, but is hardly fanciful, when we consider that Kant identifies the moral law with the law of universal reason, and that he continues in the critical period to identify the structure of all reason with the divine understanding (see pp. 144–49). Because of this identification, and because God freely commands that which is given by his nature, Kant can speak of the laws of morality as divine commands, while also insisting that, because moral laws 'are practically necessary', therefore not even the deity 'is an originator of moral laws, since they have not arisen from choice, but are practically necessary'. 'If they were

---

[16] See Firestone, *Kant and Theology at the Boundaries of Reason*, 149 ff.; Christopher McCammon 'Overcoming Deism: Hope Incarnate in Kant's Rational Religion', in Chris L. Firestone and Stephen R. Palmquist (eds), *Kant and the New Philosophy of Religion* (Bloomington and Indianapolis: Indiana University Press, 2006), 79–89.

[17] Firestone, *Kant and Theology at the Boundaries of Reason*, ch. 5.

[18] Palmquist, *Kant's Critical Religion*, 137.

[19] Palmquist, *Kant's Critical Religion*, 298–323.

not so', Kant writes, 'it might even be the case that lying was a virtue'. God is 'a lawgiver, though not an originator; just as God is no originator of the fact that a triangle has three corners' (*Coll.* 27: 283). This is just as we would expect, given Kant's continuous commitment to an intellectualist strand of rationalist theology. In terms of the distinction drawn in 1763 between moral and non-moral dependence, the law of universal reason is non-morally dependent upon the divine understanding, which grounds all possibilities. Although the divine will cannot *choose* the structure of the law of reason, it depends upon an aspect of the divine nature. The divine will can and must command the moral law, and in this sense is the law-giver, without the divine will being the 'originator' of the moral law.

In a related vein, Jacqueline Mariña defends Kant against some theological critics, by arguing that there is a deep structure of 'grace', in the sense of unmerited and universal favour to all human beings, within Kant's whole conception of our capacity to receive and follow the moral law. Mariña draws on a passage where Kant writes that '*receptivity* is all that we, on our part, can attribute to ourselves, whereas a superior's decision to grant a good for which the subordinate has no more than (moral) receptivity is called *grace*' (*Rel.* 6: 75). Mariña argues that 'there is an intrinsic connection between the universality of the moral law, grounded in the absolute worth of *all* rational creatures, and the concept of *unmerited* grace': 'Only if we think of a holy will as gracious to all rational creatures, and as therefore universal in scope, can we preserve a significant sense of the *unmerited* character of grace.'[20] In this sense, Mariña suggests, the grace is 'unmerited', as 'God's favour' does not 'rest on some hidden ground, a characteristic in virtue of which some are special and others not'. Rather in 'Kantian morality' there is a 'level playing field', which 'stipulates that *all* rational agents are of unconditioned worth and are ends in themselves': 'God assigns an absolute worth to all rational beings and does not favour some over others. This is the deep structure of the *unmerited* character of God's grace.'[21] We can grant that there is a case for all of these considerations: the integrity of Kant's rationalist philosophical theology, the role of faith, the irreducible role of historical examples, and the possibility of real insight coming from historical religion, the importance of God in conceiving of both morality and teleology, and the deep theological structure to Kant's whole conception of the moral law. Allowing that there are positive cases to be made on these fronts should be part of any balanced theological reception of Kant's legacy. Nonetheless, I submit that even when all these considerations are taken into account, we still have an incomplete assessment of Kant's legacy for Christian theologians. This book has been concerned to uncover an issue in Kant's philosophy that gets to the heart of his thought, and that in part

---

[20] Mariña, 'Kant on Grace: A Reply to his Critics', 384.
[21] Mariña, 'Kant on Grace: A Reply to his Critics', 384.

generates the epistemic shift in his critical period, and which theologians working within the orthodox pale will always struggle with: that is, how Kant conceives of the relationship between divine and creaturely action, an issue that comes to a head when attending to human freedom.

Kant's rejection of *concursus* is explicit and knowing, and is implicitly written into his thought from the 1760s onwards, when he begins to struggle to relate divine and human action. Kant's rejection of concurrence models of divine and human freedom plays an irreducible part in the emergence of transcendental idealism. This dismissal of concurrence is not only to be found in a discrete and easily separable area of Kant's philosophy of religion, in his rational theology, or in his translation of doctrines into the categories of practical reason, but is found within his metaphysical struggles from the 1760s onwards. It is 'Kant's theological problem', in that it constitutes a theological issue at the heart of his philosophy, which itself sets the framework for, rather than appearing within, the schema of the two concentric circles, the outer circle of historical faith, and the inner circle of purely rational religion. Kant's conception of the relationship between divine and human freedom is not an item of historical belief that is translated; rather, this conception sets the terms of the 'translation' process from the outer circle to the inner.

To acknowledge Kant's denial of concurrence will be important for both supporters of Kant, and those who have a more ambivalent attitude. Theologians who have misgivings about Kant might find some illumination as to why they can feel uneasy in his company; where these misgivings are already well articulated, the denial of concurrence might be added to a list, which could include Kant's neglect of core doctrines such as the Trinity and divine simplicity, or his brisk translation (into terms useful to practical reason) of the bodily resurrection (*Rel.* 6: 129; *CF* 7: 40), and the hypostatic union of God and man in Jesus (*Rel.* 6: 60–6).[22] It is perhaps more important that Kant's denial of concurrence be acknowledged and addressed by thinkers who draw heavily upon Kant to reconceive, or to defend, philosophy of religion or philosophical theology. Such thinkers might endorse Kant's conception of the relationship between divine and human action, and even argue—contra Aquinas, Suarez, Leibniz, Freddoso, and others—that it is perfectly orthodox. Even if it is not

---

[22] For a critical treatment of Kant's usefulness for orthodox Christian theology, see Yandell, 'Who is the True Kant?', *Philosophia Christi*, 9/1 (2007), 81–97. Yandell is concerned with all the doctrines listed, except that of divine simplicity, which he rejects as incompatible with the Incarnation, see 'Divine Necessity and Divine Goodness', 318. For an attempt to reintegrate the doctrine of the Trinity on Kantian grounds, see Firestone, *Kant and Theology at the Boundaries of Reason*, ch. 7. For other critical accounts of the attempt to reconcile Kant's religion with orthodox Christianity, see George di Giovanni, 'On Chris L. Firestone and Nathan Jacob's In Defense of Kant's Religion: a Comment', *Faith and Philosophy*, 26/2 (2012), 163–9, and Gordon E. Michalson, 'In Defense of Not Defending Kant's Religion', *Faith and Philosophy*, 29/2 (2012), 181–92.

'perfectly orthodox'—from within certain historical paradigms—they might claim (especially if they are theoreticians more than grammarians) that this is so much the worse for perfect orthodoxy. Philosophical theology must be *philosophically coherent*, the argument might go, and theology must be a witness to the *truth*. If concurrence is incoherent, the argument might go, it cannot be true, and philosophical theologians must push for a new paradigm of 'correct belief', of orthodoxy. Alternatively, Kantians might want to avoid Kant's position on divine and human action, while appropriating other strands of Kant's thought, such as his textured epistemology, or his claim that morality must be grounded in religious hope. I see no reason why this should be an impossible project, and I offer a possible reconstruction along these lines below; but the project will be better served if we are aware of the pitfalls and difficulties.

GRACE AND ATONEMENT

How theologians and philosophers of religion respond to Kant's denial of concurrence, and the precise textures of transcendental freedom and transcendental idealism that arise from this, will depend upon some fundamental doctrinal options. At the heart of the issue is the question of the relationship between the creator and the creature. On the one hand, the theologian might think that for human freedom to be possible, God needs to withdraw from the creature, thus enabling the creature to adopt, in a partial way, the same sort of freedom that is enjoyed by God. On the other hand, we might think that for human freedom to be possible the creature needs to move into a closer and more intimate participation with God, such that a withdrawal from God, or by God, can only lessen the freedom of the creature. In the first case, we share the same sort of freedom as God (qualitatively speaking) by virtue of God's withdrawal; in the second case, we actually participate somehow in the very same freedom that God enjoys (quantatively speaking).

Kant's denial of concurrence is part of his theological infrastructure, and it shows itself when Kant is explicitly doing positive and affirmative theological work. In particular, the difficulty becomes visible when Kant approaches doctrines that focus upon divine action in relation to human freedom: grace and atonement. It is important to note that the problem becomes more *visible* here, but does not *only* arise in relation to divine action that is described as 'grace'. Divine action is considered to be 'grace' when God transforms the creature, taking the creature beyond his or her 'natural' capacities and ends, to a life with God that goes beyond the natural, without destroying nature. Concurrence, as we have seen, is intended as an account of ordinary and ubiquitous divine action in the world, and not only of those divine actions that are described as instances of 'grace'. The point is that problems across the board in relating divine and human action reach a particular intensity and visibility, when we need to give an account of divine action upon the creature that goes beyond the 'natural'.

First of all, I look at the concept of grace in Kant's work, which will lead us into the doctrine of the atonement. A problem arises when we consider whether divine assistance could actually bring about the revolution in the human will that constitutes our choosing the moral law over heteronomous self-love, given the importance that Kant attaches to it being by our own freedom that we choose the moral law. There is a highly critical literature on Kant, which argues for the root and branch incoherence of Kant's account of extra-human assistance to human moral endeavour.[23] I turn here to a more sympathetic defence of Kant's position, presented by Mariña. In this way, I show that the theological problem remains in place, even when Kant is given a charitable hearing. Mariña distinguishes two ways in which Kant talks about grace: one more problematic than the other, both for Kant and his interpreters. First of all, I discuss the supposedly unproblematic conception of grace.

Grace in the less problematic sense involves a kind of 'divine aid which must be *laid hold* of by the person'.[24] This conception does not generate fundamental difficulties in relation to our human freedom and our responsibility to turn to the moral law, because it 'does not alter a person's will at the outset', but is rather

some historical occurrence—a person or situation—to which the person must *respond* in some way. Only after the practical and existential import of the person or situation has been assessed and interiorized by the individual can it affect a person's character.[25]

Such an act of grace comes after the 'free choice of the individual', and indeed must do so if 'the concept of grace is not to be one that ignores the agent *qua* agent'.[26] The individual begins the 'journey towards holiness' by him or herself, rather than by supernatural assistance. Extra assistance comes into play when dealing with the 'residual consequences of the propensity to evil' that 'will still haunt the person', where 'growth in virtue will only be achieved through an incessant counteracting of these effects'.[27] As Kant puts it, the

---

[23] See, for example, Michalson, Jr, *Fallen Freedom*; and Nicholas Wolterstorff, 'Conundrums in Kant's Rational Religion', in Philip J. Rossi and Michael Wreen (eds), *Kant's Philosophy of Religion Reconsidered* (Bloomington and Indianapolis: Indiana University Press, 1991), 40–53.

[24] Mariña, 'Kant on Grace: A Reply to his Critics', 386. Desmond Hogan provides a more critical discussion of the relationship between grace and *concursus*, finding grounds to support the 'traditional verdict' that Kant's mature theory of grace is Pelagian', in 'Kant's Theory of Divine and Secondary Causation', pp. 32–4, manuscript (p. 33).

[25] Mariña, 'Kant on Grace: A Reply to his Critics', 386.

[26] Mariña, 'Kant on Grace: A Reply to his Critics', 388.

[27] Mariña, 'Kant on Grace: A Reply to his Critics', 388.

individual must 'make himself antecedently worthy of receiving' the grace as assistance (*Rel.* 6:44); the moral agent must freely '*accept* this help', which might consist in the 'diminution of obstacles' or 'positive assistance' (*Rel.* 6:44). Such assistance serves to 'supplement the deficiency' of our 'moral capacity', where we regard the two causes (the divine and human) as 'together effective causes of a disposition sufficient to a conduct of a life well-pleasing to God' (*Rel.* 6: 173–4). The task of *Religion* is to see what use practical reason can make of Christian doctrines; and this is the use that practical reason can make of the notion of grace, as supernatural assistance. All the same, Kant is careful to insist that we avoid any attempt to 'distinguish the effects of grace from those of nature (virtue)' (*Rel.* 6: 174). This would constitute '*enthusiasm*', as 'nowhere in experience can we recognize a supersensible object':

To want to *perceive* heavenly influences is a kind of madness in which, no doubt, there can also be method (since those alleged inner revelations must always attach themselves to moral, and hence rational, ideas), but which nonetheless always remains a self-deception detrimental to religion. To believe that grace may have its effects, and that perhaps there must be such effects to supplement the imperfection of our striving for virtue, is all that we can say on the subject; for the rest we are not capable of determining anything concerning their distinguishing marks and even less of doing something toward their production. (*Rel.* 6: 174)

The model of divine action that we have here is similar to the conjunction of parallel divine–human action discussed in Chapter 9 (pp. 214–218), which is not what is meant by a traditional notion of concurrence. Nonetheless, the notion need not be theologically 'inadmissible' or incoherent on some interpretations. As Tanner explains, within a concurrentist framework, we can conceive of 'special interventions, supplementation, and composite acts', as long as God is still directly the cause of both the ordinary insufficient cause, and the supplementing and sufficient cause:

If created causes are insufficient to produce created effects, the theologian may use synergistic language: divine agency may be said to remedy by addition or intervention the deficiencies of created causes. If created causes are allegedly inoperative, either in general or in particular cases, the theologian may say that a creature acts by the infusion of a divine power—the creature acts not by its own power but by the power of god. Divine operations take the place of created ones. In all these cases talk of the created order suggests a composition of the divine and the non-divine.[28]

The concurrentist can permit such statements as long as they 'avoid implying a distinction within the created order between what is and is not the direct

---

[28] Tanner, *God and Creation in Christian Theology*, 100.

effect of divine agency', as God is 'directly behind both the created effect and the created beings that are without sufficient power to produce the effect'.[29]

Nonetheless, for the traditional theologian, there is, and there needs to be, more to the concept of divine grace than the divine assistance that is operative after human freedom has made the 'right move'. 'Grace' involves a divine action that brings about the fundamental transformation in the human creature, bringing about the very revolution in the will that makes the creature worthy of assistance. There is some evidence in Kant's own texts that he seems to need just such a conception of grace, when he writes that the propensity to evil in humanity is radical, such that it cannot be overcome by human endeavour, 'since extirpation could occur only through good maxims, and cannot take place when the ultimate subjective ground of all maxims is postulated as corrupt' (*Rel.* 6: 53).

Kant explains that the conception of grace that would make possible this fundamental turning of the human will is not one that theoretical or practical reason can make use of:

For it is impossible to make these effects *theoretically* cognizable (that they are effects of grace and not of immanent nature), because our use of the concept of cause and effect cannot be extended beyond the objects of experience, and hence beyond nature; moreover, the presupposition of a *practical* employment of this idea is wholly self-contradictory. For the employment would presuppose a rule concerning what good we ourselves must *do* (with a particular aim [in mind]) in order to achieve something; to expect an effect of grace means, however, the very contrary, namely that the good (the morally good) is not of our doing, but that of another being—that we, therefore, can only *come by* it by *doing nothing*, and this contradicts itself. Hence we can admit an effect of grace as something incomprehensible but cannot incorporate it into our maxims for either theoretical or practical use. (*Rel.* 6: 53)

Mariña observes correctly that the notion of 'God's supernatural cooperation in our becoming better persons' is not for Kant something that we *know* to be 'impossible'; rather 'its possibility remains inscrutable' such that, 'even if it were posited, on a practical level we wouldn't be able to make use of such a supposition'.[30] Kant concedes that although the possibility of the 'supernatural [something] we might want to assume as surrogate for the independent yet deficient determination of freedom' is 'incomprehensible to us', so too is the concept of 'freedom itself, though not containing anything supernatural in its concept' (*Rel.* 6: 191). In the *Lectures on the Philosophical Doctrine of Religion*, Kant makes a similar point, when he asks: 'But how does it stand with free actions? Can a *concursus divinus* be affirmed of them?' (*LPR* 28:

---

[29] Tanner, *God and Creation in Christian Theology*, 101.
[30] Mariña, 'Kant on Grace: A Reply to his Critics', 385–6.

1106). Kant comments that it is 'not in the least conceivable how God might concur in our actions despite our freedom, or how he could concur as a cooperating cause of our will', as in that case 'we would not be the author of our own actions, or at least not wholly so' (*LPR* 28: 1106). At the same time, Kant comments that our very idea of freedom itself is 'one which belongs to the intelligible world', such that 'we are acquainted with nothing of it beyond the fact that it exists', without knowing the 'laws by which it is governed' (*LPR* 28: 1106). Consequently, 'our reason cannot deny the possibility of this *concursus*' (*LPR* 28: 1106).

The way in which Kant describes what *concursus* amounts to here is not easily dismissed by the traditional concurrentist. Further down, Kant states the following:

> But as regards a *concursum moralem* of God's free cooperation in the free actions of human beings, such a thing cannot be comprehended in the nature of freedom, but at the same time it cannot be regarded as impossible. For if it is presupposed that every rational being could from itself act even against the plan of God, hence entirely free and independently of the whole mechanism of nature, then it is indeed possible that God, in order to make rational creatures use their freedom in a manner agreeable to his highest will, could cooperate as a *concausa*. (*LPR* 28: 1110)

Although only talking about divine concurrence with free actions, and not with natural occurrences, Kant seems to envisage here something more like a single action: God as a 'cooperating cause of our own will'. It is at least not obvious that this is either a case of a conjunction of two actions: our own, and God's supplementing action. We should concede here, I think, that what Kant means by 'concurrence' is something that a traditional defender of the notion could recognize. Significantly, it is *this* notion of concurrence with respect to freedom that Kant claims 'cannot be comprehended', and for which we have no rational use.

The precise nuance of Kant's denial of the possibility of genuine concurrence is as follows: neither theoretical *nor* practical reason can make any use of a genuinely concurring divine action with our free actions. Therefore, we can make no use of such a concept, even if theoretical reason cannot know that it is impossible. This strand of apophaticism with respect to concurring grace is interesting, and I will return to it in the concluding section. Nonetheless, a concept that neither theoretical nor practical reason can make any use of is not, in the end, in Kant's own terms, a very useful or important concept, and this is the case with concurring divine grace and human action.

Even within more immanent interpretative terms, Kant's own inability to make use of a more robust account of divine action with respect to grace and atonement has led even sympathetic commentators to conclude that Kant's project of translating revealed doctrines into the categories of pure rationalism fails on this point. So, for example, John Hare writes that 'given the premiss about natural (though imputable depravity)', Kant needs 'the possibility of extra-human assistance' prior to the free act of the will, as 'in our original condition before the revolution we do not have a good will'. Problematically, Kant's '*own* final translation of these doctrines does not allow them to play this role', as 'his own account within the pure religion of reason assumes that we can by our own devices reach an upright disposition'.[31] At most, it seems divine assistance can be a supplementary action, along the lines of Mariña's first conception of grace, which is initiated only after we have by our own 'earnest endeavour' become 'worthy of heavenly assistance' (*Rel.* 6: 192).

Kant's problems around the concept of grace and divine action manifest themselves when Kant discusses the notion of vicarious atonement.[32] In Part Two of *Religion* Kant reflects that even where, through our free action, we have acquired a 'good disposition', there is a debt of guilt left over, given that we '*nevertheless started from evil*' (*Rel.* 6: 72). We have in the past acted culpably from heteronomous principles; as it was the past, there is nothing we can do now or in the future that will alter this having happened. It is not enough that from a point in time our disposition has been entirely good, as we 'cannot regard the fact that, after his change of heart, he has not incurred new debts as equivalent to his having paid off the old ones' (*Rel* 6:72). There is a surplus to our previous debts that cannot be paid off by present or future actions.

The theological answer that usually emerges into view, when the issue is put in this forensic way, is vicarious atonement: if we cannot pay the debt, because of its enormity, then someone else will need to pay it vicariously. Although we are unable to pay the debt, Jesus as the innocent Son of God is able to make that payment for us, in such a way that God will reckon us as righteous. Such an approach to atonement relies on some notion of representative participation: that somehow I am represented by, and participate in, the sin of Adam (the 'old man'), and that I can be redeemed by being represented by, and participating in, the atoning punishment received by Christ (the 'new man'). When Jesus is crucified, the sinful 'old man' in whose guilt we now participate, is put to death, such that a new man becomes possible.[33]

Kant has a version of this vicarious atonement that enables God to reckon us as righteous, in spite of our unpayable debt. When, in our unconditioned

---

[31] Hare, *The Moral Gap*, 65.

[32] For Wood's treatment of this material, see *Kant's Moral Religion*, ch. 5. Wood does not draw attention to the replacement of the sacrificial figure of Christ with the noumenal self.

[33] Such penal accounts of vicarious atonement, associated standardly with Anselm and Luther, have long been controversial among theologians. For critical accounts and alternatives, see Paul Fiddes, *Past Event and Present Salvation: The Christian Idea of Atonement* (London: Dartman, Longman and Todd, 1989), and Timothy Gorringe, *God's Just Vengeance: Crime, Violence and the Rhetoric of Salvation* (Cambridge: Cambridge University Press, 1996).

freedom, we choose the 'good principle', then something akin to the crucifixion of Christ takes place:

The good principle is present, therefore, just as much in the abandonment of the evil as in the adoption of the good disposition, and the pain that by rights accompanies the first derives entirely from the second. The emergence from the corrupted disposition into the good is in itself already sacrifice (as 'the death of the old man', 'the crucifying of the flesh') and entrance into the long train of life's wills which the new human being undertakes in the disposition of the Son of God, that is, simply for the sake of the good, yet are still fitting *punishment* for someone else, namely the old human being (who, morally, is another human being). (*Rel.* 6: 74)

The death of Christ is now an 'example' of what happens in each noumenal self when it turns away from heteronomy. It is no longer the death of Christ that brings vicarious atonement. Rather the noumenal self takes on the role of Christ, dying to the old self, and making the vicarious atonement. In 'his new disposition (as an intelligible being)' Kant tells us that 'in the sight of a divine judge . . . he is *morally* another being' (*Rel.* 6: 74). The traditional depiction of Christ's atoning sacrifice, for Kant, is a 'way of imagining . . . as a death suffered once and for all' the 'suffering which the new human being must endure while dying to the *old* human being' (*Rel.* 6: 74).

We have a case of human action doing the atoning work, rather than divine action. It is our intelligible selves who do the atoning work, which is exemplified symbolically in traditional theological language about Jesus. Kant puts this explicitly:

This [good] disposition which he [the intelligible self] has incorporated in all its purity, like unto the purity of the Son of God—or (if we personify this idea) this very *Son of God*—bears as *vicarious substitute* the debt of sin for him, and also for all who believe (practically) in him. (*Rel.* 6: 74)

The intelligible self becomes both the '*saviour*' satisfying 'the highest justice through suffering and death', and the '*advocate*' making it possible 'for them to hope that they will appear justified before their judge' (*Rel.* 6: 74). The 'ideal of the Son of God' is conceived in exemplary terms, as a 'model' of a human being who freely follows the moral law (*Rel.* 6: 66), a 'divinely disposed teacher . . . in fact totally human' presented to us '*as an example to be emulated*' (*Rel.* 6: 66). The sense in which Jesus can be called the Son of God is not qualitatively different from the sense in which each intelligible being can display 'incarnate in him' the 'ideal of goodness' (*Rel.* 6: 64–65). Our own human action is the key. Through a noumenal free action our intelligible selves acquire a good disposition, by dying to evil (heteronomous) principles; this death has the quality of a sacrifice. Once again, the grace we are required to have faith in is more like divine assistance, in the form of the removal of obstacles, which then enables our own intelligible free action. Traditional Christian accounts would have more to say about divine action on our behalf, or concurring divine action upon us. It might be, as has been argued by Nathan Jacobs, that within practical reason there is an essential role for the symbolic narrative of Christ as the prototype of 'humanity . . . in its moral perfection'; but this is a thesis about the indispensability of symbols, not about the need for divine action.[34]

In summary, we can see that a recurring problem for interpreters of *Religion* is that the conceptual space permitted for divine action is restricted at best, and incoherent at worst. This is particularly the case in areas such as grace and atonement, where one would expect to hear a lot about divine action. This is not a quirk of Kant's translation of the historical doctrines of Christianity into the categories of practical reason, but arises as a visible theological flashpoint for a problem that is shot through his metaphysics: how to say that we are created free, given that we are created by God?

THE FINAL TWIST: KANT AS CONCURRENTIST

Both in his explicit statements, and in implicit commitments, Kant denies concurrentist accounts of the relationship between divine and creaturely action. God creates and conserves noumenal substances, but the phenomena that arise from the interaction of noumenal substances are not creations, and are not directly caused by God. This is, for Kant, an aspect of transcendental idealism, which makes possible human transcendental freedom, and protects the divine nature from inappropriate spatialization and temporalization.

There is a clean and clear way of addressing what Kant's legacy might be for Christian theology, given his denial of concurrence. We could say that on this front, for theologians and philosophers of religion who endorse concurrentism, Kant is mistaken, and his influence pernicious, inasmuch as the mistake does work in his wider philosophy. Theologians and philosophers of religion who endorse mere conservationism, on the other hand, can find more in common with Kant on this point. There is perhaps a curious irony that some of Kant's more 'constructivist' sounding pronouncements ('space is not a thing as a divine work'), which are often objected to by analytical philosophers of religion, in fact arise from a commitment that many of the same analytical philosophers of religion would share with Kant, that is, a denial of concurrentism between divine and human action.

---

[34] Nathan Jacobs, 'Kant's Prototypical Theology: Transcendental Incarnation as a Rational Foundation for God-Talk', in Chris L. Firestone and Stephen R. Palmquist (eds), *Kant and the New Philosophy of Religion* (Bloomington and Indianapolis: Indiana University Press, 2006), 124–40 (p. 132).

There is also, though, a more nuanced approach to the question, which involves asking how much of what matters to the critical Kant could in fact be preserved within a concurrentist framework, if we were to engage in an explicit and self-conscious reconstruction. Such a project might be of interest to a theologian or philosopher of religion who wanted to draw upon Kant's insights, while avoiding mere conservationism. A case can be made that quite a lot of Kant's commitments could be preserved, and some of them positively assisted.

Kant could adopt a concurrentist approach to divine and human inter-action, while preserving transcendental freedom, with respect to our first causation in relation to other created substances. We saw in Chapter 8 that Schleiermacher arguably explores this line of thought. Kant already shows himself to be aware of a qualitative difference between dependence upon God for our existence, and dependence upon other creatures. In the *Reflexion* where Kant claims that space is 'not a thing as a divine work' (*R* 6057, 18: 439–40). Kant also writes that 'God has not given human beings independ-ence from himself, but from the incentives of sensibility'. Kant could also continue to insist that space and time are forms of our intuition, rather than being in things in themselves. In this way, transcendental idealism could remain an important consideration in his protection of our transcen-dental freedom with respect to other created spatio-temporal phenomenal substances, and also with respect to ensuring that space and time are not conceived of as infinite things-in-themselves that threaten the impassibility of the divine nature. All that would be required is that space and time are forms of intuition, but that God is the direct creator and cause of their being our forms of intuition.

There are other aspects of Kant's moral philosophy that resonate positively with the adoption of concurrentism. These are the intellectualist theological strands that go right back to his earliest writings, explored in Chapters 2 and 3. Given his philosophical theology, Kant has resources, which some other theological systems and intuitions do not provide, for explaining how we can be free in relation to God, even where we are not able to do other than we do, and even where we are not ultimately responsible for our actions. This is because freedom, for Kant, in its paradigmatic divine form, does not involve an ability to do otherwise: it involves, rather, a capacity to do the good, and to express and conform to the divine nature. Where there is such an understand-ing of freedom at work, it need not violate fundamental intuitions to explain that with respect to the uncreated good that is God, to be drawn into participation with God, where God acts in our actions, can only enlarge and fulfil our freedom.

A number of commentators have argued that Kant's critical conception of 'autonomy' should be interpreted as our capacity to follow an objective moral law on the grounds of its rationality, rather than because of heteronomous impulses, or the command of a 'superior'.[35] We might sum this up by saying that the force of autonomy ('giving oneself the law') is 'it is the law, grounded upon rationality, and we give it to ourselves, because it is the law', rather than 'we construct the law for ourselves, and it is the law because of our constructive activity'. Although I do not show it here, I am convinced that these realist and anti-constructivist interpretations of autonomy are correct accounts of what Kant intends. If this is right, then concurrence would be deeply compatible with autonomy. Where concurrence is properly understood and assented to, God would be conceived of as an autonomous rather than a heteronomous influence on the creature, part of the creature's own movement, rather than 'vying' with the creature. When I act to give the law to myself, because it is the law, grounded upon rationality, then God also acts in my action of giving myself the law. We hit deeper theological harmonics if we go on to join together aspects of Kant's thought more explicitly than he does himself, along the lines I have set out (see pp. 230–231). If we consider that the law is grounded by rationality, which is itself grounded by, and constitutive of, the divine understanding, then my action of giving myself the law, in which God acts, becomes also a form of participation in the divine nature. God would act in the action by which I move closer to the divine nature.

We saw in the first section of this chapter that one of the obstacles to a concurrentist account of divine and human action is the need to 'explain' evil actions, where human beings turn away from the good. Among those philosophers and theologians who reject concurrentism, the problem of theodicy features prominently. Significantly, this is not a consideration that motivates Kant in any way. As we saw in Chapter 6 (pp. 127–134), Kant is convinced that our turning away from the good is fundamentally inexplicable: our ability to do otherwise does not explain this turning-away, but is in fact a consequence of it. Losing any putative explanatory power that comes from denying concurrentism, when accounting for the origin of evil, would not be a problem for Kant, as he makes no recourse to such patterns of explanation. In fact, Kant's line on the systematic and fundamental inexplicability of evil puts him, by contingent association at least, in the company of theologians and philosophers who endorse concurrentism. As we saw in the first section of the chapter, theologians and philosophers of religion who endorse concurrentism often know that they do not have an explanation of evil, whilst considering this a rational inevitability, given the nature of evil itself.

---

[35] See, for example, Stern, *Understanding Moral Obligation*, ch. 1; Terence Irwin, 'Continuity in the History of Autonomy', *Inquiry: An Interdisciplinary Journal of Philosophy*, 54/5 (2011), 442–59, and *The Development of Ethics, Volume III: From Kant to Rawls*, 147–72; Allen W. Wood, *Kant's Ethical Thought*, and *Kantian Ethics*, 66–122; and Patrick Kain, 'Self-Legislation in Kant's Moral Philosophy', *Archiv für Geschichte der Philosophie*, 86 (2004), 257–306.

At this point, we might reflect more on the 'inconceivability' of a traditional conception of concurrence. We have seen that there are passages where Kant does discuss the traditional conception of concurrence, and refuses to state that we know it to be impossible (*Rel.* 6: 192; *LPR* 28: 1106–11). When Kant comments that it is 'not in the least conceivable how God might concur in our actions despite our freedom', this could be read straightforwardly as expressing a theoretician's distaste for the grammarian's insistence on *concursus*, which amounts to a dismissal. We need to weigh in the balance here that 'incomprehensible' propositions can play an important and positive role in Kant's thought. As we have seen, Kant reflects that there is something 'incomprehensible' in the concept of freedom itself: the idea of freedom is one that belongs to the intelligible world, and we are 'acquainted with nothing of it beyond the fact that it exists', without knowing the 'laws by which it is governed' (*LPR* 28: 1106). This opens a door for a Kantian theologian, although not a door that Kant himself actually went through.

There are structural features of Kant's defence of the notion of noumenal first causation that could apply similarly to a Kantian defence of *concursus*. We recall that the defence of the commitment to noumenal first causation involved first of all the admission that it was not demonstrably impossible. Kant says in the passage above that 'our reason cannot deny the possibility of this *concursus*'; in fact to do so would be to go beyond the proper limits of reason. The defence of noumenal first causation involved a commitment to making morality work; we might call this the 'grammatical' bedrock of this part of Kant's philosophy. That we are committed to assenting to the only grounds that will make morality work is a non-negotiable starting point for a further argument, rather than being the result of an argument. For Kant, we can have an argument about whether a commitment to noumenal first causation is the only way to make morality work; but if we agree that such a commitment provides the only grounds that genuinely make morality work, and if noumenal first causation is not theoretically impossible, then we must subscribe to this commitment. If the Kantian theologian makes it a grammatical point that God and the creature *must* cooperate in their actions if moral theology is to be possible, then we might be able to run a structurally similar argument: if divine concurrence with human actions, in a full and traditional sense, is the only grounds upon which moral theology can really work, then we must ascribe to this commitment. In another passage, Kant pushes this door slightly further open:

For to be a creature and, as a natural being, merely the result of the will of the creator; yet to be capable of responsibility as a freely acting being (one which has a will independent of external influence and possibly opposed to the latter in a variety of ways) but again, to consider one's own deed at the same time also as an effect of a higher being—this is a combination of concepts which we must indeed think together in the idea of a world and of a highest good, but which can be intuited only by one who penetrates to the cognition of the supersensible (intelligible) world and sees the manner in which this grounds the sensible world. (*MPT* 263–64)

Here we move even closer, albeit only suggestively, towards a more traditional notion of concurrence, as we consider our 'own deed at the same time also as an effect of a higher being', without any indication that we have here a conjunction of two deeds, our own and then a supplementing divine action. As with noumenal first causation, we have a mixture of epistemic discipline, verging on the apophatic, which at the same time makes possible a firm assent to propositions on non-theoretical moral grounds. Here at least there is the suggestion even that 'we must indeed think together' the action of the creator and the creature, albeit knowing that we can never know or explain such a cooperation. In another passage from *Religion* we find a similar thought:

It is, however, totally incomprehensible to our reason how beings can be *created* to use their powers freely, for according to the principle of causality we cannot attribute any other inner ground of action to a being, which we assume to have been produced, except that which the producing cause has placed in it. And, since through this ground (hence through an external cause) the being's every action is determined as well, the being itself cannot be free. So through our rational insight we cannot reconcile the divine and holy legislation, which only applies to free beings, with the concept of the creation of these beings, but must simply presuppose the latter as already existing free beings who are determined to citizenship in the divine state, not in virtue of their creation, but because of a purely moral necessitation, only possible according to the laws of freedom, i.e. through a call. So the call to this end is morally quite clear; for speculation, however, the possibility of beings who are thus called is an impenetrable mystery. (*Rel.* 6: 142–3)

Here Kant does not seem to follow a mere conservationist line, when he writes that God as the 'producing cause' must be the 'inner ground of action' of a being. Kant is unable to find a way to reconcile this with the claim that we are free, as he worries that 'through this ground' the 'being's every action is determined as well'. Kant's unrelenting honesty about the limits of knowledge, alongside his attention to the deep needs of human reason that go beyond these limitations, where such needs of reason permit or even require assent to 'impenetrable mysteries', might be the key for Kantian theologians who want to affirm with Aquinas that

God does act sufficiently within things as the first agent cause and that does not imply that the activity of secondary causes is superfluous. The one action does not issue from two agents of the same level; there is, however, nothing against one and the same action's issuing from a primary and secondary agent. God does not merely impart forms to things, but upholds them in existence, applies them to their actions and is the end of all actions.[36]

---

[36] Aquinas, *Summa Theologiae*, 1a.105.5.

Bibliography

Abegg, Johann Friedrich, *Reisetagebuch von 1798* (Frankfurt: Insel Verlag, 1976).

Adams, Robert, 'Things in Themselves', *Philosophy and Phenomenological Research*, 57/4 (1997), 801–25.

Adams, Robert, 'God, Possibility and Kant', *Faith and Philosophy*, 17/4 (2000), 425–40.

Adickes, Erich, *Kant und das Ding an sich* (Berlin: Pan Verlag, 1924).

Allison, Henry, 'Kant's Critique of Spinoza', in Richard Kennington (ed.), *The Philosophy of Baruch Spinoza* (Washington: Catholic University of America Press, 1980).

Allison, Henry, *Kant's Transcendental Idealism: An Interpretation and Defense* (New Haven, CT: Yale University Press, 1983).

Allison, Henry, *Kant's Theory of Freedom* (Cambridge: Cambridge University Press, 1995).

Allison, Henry, 'Kant's Transcendental Idealism', in Graham Bird (ed.), *A Companion to Kant* (Oxford: Wiley-Blackwell, 2010), 111–24.

Ameriks, Karl, *Kant and the Fate of Autonomy* (Cambridge: Cambridge University Press, 2000).

Ameriks, Karl, *Kant's Theory of Mind: An Analysis of the Paralogisms of Pure Reason* (Oxford: Oxford University Press, 2000).

Ameriks, Karl, *Interpreting Kant's Critiques* (Oxford: Oxford University Press, 2003).

Ameriks, Karl, 'The Critique of Metaphysics: Kant and Traditional Ontology', in Ameriks, *Interpreting Kant's Critiques* (Oxford: Oxford University Press, 2003), 112–34.

Anderson, Pamela Sue, 'The Philosophical Significance of Kant's Religion: "Pure Cognition" or "Belief" in God', *Faith and Philosophy*, 29/2 (2012), 151–62.

Anderson, Pamela Sue, and Bell, Jordan, *Kant and Theology* (London and New York: T&T Clark International, 2010).

Anselm, *De libertate arbitrii*, in *S. Anselmi Cantuariensis Archiepiscopi Opera Monia*, ed. F. S. Schmitt (Stuttgart-Bad Canstatt: Friedrich Fromann Verlag, 1968).

Aquinas, Thomas, *De Potentia*, in *Quaestiones Disputatae*, vol. 2 (Taurini: Marietti, 1965), 6.2.3.

Aquinas, Thomas, *Summa Contra Gentiles*, ed. and trans. Vernon J. Bourke (Notre Dame, IN: University of Notre Dame Press, 1975).

Aquinas, Thomas, *Summa Theologiae*, Blackfriars Edition, ed. Thomas Gilby OP et al., 60 vols (Cambridge: Cambridge University Press, 2006).

Aquinas, Thomas, *De Veritate*, trans. T. C. O'Brien, in Thomas Aquinas, *Summa Theologiae*, Blackfriars Edition, ed. Thomas Gilby OP et al., 60 vols (Cambridge: Cambridge University Press, 2006), vol. 31, appendix 4, 205–15.

Audi, Robert, 'Belief, Faith and Acceptance', *International Journal for Philosophy of Religion*, 63/1 (2008), 87–102.

Augustine, *De Libero Arbitrio. On Free Choice of the Will*, trans. Thomas Williams (Cambridge and Indianapolis: Hackett Publishing Company, 1993).

Barclay, John, 'By the Grace of God I Am What I Am: Grace and Agency in Philo and Paul', in John M. G. Barclay and Simon J. Gathercole (eds), *Divine and Human Agency in Paul and his Cultural Environment* (London and New York: T&T Clark, 2007), 140–57.

Basile, Pierfrancesco, 'Kant, Spinoza and the Metaphysics of the Ontological Proof', *Metaphysica: International Journal for Ontology and Metaphysics*, 11/1 (2010), 17–37.

Baumgarten, Alexander, *Metaphysica*, 4th edn (Halle: Carl Hermann Hemmerde, 1757).

Beck, Lewis White, *A Commentary on Kant's Critique of Practical Reason* (Chicago: University of Chicago Press, 1960).

Beck, Lewis White, *Early German Philosophy: Kant and his Predecessors* (Cambridge, MA: Harvard University Press, 1969).

Beck, J. S., *Erläutender Auszug aus den kritischen Schriften des Herrn Prof. Kant, auf Anrathen desselben* (Riga, 1795).

Beiser, Frederick, 'Moral Faith and the Highest Good', in *The Cambridge Companion to Kant and Modern Philosophy*, ed. Paul Guyer (Cambridge: Cambridge University Press, 2006), 588–639.

Bennett, Jonathan, *Kant's Analytic* (Cambridge: Cambridge University Press, 1966).

Bennett, Jonathan, *Kant's Dialectic* (Cambridge: Cambridge University Press, 1974).

Bergman, Michael, and Cover, J. A., 'Divine Responsibility without Freedom', *Faith and Philosophy*, 23/4 (2006), 381–408.

Burrell, David, *Freedom and Creation in Three Traditions* (Notre Dame, IN: University of Notre Dame Press, 1993).

Burrell, David, 'Divine Action and Human Freedom in the Context of Creation', in *The God Who Acts: Philosophical and Theological Explorations* (University Park, PA: Pennsylvania University Press, 1994), 103–9.

Byrd, Jeremy, 'Kant's Compatibilism in the New Elucidation of the First Principles of Metaphysical Cognition', *Kant-Studien*, 99/1 (2008), 68–79.

Byrne, Peter, *Kant on God* (Aldershot: Ashgate Publishing, 2007).

Cassirer, Ernst, *Rousseau–Kant–Goethe: Two Essays* (Princeton: Princeton University Press, 1947).

Chignell, Andrew, 'Belief in Kant', *Philosophical Review*, 116/3 (2007), 323–60.

Chignell, Andrew, 'Kant's Concepts of Justification', *Noûs*, 41/1 (2007), 33–63.

Chignell, Andrew, 'Kant, Modality, and the Most Real Being', *Archiv für Geschichte der Philosophie*, 91/2 (2009), 157–92.

Chignell, Andrew, 'Real Repugnance and Belief about Things-in-Themselves: A Problem and Kant's Three Solutions', in Benjamin Lipscomb and James Krueger (eds), *Kant's Moral Metaphysics: God, Freedom and Immortality* (Berlin and New York: de Gruyter, 2010), 177–209.

Chignell, Andrew, 'Real Repugnance and our Ignorance of Things-in-Themselves: A Lockean Problem in Kant and Hegel', in F. Rush, K. Ameriks, and J. Stolzenberg (eds), *Internationales Jahrbuch des Deutschen Idealismus 7* (Berlin: Walter de Gruyter, 2010).

Chignell, Andrew, 'Introduction: On Defending Kant at the AAR', *Faith and Philosophy*, 26/2 (2012), 144–50.

Chignell, Andrew, 'Kant, Real Possibility and the Threat of Spinoza', *Mind* (forthcoming).

Cohen, Hermann, *Kant's Theorie der Erfahrung* (2nd edn; Berlin: Dümmler, 1885).

Cohen, Jonathan, 'Belief and Acceptance', *Mind*, 98/391 (1989), 367–89.

Crusius, Christian August, *Entwurf der notwendigen Vernunfwahrheiten* (1745), in *Die philosophischen Hauptschriften*, ed. G. Tonelli (Hildesheim: Olms Verlag, 1964–).

Crusius, Christian August, *Anweisung, Vernünftig zu Leben* (Leipzig: J. F. Gleditsch, 1767).

Dalbosco, C. A., *Ding an sich und Erscheinung: Perspektiven des transzendentalen Idealismum bei Kant* (Würzberg: Königshausen und Neumann, 2002).

Davidovich, Adina, *Religion as a Province of Meaning* (Minneapolis: Fortress Press,1993).

Durandus, William, *In Sententias Theologicas Petri Lombardi Commentariorum Libri Quattuor* (Venice, 1571; reprinted at Ridgewood, NJ: Gregg Press, 1964).

Falkenstein, Lorne, *Kant's Intuitionism: A Commentary on the Transcendental Aesthetic* (Toronto: University of Toronto Press, 2004).

Ficara, Elena, *Die Ontologie in der 'Kritik der reinen Vernunft'* (Würzberg: Königshausen und Newmann, 2006).

Fichte, J. G., *Erst Einleitung in die Wissenschaftslehre* (1797), in *Fichtes Werke*, ed. I. H. Fichte, Band 1 (Berlin: Bruno Cassirer, 1906).

Fiddes, Paul, *Past Event and Present Salvation: The Christian Idea of Atonement* (London: Dartman, Longman and Todd, 1989).

Firestone, Chris L., *Kant and Theology at the Boundaries of Reason* (Aldershot: Ashgate Publishing, 2009).

Firestone, Chris L., and Jacobs, Nathan, *In Defense of Kant's Religion* (Bloomington, IN: Indiana University Press, 2008).

Firestone, Chris L., and Palmquist, Stephen R. (eds), *Kant and the New Philosophy of Religion* (Bloomington and Indianapolis: Indiana University Press, 2006).

Fisher, Mark, and Watkins, Eric, 'Kant on the Material Ground of Possibility: From "The Only Possible Argument" to the "Critique of Pure Reason"', *Review of Metaphysics*, 52/2 (1998), 369–95.

Flikshuh, Katrin, *Kant and Modern Political Philosophy* (Cambridge: Cambridge University Press, 2000).

Flint, Thomas, 'Two Accounts of Providence', in Thomas V. Morris (ed.), *Divine and Human Action: Essays in the Metaphysics of Theism* (Ithaca, NY, and London: Cornell University Press, 1988), 147–81.

Förster, Eckart, *Kant's Final Synthesis: An Essay on the Opus Postumum* (Cambridge, MA, and London: Harvard University Press, 2000).

Freddoso, Alfred J., 'Medieval Aristotelianism and the Case against Secondary Causation in Nature', in Thomas V. Morris (ed.), *Divine and Human Action: Essays in the Metaphysics of Theism* (Ithaca, NY, and London: Cornell University Press, 1988), 74–118.

Freddoso, Alfred J., 'God's General Concurrence with Secondary Causes: Why Conservation is not Enough', *Philosophical Perspectives*, 5 (1991), 553–85.

Freddoso, Alfred J., 'God's General Concurrence with Secondary Causes: Pitfalls and Prospects', *American Catholic Philosophical Quarterly*, 67 (1994), 131–56.

Freddoso, Alfred J., 'Introduction', in Francisco Suarez, SJ, *On Creation, Conservation and Concurrence: Metaphysical Disputations 20–22*, trans. with introduction by Alfred J. Freddoso (South Bend, IN: St Augustine's Press, 2002), pp. xi–cxxiii.

Friedman, Michael, *Kant and the Exact Sciences* (Cambridge, MA.: Harvard University Press, 1992).

Frierson, Patrick, *Freedom and Anthropology in Kant's Moral Psychology* (Cambridge: Cambridge University Press, 2003).

Garber, Daniel, 'What Leibniz Really Said?', in Daniel Garber and Béatrice Longuenesse (eds), *Kant and the Early Moderns* (Princeton: Princeton University Press, 2008), 64–78.

Gardner, Sebastian, 'The Primacy of Practical Reason', in Graham Bird (ed.), *A Companion to Kant* (Oxford: Wiley-Blackwell, 2010), 259–74.

Gawlick, Hans, and Kriemendahl, Lothar, *Hume in der deutschen Aufklärung: Umrisse der Rezeptionsgeschichte* (Stuttgart: Fromann-Holzboog, 1987).

Giovanni, George di, 'On Chris L. Firestone and Nathan Jacob's In Defense of Kant's Religion: A Comment', *Faith and Philosophy*, 26/2 (2012), 163–9.

Gorringe, Timothy, *God's Just Vengeance: Crime, Violence and the Rhetoric of Salvation* (Cambridge: Cambridge University Press, 1996).

Guyer, Paul, *Kant and the Claims of Knowledge* (Cambridge: Cambridge University Press, 1987).

Guyer, Paul, *Kant on Freedom, Law, and Happiness* (Cambridge: Cambridge University Press, 2000).

Guyer, Paul, 'The Unity of Nature and Freedom: Kant's Conception of the System of Philosophy', in Sally Sedgwick (ed.), *The Reception of Kant's Critical Philosophy: Fichte, Schelling, and Hegel* (Cambridge: Cambridge University Press, 2007), 19–53.

Guyer, Paul, 'Beauty, Systematicity, and the Highest Good: Eckart Förster's *Kant's Final Synthesis*', *Inquiry*, 46/2 (2003), 195–214.

Hare, John, *The Moral Gap: Kantian Ethics, Human Limits, and God's Assistance* (Oxford: Clarendon Press, 1996).

Hare, John, 'Kant's Divine Command Theory and its Reception within Analytical Philosophy', in D. Z. Phillips and Timothy Tessin (eds), *Kant and Kierkegaard on Religion* (New York: Palgrave Macmillan, 2000), 263–77.

Hare, John, 'Kant on Recognizing our Duties as God's Commands', *Faith and Philosophy*, 17 (2000), 459–78.

Hare, John, *God's Call: Moral Realism, God's Commands, and Human Autonomy* (Grand Rapids: William B. Eerdmans, 2001).

Hare, John, 'Kant on the Rational Instability of Atheism', in Chris L. Firestone and Stephen R. Palmquist (eds), *Kant and the New Philosophy of Religion* (Bloomington and Indianapolis: Indiana University Press, 2006), 62–78.

Hare, John, *God and Morality: A Philosophical History* (Oxford: Wiley-Blackwell, 2009).

Hasker, William, 'God the Creator of Good and Evil?', in Thomas F. Tracy (ed.), *The God Who Acts* (University Park, PA: Pennsylvania University Press, 1994), 137–46.

Heimsoeth, Heinz, 'Metaphysical Motives in the Development of Critical Idealism', in Moltke S. Gram (ed. and trans.), *Kant: Disputed Questions* (Atascadero, CA: Ridgeview Publishing Company, 1984), 194–235.

Hill, Thomas, *Dignity and Practical Reason* (Ithaca, NY: Cornell University Press, 1993).

Hogan, Desmond, 'How to Know Unknowable Things in Themselves', *Noüs*, 43/1 (2009), 49–63.

Hogan, Desmond, 'Noumenal Affection', *Philosophical Review*, 118/4 (2009), 501–32.

Hogan, Desmond, 'Three Kinds of Rationalism and the Non-Spatiality of Things in Themselves', *Journal of the History of Philosophy*, 47/3 (2009), 355–82.

Hogan, Desmond, 'Kant's Copernican Turn and the Rationalist Tradition' in *The Cambridge Companion to Kant's* Critique of Pure Reason, ed. Paul Guyer (Cambridge: Cambridge University Press, 2010), 21–40.

Hogan, Desmond, 'Kant's Theory of Divine and Secondary Causation', in Brandon Look, *Leibniz and Kant* (Oxford: Oxford University Press, forthcoming).

Insole, Christopher J., *The Realist Hope: A Critique of Anti-Realist Approaches in Contemporary Philosophical Theology* (Aldershot: Ashgate Press, 2006).

Insole, Christopher J., 'The Irreducible Importance of Religious Hope in Kant's Conception of the Highest Good', *Philosophy*, 83/325 (2008), 333–51.

Insole, Christopher J., 'Intellectualism, Relational Properties and the Divine Mind in Kant's Pre-Critical Philosophy', *Kantian Review*, 16/3 (2011), 399–428.

Insole, Christopher J., 'Kant's Transcendental Idealism, Freedom and the Divine Mind', *Modern Theology*, 27/4 (2011), 608–38.

Insole, Christopher J., 'Kant's Transcendental Idealism and Newton's Divine Sensorium', *Journal of the History of Ideas*, 72/3 (2011), 413–36.

Insole, Christopher J., 'Realism and Anti-Realism', in *The Oxford Handbook to the Epistemology of Theology*, ed. Richard Aquino (Oxford: Oxford University Press, forthcoming).

Irwin, Terence, *The Development of Ethics: A Historical and Critical Study. Volume III: From Kant to Rawls* (Oxford: Oxford University Press, 2009).

Irwin, Terence, 'Continuity in the History of Autonomy', *Inquiry: An Interdisciplinary Journal of Philosophy*, 54/5 (2011), 442–59.

Jacobi, F. H., *David Hume über den Glauben; oder Idealismus und Realismus* (1787), repr. in F. H. Jacobi, *Werke* (Leipzig: Gerhard Fleischer, 1815), vol. 2.

Jacobs, Nathan, 'Kant's Prototypical Theology: Transcendental Incarnation as a Rational Foundation for God-Talk', in Chris L. Firestone and Stephen R. Palmquist (eds), *Kant and the New Philosophy of Religion* (Bloomington and Indianapolis: Indiana University Press, 2006), 124–40.

Janz, Paul, *The Command of Grace: A New Theological Apologetics* (London: T&T Clark, 2009).

Jauernig, Anja, 'Kant's Critique of the Leinizian Philosophy: *Contra* the Leinizians, but *Pro* Leibniz', in Daniel Garber and Bétrice Longuenesse (eds), *Kant and the Early Moderns* (Princeton and Oxford: Princeton University Press, 2008), 41–64.

Kain, Patrick, 'Self-Legislation in Kant's Moral Philosophy', *Archiv für Geschichte der Philosophie*, 86 (2004), 257–306.

Kain, Patrick, 'Realism and Anti-Realism in Kant's Second *Critique*', *Philosophy Compass*, 1 (2006), 449–65.

Kain, Patrick, 'The Development of Kant's Conception of Divine Freedom', in Brandon Look (ed.), *Leibniz and Kant* (Oxford: Oxford University Press, forthcoming).

Kane, Robert, *The Significance of Free Will* (Oxford: Oxford University Press, 1998).

Kilby, Karen, 'Evil and the Limits of Theology', *New Blackfriars*, 84/983 (2003), 13–29.

Kopper, J., 'Kants Gotteslehre', *Kant-Studien*, 47 (1955-6), 31–63.

Korsgaard, Christine M., 'The Normativity of Instrumental Reason', in Garrett Cullity and Berys Gaut (eds), *Ethics and Practical Reason* (Oxford: Clarendon Press, 1997).

Kretzmann, Norman, 'A General Problem of Creation' in Scott MacDonald (ed.), *Being and Goodness: The Concept of the Good in Metaphysics and Philosophical Theology* (Ithaca, NY: Cornell University Press, 1991), 208–49.

Kuehn, Manfred, *Kant: A Biography* (Cambridge: Cambridge University Press, 2001).

Laberge, Pierre, *La Théologie Kantienne précritique* (Ottawa: Éditions de L'Université d'Ottawa, 1973).

Langton, Rae, *Kantian Humility: Our Ignorance of Things in Themselves* (Oxford: Oxford University Press, 2004).

Langton, Rae, 'Kant's Phenomena: Extrinsic or Relational Properties? A Reply to Allais', *Philosophy and Phenomenological Research*, 73/1 (2006), 170–85.

Langton, Rae, 'Humility and Co-Existence in Kant and Lewis: Two Modal Themes, with Variations', in Barry Loewer and Jonathan Schaffer (eds), *The Blackwell Companion to David Lewis* (Oxford: Blackwell, forthcoming).

Lavin, Douglas, 'Practical Reason and the Possibility of Error', *Ethics*, 114 (2004), 424–57.

Laywine, Alison, *Kant's Early Metaphysics and the Origins of the Critical Philosophy* (Atascadero, CA: Ridgeview Publishing Company, 1993).

Lee, Sukjae, 'Leibniz on Divine Concurrence', *Philosophical Review*, 113/2 (2004), 203–48.

Leibniz, Gottfried Wilhelm, 'Letter to Wedderkopf' (May 1671), in *Philosophical Papers and Letters*, ed. and trans. Leroy E. Loemker, 2nd edn (Dordrecht: Kluwer Academic Publishers, 1989), 146–7.

Leibniz, Gottfried Wilhelm, 'Necessary and Contingent Truths' (*c*.1686), in *Philosophical Writings*, ed. and trans. Mary Morris and G. H. R. Parkinson (London: Dent, 1973), 96–105.

Leibniz, Gottfried Wilhelm, *Discourse on Metaphysics* (1686), in *Philosophical Essays*, ed. Roger Ariew and Daniel Garber (Indianapolis and Cambridge: Hackett, 1989), 35–68.

Leibniz, Gottfried Wilhelm, *Dialogue on Human Freedom and the Origin of Evil* (25 January 1695), in *Philosophical Essays*, ed. Roger Ariew and Daniel Garber (Indianapolis and Cambridge: Hackett, 1989), 111–17.

Leibniz, Gottfried Wilhelm, *A New System of the Nature and Communication of Substances, and of the Union of the Soul and Body* (1695), in *Philosophical Essays*, ed. Roger Ariew and Daniel Garber (Indianapolis and Cambridge: Hackett, 1989), 138–45.

Leibniz, Gottfried Wilhelm, 'Extract from a Letter Written by Monsieur Leibniz about his Philosophical Hypothesis (1696) ("Third Explanation of the New System")', in *Philosophical Texts*, ed. and trans. R. S. Woolhouse and Richard Francks (Oxford: Oxford University Press, 1998), 191–3.

Leibniz, Gottfried Wilhelm, *The Ultimate Origination of Things* (1697), in *Philosophical Essays*, ed. Roger Ariew and Daniel Garber (Indianapolis and Cambridge: Hackett, 1989), 149–155.

Leibniz, Gottfried Wilhelm, *Monadology* (1714), in *Philosophical Essays*, ed. Roger Ariew and Daniel Garber (Indianapolis and Cambridge: Hackett, 1989), 268–81.

Leibniz, Gottfried Wilhelm, *Causa Dei Asserta per Justitiam Eius*, in *Die Philosophischen Schriften*, ed. C. I. Gerhardt, 7 vols (Berlin: Weidmann, 1875–90), 6: 440–62.

Leibniz, Gottfried Wilhelm, *De Libertate Fato Gratia Dei*, in *Textes Inédites d'après les manuscrits de la Bibliothèque provinciale de Hanovre*, ed. Gaston Grua (Paris: Gaston Grua, 1948).

Leibniz, Gottfried Wilhelm, *Philosophical Essays*, ed. Roger Ariew and Daniel Garber (Indianapolis and Cambridge: Hackett, 1989).

Leibniz, Gottfried Wilhelm, *Philosophical Texts*, ed. and trans. R. S. Woolhouse and Richard Francks (Oxford: Oxford University Press, 1998).

Leibniz, Gottfried Wilhelm, *Theodicy: Essays on the Goodness of God, the Freedom of Man and the Origin of Evil*, ed. Austin M. Farrer and trans. E. M. Huggard (New York: Cosimo, 2009).

Lord, Beth, *Kant and Spinoza: Transcendental Idealism and Immanence from Jacobi to Deleuze* (Basingstoke: Palgrave Macmillan Press, 2011).

Ludwig, Bernd, 'Die "consequente Denkungsart der speculativen Kritik": Kants radikale Umgestaltung seiner Freiheitslehre im Jahre 1786 und die Folgen für dir Kritische Philosophie als Ganze', *Deutsche Zeitschrift für Philoosphie*, 58/4 (2010), 595–628.

McCammon, Christopher, 'Overcoming Deism: Hope Incarnate in Kant's Rational Religion', in by Chris L. Firestone and Stephen R. Palmquist (eds), *Kant and the New Philosophy of Religion*, ed. by Chris L. Firestone and Stephen R. Palmquist (Bloomington and Indianapolis: Indiana University Press, 2006), 79–89.

McDonough, Jeffrey K., 'Leibniz: Creation *and* Conservation *and* Concurrence', *Leibniz Review*, 17 (2007), 31–59.

McDowell, John, *Mind and World* (Cambridge, MA: Harvard University Press, 1996).

Mackie, J. L., *The Miracle of Theism*, (Oxford: Oxford University Press, 1982).

MacKinnon, Donald, *Themes in Theology: The Three-Fold Cord: Essays in Philosophy, Politics, and Theology* (Edinburgh: T&T Clark, 1987).

Mariña, Jacqueline, 'Kant on Grace: A Reply to his Critics', *Religious Studies*, 33/4 (1997), 379–400.

Mariña, Jacqueline, *Transformation of the Self in the Thought of Friedrich Schleiermacher* (Oxford: Oxford University Press, 2008).

Meier, Georg Friedrich, *Metaphysik* (Halle: Carl Hermann Hemmerde, 1757).

Michalson, Gordon E., Jr., *Fallen Freedom: Kant on Radical Evil and Moral Regeneration* (Cambridge: Cambridge University Press, 1990).

Michalson, Gordon E., Jr., *Kant and the Problem of God* (Oxford: Blackwell, 1999).

Michalson, Gordon E., Jr., 'In Defense of Not Defending Kant's Religion', *Faith and Philosophy*, 29/2 (2012), 181–92.

Molina, Luis de, *On Divine Foreknowledge: Part IV of the 'Concordia'*, trans. with introduction and notes by Alfred J. Freddoso (Ithaca, NY: Cornell University Press, 1988).

Moore, A. W., *Noble in Reason, Infinite in Faculty: Themes and Variations in Kant's Moral and Religious Philosophy* (London: Routledge, 2003).

Morris, Thomas V., 'Absolute Creation', in *Anselmian Explorations: Essays in Philosophical Theology* (Notre Dame, IN: Notre Dame University Press, 1987), 161–78.

Morrison, J. C., 'Christian Wolff's Criticism of Spinoza', *Journal of the History of Philosophy*, 31/3 (1993), 405–20.

Morrison, Wes, 'Is God Free? Reply to Wierenga', *Faith and Philosophy*, 23/1 (2006), 93–8.

Natorp, Paul, *Die logischen Grundlage der exacten Wissenschaften* (Leipzig and Berlin: Teubner, 1910).

Natorp, Paul, 'Kant und die Marburger Schule', *Kant-Studein*, 17 (1912), 193–221.

O'Neill, Onora, *Constructions of Reason: Explorations of Kant's Practical Philosophy* (Cambridge: Cambridge University Press, 1989).

Orr, James, 'Natural Purposiveness as a Theological Problem in Kant's Pre-Critical and Critical Philosophy', unpublished manuscript.

Palmquist, Stephen R., *Kant's System of Perspectives: An Architectonic Interpretation of the Critical Philosophy* (Lanham, MD: University Press of America, 1993).

Palmquist, Stephen R., *Kant's Critical Religion: Volume Two of Kant's System of Perspectives* (Aldershot: Ashgate Publishing, 2000).

Palmquist, Stephen R., *Kant's Critical Religion: Volume Two of Kant's System of Perspectives* (Aldershot: Ashgate Publishing, 2000).

Pereboom, Derk, 'Kant on Transcendental Freedom', *Philosophy and Phenomenological Research*, 73/3 (2006), 537–64.

Plantinga, Alvin, *God, Freedom and Evil* (Grand Rapids, MI: William B. Eerdmans, 1974).

Prauss, Gerard, *Kant und das Problem der Dinge an Sich* (Bonn: Bouvier, 1974).

Pruss, Alexander, 'A New Free Will Defence', *Religious Studies*, 39 (2003), 211–33.

Radner, Michael, 'Substance and Phenomenal Substance', in Kenneth F. Barber and Jorge J. E. Gracia (eds), *Individuation and Identity in Early Modern Philosophy* (Albany, NY: State University of New York Press, 1994), 245–66.

Redmann, H.-G., *Gott und Welt: Die Schöpfungstheologie der vorkritischen Periode Kants* (Göttingen: Vandenhoeck and Ruprecht, 1962).

Rossi, Phillip J., and Wreen, Michael (eds), *Kant's Philosophy of Religion Reconsidered* (Bloomington and Indianapolis: Indiana University Press, 1991).

Rowe, William L., *Can God be Free?* (Oxford: Oxford University Press, 2004).

Schleiermacher, Friedrich, *The Christian Faith*, trans. H. R. Mackintosh and James Stuart (Edinburgh: T&T Clark, 1928), reprint with a foreword by B. A. Gerrish (Edinburgh: T&T Clark, 1999).

Schmaltz, Tad M., *Descartes and Causation* (Oxford: Oxford University Press, 2008).

Schmuker, Joseph, 'Die Gottesbeweise beim vorkritischen Kant', *Kantstudien*, 54/4 (1963), 445–63.

Schönfeld, Martin, *The Philosophy of the Young Kant: The Precritical Project* (NewYork: Oxford University Press, 2000).

Schulze, G. E., *Aenesidemus* (Helmstadt, 1792).

Smit, Houston, 'The Role of Reflection in Kant's *Critique of Pure Reason*', *Pacific Philosophical Quarterly*, 80/2 (1999), 203–23.

Stalnaker, Robert, *Inquiry* (Cambridge MA.:, Bradford Books, 1984).

Stang, Nicholas, 'Kant's Possibility Proof', *History of Philosophy Quarterly*, 27/3 (2010), 275–99.

Stang, Nicholas, 'Did Kant Conflate the Necessary and the A Priori?', *Noûs*, 45/3 (2011), 443–71.

Stauffer, F. Ernest, *German Pietism during the Eighteenth Century* (Leiden: E. J. Brill, 1973).

Stern, Robert, *Understanding Moral Obligation: Kant, Hegel, Kierkegaard* (Cambridge: Cambridge University Press, 2012).

Stevenson, Leslie, 'Opinion, Belief or Faith, and Knowledge', *Kantian Review*, 7 (2003), 72–101.

Strawson, Peter, *The Bounds of Sense: An Essay on Kant's* Critique of Pure Reason (London: Methuen, 1966).

Stump, Eleonore, *Aquinas* (London and New York: Routledge, 2003).

Stump, Eleonore, and Kretzmann, Norman, 'Absolute Simplicity', *Faith and Philosophy*, 2/4 (1985), 353–82.

Suarez, Francisco, SJ, *On Efficient Causality: Metaphysical Disputations 17–19*, trans. Alfred Freddoso, in *The Yale Library of Medieval Philosophy*, ed. by Norman Kretzmann, Eleanore Stump, and John Wippel (New Haven, CT: Yale University Press, 1994).

Suarez, Francisco, SJ, *On Creation, Conservation and Concurrence: Metaphysical Disputations 20–22*, trans. with introduction by A. J. Freddoso (South Bend, IN: St Augustine's Press, 2002).

Swinburne, Richard, *The Coherence of Theism* (Oxford: Clarendon Press, 1993).

Talbott, Thomas, 'On the Divine Nature and the Nature of Divine Freedom', *Faith and Philosophy*, 5 (1988), 3–24.

Tanner, Kathryn, 'Human Freedom: Human Sin, and God the Creator', in Thomas F. Tracy (ed.), *The God Who Acts* (University Park, PA: Pennsylvania University Press, 1994), 111–36.

Tanner, Kathryn, *God and Creation in Christian Theology: Tyranny or Empowerment* (Minneapolis: Fortress Press, 2005).

Thorpe, Lucas, 'Is Kant's Realm of Ends a *Unum per Se*? Aquinas, Suarez, Leibniz and Kant on Composition', *British Journal for the History of Philosophy*, 18/3 (2010), 461–85.

Tracy, Thomas F. (ed.), *The God Who Acts* (University Park, PA: Pennsylvania State University Press, 1994).

Ullman-Margalit, Edna, and Margalit, Avishai, 'Holding True and Holding as True', *Synthese*, 92/2 (1992), 167–87.

Vaihinger, Hans, *Commentar zu Kant's Kritik der reinen Vernunft*, 2 vols (Stuttgart: W. Spemann und Union Deutsche Verlagsgesellschaft, 1881–92).

Vailati, Ezio, 'Leibniz on Divine Concurrence with Secondary Causes', *British Journal for the History of Philosophy*, 10/2 (2002), 209–30.

Van Cleve, James, *Problems from Kant* (Oxford: Oxford University Press, 1995).

Van Inwagen, Peter, *An Essay on Free Will* (Oxford: Clarendon Press, 1983).

Velkley, Richard L., *Freedom and the End of Reason: On the Moral Foundation of Kant's Critical Philosophy* (Chicago and London: University of Chicago Press, 1989).

Walker, Ralph, *Kant* (London: Routledge and Kegan Paul, 1978).

Ward, Keith, *The Development of Kant's View of Ethics* (Oxford: Blackwell, 1972).

Warda, Arthur, and Driesche, Carl (eds), *Briefe von und an Scheffner*, 5 vols (Munich and Leipzig: Dunker and Humblot, 1916).

Watkins, Eric, *Kant and the Metaphysics of Causality* (Cambridge: Cambridge University Press, 2005).

Westphal, Merold, 'Theological Anti-Realism', in Andrew Moore and Michael Scott (eds), *Realism and Religion: Philosophical and Theological Perspectives* (Aldershot: Ashgate Publishing, 2007), 131–45.

Wierenga, Edward, 'The Freedom of God', *Faith and Philosophy*, 19/4 (2002), 425–36.

Wierenga, Edward, 'Perfect Goodness and Divine Freedom', *Philosophical Books*, 48/3 (2007), 207–16.

Williams, Thomas, and Visser, Sandra, 'Anselm's Account of Freedom', *Canadian Journal of Philosophy*, 31/2 (2001), 221–44.

Wittgenstein, Ludwig, *Philosophical Investigations* (Oxford: Blackwell, 1973).

Wolff, Christian, *Theologia Naturalis Methodo Scientifica Pertracta* (Frankfurt and Leipzig, 1736).

Wolterstorff, Nicholas, 'Conundrums in Kant's Rational Religion', in Philip J. Rossi and Michael Wreen (eds), *Kant's Philosophy of Religion Reconsidered* (Bloomington and Indianapolis: Indiana University Press, 1991), 40–53.

Wolterstorff, Nicholas, 'Is it Possible and Desirable for Theologians to Recover from Kant?', *Modern Theology*, 14/1 (1998), 1–18.

Wood, Allen W., *Kant's Moral Religion* (Ithaca, NY, and London: Cornell University Press, 1970).

Wood, Allen W., *Kant's Rational Theology* (Ithaca, NY: Cornell University Press, 1978).

Wood, Allen W., 'Translator's Introduction', in Kant, *Lectures on Philosophical Theology* (Ithaca, NY: Cornell University Press, 1978), 9–18.

Wood, Allen W., 'Kant's Compatibilism', in Allen W. Wood (ed.), *Self and Nature in Kant's Philosophy* (Ithaca, NY, and London: Cornell University Press, 1984), 73–101.

Wood, Allen W., *Kant's Ethical Thought* (Cambridge: Cambridge University Press, 1999).

Wood, Allen W., 'Kant's Formulations of the Moral Law', in Graham Bird (ed.), *A Companion to Kant* (Oxford: Wiley-Blackwell, 2010), 291–307, and in *Kant's Ethical Thought* (Cambridge: Cambridge University Press, 1999), 274–82, 309–20.

Wood, Allen W., *Kantian Ethics* (Cambridge: Cambridge University Press, 2008).

Wood, Allen W., 'Kant's Life and Works', in Graham Bird (ed.), *A Companion to Kant* (Oxford: Wiley-Blackwell, 2010), 10–31.

Wuerth, Julian, 'The Paralogisms of Pure Reason', in *The Cambridge Companion to Kant's* Critique of Pure Reason, ed. Paul Guyer (Cambridge: Cambridge University Press, 2010), 210–44.

Wundt, Max, *Kant als Metaphysiker; ein Betrag zur Geschichte der deutschen Philosophie im 18ten Jahrhundert* (Stuttgart: F. Enke, 1924).

Xie, Simon Shengjian, 'What is Kant: A Compatibilist or an Incompatibilist? A New Interpretation of Kant's Solution to the Free Will Problem', *Kant-Studien*, 100/1 (2009), 53–76.

Yandell, Keith, 'Divine Necessity and Divine Goodness', in Thomas V. Morris (ed.), *Divine and Human Action* (Ithaca, NY, and London: Cornell University Press, 1988), 313–44.

Yandell, Keith, 'Who is the True Kant?', *Philosophia Christi*, 9/1 (2007), 81–97.

Zoller, Coleen P., 'The Pre-Critical Roots of Kant's Compatibilism', *Philosophy and Theology*, 19/1–2 (2007), 197–213.

Index

Figures and items in footnotes listed in bold.